THE CHINESE IMPACT UPON
ENGLISH RENAISSANCE LITERATURE

The Chinese Impact upon English Renaissance Literature examines how English writers responded to the cultural shock caused by the first substantial encounter between China and Western Europe. Author Mingjun Lu explores how Donne and Milton came to be aware of England's participation in 'the race for the Far East' launched by Spain and Portugal, and how this new global awareness shaped their conceptions of cultural pluralism. Drawing on globalization theory, a framework that proves useful to help us rethink the literary world of Renaissance England in terms of global maritime networks, Lu proposes the concept of 'liberal cosmopolitanism' to study early modern English engagement with the other. The advanced culture of the Chinese, Lu argues, inculcated in Donne and Milton a respect for difference and a cosmopolitan curiosity that ultimately led both authors to reflect in profound and previously unexamined ways upon their Eurocentric and monotheistic assumptions. The liberal cosmopolitan model not only opens Renaissance literary texts to globalization theory but also initiates a new way of thinking about the early modern encounter with the other beyond the conventional colonial/postcolonial, nationalist, and Orientalist frameworks. By pushing East-West contact back to the period in 1580s–1670s, Lu's work uncovers some hitherto unrecognized Chinese elements in Western culture and their shaping influence upon English literary imagination.

Transculturalisms, 1400–1700

Series Editors:
Mihoko Suzuki, University of Miami, USA,
Ann Rosalind Jones, Smith College, USA, and
Jyotsna Singh, Michigan State University, USA

This series presents studies of the early modern contacts and exchanges among the states, polities and entrepreneurial organizations of Europe; Asia, including the Levant and East India/Indies; Africa; and the Americas. Books will investigate travelers, merchants and cultural inventors, including explorers, mapmakers, artists and writers, as they operated in political, mercantile, sexual and linguistic economies. We encourage authors to reflect on their own methodologies in relation to issues and theories relevant to the study of transculturism/translation and transnationalism. We are particularly interested in work on and from the perspective of the Asians, Africans, and Americans involved in these interactions, and on such topics as:

- Material exchanges, including textiles, paper and printing, and technologies of knowledge
- Movements of bodies: embassies, voyagers, piracy, enslavement
- Travel writing: its purposes, practices, forms and effects on writing in other genres
- Belief systems: religions, philosophies, sciences
- Translations: verbal, artistic, philosophical
- Forms of transnational violence and its representations.

Also in this series:

English Colonial Texts on Tangier, 1661–1684
Imperialism and the Politics of Resistance
Karim Bejjit

Early Modern Catholics, Royalists, and Cosmopolitans
English Transnationalism and the Christian Commonwealth
Brian C. Lockey

The Spanish Presence in Sixteenth-Century Italy
Images of Iberia
Edited by Piers Baker-Bates and Miles Pattenden

Negotiating Transcultural Relations in the Early Modern Mediterranean
Ottoman-Venetian Encounters
Stephen Ortega

The Chinese Impact upon English Renaissance Literature

A Globalization and Liberal Cosmopolitan Approach to Donne and Milton

MINGJUN LU

ASHGATE

© Mingjun Lu 2015

All rights reserved. No part of this publication may be reproduced, stored in a retrieval system or transmitted in any form or by any means, electronic, mechanical, photocopying, recording or otherwise without the prior permission of the publisher.

Mingjun Lu has asserted her right under the Copyright, Designs and Patents Act, 1988, to be identified as the author of this work.

Published by
Ashgate Publishing Limited
Wey Court East
Union Road
Farnham
Surrey, GU9 7PT
England

Ashgate Publishing Company
110 Cherry Street
Suite 3-1
Burlington, VT 05401-3818
USA

www.ashgate.com

British Library Cataloguing in Publication Data
A catalogue record for this book is available from the British Library

The Library of Congress has cataloged the printed edition as follows:

Lu, Mingjun, 1970–
   The Chinese impact upon English Renaissance literature: a globalization and liberal cosmopolitan approach to Donne and Milton / by Mingjun Lu.
    pages cm. — (Transculturalisms, 1400–1700)
   Includes bibliographical references and index.
   ISBN 978-1-4724-6125-4 (hardcover: alk. paper) -- ISBN 978-1-4724-6126-1 (ebook) — ISBN 978-1-4724-6127-8 (epub)
   1. English literature—Early modern, 1500–1700—History and criticism. 2. English literature—Chinese influences. 3. Literature and globalization. I. Title.
   PR421.L86 2015
   820.9'003—dc23

2015006927

ISBN: 9781472461254 (hbk)
ISBN: 9781472461261 (ebk – PDF)
ISBN: 9781472461278 (ebk – ePUB)

Printed in the United Kingdom by Henry Ling Limited, at the Dorset Press, Dorchester, DT1 1HD

To Tianhao, Tianqi, and Rongzhou

Contents

Acknowledgements	*vii*
Introduction: China in Early Modern Globalization: A Liberal Cosmopolitan Model	1
1 Global Silver-Gold Flows: The Chinese Resonance of Donne's "Unfil'd Pistolets"	35
2 The Anyan Strait: Donne's Global Vision and Theological Cosmopolitanism	57
3 Chinese Chronology and Donne's Apologetic Exegesis in *Essayes in Divinity*	81
4 The Resonance of Chinese Antiquity in Milton's *Paradise Lost*	109
5 Webb's Chinese Linguistic Model and the Primitive Language in Milton's *Paradise Lost*	141
6 The Mongol Tartars' World Imperialism and Milton's Vision of Global Governance	173
Conclusion	201
Bibliography	*203*
Index	*233*

Acknowledgements

This book is about East-West contact in the Renaissance. In the book, I make the case that even in the formative period of colonialism and when a Eurocentric outlook reigned supreme, enlightened thinkers showed a remarkable liberal cosmopolitanism to embrace and engage cultural pluralism. The conceptual framework governing the book has been inspired by some real liberal cosmopolitan minds, without which the book could not have taken its present form.

I owe the book both to the supervisory committee of my PhD dissertation and professors and friends at the University of Toronto. With a remarkable cosmopolitan spirit, my supervisor Professor Elizabeth Harvey embraces the cultural diversity epitomized in me. Elizabeth supported the project when I first proposed it: she believed in its worth and feasibility, even when I myself was in doubt. Without Elizabeth's ardent passion and firm faith in the project, I could not have brought it to completion. All along the way, Elizabeth has remained the lighthouse she always is—an infinite source of inspiration that prompts me to scale new intellectual heights. My profound gratitude to Elizabeth transcends any verbal expressions. My heartfelt thanks also go to my co-supervisor Professor Mary Nyquist. A strict, highly demanding, and ever-inspiring mentor, Mary has trained me in the very art of the discipline. Under her rigorous training, my thought has become precise and my reasoning cogent. I am indebted to Mary for not only her intellectual mentorship but also for the extraordinary cosmopolitan generosity she has extended towards those around her. If Elizabeth has led me into a new field and Mary disciplined me in the art of the trade, my committee member Professor David Galbraith has guided me to explore new terrain. It is David who has guided me through the entangled jungle of exegetical literature and discovery stories, a journey that has helped shape the broad contour of the book. I owe David a debt for both his generous support and his special offer to help proofread the whole manuscript. I also warmly thank my graduate instructors Professor Lynne Magnusson and Professor Paul Stevens for their recognition of my humble gifts and for the kindness they have shown me during my first years of study in Canada. My sincere thanks go to Esther de Bruijn as well, a great friend who spared her precious time to proofread the chapters amidst the intense writing of her own dissertation.

In addition to professors at the University of Toronto, I also gratefully acknowledge mentors and friends from other institutions. My special thanks are reserved for my external examiner Professor David Porter from the University of Michigan. As one of those path-breaking pioneers in East-West studies in early modern literature, Porter's own remarkable achievements have proved a rich resource of inspiration. Porter was instrumental in helping turn my dissertation into a book, and those highly inspirational conversations with him were crucial to the refining of the theoretical framework of the project. I am also grateful to Professor Anthony Grafton at Princeton University for his insightful instruction on my knowledge of Joseph Scaliger's chronology. I'm equally indebted to Professor Yan Haiping at the Tsinghua University for helping me reorient my research towards a more comparative and intercultural focus. My new friend Professor Wen Jin at the Fudan University also deserves a special remark here. The sharp and pertinent questions she asked about my methodology have compelled me to think deep, a rethinking that has given a finishing touch to the book.

My warm thanks extend to my editor Erika Gaffney and the anonymous reader of my manuscript at Ashgate Publishing too. Erika is an amazing editor. The undoubting faith she has placed in my work and her ever-positive and encouraging words have made the publishing process a truly enjoyable experience. I am very grateful to the anonymous reader for her/his careful and patient reading of my manuscript. My thesis has improved every time I tried to respond to her/his thought-provoking questions.

I gratefully acknowledge here the various scholarships that contributed substantially to the completion of the book: an Ontario Graduate Scholarship (OGS)—a named Thomas and Beverley Simpson/OGS at the Faculty of Arts and Science and fellowships from the University of Toronto. My project has profited hugely from the two prestigious scholarships from SSHRC—a Canada Graduate Scholarship and the SSHRC William E. Taylor Fellowship for the most outstanding doctoral award recipient for the year 2006. These generous scholarships have allowed me to concentrate on the research without financial concerns.

Earlier versions of several chapters appear in the following journals. Chapter 3, "Chinese Chronology and Donne's Apologetic Exegesis in *Essayes in Divinity*," was published in the *John Donne Journal*. A revised version of Chapter 6, "The Mongol Tartars' World Imperialism and Milton's Vision of Global Governance," saw print in *Early Modern Literary Studies*. The original version of Chapter 2, "The Strait of Anyan: Donne's Global Vision and Theological Cosmopolitanism," will appear in a forthcoming issue in *Criticism: A Quarterly for Literature and the Arts*, scheduled for publication by Wayne State University Press in 2015. I am grateful to the publishers for permission to use this material.

I owe my achievements to my husband Rongzhou, whose unyielding support and sacrificial spirit has been a constant source of solace and strength. Rongzhou is the pillar that buttresses the roof under whose protection I read and wrote without worries. The book is a crystallization of my love for my two sons Tianhao and Tianqi. Tianhao's natural liberality and Tianqi's natural brightness have been two pure springs of comfort and inspiration. I'm no less indebted to my brothers Weibo and Weiguang, two loyal companions who have not only shared an eventful life with me but also unconditionally supported me, rain or shine. My heartfelt gratitude also goes to my parents-in-law, whose selfless care of their grandsons has given me the necessary time to accomplish the book.

All my thoughts derive ultimately from a simple and modest fountain—my parents and the rural community they live in. Humble and illiterate peasants as my parents are, their silent endurance, happy optimism, and earthy wisdom go into the veins of every word in this book. My profound indebtedness to my parents goes hand in hand with that to my neighbors in my native village, whose genuine concern and admiration has ever been a warm and strong current that penetrates to the very roots of my life. What animates the spiritual fabric of the book is ancient Chinese wisdom epitomized in my parents and neighbors—the most enduring and faithful carrier of the Chinese culture.

This book was made possible through the cosmopolitan generosity of all the people and institutions acknowledged here. I alone am responsible for any remaining defects and infelicities.

Introduction
China in Early Modern Globalization: A Liberal Cosmopolitan Model

I: China's Material and Cultural Presence in Early Modern Europe

The rise of China has attracted worldwide attention in modern global affairs. When China replaced Japan as the world's second largest economy and global economic gravity started to shift back to the East, Chinese culture took on an unprecedented appeal.[1] But the source of this attraction emanates more from cultural and artistic forms than universal values or ideals. China should, some native scholars propose, construct a conceptual framework that can not only induce social and cultural integration but also endow traditional Chinese values with a universality comparable to Western freedom, democracy, and the rule of law. To formulate such a framework, these scholars suggest learning from the humanist model of the Renaissance. Since the Renaissance model is noted for its successful resurrection of the classical past, they argue, a similar paradigm might help the Chinese capitalize on its ancient culture epitomized in Confucian ethics and Taoist philosophy.

In proposing to learn from the West, these scholars ignored a significant aspect of East-West contact, that is, the Chinese inspiration of the Renaissance model. The unparalleled intellectual enlightenment and cultural advancement characterizing early modern Europe has been inspired by not only the Greek and Roman but also Chinese culture.[2] John M. Hobson identifies a host of "eastern origins" of Western civilization during 500–1800.[3] For Michael Edwardes, "the Renaissance, for all its Classical face, was alive with influences from the East, often disguised, their source almost always unrecognized."[4] Though largely hidden to the West

---

[1] David Shambaugh, *China Goes Global: The Partial Power* (Oxford: Oxford UP, 2013); Joshua Kurlantzick, *Charm Offensive: How China's Soft Power Is Transforming the World* (New Haven: Yale UP, 2007).

[2] For early modern Europe's interactions with other worlds see, Mary B. Campbell, *The Witness and the Other World: Exotic European Travel Writing, 400–1600* (Ithaca, NY: Cornell UP, 1988); Stephen Greenblatt, *Marvelous Possessions: The Wonder of the New World* (Chicago: U of Chicago P, 1992); Jerry H. Bentley, *Old World Encounters: Cross-Cultural Contacts and Exchanges in Pre-Modern Times* (New York: Oxford UP, 1993); and Matthew Birchwood and Matthew Dimmock, eds. *Cultural Encounters Between East and West: 1453–1699* (London: Cambridge Scholars, 2005).

[3] John M. Hobson, *The Eastern Origins of Western Civilisation* (Cambridge: Cambridge UP, 2004).

[4] Michael Edwardes, *East-West Passage* (New York: Taplinger, 1971), 94.

before maritime discoveries, China came to the full view of western Europe in the sixteenth and seventeenth centuries. The global trade of gold and silver set in motion by Spain's discovery of American mines, the staggering demand for new world silver by Ming China, as well as the Jesuits' apostolic enterprise—all these transnational activities combined to alert the West to the existence of the Middle Kingdom towering in the Far East.[5] What was disturbing to early modern Europeans is that this formidable Eastern empire boasted of not only a powerful economy but also a long history and cultural heritage. According to Eric R. Wolf, the West propagates a historical lineage that runs from ancient Rome and Greece through Renaissance Europe all the way to the United States.[6] But the truth is that the primacy of this Eurocentric narrative of world history was already challenged by the Chinese culture in the early modern period, a challenge that appeared the more revealing because China was once contemporaneous with ancient Greece and Rome. Moreover, the Eastern civilization demonstrated a highly advanced level of civility in its political, ethical, economic, and cultural systems, a superiority that compelled the West to reflect upon both its Eurocentric cultural assumptions and its monotheistic religious discourse. The intervention of Chinese culture in the heyday of Western civilization thus at once questions the Eurocentric master narrative and indicates a Chinese origin of "early modernities."[7]

In reality, in their historical evolution, Western liberal values such as freedom and democracy have been informed by as diverse sources as the Chinese, Russian, Islamic, Mexican, Peruvian, and African cultures. As Barry Buzan puts it, "During its putative first phase, Europe was neither isolated nor powerful. It was a relatively poor, weak and backward place on the periphery of a Eurasian system of powerful empires, and was absorbing from other more advanced cultures many of the ideas that were to play strongly in its own development."[8] Likewise, David Porter argues that the development of world history from 1100 to 1800 was a concerted effort of all existing civilizations and that "early modernities" tell a story of transnational influences and cross-cultural communications no less robust than the modern ones.[9] In particular, the high civility, antiquity, and uninterrupted continuity of the Chinese civilization make it a unique test case for any culture that presumes upon a monotheistic origin. So a credible evaluation of the progress of human history cannot overlook the Chinese element. One objective of this book is to tease out the Chinese sources in early modern European culture, especially English literature.

---

[5] By the "New World," I refer exclusively to "America," and by "new worlds" I mean all the new regions discovered by early modern explorers, China and the Far East included.

[6] Eric R. Wolf, *Europe and the People without History*, foreword Thomas H. Eriksen, 2nd ed. (Berkeley: U of California P, 2010), 5.

[7] David Porter ed. *Comparative Early Modernities: 1100-1800* (London: Palgrave, 2012), 1-12.

[8] Barry Buzan, "Culture and International Society," *International Affairs* 86.1 (2010): 1–25, 12.

[9] Porter, ed., *Comparative Early Modernities*.

According to Porter, since the "complex and dramatically ambivalent responses" occasioned by China's "re-emergence" as a world power "resonate unmistakably with those evoked by the emergence of China ... in English consciousness in the eighteenth century," time is ripe for reconsidering "the historical dynamics of this encounter."[10] Whereas Porter explores "the Chinese taste" in the eighteenth century, I trace the "historical dynamics" back to the end of the sixteenth century, examining how early modern Europe responded to its initial contact with the Chinese culture. As is forcefully demonstrated by Porter and Robert Markley's pioneering works on early modern East-West studies, though the impact of China upon England gathered momentum in the latter part of the seventeenth and the eighteenth centuries, its inception occurred around 1600.[11] This book traces the starting point further back to 1553, the year in which England decided to join the "race for the Far East" (PN 12:8) initiated by the Iberian countries.[12] The time frame of this book spans, therefore, from the 1580s to the 1670s, a period that witnessed the first substantial encounter between China and England. In his *The English Voyages of the Sixteenth Century* (1905), the historian W. A. Raleigh writes, "modern travel and geography owe their chief advances to the search for the fabled realm of Cathay," and it is through "the discovery of a passage through one of the innumerable inlets of the North" that "the story of the English Voyages begins" (PN 12:10).[13] The "passage" here refers to the Northeast and Northwest Passages project inaugurated by the English to reach the Far East. England's "search for the fabled realm of Cathay," therefore, constitutes the broader backdrop that defines the historical span, geographical terrain, and thematic scope of my study of imaginative responses to the discovery of the Pacific region as is revealed in Renaissance English literature.

At the turn of the seventeenth century, England's Far Eastern enterprise, which involved not only such notable figures as John Dee (1527–c. 1608) and Sir Humphrey Gilbert (1539–83) but also Queen Elizabeth and her court, generated great enthusiasm for China. Consequently, Chinese goods started to enjoy wide popularity in the English market. Ben Jonson dramatizes this craze for Eastern wares in his *The Entertainment at Britain's Burse* (1609), a lost masque uncovered

---

[10] Porter, *The Chinese Taste in Eighteenth-Century England* (Cambridge: Cambridge UP, 2010), 11.

[11] Porter, *Ideographia: The Chinese Cipher in Early Modern Europe* (Stanford: Stanford UP, 2001); Robert Markley, *The Far East and the English Imagination, 1600–1730* (Cambridge: Cambridge UP, 2006).

[12] Quoted from Richard Hakluyt, *Principal Navigations, Voiages, Traffiques and Discoveries of the English Nation*, 12 vols. (Glasgow: James Maclehose & Sons, 1903–1905). Hakluyt's work will be referred to as "PN" and quoted by volume and page number.

[13] W. A. Raleigh's work was incorporated in volume 12 of Hakluyt's *Principal Navigations*. For an equally majestic study of early modern maritime discovery also see O. H. K. Spate, *The Pacific Since Magellan*, vol. 2., *Monopolists and Freebooters* (Canberra: Australian National UP, 1983).

in 1977 by James Knowles in the State Papers Domestic of the Public Record Office.[14] The masque was commissioned by Sir Robert Cecil (1563–1612), Secretary of the State, to commemorate the opening of the New Exchange. The performance takes places in a "China howse," one of the "diuers" in London, as we learn from "The Master," whose "more gently" way of advertising the commodities tends to locate every item in a context, especially those that evoke commercial rivalries within domestic and European markets. Apart from the knowledgeable Master, two other actors feature in the masque: the "Key Keeper" who claims to be a "compasse" guiding the customer-audience navigating a vast array of Eastern merchandise, and the "Shop-Boy" who is energetically touting the goods.[15] What is striking about Jonson's *Entertainment* is the sheer number and variety of commodities the Burse puts on show, a profusion vividly dramatized through a long inventory enumerated by the Shop-Boy. After the Key Keeper introduces the occasion of the entertainment, we hear the Boy crying:

> What doe you lacke? What is't you buy? Veary fine China stuffes, of all kindes and quallityes? China Chaynes, China Bracelett, China scarfes, China fannes, China girdles, China kniues, China boxes, China Cabinetts, Caskets, vmbrellas, Sundyalls, Hower glasses, looking glasses, Burninge glasses, Concaue glasses, Triangular Glasses, Conuexe glasses, Christall globes, Waxen pictures, Estrich Egges, Birds of Paradise, Muskcads, Indian Mice, Indian ratts, China dogges and China Cattes? Flow[l]rs of silke, Mosaick fishes? Waxen fruict, and Purslane dishes? Very fine Cages for Birds, Billyard Balls, Purses, Pipes, rattles, Basons, Ewers, Cups, Cans, Voyders, Toothpicks, Targets, falchions, Beards of all ages, vizards, Spectacles! See what you lack.

Displayed here is a mélange of material objects running the whole gamut from staple Chinese goods like silk and porcelain to ordinary necessities, decorative trappings, entertaining trinkets, mechanical devices, and even domestic animals, a rich variety that implies a flourishing and multifaceted transnational trade.

In putting exclusively Chinese goods on display, Jonson's *Entertainment* stages a snapshot of an embryonic global trade with the Far East. Compared with the Portuguese and the Spanish who had been immensely enriched by trading with

---

[14] James Knowles announced his discovery of the *Entertainment at Britain's Burse* in "Cecil's Shopping Centre: The Rediscovery of a Ben Jonson Masque in Praise of Trade," *Times Literary Supplement* (February 7, 1997): 14–15. The text of *Entertainment* appears in Knowles, ed., *Ben Jonson, The Key Keeper: A Masque for the Opening of Britain's Burse April 19, 1609* (Tunbridge Wells: Foundling, 2002). But all my quotes about this masque are from the edited text of Knowles, "Jonson's Entertainment at Britain's Burse," in *Re-presenting Ben Jonson: Text, History, Performance*, ed. Martin Butler (New York: St. Martin's, 1999). For Jonson's masque also see David J. Baker, "'The Allegory of a China Shop': Ben Jonson's 'Entertainment at Britain's Burse' and 'Volpone,'" in Baker, *On Demand: Writing for the Market in Early Modern England* (Stanford: Stanford UP, 2010), 93–120.

[15] Jonson, *Entertainment*, 132, 134.

Far Eastern countries, England was a latecomer and thereby novice in learning how to exploit the Chinese market.[16] Jonson's masque aptly captures England's new experience of dealing with the commercial opportunities offered by Chinese goods. At the early stage of East-West contact, Porter remarks, Chinese imports "were bona fide Chinese goods reflecting contemporary Chinese rather than European tastes," and "the alien aesthetic had yet not been stylistically assimilated to a European sensibility, their imaginative valences and uses within a Western context were as yet largely unsettled and indeterminate."[17] This "unsettled and indeterminate" halo encircling genuine Chinese commodities incited both appetite and anxiety from the customer-audience in an English China house. The Key Keeper tells us that everyone he meets wants to know about the new Burse: "About the howse, the roomes, the floore, the roofe, the lightes, the shops, the very barres and padlockes; Not a grayne in the waynscot, but they haue hade my affadauit for." Being thus harassed, he complains to the king, "I haue had more interrogatorys geuen me in one hower, then all your lawe courtes euer knewe in a Michaelmas Terme." Further, the questions addressed to the Keeper are of such a nature that he thinks "the wisest Contantables, that euer were, could not inuente." Not only commoners but also would-be patrons appear confused by the new Burse. To illustrate such "perplexityes," the Keeper evokes an imaginary chorus that makes various conjectures about the prospect of a Chinese Burse "before the shops were vp." Some would "haue it a publique banque, where money should be lente," others would like it to be "a lombarde, to deale with all manner of pawnes," a "library," or even "an Arsenall for decayed citizen." These remarks are so random, the Key Keeper says, that "I wonder how such men could keepe theyr braynes from being guilty of imagining it, rather, a place to twiste silke in, or make ropes, or play a shittlecocke, better then nothing." The arbitrary feature of these surmises vividly bears out some disturbing uncertainty over investing in Chinese trade in the beginning of the seventeenth century. The English investors simply cannot grasp how to use a shop that carries Chinese wares: as a "banque," "library," "pawnes" shop, or an "Arsenall."

King James was not exempt from this general concern. That the king had no clearer idea of England's position in trading with "the newe region" represented by China is pointedly articulated by the Key Keeper:

> Your Maiestie will pardon me? I thinke you scarse knowe, where you are now nor by my troth can I tell you, more then that you may seeme to be vppon some lande discouery of a newe region here, to which I am your compasse.

---

[16] For England's venture into the Eastern market in the early seventeenth century see Markley, *The Far East and the English Imagination*, 30–69; and Barbara Sebek and Stephen Deng, eds. *Global Traffic: Discourses and Practices of Trade in English Literature and Culture from 1550* (New York: Palgrave, 2008)

[17] Porter, *The Chinese Taste*, 135.

Since the Key Keeper is addressing the king in person, he most probably perceives James I's bewilderment by his looks and manners—that puzzlement typical of those confronted with the "discouery of a newe region." His remark that the king "scarse knowe[s]" where he stands alludes to the irresolute nature of the state policy concerning commerce with China. The masque at once helps the king visualize the prospect and offers him first-hand knowledge of the Asian trade, though rather than reflecting the reality of this trade, the "entertainment" is sampled and specially orchestrated for the royal view. The Keeper says that to act as the king's "compass," he has "walked the rounde this fortnight in my present place, and office," a confession that indicates hard work before making a presentation in the royal presence. Meanwhile, the Master seems bent on turning the members of the royalty into customers when he addresses the king, "ye looke like a man that would geue good handsell," and the queen "ye looke like a good customer too."[18] What the Master actually has in mind is to enhance the attraction of Chinese goods to the king and thereby influence state policy in favor of the Eastern trade. Such trivial stuff as Chinese toothpicks did seem to appeal to royal fancy at the turn of the seventeenth century. In William Shakespeare's *Much Ado about Nothing* (1598–99), the young Lord of Padua, Benedick, says to Don Pedro, Prince of Aragon, "I will fetch you a tooth-picker from the furthest inch of Asia" (2.1.249–51).[19]

Jonson's catalogue of Eastern goods bespeaks not only transnational trade but also the presence of China in early modern England. This presence was tangible enough to be felt, sold, and bartered as material objects. Martin Butler maintains that Jonson's *Entertainment* "celebrates the expansion of British trade into Asian markets, and dwells approvingly on the luxury goods that could be bought from Salisbury's marvelous mall."[20] In fact, the copious wares showcased in Jonson's China Shop struck their English audience-customers as more than luxury goods. By the early modern period, the gateway to the Far East, that is, the Mediterranean and the Red Sea, were firmly controlled by the Turks, Venetians, and Egyptians, so Eastern goods had indeed been exotic luxuries in Western markets.[21] But ever since Vasco Da Gama's (1460–1524) arrival at Calcutta in 1498, a large amount of Eastern riches started to be imported into western Europe through the Cape

---

[18] Jonson, *Entertainment*, 132, 133, 134, 140.
[19] Quotes on William Shakespeare are from *The Arden Shakespeare Complete Works*, ed. Richard Proudfoot, Ann Thompson, and David S. Kastan, 2nd ed. (London: Thomson, 2001).
[20] Martin Butler, "Jonson's London and Its Theatres," in *The Cambridge Companion to Ben Jonson*, ed. Richard Harp and Stanley Stewart (Cambridge: Cambridge UP, 2000), 15–29, 18.
[21] For the practice of fetishizing commodities see, Baker, "Allegory of China Shop," 159; Arjun Appadurai, "Introduction: Commodities and the Politics of Value," in *The Social Life of Things: Commodities in Cultural Perspective*, ed. Appadurai (Cambridge: Cambridge UP, 1986), 3–63; and David Hawkes, *Idols of the Marketplace: Idolatry and Commodity Fetishism in English Literature, 1580–1680*, 1st ed. (New York: Palgrave, 2001).

of Good Hope, and the establishment of the East India Company in 1600 greatly augmented England's traffic in Eastern merchandise. As Robert K. Batchelor points out, "from the 1550s, London began to import and re-export increasingly large amounts of goods from the Americas and Asia."[22] Thus by the first decade of the seventeenth century, Eastern commodities were no longer luxury items for the English.

The goods in Jonson's masque sounded exotic because they evoked a powerful alien culture. Material goods are marvelous carriers of cultural codes, David Harvey says, for "if we view culture as that complex of signs and significations (including language) that mesh into codes of transmission of social values and meanings," then "money and commodities are themselves the primary bearers of cultural codes."[23] Even if the appeal of Chinese wares arose from their exotic nature, Porter observes, this exoticism is "a novelty with a four-thousand-year-old lineage," and it is precisely because of the rich cultural legacy they encode that "the Chinese-styled goods potentially evoked a far more complex range of responses than did other contemporary fashions and commodities."[24] For David Baker, these "cultural codes" are "epistemic conundrums" that contribute no less than commercial profit to the appeal of the Asian commodities in Jonson's burse.[25] Indeed, the cultural message entailed in Chinese goods is explicitly articulated by Jonson's Master, who declares that "I assure you he that would study but the Allegory of a China shop, might stand worthily to be the Rector of an Academy." What is suggested here is that those alien goods impart a cultural "allegory," the interpretation of which enables one to "stand worthily to be the Rector of an Academy." The deciphering of what Porter calls "the Chinese Cipher" is especially enlightening because, the Master says, China is "The onely wise nation vnder the Sun: They had all the knowledge of all manner of Arts and letters, many thousand[s]years, before any of these parts could speake."[26]

The Master's praise is not singular. Instead, it is representative of early modern response to China at the first stage of East-West contact, a reaction marked by genuine awe and admiration. In his *The History of Great and Mighty Kingdom of China* (1585), the Augustinian friar González de Mendoza (1540–1617) expressly states that the Chinese "without all doubt seemed to exceede the Greekes, Carthagenians, and Romanes" in the level of their civilization.[27] The

---

[22] Robert K. Batchelor, *London: The Selden Map and the Making of a Global City, 1547–1689* (Chicago: U of Chicago P, 2014), 8.
[23] David Harvey, "Time-Space Compression and the Postmodern Condition," in Liam Connell and Nicky Marsh, ed., *Literature and Globalization: A Reader* (London: Routledge, 2010), 6–21, 12.
[24] Porter, *The Chinese Taste*, 21, 24.
[25] Baker, *On Demand*, 101.
[26] Jonson, *Entertainment*, 136–37; Porter, *Ideographia*.
[27] Juan González de Mendoza, *The History of Great and Mighty Kingdom of China and the Situation Thereof* (1588), trans. Robert Parke and ed. Sir George T. Staunton, 2 vols. (London: Hakluyt Society, 1854), vol. 1, 92.

French essayist Michel de Montaigne (1533–92) was equally unreserved in his praise of China, which was, he writes in his "On Experience," "a kingdom whose polity and sciences surpass our own exemplars in many kinds of excellence" and "whose history teaches me that the world is more abundant and diverse than either the ancients or we realized."[28] Like Montaigne, the famous chronologer Joseph Scaliger (1540–1609) also recognized "exemplars" for the West in Chinese culture. For the chronological reformer, the Eastern empire "governs itself excellently" and "its fine control of public order [*bonne police*] wins admiration and condemns us Frenchmen." The reason is that, Scaliger explains, while the French "have only a small kingdom by comparison with theirs, and yet we cannot bear to get along with one another, and we cut each other's throats on credit," the Chinese "live in tranquility, and have a system of justice so well administered that although they worship devils, they put Christianity to shame."[29] Likewise, in his *The New Organon* (1620), Francis Bacon (1561–1626) showed no less regard for the ingenuity of the Eastern people. The three inventions of China, that is, "printing, gunpowder and the magnet," the Lord Chancellor declares, "have changed the whole face and state of things throughout the world; the first in literature; the second in warfare; the third in navigation."[30]

China had thus a double presence in early modern Europe: in the cultural sphere as well as in transnational trade. China was known to the medieval West as "Cathay" through the narratives of the Venetian traveler Marco Polo (1254–1324) and Sir John Mandeville, the fourteenth-century English Benedictine monk.[31] Cathay also showed up in the accounts of the pontifical legates to the Mongol court, such as the Franciscan friar John of Plano Carpini's (1182–1252) *The History of the Mongols which we Call Tartars* (1247) and the Flemish Franciscan William of Rubruck's (1220–93) *The Journey of William Rubruck* (1253–55).[32] By "Cathay," medieval travelers meant the Song Empire (996–1271) before its conquest by the Mongol Tartars. After the Mongols overthrew the Song and established the Yuan dynasty (1271–1368), "Cathay" referred specifically to the northern part of China. The Mongol conquerors called the Han Chinese living in the south "Mangi," a

---

[28] Michel de Montaigne, "On Experience," in *The Complete Essays*, trans. and ed. M. A. Screech (London: Penguin, 2003), 1215.

[29] Scaliger to Dupuy, August 25, 1587, quoted in Anthony Grafton, *Joseph Scaliger: A Study in the History of Classical Scholarship*, 2 vols. (Oxford: Oxford UP, 1983–1993), vol. 2. *Historical Chronology*, 362.

[30] Francis Bacon, *The New Organon, and Related Writings*, ed. Fulton H. Anderson (Indianapolis: Bobbs-Merrill, 1960), 118.

[31] *The Travels of Marco Polo*, trans. Ronald Latham (London: Penguin, 1958); and *The Book of John Mandeville with Related Texts*, ed. and trans. Iain M. Higgins (Indianapolis: Hackett, 2011). For more on Polo see Suzanne C. Akbari and Amilcare Iannucci, eds., *Marco Polo and the Encounter of East and West* (Toronto: U of Toronto P, 2008).

[32] For Carpini and Rubruck's works, see *The Mongol Mission: Narratives and Letters of the Franciscan Missionaries in Mongolia and China in the Thirteenth and Fourteenth Centuries*, ed. Christopher Dawson (New York: Sheed and Ward, 1955).

derogatory term that meant southern barbarians.[33] By the time Jonson composed his *Entertainment*, however, though Cathay still lingered in Western minds through the wide dissemination of Polo and Mandeville's works, there started to circulate another portrait of the Far East in the reports of the Jesuit missionaries.[34] After the Ming Empire (1368–1644) toppled the Yuan Dynasty built by the Mongol Tartars in 1368, the overland routes to China were largely blocked, which basically cut off Western access to the Far East. Consequently, regions along the Pacific Ring disappeared from Western view until the Iberian adventurers rediscovered them in the sixteenth century. As is pointed out by Matteo Ricci (1552–1610) and Nicholas Trigault (1577–1628), two Jesuit pioneers of the Chinese mission, "China," the Ming Empire or the so-called Middle Kingdom existing alongside early modern Europe, proved none other than the medieval Cathay.[35] Jonson's Master recalls this Western tradition of representing the Far East when he remarks that "Sir John Mandeville was the first [English author], that brought scynece from thence into our climate, and so dispensed it into Europe and in such Hieroglyphiks as these."[36]

II: Early Modern Reports of China and Outline of the Book

This book positions itself in relation to two major bodies of literature—Western reports on China and sinological studies. My first primary source comes from the Western tradition of representing the Far East. This tradition is embodied in Polo and Mandeville's travel accounts, the reports of the pontifical legates to the

---

[33] For "Mangi," see Polo, *Travels*, 164. It should be noted that whereas "Cathay" was a term used by Western observers, "Mangi" was used by the Mongols themselves.

[34] Some 300 manuscripts of Mandeville's travel account have survived. Mandeville's work was available in almost every major European language by 1400, and nine English editions appeared in the seventeenth century. Still extant are 119 of Polo's *Travels*, and John Brampton translated it into English in 1579. Both Polo and Mandeville's accounts were adapted in Giovanni Battista Ramusio's *Delle navigationi et viaggi* (1550–54) and Samuel Purchas's *Hakluytus Posthumus or Purchas His Pilgrimes* (1625), 20 vols. (Glasgow: James MacLehose and Sons, 1905–1907). For Mandeville and Polo's accounts in Purchas see vol. 11, 188–306; 365–94.

[35] For the name of "Middle Kingdom" see *China in the Sixteenth Century: The Journals of Matthew Ricci: 1583–1610*, ed. Nicolas Trigault and trans. Louis J. Gallagher, S.J. (New York: Random House, 1953), 7. Matteo Ricci reached Macao in 1582. At his death in Beijing in 1610, Ricci left a journal recording both Chinese culture and the apostolic cause in China. Trigault, a fellow missionary in China, brought Ricci's journal from Macao to Rome in 1614. Trigault arrived in China in 1611. A year later, he went to Rome to recruit new missionaries, returned in 1618, and died in China in 1628. Trigault translated Ricci's journal into Latin and published it under the title of *De christiana expeditione apud Sinas* (Augsburg, 1615). Trigault's translation went through 11 editions between 1615 and 1625. Since Trigault prefaced Ricci's journal with an extensive introduction of Chinese culture, Gallagher's modern edition will be referred to as Ricci-Trigault.

[36] Jonson, *Entertainment*, 136.

Mongol court, Mendoza's *Mighty Kingdom of China*, Ricci and Trigualt's *Journals* or *De christiana expeditione apud Sinas* (1615), and the Jesuit historian Martino Martini's (1614–61) *Sinicae historiae decas prima* (1658). Travel compilations such as Richard Hakluyt's (1552–1616) *Principal Navigations* (1589–1600), Samuel Purchas's (1575–1626) *Hakluytus Posthumus* or *Purchas His Pilgrimes* (1625), and Peter Heylyn's (1599–1662) *Cosmographie* (1657) also come under this heading. A second primary source consists in sinological scholarship, especially the so-called Jesuit sinophile literature,[37] interpretative or critical works on the early modern reception of the Far East. George H. Dunne's *Generation of Giants* and David E. Mungello's *Curious Land* belong to this category.[38]

As the backbone of my primary sources, I pay special attention to the Jesuits' accounts of China.[39] In effect, the encounter between East and West could not have been that fruitful without the intervention of Jesuit missionaries. By the first two decades of the seventeenth century, the Christian expedition in China envisioned and passionately pursued by St. Francis Xavier (1506–52) had been greatly expanded by his successors Alessandro Valignano (1539–1606), "the Official

---

[37] For Renaissance sinological scholarship see, Arnold H. Rowbotham, *Missionary and Mandarin: The Jesuits at the Court of China* (Berkeley: U of California P, 1942), 241–76; George H. Dunne, *Generation of Giants: The Story of the Jesuits in China in the Last Decades of the Ming Dynasty* (Notre Dame, IN: U of Notre Dame P, 1962); and David E. Mungello, *Curious Land: Jesuit Accommodation and the Origins of Sinology* (Honolulu: U of Hawaii P, 1989). Rowbotham calls this kind of works "Jesuit sinophile literature."

[38] Notable sinological works also include: Friedrich Hirth, *China and the Roman Orient* (Shanghai: Kelly & Walsh, 1885); Sir Henry Yule, trans. and ed., *Cathay and the Way Thither: Being a Collection of Medieval Notices of China*, 4 vols. (Taipei: Ch'eng-Wen, 1966); Geoffrey F. Hudson, *Europe and China: A Survey of their Relations from the Earliest Times to 1800* (London: Arnold, 1931); Shou-yi Ch'en, "Sino-European Cultural Contacts since the Discovery of the Sea Route," *Nankai Social and Economic Quarterly* 8.1 (1935): 44–74; Joseph Needham, et al., eds. *Science and Civilisation in China*, 7 vols. (Cambridge: Cambridge UP, 1954–2008); Raymond S. Dawson, *The Chinese Chameleon: An Analysis of European Conceptions of Chinese Civilization* (Oxford: Oxford UP, 1967); Donald F. Lach, *China in the Eyes of Europe: The Sixteenth Century* (Chicago: U of Chicago P, 1965); Lach and Edwin J. van Kley, *Asia in the Making of Europe*, 3 vols. (Chicago: Chicago UP, 1993); J. J. Clarke, *Oriental Enlightenment: The Encounter between Asian and Western Thought* (New York: Routledge, 1997); Lionel M. Jensen, *Manufacturing Confucianism: Chinese Traditions and Universal Civilization* (Durham, NC: Duke UP, 1997); Jonathon Spence, *The Chan's Great Continent: China in Western Minds* (London: Penguin, 2000); and John E. Wills, Jr., ed. *China and Maritime Europe, 1500–1800: Trade, Settlement, Diplomacy, and Missions* (New York: Cambridge UP, 2011).

[39] For works on the Jesuits' Chinese mission in the Renaissance see Rowbotham, *Missionary and Mandarin*; Mungello, *Curious Land*; Mungello, *The Great Encounter of China and the West* (Lanham, MD.: Rowman & Littlefield, 1999); Liam M. Brockley, *Journey to the East: The Jesuit Mission to China, 1579–1724* (Cambridge, MA: Harvard UP, 2007); and R. Po-Chia Hsia, *A Jesuit in the Forbidden City: Matteo Ricci, 1552–1610* (Oxford: Oxford UP, 2010).

Visitor of the Society [of Jesus] to the entire Orient,"[40] and Matteo Ricci, who was appointed by Valignano as "the Superior" of the China mission.[41] These pioneering missionaries made it a mandate to study the Chinese culture, and they transmitted what they had absorbed from China back to Europe through complex and far-ranging communication networks.[42] According to Steven J. Harris, the Society of Jesus established an "organizational structure" that "effectively combined spatially distributed networks (the Society's overseas missions) with multiple nodal points or nexus (Jesuit Colleges and universities) which served as the locally conditioned centers for the gathering, collation, distillation, and dissemination of much of Jesuit science."[43] It is precisely because of this highly ordered regulation and dissemination network, Donald F. Lach and Edwin van Kley argue, that "hundreds of Jesuit letterbooks, derivative accounts, travel accounts … pamphlets, newssheets, and the like" were circulated and preserved. These various accounts, Lach and van Kley state, "were published in all European languages, frequently reprinted and translated, collected into the several large compilations of travel literature published during the century, and regularly pilfered by later writers or publishers."[44] Chinese culture as interpreted and transmitted by Jesuit missionaries provided a valuable resource for Renaissance interest in China, an interest that inspired, in turn, some intellectual enterprises whose "origins" could be traced, whether directly or indirectly, to the Far East.

The large volume of Chinese culture introduced to Europe through Jesuit missionaries spilled inevitably into literature. Renaissance literature, as a sensitive cultural barometer that responded aptly to changes both in the physical and intellectual worlds, could not have been deaf to the name of China shouted 11 times by Jonson's Shop-Boy. In fact, alongside multitudes of Jesuit reports, Lach and van Kley note,

> Hundreds of books about Asia, written by missionaries, merchants, sea-captains, physicians, sailors, soldiers, and independent travelers, appeared during the [seventeenth] century. There were at least twenty-five major descriptions of South Asia alone, another fifteen devoted to mainland Southeast Asia, about twenty to the archipelagoes, and sixty or more to East Asia.

---

[40] Ricci-Trigault, *Journals*, 190. Valignano was initially appointed as "Official Visitor to the whole India Mission." Later, "by order of the General of the Society of Jesus," he "had ceased to govern the Mission of India. His authority then, under the title of Official visitor, extended only to Japan and to the China Mission." Ricci-Trigault, *Journals*, 130, 290.

[41] Ricci-Trigault, *Journals*, 295.

[42] Steven J. Harris, "Mapping Jesuit Science: The Role of Travel in the Geography of Knowledge," in *The Jesuits: Cultures, Sciences, and the Arts, 1540–1773*, ed. John W. O'Malley, Gauvin A. Bailey, and Steven. J. Harris (Toronto: U of Toronto P, 1999), 212–40.

[43] Harris, "Mapping Jesuit Science," 214, 215.

[44] Lach and van Kley, *Asia in the Making of Europe*, vol. 3., 1890; see also Hobson, *Eastern Origins*, 200; and Clarke, *Oriental Enlightenment*, 40.

Given this plenitude of works on the Far East, Lach and van Kley conclude, "few literate Europeans could have been completely untouched by it, and it would be surprising indeed if its effects could not have been seen in contemporary European literature, art, learning, and culture."[45] Indeed, apart from the abundant references in Jonson's masque, the image of China showed up in other literary works as well.[46] China or Cathay figures prominently in Ludovico Ariosto's *Orlando Furioso* (1516) and Francois Rabelais's *Pantagruel* (1532). Ariosto's epic poem relates the return of Orlando from Tartary, India, and Meida to the West, and the girl he has been long in love was "Angelica," a native of Cathay.[47] Rabelais situates the "Land of Utopia" and the "City of the Amaurots" in China. The trans-Pacific journey represented in Bacon's *New Atlantis* (1627) starts from "Peru" towards "China and Japan."[48] George Puttenham comments on Chinese poetry in *The Arte of English Poesie* (1589).[49] In *The Anatomy of Melancholy* (1621), Robert Burton identifies various aspects of Chinese culture that are either adverse or conducive to the disease of melancholy.[50] In Shakespeare's *Much Ado About Nothing* the young Lord of Padua says to the Prince of Aragon:

> Will your Grace command me any service to the world's end? I will go on the slightest errand now to the Antipodes that you can devise to send me on; I will fetch you a tooth-picker from the furthest inch of Asia; bring you the length of Prester John's foot; fetch you a hair off the great Cham's beard; do you any embassage to the Pigmies. (2.1.249–53)

In addition, Shakespeare also mentions a "Cathayan" or "Cataian" in *Merry Wives of Windsor* (2.1.130) and *Twelfth Night* (2.3.75), and speaks of "China dishes" in *Measure for Measure* (2.1.92).[51] John Donne and John Milton's portrayals of China prove part of this literary tradition of depicting the Far East.

---

[45] Lach and van Kley, *Asia in the Making of Europe*, vol. 3., 1890.

[46] For the impact of geographical discovery upon imaginative literature, see Robert R. Cawley, *Unpathed Waters: Studies in the Influence of the Voyagers on Elizabethan Literature* (Princeton: Princeton UP, 1940); and Neil Rennie, *Far-Fetched Facts: The Literature of Travel and the Idea of the South Seas* (Oxford: Clarendon, 1995).

[47] Ludovico Ariosto, *Orlando Furioso* (1516), trans. Guido Waldman (Oxford: Oxford UP, 1998), 100, 101.

[48] Francis Bacon, *New Atlantis*, in *Three Early Modern Utopias*, ed. Susan Bruce (Oxford: Oxford UP, 1999), 152.

[49] George Puttenham, *The Arte of English Poesie*, ed. Gladys Willcock and Alice Walker (Cambridge: Cambridge UP, 1936), 91–94, 106–07.

[50] Robert Burton, *The Anatomy of Melancholy*, ed. A. F. Bullen, 3 vols. (London: Bohn's Popular Library, 1923), vol. 1., 87, 102, 104–5, 115–16, 249, 265, 304, 419–20; vol. 2., 173, 199.

[51] For Shakespeare and maritime exploration see Walter Cohen, "The Undiscovered Country: Shakespeare and Mercantile Geography," in *Marxist Shakespeares*, ed. Jean E. Howard and Scott C. Shershow (London: Routledge, 2001), 128–58; and Carole Levin, *Shakespeare's Foreign Worlds: National and Transnational Identities in the Elizabethan Age* (Ithaca, NY: Cornell UP, 2009).

The English reception of the Chinese culture as is filtered by the Jesuits, however, tends to be complicated by the polemical wars waged between the reformed Church of England and the Roman Catholic Church. The post-Reformation era witnessed an intense rivalry between the reformed and Catholic churches for theological legitimacy and jurisdictional authority, a competition that gave rise to the famous polemical battles that involved many highly renowned divines and theologians on both divides of the debate. The polemical controversy raged so high that between 1605–1625 about 500 works were published by some 150 authors from the two different camps.[52] The Gunpowder Plot engineered by the Romanish priests and Jesuits further inflamed the religious disputes. King James founded the Chelsea College in 1609 with the express purpose to engage the antipapal polemic.[53] For the English, what was at stake is not only national security but also the authority and legitimacy of the Anglican Church, the spiritual foundation of the newly forged nation-state. The theological polemic provided an ideal platform for the Anglicans to defend and justify the reformed Church. As Anthony Milton points out, antipapal polemic during the Elizabethan period served as an effective means for moderate Puritans to show loyalty to the Church of England. Likewise, antipapal writers in the Jacobin times "were the most distinctive feature of English protestant theology and occupied the energies of all the principal members of the Jacobean episcopate."[54]

Given this widespread doctrinal controversy, it might sound sensible that English Protestants would reject messages conveyed by the Jesuits, the militant defenders of the Roman Church. That both Donne and Milton voiced unreservedly criticisms of the Jesuits tends to reinforce this possibility. While visiting Naples in his continental tour during 1638–39, Milton learned from some merchants "of plots laid against me by the English Jesuits, should I return to Rome" (YP 4:619).[55] In his *Doctrine and Discipline of Divorce* (1643), he criticizes the Jesuits and Arminius's mistaken notion on the author of sin, and in his *Areopagitica* (1644), he touches on the doctrinal corruption caused by the Jesuits and Sorbonists. Compared to Milton, Donne seemed more justified in discrediting the Jesuits' reports. Both his brother Henry Donne and his uncle Jasper Heywood were martyred because of their Catholic convictions, which might account for his severe critique of Catholic martyrdom in his *Pseudo-Martyr* (1610). In his *Ignatius His Conclave* (1611), Donne presents another scathing critique of the Catholic order by staging

---

[52] T. H. Wadkins, "Theological Polemic and Religious Culture in Early Stuart England," diss. Graduate Theological Union, U of California, Berkeley, 1988, 71.

[53] D. E. Kennedy, "King James's College of Controversial Divinity at Chelsea," in *Grounds of Controversy, Three Studies of Late 16th and Early 17th Century English Polemics*, ed. Kennedy (Melbourne: Melbourne UP, 1989), 97–119.

[54] Anthony Milton, *Catholic and Reformed: The Roman and Protestant Churches in English Protestant Thought 1600–1640* (Cambridge: U of Cambridge P, 1995), 31.

[55] *The Complete Prose Works of John Milton*, ed. Don M. Wolfe et. al., 8 vols. (New Haven: Yale UP, 1953–82), vol. 4. 551. This work will be referred to as YP and quoted by volume and page number, and most Milton's prose works will be cited from this collection.

a confrontation between Copernicus and Ignatius of Loyola, principal founder of the Society of Jesus and archetypal representative of the Catholic mission.[56] Here Ignatius is represented as the archenemy that tyrannizes over spiritual freedom and hinders the propagation of Copernican astronomy.

The truth is that, however, despite the seemingly irreconcilable confrontation between the Protestants and the Papists, early modern intellectuals had the wisdom and insight to distinguish between the transmitter and the culture being transmitted. Put differently, there was a tendency for enlightened thinkers to transcend doctrinal differences and embrace knowledge of the new worlds, whether this knowledge was relayed back by the Jesuits or Protestants. Both Hakluyt and Purchas's travel compilations exemplify this cosmopolitan open-mindedness. Hakluyt was an ordained priest and once personal chaplain to Sir Robert Cecil, Secretary of State. Purchas was a clergyman noted not only for his collection of Hakluyt's posthumous manuscripts but also for his compiling of *Purchas His Pilgrimage* (1613), an encyclopedia of a broad array of foreign peoples and religions. But most Jesuit reports of the newly discovered worlds were adapted and contained in Hakluyt's *Principal Navigations* and Purchas's *Hakluytus Posthumus*. So even highly reputed Anglicans like Hakluyt and Purchas showed a liberal cosmopolitanism towards the reports of the Jesuits, their avowed doctrinal enemies. Further, even if the Jesuits' accounts are colored by the Catholic agenda, in a market with few suppliers of information about China, people could only take the message available and accessible to them as it was given. In fact, since most of the Jesuits' reports were anthologized and repeatedly documented in Hakluyt, Purchas, and Heylyn's travel compilations, they tended to form a more or less consistent sinological discourse. This discourse served, in turn, as a sort of information repository to which most early modern authors turned for reference, including Donne and Milton.

A chief aim of my study is to recognize those "unrecognized" sources of China in Renaissance English culture, disclosing the "Eastern origins" of some particular images and allusions in Donne and Milton's works. Compared with other Oriental countries such as the Ottoman Empire and eastern India, Renaissance literary representations of China are few. If we pay close attention, however, we can pin down some traces and echoes, resonances that, though slight in number, are significant enough to make us aware of the impact of the Chinese culture upon early modern literature. Those seemingly simple and accidental references actually evoke the broader backdrop of maritime discovery of the Far East, and are thus symptomatic of a multifaceted intercourse between Ming China and early modern Europe. This book intends to explore this multidimensional global dialogue as it is mediated through a variety of discourses such as chronology, language, theology, and politics.

The "China" of each generation tends to serve for the West a distinct set of discursive functions and rhetorical purposes. My study focuses on how China

---

[56] John Donne, *Ignatius his Conclave*, in *John Donne, Dean of St Paul's: Complete Poetry and Selected Prose*, ed. John Hayward (London: Nonesuch, 1967): 357–409.

served as a cultural stimulus that impelled early modern Europeans to rethink their economic, theological, and political preconceptions. At the turn of the seventeenth century, China, though a profitable market for the Spanish and Portuguese, appeared to the English as not only an unforeseeable economic force but also an undecipherable cultural space. The admiration expressed by Bacon, Montaigne, and Scaliger reveals both criticism of contemporary societies and anxieties over potential challenges posed by a highly progressive pagan culture. Given that the Chinese are heathens, if their ancient annals hold true, the authority of biblical chronology would stand on shaky ground. If the pagans could maintain a political and ethical system more advanced, then how to explain the superiority of the monotheistic European culture? If the Chinese are inventors of those epoch-making instruments such as paper and the compass, then how to rationalize attempts to colonize a people apparently far superior to western Europeans? To complicate the matter, what if the formidable culture in the Far East proved no mere fiction but sustained by a powerful economic base, as a large portion of the precious metals produced in Spain's American mines ended up in the Ming Empire? This book examines how Donne and Milton grapple with some of these disturbing implications of the Chinese culture—the shocks consequent upon the discovery of the Pacific region, China's dominance in the global flow of gold and silver, Chinese antique history and seemingly primitive language, as well as the global imperialism of the Mongol Tartars.[57] I mean to show both authors' "wonder" or what Stephen Greenblatt calls "decisive emotional and intellectual experience" of the "radical difference" represented by China, how this powerful alterity obliged them to reflect upon some fundamental assumptions of their own society, and what interpretive strategies they conjure to negotiate a culture comparable to western Europe in some major aspects of civilization.[58]

Most scholarship on Renaissance literary representations of China focuses on the late seventeenth and eighteenth centuries, and the few studies that do notice the allusions to China in Elizabethan and early Stuart literature confine their discussions to some general or tangential remarks, without engaging in sustained discussions.[59] But there are notable exceptions in recent studies. Porter examines the Western reception of both Chinese ideographical characters and artistic forms

---

[57] Given the dynastic connection between the Mongol and the Yuan empire, I consider the pre-Yuan Mongol rule part of the Chinese history.

[58] Greenblatt, *Marvelous Possessions*, 14.

[59] For works on Renaissance literary representations of China see, Qian Zhongshu, "China in the English Literature of the Seventeenth Century," *Quarterly Bulletin of Chinese Bibliography* 1.4 (1940): 351–84; William W. Appleton, *A Cycle of Cathay: The Chinese Vogue in England during the Seventeenth and Eighteenth Centuries* (New York: Columbia UP, 1951); Thomas H. C. Lee, ed. *China and Europe: Images and Influences in the Sixteenth to Eighteenth Centuries* (Hong Kong: Chinese UP, 1991); Adrian Hsia, ed. *The Vision of China in the English Literature of the Seventeenth and Eighteenth Centuries* (Hong Kong: Hong Kong UP, 1988); and Hsia, *Chinesia: The European Construction of China in the Literature of the Seventeenth and Eighteenth Centuries* (Tübingen: Niemeyer, 1998).

in the early seventeenth century, and Gwee Li Sui investigates the "the specter of scientific China" in Bacon's *New Atlantis*.[60] Markley and Walter H. S. Lim bring the Far East into Milton studies.[61] Knowles, Baker, and Michael Murrin are pioneers in presenting sustained studies of literary images of China in the late sixteenth and early seventeenth centuries.[62] In studying literary portrayals of East-West contact before the 1670s, this book at once draws upon, and participates in, the sinological critical tradition established by these scholars. While scholars like Porter and Eugenia Zuroski Jenkins explore how the Chinese impact evolves and transforms early modern taste, subjectivity, and even ways of thinking, my focus is on how the Chinese culture challenges some assumptions fundamental to the Adamic heritage.[63]

My work, however, departs from previous scholarship in three key aspects. First, rather than the conventional racialist, colonialist, and Orientalist models, I adopt a globalization and liberal cosmopolitan approach to early modern receptions of the other represented by the Chinese. This methodology will be discussed in detail below. Second, by extending East-West contact to the latter part of the sixteenth century, I engage a form of encounter quite distinct from that in the eighteenth century. The initial collision between two diametrically opposite cultures provoked, apart from genuine admiration, anxieties over the threat posed by a powerful alien culture. Unlike the nicer distinction and more critical and nuanced receptions of Chinese objects characterizing the eighteenth-century cult of "Chinoiserie"—European artistic appropriation of Chinese motifs and themes in decorative arts—Western thinkers before the 1670s seemed attracted by more general and pronounced cultural patterns.[64] Such conspicuous cultural forms as

---

[60] Porter, "Writing China: Legitimacy and Representation 1606–1773," *Comparative Literature Studies* 33 (1996): 98–101, Porter, *The Chinese Taste*, and Gwee Li Sui, "Westward to the Orient: The Specter of Scientific China in Francis Bacon's *New Atlantis*," in *The English Renaissance, Orientalism, and the Idea of Asia*, ed. Debra Johanyak and Walter S. H. Lim (New York: Palgrave, 2010), 161–83.

[61] Markley, *The Far East and the English Imagination*; Walter S. H. Lim, "China, India, and the Empire of Commerce in Milton's *Paradise Lost*," in *Sinographies: Writing China*, ed. Eric Hayot, Haun Saussy, and Steven G. Yao (Minneapolis: U of Minnesota P, 2008), 115–39; and Lim, "John Milton, Orientalism, and the Empires of the East in *Paradise Lost*," in Johanyak and Lim eds., 203–35. Also see Rachel Trubowitz, "'The people of Asia and with them the Jews': Israel, Asia, and England in Milton's Writings," in *Milton and the Jews*, ed. Douglas A. Brooks (Cambridge: Cambridge UP, 2008), 151–77; and Jonathan E. Lux, " 'Shot Through with Orient Beams': Restoring the Orient to Milton's Paradise," *Milton Quarterly* 48.4 (2014): 235-47.

[62] Michael Murrin, *Trade and Commerce* (Chicago: Chicago UP, 2014);

[63] Porter, *The Chinese Taste*; Eugenia Zuroski Jenkins, *A Taste for China: English Subjectivity and the Prehistory of Orientalism* (New York: Oxford UP, 2013).

[64] For eighteenth-century reception of Chinese artistic objects and literary motifs, see Porter, *Chinese Taste*, and Chi-ming Yang, *Performing China: Virtue, Commerce and Orientalism in Eighteenth-Century England, 1660–1760* (Baltimore: Johns Hopkins UP, 2011).

Chinese antique history and imperial system proved especially destabilizing, since they called into doubt some cornerstone hypotheses of the Eurocentric and monotheistic heritage. The "unsettled and indeterminate" halo exuding from Chinese goods in Jonson's masque is symptomatic of the bewildering reactions to the Eastern culture at the earlier stage of East-West encounter. The third feature that distinguishes my study is the thematic breadth it covers. Whereas other scholars tend to deal with a particular facet of East-West contact, my work engages the manifold implications of China's emergence as a global actor in the early modern period —economic, theological, chronological, linguistic, and political. By unpacking the images and metaphors in Donne and Milton's works that encode the Chinese elements, I intend to show how China impacted Renaissance imaginative minds and how this impact impelled them to fabricate various adaptive strategies, strategies that, in turn, helped shape Western cultural and discursive practices.

III: The Ethnic, Orientalist, and Colonialist Models vs. the Jesuits' Accommodative Policy

By the early modern period, China had become a definite cultural space in Renaissance travel literature and cartographical discourse. The cartographical image of the Far East during this period shows that the region was far from fantastic and legendary; instead, it was a geographical space no less tangible than the European continent.[65] Nor did its culture and customs sound mythical any more by the turn of the seventeenth century.[66] Margaret T. Hodgen rightly notes that Carpini's, Rubruck's, and Polo's accounts of the Mongols and Cathayans have an unexpectedly ethnological character.[67] Sir Humphrey Gilbert, pioneer of England's colonial cause in America, wrote to his brother in 1566: "You might justly have charged mee with an unsetled head if I had at any time taken in hand, to discover Utopia, or any countrey fained by imagination: But Cathaia is none such

---

[65] For early modern cartographical mapping of China and the Far East see: Abraham Cresques's *Catalan World Atlas* (1375); Francisco Rodrigues's *The Atlas* (1513); Giacomo Gastaldi's *Asiae Nova Descriptio* (1570); and Abraham Ortelius's *Theatrum orbis terrarum* (1570). On modern works see Heinrich Winter, "Francisco Rodrigues' Atlas of ca. 1513," *Imago Mundi* 6 (1949): 20–26; Winter, "Catalan Portolan Maps and Their Place in the Total View of Cartographic Development," *Imago Mundi* 11 (1954): 1–12; and Toby Lester, *The Fourth Part of the World: An Astonishing Epic of Global Discovery, Imperial Ambition and the Birth of America* (New York: Free Press, 2009).

[66] For the mythological approach to the Tartars see, Gregory G. Guzman, "Reports of Mongol Cannibalism in the Thirteenth-Century Latin Sources: Oriental Fact or Western Fiction?" in *Discovering New Worlds: Essays on Medieval Exploration and Imaginatio*, Scott D. Westrem (New York: Garland, 1991), 31–68; and C. W. Connell, "Western Views of the Origin of the Tartars: An Example of the Influence of Myth in the Second Half of the Thirteenth Century," *Journal of Medieval and Renaissance Studies* 3 (1973): 115–37.

[67] Margaret T. Hodgen, *Early Anthropology in the Sixteenth and Seventieth Centuries* (Philadelphia: U of Pennsylvania P, 1971), 33.

… ."[68] Not merely exploratory navigators but also the Jesuit missionaries made a point to highlight the un-Utopian feature of the Middle Kingdom. Speaking of their *Journals*, Ricci and Trigault remark:

> We speak the native language of the country, have set ourselves to the study of their customs and laws and finally, what is of the highest importance, we have devoted ourselves day and night to the perusal of their literature. These advantages were, of course, entirely lacking to writers who never at any time penetrated into this alien world.[69]

Since most Jesuit missionaries were well-educated scholars, their accounts should be immune to charges of being fantastic. Then how did Renaissance Europe respond to the geographical and cultural space represented by China?

The ethnic or racialist, Orientalist, and colonialist frameworks are three typical approaches to the early modern conception of the foreign other. The racialist discourse deals with diverse forms of discrimination or marginalization based on "various combinations of ethnic, geographic, cultural, class, and religious difference."[70] According to Ania Loomba, "race" is an artificial construct, because "what we call race does not indicate natural or biological divisions so much as social divisions which are characterized as if they were natural or biological."[71] "Ethnicity" is a concept specially formulated to address this artificial nature of race. "To signal the mutability and constructedness of race," Loomba observes, "many writers frame the word within quote marks and others substitute it with 'ethnicity.'"[72] Thus ethnic classification *per se* does not entail racialist implications; it is the use of ethnic category to signify essential inferiority or discrimination that constitutes racism. Edward W. Said's *Orientalism*, a study of the Orientalist literature of the nineteenth century in the Middle East, sets up a new way of thinking about the racial or ethnic other. For Said, the West views the Orient through the binary oppositions between Westerners and Orientals. But "when one uses categories like Oriental and Western as both the starting and the end points of analysis, research, public policy," Said argues, "the result is usually to polarize the distinction—the Oriental becomes more Oriental, the Westerner more Western," a polarization that inevitably inhibits fruitful interactions between "different cultures, traditions, and societies."[73] So the Orientalist model allows us to see how the West constructs an Eastern other in order to "control, manipulate,

---

[68] Sir Humphrey Gilbert to Sir John Gilbert, June 30,1566, in *The Voyages and Colonising Enterprises of Sir Humphrey Gilbert*, ed. David B. Quinn, 2 vols. (London: Hakluyt Soceity,1940), vol. 1., 134.
[69] Ricci-Trigault, *Journals*, 5.
[70] Ania Loomba, *Shakespeare, Race, and Colonialism* (Oxford: Oxford UP, 2002), 2.
[71] Loomba, *Shakespeare*, 3.
[72] Loomba, *Colonialism/ Postcolonialism*, 2nd ed. (London: Routledge, 2005), 106.
[73] Edward W. Said, *Orientalism*, 25th Anniversary Edition, with a New Preface by the Author (New York: Vintage Books, 2003), 45–46.

even incorporate what is manifestly a different (or alternative and novel) world."[74] Thus like the ethnic or racial spectacles, an Orientalist lens also tends to fixate on instances of marginalization, manipulation, and exclusion rather than equal and reciprocal intercourses.

China remains largely a place name in most critical studies of the racial or foreign other in the early modern period.[75] Apart from a few works on trade with the Far East, there seems to be a systematic neglect of the Chinese in scholarship on early modern literary portrayals of the Orient before the 1670s. Loomba presents a long catalogue of the "outsiders" for Shakespearean England, which include the "Indians, gypsies, Jews, Ethiopians, Moroccans, Turks, Moors, 'savages,' the 'wild Irish,' the 'uncivil Tartars,' as well as non-English Europeans."[76] China does not show up in this exhaustive list. The Far East is excluded in Richard Barbour's *Before Orientalism: London's Theatre of the East 1576–1626*, a work that confines the Orient to the Ottoman and Mogul empires.[77] China is absent from Mary Floyd-Wilson's *English Ethnicity and Race in Early Modern Drama* as well. But in including Western depictions of China in the collection of articles in *Renaissance, Orientalism, and the Idea of Asia*, Debra Johanyak and Walter S. H. Lim chart new lines of inquiry in studies of the early modern other.

The paucity of references to China may account for this critical oversight. But another possible reason is that the Middle Kingdom simply does not fit in with the ethnocentric or Orientalist framework that presupposes various forms of inferiority. As George H. Dunne puts it, if a conceptual paradigm that presumes the superiority of European culture "proved wanting in India," "it would prove totally inept in China."[78] Michael Keevak notes that "yellowness" is a racial construct that started to circulate only in the eighteenth and nineteenth centuries, since in their initial encounter with the Asian people, Western missionaries and merchants tended to regard the Chinese and Japanese as "white."[79] Indeed, a racialist model might apply to the Turks, Moors, Indians, and Africans, as the literary images of

---

[74] Said, *Orientalism*, 12.

[75] For early modern ethnic or racialist studies see, *Women, "Race" and Writing in Early Modern England*, ed. Margo Hendricks and Patricia Parker (London: Routledge, 1994); Kim Hall, *Things of Darkness: Economies of Race and Gender in Early Modern England* (Ithaca, NY: Cornell UP, 1995); Nabil Matar, *Turks, Moors, and Englishmen in the Age of Discovery* (New York: Columbia UP, 1999); Imtiaz H. Habib, *Black Lives in the English Archives, 1500–1677: Imprints of the Invisible* (Aldershot: Ashgate, 2008); Joyce G. MacDonald, *Women and Race in Early Modern Texts* (Cambridge: Cambridge UP, 2002); Mary Floyd-Wilson, *English Ethnicity and Race in Early Modern Drama* (Cambridge: Cambridge UP, 2003); and Johanyak and Lim eds., *The English Renaissance*.

[76] Loomba, *Shakespeare*, 8.

[77] Richard Barbour, *Before Orientalism: London's Theatre of the East 1576–1626* (New York: Cambridge UP, 2003).

[78] Dunne, *Generation of Giants*, 12.

[79] Michael Keevak, *Becoming Yellow: A Short History of Racial Thinking* (Princeton, NJ: Princeton UP, 2011).

these people largely reflect their real lived conditions. As declared enemies of Christian Europe, the Spanish and Barbary Moors and their associates, Muslims and Turks in the East, had been historically viewed through a racial lens. Later, when the first cargo of African slaves were unloaded on August 8, 1444, from the exploration ships commissioned by Henry the Navigator, and when Columbus paraded with his American Indians on his way to see the Spanish sovereigns in 1492, the other represented by the Africans and Americans began to be regarded through the racial framework as well. The establishment of the two colonies of Macau and Manila by the Portuguese and Spanish in the sixteenth century brought the Far East into the orbit of the "outsiders," and, as a consequence, China was focalized through the same lens fixated on already established others. But easy as it was to categorize other non-Christian and nonwhite peoples in racialist terms, China fitted uneasily within such a parameter because the "difference" it embodied, to use Bacon's words, "comes not from soil, not from climate, not from race, but from the arts."[80] For Western observers, Chinese culture was, rather than inferior, superior to the West. Polo remarked that Cathay "surpass[es] other nations in the excellence of their manners and their knowledge of many subjects."[81] For Mandeville, "the kingdom of Cathay is the largest kingdom there is in the world, and also the Great Chan is the strongest emperor there is under the firmament."[82] Similarly, Mendoza noticed that the Chinese were "so prudent and wise in the gouernment of their common wealth, and so subtill and ingenious in all arts."[83] Ricci and Trigault even claimed a rational aspect of Eastern paganism. "Of all the pagan sects known to Europe," they say, we "know of no people who fell into fewer errors in the early ages of their antiquity than did the Chinese."[84] Put differently, the pagan philosophy of the Chinese was shot through with rational light, and thereby conformable to the Christian faith. So, heathens as the Chinese were, they boasted a high level of civilization both in physical and spiritual terms.

Since colonialism started to take shape with maritime expansions in the sixteenth and seventeenth centuries, and the racial or ethnical other has assumed an additional dimension in the "colonial discourse," colonialism is indeed a pertinent model to study western Europe's interactions with most new world others in the early modern period. As Loomba notes, though racial stereotypes could be traced back to ancient Greece and Rome, European colonialists reworked and entrenched the image of the racial other.[85] This coupling of the racial with colonial other was especially notable in the formative period of colonialism. "Colonialism" means "the conquest and control of other people's land and goods," a term that refers both to "pre-capitalist" and "capitalist European" colonial practices.[86] For Loomba,

[80] Bacon, *New Organon*, 118.
[81] Polo, *Travels*, 160.
[82] Mandeville, 139.
[83] Mendoza, *Mighty Kingdom of China*, 39.
[84] Ricci-Trigault, *Journals*, 93.
[85] Loomba, *Colonialism/ Postcolonialism*, 92.
[86] Loomba, *Colonialism/Postcolonialism*, 8, 9.

Said's *Orientalism* initiates not merely a novel way of thinking about racialism but also "a new kind of study of colonialism," that is, "colonial discourse." As a framework used to describe, explain, and theorize colonial practices, colonial discourse "indicates a new way of conceptualizing the interactions of cultural, intellectual, economic or political processes in the formation, perpetuation and dismantling of colonialism." This conceptualization, Loomba argues, "allows us to see how power works through language, literature, culture, and the institutions which regulate our daily lives."[87]

The colonial model is much adopted in scholarship on Donne and Milton's depictions of the new worlds. But this interpretive model proves inapt to account for images of China in Renaissance literary works, as most of these images derived from contemporary travel and missionary reports that emphasize the greatness and mightiness of the Eastern country. Early modern Western observers themselves recognized that the Chinese who "imagine[d] the whole world included in their kingdoms" were far from a colonial object.[88] The Chinese's remarkable sense of self-centeredness and self-sufficiency rendered the colonial approach especially irrelevant. The Chinese call their country the "Middle Kingdom" or "the center" of the world and their monarch "Lord of the Universe," Ricci and Trigault remark, because they "are of the opinion that the extent of their vast dominion is to all intents and purposes coterminous with the border of the universe." Apart from this undoubting belief in the centrality of their country, the two missionaries also note that "everything which the people need for their well-being and sustenance, whether it be for food or clothing or even delicacies and superfluities, is abundantly produced within the borders of the kingdom [China] and not imported from foreign climes."[89] The Chinese's "opinion" of their own superiority and centrality was so formidable that in his *Complete Map of Mountains, Seas, and Lands* (1602), Ricci, to accommodate this highly entrenched notion, had to place China in the very middle of the map.[90] Unlike the Eastern Indians who were, as Milton says, stained with "barbarism" and "worship as gods malevolent demons whom they cannot exorcise"(YP 4:551), China, with its powerful ethical and monarchical systems, was frequently portrayed as inhabited by a people who were comparable with, and even superior to, western Europeans. People in America and Africa were regarded as some "historyless" ancestors at an earlier, infant-like stage.[91] In contrast, Ming

---

[87] Loomba, *Colonialism/Postcolonialism*, 43, 45, 50–51.
[88] Ricci-Trigault, *Journals*, 43.
[89] Ricci-Trigault, *Journals*, 7, 10.
[90] On Ricci's map see J. F. Baddeley, "Father Matteo Ricci's Chinese World Maps, 1584–1608," *Geographical Journal* 53 (1919): 254–70; and Bolesław Szcześniak, "Matteo Ricci's Maps of China," *Imago Mundi* 11 (1954): 127–36.
[91] The term "historyless people" was first used by Marx and Engels to describe those primitive aboriginals who could only subject themselves to be assimilated by the colonizers. For a critique of the "historyless" doctrine see Wolf, *People without History*; Mary Nyquist, "Contemporary Ancestors of de Bry, Hobbes, and Milton," *University of Toronto Quarterly* 77.3 (2008): 837–75; and Hodgen, *Early Anthropology*, 338–39.

China, once contemporaneous with ancient Egypt, Greece, and Rome, has been enjoying a long and uninterrupted history that, as Donne put it in 1614, "vex[es] us at this day."[92]

The Jesuits' accommodative model that regards the Chinese culture in its own right proves a fruitful though limited approach.[93] Unlike the Portuguese and the Spanish who tried to open the door of the Middle Kingdom by cannons, Jesuit missionaries adopted an accommodative approach.[94] In their *Journals*, Ricci and Trigualt keep an entry on the accommodative policy introduced by Valignano. "Judging from the immense expanse of this empire [China]," "the nobility of character of its people," and "the fact that they had lived in peace for centuries," Valignano says, "surely the wisdom of their system of public administration and the well known prudence of their governing Magistrates would seem to favor the proposed [evangelical] expedition." The reason is that, Valignano further explains, "a clever and accomplished people, devoted to the study of fine-arts" should have the sagacity to "accept a few strangers, who were also distinguished for their learning and virtue, to come and dwell among them, especially if their visitors were well versed in the Chinese language and literature."[95] It is in consideration of the "nobility," "wisdom," "prudence," and "learning and virtue" of the Chinese people that Valignano proposed the policy to accommodate rather than denounce this religious and cultural other. Valignano's proposal received official sanction from the Sacred Congregation for the Propagation of the Faith (known as the Propaganda Fide) in 1659, which stipulated: "Do not try to persuade the Chinese to change their rites, their customs, their ways, as long as these are not openly opposed to religion and good morals. What would be sillier than to import France, Spain, Italy, or any other country of Europe into China? Don't impose these, but the faith."[96] The Jesuits' respect for Chinese culture paid off. In 1692, Emperor Kangxi (1662–1722) promulgated a decree of toleration for Christianity.[97] The encoding of the accommodative policy in pontifical and royal edicts marked the high water of the intercourse between East and West in the Renaissance.

The accommodative framework does not, however, preclude the deeper cultural differences that hinder a real reciprocal communication. As is instanced in the famous "Rites Controversy," Western responses to Chinese culture could not be

---

[92] John Donne, *Essayes in Divinity: Being Several Disquisitions Interwoven with Meditations and Prayers*, ed. Anthony Raspa (Montreal: McGill-Queen's UP, 2001), 22.

[93] Benjamin A. Elman, *On Their Own Terms: Science in China, 1550–1900* (Cambridge: Harvard UP, 2005).

[94] Mungello, *Curious Land*, 13. Hudson calls it a policy of "concession," *Europe and China*, 303.

[95] Ricci-Trigault, *Journals*, 130.

[96] *100 Roman Documents Relating to the Chinese Rites Controversy (1645–1941)*, trans. Donald F. St. Sure S. J. and ed. Ray R. Noll (San Francisco: Ricci Institute, 1992), 6. For Valignano's policy also see Andrew C. Ross, "Alesssandro Valignano: The Jesuits and Culture in the East," in O'Malley et al. eds., 337–51.

[97] S. Neill, *A History of Christian Missions* (Harmondsworth: Penguin, 1964), 189–90.

covered by the umbrella concept of "accommodation," and there existed equally powerful competing interpretative alternatives.[98] The "Rites Controversy" was sparked by different attitudes within the missionary camp towards Chinese funeral rites and ritual veneration of Confucius (551–479 BC). Whereas most Jesuits opted for compromise and respect for Confucian rites, considering them civil and political rather than religious ceremonies, the Franciscans and Dominicans condemned them as superstitious and idolatrous. The flame of this debate raged so high that it lasted from ca. 1630 until 1745, involving such notable figures as the popes, bishops, Chinese emperors, the Jansenists, as well as the Sorbonne University in Paris. Since Pope Clement XI (1649–1721) supported the Dominican line of interpreting the Eastern culture, the pontifical legate to Emperor Kangxi in 1705–7 was driven out of the imperial capital. Ignoring this royal displeasure, the pope continued the hostile policy, issuing the papal bull *Ex illa die* on March 19, 1715, to officially repudiate Chinese rites. In response, the Chinese emperor proclaimed the Decree of Kangxi (1721), stipulating that "From now on, Westerners should not be allowed to preach in China, to avoid further trouble."[99] The Eastern door shut resolutely against the missionaries at the imperial decree, and the golden age for East-West contact came to an end until it was reopened in modern times. Both the internal dissention within the Catholic Church and the resolute measures taken by the pontifical and imperial heads speak of the irreconcilable elements inherent in the two widely distinct cultures.

IV: A Globalization and Liberal Cosmopolitan Model

Given the inadequacy of the conventional interpretive frameworks, I propose a globalization approach to the early modern encounter with China.[100] Manfred B. Steger differentiates between "globality" and "globalization." By "globality," he means "*a social condition* characterized by tight global economic, political, cultural, and environmental interconnections and flows that make most of the current existing borders and boundaries irrelevant." In contrast, "globalization" indicates "*a set of social processes* that appear to transform our present social conditions of weakening nationality into one of globality."[101] Since various forms of global "interconnections and flows" mark the transcontinental intercourse in

---

[98] For the "Rites controversy," see David E. Mungello, ed., *The Chinese Rites Controversy: Its History and Meaning* (Nettetal: Steyler Verlag, 1994); and Porter, *Ideographia*, 108–21.

[99] *China in Transition, 1517–1911*, trans. Dan J. Li (New York: Van Nostrand Reinhold, 1969), 22.

[100] For the necessity to approach early modern literature from a globalization perspective see Daniel Vitkus, "Introduction: Toward a New Globalism in Early Modern Studies," *Journal for Early Modern Cultural Studies* 2.1 (2002): v–viii.

[101] Manfred B. Steger, *Globalization: A Very Short Introduction*, 2nd ed. (Oxford: Oxford UP, 2009), 8, 9.

the Renaissance, Dennis Flynn and Arturo Giráldez argue, "a global perspective instead of the predominant Eurocentric view" provides a more apt lens to study the transoceanic trade of precious metals between Europe, the New World, and Ming China.[102] As the so-called Manila Galleons connected the Atlantic and the Pacific for the first time in history, Flynn and Giráldez propose, the establishment of the Manila colony by the Spanish in 1571 marks the "birth" of early modern globalization.[103] The ascendancy of Ming China in the global economy, especially through its leadership in the silver trade, constitutes the central evidence for claims of an early modern globalization. Andre Gunder Frank argues that it is China, not Europe, that held the center stage in the early modern world trade.[104] For Kenneth Pomeranz, the Far East was an "'active' force in creating a global economy," because "somewhere between one-third and one-half" of the silver bullion looted by the Europeans from the New World "wound up in China."[105] Hobson asserts that "the East enabled the rise of the West" during 500–1800, and "China's economy was pivotal insofar as it constituted a silver sink into which much of the world's silver was channeled."[106] Baker claims that it is precisely "the Asian demand for New World silver that makes possible" the flood of Chinese goods in a British Burse.[107]

Although the global flows of precious metals in the early modern period do not necessarily constitute "globalization," they do exemplify processes that are "global." Technological and communicative constraints did not obstruct the globalizing processes precipitated by maritime explorations. One cannot deny the global scope of England and Spain's colonial enterprises in the early modern period on the grounds of the lack of modern Internet and other information technologies. The much-talked-of delays marking early modern transnational communications do not mean that global cultural transmissions did not happen.[108] Though the intensification and acceleration of communication is crucial to the modern definition of globalization, and these characteristics are obviously lacking in the early modern globalizing processes, the worldwide commercial and cultural activities set in

---

[102] Dennis O. Flynn and Arturo Giráldez, "Born with a 'Silver Spoon': The Origin of World Trade in 1571," *Journal of World History* 6.2 (1995): 201–21, 203.

[103] Flynn and Giráldez, *China and the Birth of Globalization in the 16th Century* (Aldershot: Variorum, 2010). Though most of Flynn and Giraldez's articles quoted in this dissertation are comprehended in this work, I use their original publications as much as possible. Also see Howard J. Erlichman, *Conquest, Tribute, and Trade: the Quest for Precious Metals and the Birth of Globalization* (Amherst, NY: Prometheus Books, 2010).

[104] Andre Gunder Frank, *ReORIENT: Global Economy in the Asian Age* (Berkeley: U of California P, 1988).

[105] Kenneth Pomeranz, *The Great Divergence: China, Europe, and the Making of the Modern World Economy* (Princeton: Princeton UP, 2000), 161, 190.

[106] Hobson, *Eastern Origins*, 2, 66.

[107] Baker, *On Demand*, 99.

[108] For such delays see Miles Ogborn, *Indian Ink: Script and Print in the Making of the English East India Company* (Chicago: U of Chicago P, 2008).

motion by navigators, travelers, merchants, and evangelical Jesuits are nevertheless irrefutable historical facts. Apart from the interconnections enabled by commercial trade, the Jesuits' missionary work opened up various cultural circuits throughout the world, and the slave trade enacted a global labor flow.[109]

The global consciousness awakened by early modern transnational communications is vividly captured by a growing craze for images of the earth. According to Fred Spier, the plethora of globes and maps in the Renaissance played a great part in raising contemporary consciousness of a globalized world. The "first wave of true globalization," Spier says, generated "the first *Earth Icons*," that is, "images of our planet used by people to show that they were global players," and that many early modern maps and books contain such images "points to a vivid global awareness in this city [Amsterdam] at that time."[110] By "global awareness," Spier means the sudden enlightenment brought about by perception of a globalized world.

Rather than economic globalization *per se*, however, this book focuses on the cultural consequences caused by this "first wave of true globalization." Specifically, I examine the encounter between the old and new cultures triggered by global interactions or the so-called cultural globalization that "refers to the intensification and expansion of cultural flows across the globe." By "culture," I mean "the symbolic construction, articulation, and dissemination of meaning."[111]

---

[109] Luke Clossey, *Salvation and Globalization in the Early Jesuit Missions* (Cambridge: Cambridge UP, 2008); and Patrick Manning, ed. *Slave Trades, 1500–1800: Globalization of Forced Labour* (Ashgate: Variorum, 1996). For the various global interconnections in the Renaissance also see, Wendy F. Kasinec and Michael A. Polushin, ed. *Expanding Empires: Cultural Interaction and Exchange in World Societies from Ancient to Early Modern Times* (Wilmington, DE: SR Books, 2002); Denis O. Flynn, Arturo Giráldez, and Richard von Glahn, eds. *Global Connections and Monetary History 1470–1800* (Aldershot: Ashgate, 2003); Geoffery Gunn, *First Globalization: The Eurasian Exchange, 1500–1800* (Lanham, MD: Rowman & Littlefield, 2003); and Charles H. Parker, *Global Interactions in the Early Modern Age, 1400–1800* (New York: Cambridge UP, 2010).

[110] Fred Spier, "Histories Big and Small: A Critique of Wolf Schäfer's New Global History," *Erwägen Wissen Ethik* 14 (2003): 118–20, 119. For globe making in early modern England and its influence upon literature see, Victor Morgan, "The Literary Image of Globes and Maps in Early Modern England," in *English Map-Making 1500–1650: Historical Essays*, ed. Sarah Tyacke (London: British Library, 1983), 46–56; J. B. Harley, "Meaning and Ambiguity in Tudor Cartography," in Tyacke ed., *English Map-Making*, 22–45; Frank Lestringant, *Mapping the Renaissance World: The Geographical Imagination in the Age of Discovery*, trans. David Fausett (Berkeley: U of California P, 1994); and Adam M. Cohen, "Englishing the Globe: Molyneux's Globes and Shakespeare's Theatre Career," *Sixteenth Century Journal* 37 (2006): 963–84.

[111] Steger, *Globalization*, 71. On cultural globalization theory, see Arjun Appadurai, *Modernity at Large: Cultural Dimensions of Globalization* (Minneapolis: U of Minnesota P, 1996); Fredric Jameson and Masao Miyoshi, eds. *The Cultures of Globalization* (Durham: Duke UP, 1998); and John Tomlinson, *Globalization and Culture* (Chicago: U of Chicago P, 1999).

As Liam Connell and Nicky Marsh point out, cultural globalization allows us to see at once "globalization's economic and discursive form" or "its material base and its cultural superstructure."[112] My chapter on the resonance of the global flow of precious metals in Donne's works seeks precisely to illustrate the "economic form" or "material base" of early modern cultural globalization to be elaborated in the ensuing chapters. The Jesuits' transnational apostolic mission that undertook to propagate European culture exemplifies the cultural dimension of early modern global commerce.[113]

As a conceptual paradigm that has generated a host of analytical categories such as hybridity, cosmopolitanism, and identity politics, globalization theory helps us rethink the literary world of seventeenth-century England against the backdrop of global trade networks. Situating my argument within the broader framework of globalization theory, I propose the concept of *liberal cosmopolitanism* to study Europe's receptions of the new others disclosed by the early modern globalization. By liberal cosmopolitanism I mean a set of liberal principles that guide early modern English interactions with some newly discovered global others. Suman Gupta defines cosmopolitanism as "the determination and cultivation of political and ethical and social principles that are consistent with a globalized world."[114] For Kwame A. Appiah, "universal concern and respect for legitimate difference" generate a "cosmopolitan curiosity" to engage "alternative ways of thinking, feeling, and acting."[115] I argue that even in the formative period of colonialism and when a Eurocentric outlook reigned supreme, some enlightened thinkers nevertheless displayed a remarkable liberal cosmopolitanism to embrace and engage cultural pluralism. As is shown in the Jesuits' accommodative policy, liberal cosmopolitan principles were consciously adopted in Europe's contact with such advanced others as Ming China and the Azuchi-Momoyama Japan (c. 1573–1600).[116] In particular, the superior culture of the Chinese prompted in Donne and Milton a respect for difference and a "cosmopolitan curiosity" that led both authors to engage it on its own terms. This engagement, in turn, compels them to reflect in profound and previously unexamined ways upon their Eurocentric and monotheistic assumptions and to reconsider the place of Renaissance Europe within a rapidly expanding world. Ulbrich Beck states that cosmopolitanism reflects a "reflexive awareness" of "how globality overcomes and reconfigures differentiation."[117] The liberal cosmopolitan model allows us precisely to see how

---

[112] Connell and Marsh eds., *Literature and Globalization*, 3.
[113] For the cultural globalization enacted by the Jesuits see Clossey, *Globalization in the Early Jesuit Missions*.
[114] Suman Gupta, *Globalization and Literature* (London: Polity, 2009), 48.
[115] Kwame A. Appiah, *Cosmopolitanism: Ethics in a World of Strangers* (New York: Norton, 2006), 97, xv.
[116] For Early modern approaches to Japan see Ikuo Higashibaba, *Christianity in Early Modern Japan: Kirishitan Belief and Practice* (Leiden, Boston & Köln: Brill, 2001); also see Keevak, *Becoming Yellow*.
[117] Ulrich Beck, *The Cosmopolitan Vision* (Cambridge: UK, Polity, 2006), 3. 4.

encounters with a superior and radical other obliged early modern Europeans to redefine cultural difference or "reconfigure differentiation" along some liberal cosmopolitan lines. This enlightened cosmopolitanism enabled by encounters with some advanced non-Western cultures, I would suggest, planted the very seeds of Western liberalism that was to witness a full blossoming in the eighteenth-century Enlightenment.[118] A cosmopolitan approach to global diversities, however, does not necessarily imply moral approbation, nor is the willingness to engage cultural difference incompatible with the desire to subsume, appropriate, or neutralize it.

The liberal cosmopolitan model assumes immediate relevance for those who were confronted with, for the first time in history, a newly revealed globe. In the early modern period when the earth seemed to have assumed a motive and global dimension overnight, enlightened minds were apt to acquire a more capacious outlook. Copernican astronomy reversed the roles of the sun and the earth, a revolution that directly challenged the Christian establishment premised upon a sedentary earth. Meanwhile, the meeting of the Far East with the Far West transformed the "flat" earth into a rounded globe, a transformation that raised doubts about the old world center. Inspired by these paradigmatic shifts, those inquisitive minds started to construct new models to conceptualize a radically changed cosmos. Liberal cosmopolitanism is numbered among those experimental paradigms that sought to replace the old outdated conceptual frameworks.

That the term *cosmopolitan* first appeared in the Renaissance also indicates the dawning of such a perspective in this particular era. Cosmopolitanism comes from *cosmopolite*, a word that means a "citizen of the world" or "one who regards or treats the whole world as his country." With "no national attachments or prejudices," a cosmopolite is usually used as a counterpart to a "patriot" who harbors intense national feelings.[119] Thomas Blount's *Glossographia* (1656) is the first English dictionary to include an entry for cosmopolite, by which he means "a Citizen of the World; or Cosmopolitan."[120] In reality, there was a rising tendency in the Renaissance for enlightened minds to consciously identify themselves as cosmopolitans. In his *Epistolæ Ho-Elianæ* (1645), James Howell says, "I came tumbling out into the World a pure *Cadet*, a true *Cosmopolite*; nor Born to Land, Lease, House or Office."[121] Similarly, in his *Principal Navigations*, Hakluyt remarks that a perfect cosmographer "finde[s] himselfe Cosmopolites, a citizen and a member of the whole and onely mysticall citie vniuersall, and so consequently to meditate of the Cosmopoliticall government thereof" (PN 1:16). As a newly added dictionary item, however, the word *cosmopolitan* had not yet acquired the full-spectrum meaning it possesses now, and most of the time it

---

[118] For the evolution of the liberal tradition see Porter, "What Is Universal about Universal Human Rights?" *CICS International Connections* 3.2 (2011): 6–10.
[119] "cosmopolite, n. and adj." 2nd ed. 1989. *OED Online*. June 5, 2012.
[120] Thomas Blount, *Glossographia, or A Dictionary Interpreting all such Hard Words* (London, 1656), sig. L4r.
[121] James Howell, *Epistolæ Ho-Elianæ* (London, 1688), 285.

meant a narrow openness to the others within the national or European borders. Cosmopolitan attentiveness to the non-Western others in such newly discovered worlds as Peru and Mexico was quite rare, especially when considering the colonial underpinning of those exploratory ventures. But there are some liberal moments in open-minded thinkers like Donne and Milton that signal a global consciousness and cosmopolitan tolerance of cultural pluralism. In effect, such enlightened moments were substantial enough to constitute some identifiable and distinct forms of cosmopolitanism. Renaissance cosmopolitanism, Alison Games argues, distinguishes by its multivocal and pluralistic responses to global diversities. For instance, the merchants' "cosmopolitanism" was expressed by the clerics as "ecumenism," that is, a wish to embrace religious diversification through the evangelical mission, and the colonialists articulated their cosmopolitan will in "their willingness to adapt and to learn from the examples of rivals and predecessors."[122]

The liberal spirit marking Renaissance cosmopolitans resonates Bacon's injunction to globalize learning or knowledge. Maritime cosmopolitanism expresses not only as a cosmopolitan willingness to engage alien cultures but also a liberal impulse to propagate Western knowledge to foreign lands. This outbound liberal strand finds a theoretical articulation in Bacon's *The Advancement of Learning* (1605). Capitalizing on images and metaphors supplied by maritime explorations, Bacon argues,

> if the invention of the ship was thought so noble, which carrieth riches and commodities from place to place, and much more are letters to be magnified, which as ships pass through the vast seas of time, and make ages so distant to participate of the wisdom, illuminations, and inventions, the one of the other.[123]

What Bacon calls forth here is the compulsion to globalize and circulate Western knowledge for mutual learning, which shows none other than a cosmopolitan generosity to distribute and share common intellectual property. For Bacon, "letters" are "ships" that allow people to transcend time and space and enjoy each other's "wisdom, illuminations, and inventions." In an age of unprecedented adventure, the Lord Chancellor urges, those "received authors" embodying European learning "should stand up like Hercules' Columns, beyond which there should be" both "sailing" and "discovering."[124] Simply put, scholars should, like maritime explorers, venture out both to promote European learning and learn from others.

Bacon's injunction of global knowledge circulation and sharing was not a utopian vision but empirically tried out by the Jesuit missionaries. To bring the new

---

[122] Alison Games, *The Web of Empire: English Cosmopolitans in an Age of Expansion, 1560–1660* (New York: Oxford UP, 2008), 10.

[123] Francis Bacon, *The Advancement of Learning*, in *Francis Bacon: A Critical Edition of the Major Works*, ed. Brian Vickers (Oxford: Oxford UP, 2002), 168.

[124] Bacon, *Advancement of Learning*, 169.

pagans to the fold of the Christian God, the Jesuits dispersed themselves throughout the globe, setting in motion various forms of global cultural "interconnections and flows." Though proceeding under the banner of Christianity, the evangelical cause was simultaneously a cultural enterprise, for, as George H. Dunne remarks:

> To the body of revealed truths, Christianity had developed cultural forms. It had accommodated itself and contributed to the development of European art forms, social customs, modes of dress, of language, of thought. It had also developed a body of ecclesiastical laws, Roman in character, regulating the discipline of Catholic life. A part of history as they were, these cultural and juridical forms were not divinely revealed.

So what the Jesuits carried with them was not only Christian faith but also the "European cultural forms" accruing to that faith. Like other human constructs, however, European culture possesses "no absolute values," and as such, it is susceptible to the influence of any host culture.[125] In other words, the early modern apostolic enterprise has practically galvanized interactions between Western and non-Western cultures. It is not my intention, however, to study the global impact on China left by European cultural forms disseminated by the learned men of the West. Rather, my goal is to explore the influence of Chinese cultural forms as they were transmitted by travelers and missionaries upon Renaissance English literature.[126]

Though addressing the special case of England, the cosmopolitan framework also applies to China's receptions by other major European countries. The Spanish, Portugal, French, and Dutch responded differently to the discovery of the Pacific region, but a consistent pattern indicative of a cosmopolitan tendency can nevertheless be discerned, especially in Spain. As Christina Lee notes, the Spanish writer Alonso Ercilla's (1533–94) epic *La Araucana* features a remarkable sinocentric perspective, in which it is the Far East that takes the center stage and Europe appears but as a peripheral prop. Juan Gil and Tatiana Seijas examine how Chinese travelers who happened to land in Spain negotiated their identity, subjectivity, and agency in light of their brushes with the Spanish legal system. The success of most of the legal cases involving the Chinese indicates signs of cosmopolitan tolerance towards the Far Eastern other in early modern Spain.[127] These various cosmopolitan strands entailed in national conceptions of the Far East, though hardly visible, nevertheless signal an emerging discourse that sought to engage the newly discovered others on their own terms.

Renaissance liberal cosmopolitanism expresses most eloquently in its universal endeavors to comprehend the whole world within the conceptual frameworks

---

[125] Dunne, *Generation of Giants*, 227–28.
[126] For the Chinese influence upon the Jesuits, see Nicolas Standaert, "Jesuit Corporate Culture as Shaped by the Chinese," in O'Malley et al. eds., 352–62.
[127] See Christina H. Lee, ed. *Western Visions of the Far East in a Transpacific Age, 1522–1657*. Christina H. Lee (Aldershot: Ashgate, 2012).

offered by the European civilization. The universal or global outlook expressed by Renaissance thinkers was not a utopian vision but had a very specific historicity—it was a necessary outcome of physical expansions and discoveries. Though initially spurred by a cosmopolitan desire to know and understand the whole known world, universalism has evolved into a concept freighted with ideological valences. In modern globalization theory, universalism is often faulted for having spawned such exclusive ideologies as "Eurocentrism, colonialism, imperialism, racialism, nationalism, sexism, paternalism, heterosexism, and more."[128] But a universal perspective meant quite a different thing in the Renaissance—it was a lens put on in immediate responses to a newly revealed globe, and as such it symbolized, rather than claims of exhaustive knowledge or an ideological and essentialist construct, a real mental outlook of some early modern thinkers. In fact, this universal vision signifies not only a new horizon but also a real revolutionary force, a force that has practically fomented two large-scale intellectual movements. One is the "universal history" project represented by Jean Bodin's *Method for the Easy Comprehension of History* (1566), and the other is the "universal language" reform culminated in the famous linguist John Wilkins's *An Essay towards a Real Character and a Philosophical Language* (1668). A cosmopolitan engagement with the new historical data and species of languages in the recently discovered worlds proved the key driver behind the early modern historical and linguistic revolutions.

Early modern, however, differs from modern cosmopolitanism. Modern cosmopolitanism refers both to a physical and spiritual state, as the high-speed transportation and information systems that allow free traversing across cultural and national borders literally create cosmopolitan cities and conditions. In contrast, Renaissance cosmopolitanism presents itself more as thought experiment than practical engagement. By *thought experiment* I mean a form of encounter that remains largely at the imaginative or contemplative level, since neither Donne nor Milton, or even Hakluyt, the self-styled cosmopolitan cosmographer, had ventured beyond the European borders. These authors' responses to the new global others were mediated by a multitude of reports transmitted by navigators, merchants, and missionaries who physically travelled to the foreign lands and sensibly felt the difference of the other. It is in the attempt to make sense of the alien other represented by these various global travelers that authors like Donne and Milton came up with their own interpretive strategies, strategies that, I propose, reflect a cosmopolitan willingness to negotiate cultural pluralism. In this sense, Renaissance cosmopolitanism presents itself largely as an intellectual awareness of, and conceptual adaptation to, peoples and cultures beyond the Adamic heritage. Further, cosmopolitanism, whether modern or early modern, is unavoidably conditioned by cultural and national constraints. The cosmopolitans cannot transcend the symbolic system they are born with—the concepts and repertoire they employ come necessarily from specific cultural and nationalist discourses.

---

[128] Sue-Im Lee, "'We Are Not the World': Global Village, Universalism, and Karen Tei Yamashita's *Tropic of Orange*," *Modern Fiction Studies* 52.3 (2007): 501–27, 504.

Thus naturally colored by the monotheistic and Eurocentric outlook unique to the early modern period, Donne and Milton's cosmopolitan impulse to engage the Chinese culture does not preclude the desire to neutralize and assimilate it.

A globalization and liberal cosmopolitan methodology obviously challenges the Eurocentric and nationalist frameworks frequently adopted in studies of early modern interactions with the new worlds. On the one hand, J. M. Blaut defines "Eurocentrism" as "a *unique* set of beliefs" that represents "the intellectual and scholarly rationale for one of the most powerful social interests of the European elites." As such, Blaut argues, "Eurocentrism is quite simply the colonizer's model of the world."[129] In a Eurocentric account, Hobson says, "the East has been a passive bystander in the story of world historical development as well as a victim or bearer of Western power," and this narrative has "legitimately marginalised [the East]from the progressive story of world history."[130] Rather than presuming European superiority, the liberal cosmopolitan model values cultural pluralism, recognizing the contributions of both East and West to the progress of world history. The nationalist methodology or "methodological nationalism," on the other hand, assumes that "the nation-state creates and controls the 'container' of society."[131] Methodological nationalism, especially in Milton studies, has been an entrenched critical practice.[132] A purely nationalist framework is, however, insufficient to account for the various "forces that were drawing the continents into more encompassing relationships" and making the world "a unified stage for human action" in the early modern period.[133] If European nations were actors in this "unified stage," they were actors performing roles with global amplifications. Early modern cosmopolitan metropolises such as London and Lisbon epitomized the global reach of those emerging nation-states. London was a veritable global city, because, Robert K. Batchelor argues, "changes taking place in Asia and on a global scale were translated through London into apparently national developments."[134] So "London developed not just as a market town ... but a place that enabled and indeed fostered global commerce between Asia, the Atlantic World, and Europe." Not only London but also other early modern urban centers closely tied to the

---

[129] James Blaut, *The Colonizer's Model of the World: Geographical Diffusionism and Eurocentric History* (New York: Guilford, 1993), 10.

[130] Hobson, *Eastern Origins*, 4. For anti-Eurocentrism see Janet L. Abu-Lughod, *Before European Hegemony: The World System A. D. 1250–1350* (Oxford: Oxford UP, 1989); Roy Bin Wong, *China Transformed: Historical Change and the Limits of European Experience* (Ithaca, NY: Cornell UP, 1997).

[131] Beck, *Cosmopolitan Vision*, 2.

[132] The nationalist approach to Milton culminates in David Loewenstein and Paul Stevens, ed. *Early Modern Nationalism and Milton's England* (Toronto: U of Toronto P, 2008). See also Richard Helgerson, *Forms of Nationhood* (Chicago: U of Chicago P, 1994); and Claire McEachern, *The Poetics of English Nationhood 1590–1612* (Cambridge: Cambridge UP, 1996).

[133] Wolf, *People without History*, 24.

[134] Batchelor, *London*, 22.

Asian-European-American trade, such as Delft, Antwerp, Lisbon, Seville, and Amsterdam, were global emporiums.[135]

My chapters unfold as follows. The introduction, "China in Early Modern Globalization: A Liberal Cosmopolitan Approach," establishes the broad historical backdrop and the overall methodological framework governing subsequent discussions. Chapter 1, "Global Silver-Gold Flows: The Chinese Resonance of Donne's 'unfil'd Pistolets'," studies how Donne's image of Spanish coinage in his elegy "The Bracelet" captures the global flow of precious metals dominated by Ming China, and how this global commerce provides the material base for early modern transnational cultural interactions. Chapter 2 is entitled "The Anyan Strait: Donne's Global Vision and Theological Cosmopolitanism." Referring to Hakluyt's account of the Northeast and Northwest passages program, I examine how Donne's image of Anyan in his "Hymn to God, My God, in My Sickness" bears on his awareness of early modern transnational exploratory processes, and how this global vision helps shape his cosmopolitan spirit. I propose that the theological adjustment to the Western discovery of the Far East symbolized by the Anyan strait suggests a *theological cosmopolitanism*, by which I mean an attempt to resituate biblical discourse within a global context.

In Chapter 3, "Chinese Chronology and Donne's Apologetic Exegesis in *Essayes in Divinity*," I explore Donne's engagement with the chronological controversy caused by Mendoza's the *Great and Mighty Kingdom of China* and Scaliger's problematic reactions to Mendoza's account in formulating his chronological theory. I argue that in embedding his image of the Eastern annals within an extensive exegesis of Genesis and Exodus, Donne evinces a cosmopolitan willingness to accommodate chronological difference to the scriptural timeline. Chapter 4 is entitled "The Resonance of Chinese Antiquity in Milton's *Paradise Lost*." Here I investigate how the chronological debate ignited by Mendoza's work was intensified by the publication of Martini's *Sinicae historiae decas prima*. I suggest that the chronological dispute centering on Chinese antiquity helps reveal Milton's liberal cosmopolitanism to engage alternative accounts of time in both his representation of a biblical timeline and his synopsis of world histories in *Paradise Lost*.

Chapter 5, "Webb's Chinese Linguistic Model and the Primitive Language in *Paradise Lost*," considers the linguistic scheme outlined in Milton's epic poem in relation to Webb's *An Historical Essay* that champions the primacy of the Chinese language. The powerful linguistic framework represented in *Paradise Lost*, I propose, resonates in Webb's Chinese model, a resonance that brings to light Milton's unique response to the early modern linguistic reform inspired by Chinese "real" characters. Chapter 6, "The Mongol Tartars' World Imperialism

---

[135] Batchelor, *London*, 8; Timothy Brook, *Vermeer's Hat: The Seventeenth Century and the Dawn of the Global World* (Toronto: Penguin, 2008), also see Brook, *Mr. Selden's Map of China: Decoding the Secrets of a Vanished Cartographer* (New York: Bloomsbury, 2013).

and Milton's Vision of Global Governance," examines Milton's various allusions to the Tartars in *Paradise Lost* in light of the Mongols' western campaigns in the thirteenth century. I argue that the world empire forged by the Mongol Tartars was one of the imperial models that inspired Milton's representation of the contest for empire in his epic poem, and that the lessons learned from the Mongol model compelled Milton to imagine a new global cosmopolis in the rule of the Son. That Milton ultimately rejects the Mongols' imperial governance does not contradict his cosmopolitan spirit; instead, it bespeaks an intellectual cosmopolitanism informed by cultural comparisons.

Donne and Milton are exemplars of Renaissance imaginative receptions of the Chinese culture. Alongside the fluid cosmopolitanism represented by mobile travelers described by Games, the Renaissance also witnessed another kind of cosmopolitans—sedentary travelers who imagined the world by absorbing messages transmitted by those active cross-cultural agents. According to the historian W. A. Raleigh, "action and imagination went hand in hand … Shakespeare and Marlowe were, no less than Drake and Cavendish, circumnavigators of the world" (PN 12:95). I would call these poetic "circumnavigators" who creatively engaged issues of global dimension and relevance "imaginary cosmopolitans." Both Donne and Milton are numbered, like Shakespeare and Christopher Marlowe, among these imaginary cosmopolitans who have not only helped articulate and shape contemporary reception of the other but also turn cultural forms into global assets.[136] China and the Far East started to assume significance in world culture and history as never before, when Donne and Milton, two literary geniuses in the Renaissance, undertook to engage its trade, politics, language, and chronology in startlingly fresh and revealing ways.

---

[136] For English poets and the new world see David McInnis, "The Golden Man and the Golden Age: The Relationship of English Poets and the New World Reconsidered," *Early Modern Literary Studies* 13.1 (2007): 1–19.

Chapter 1
Global Silver-Gold Flows: The Chinese Resonance of Donne's "Unfil'd Pistolets"

With the rise of modern China, how to deploy global strategies to tap into the high growth engine powered by the Chinese economy has become the top agenda of almost every Western country. The United States is rebalancing to Asia, with a view to arresting China's growing importance in international economy and relations. The European Union regards China as a key source of strength that can help revitalize its sluggish economy, and Canada is seeking any means possible to project a commercial presence in the Chinese market. People from different countries, whether big or small, are flocking to China as if attracted by an irresistible magnet. History is repeating itself. Similar stories happened about 400 years ago when Ming China was also looked up to by Western countries as the lodestar of world economy. This chapter studies the literary implications of the early modern globalization dominated by the Chinese economy. The transnational trade triggered by the "race for the Far East," and the global market dominated by Ming China's insatiable demand for the precious metals produced in the New World, I propose, constitute the powerful "material base" that helped shape the global perspective of early modern cosmopolitans like Donne.

According to the historian W. A. Raleigh, Hakluyt's seemingly formless *Principal Navigations* is governed by a "single thread of interest"—"the long struggle of the nations of Europe for commercial supremacy and the control of the traffic with the east." Following this "thread," we can find that "there is the same glitter of gold and precious stones, the same odour of far-fetched spices" in "all the dreams of the politicians and merchants, sailors and geographers, who pushed back the limits of the unknown world" (PN 12:2–3). Ever since Magellan discovered the southwest way "across the Pacific to the Philippines" in 1519–21, Raleigh remarks, "the aim of the European navigators was not to explore or settle America, rather to discover a passage whereby America might be avoided, and a way opened to the lands beyond." "Cathay, the ultimate goal of all Eastern travel," Cipangu [Japan], "the richest island in the world for gold and spices," and the Spice Islands in Southeast Asia, proved to be those "lands beyond." (PN 12:4) Together, these three eastern regions along the Pacific Rim constituted a powerful magnet that orientated the "race for the Far East."

The topic of this chapter concerns the economic and social implications caused by this fascination with Chinese gold and the Western rivalry for the Eastern market. Representations of precious metals are everywhere in Renaissance literature, but most studies deal with their origins in trade either within the European continent or between Europe and the New World.[1] Adding the Far East to the picture, I explore how the Europe-America-China global commerce of gold and silver is reflected in Donne's image of "unfil'd Pistolets" (31) in his elegy "The Bracelet" (1593–94).[2] Metaphors of coins pervade Donne's poems and sermons, which indicates his unusual concern with financial and economic issues.[3] But his particular image of Spanish coinage, that is, "unfil'd Pistolets," signals an attention not only to European but also the global trade of precious metals in the early modern period. In "The Bracelet," Donne writes,

> Or were they Spanish Stamps, still travailing,
> That are become as Catholique as their King;
> These unlick'd beare-whelps, unfil'd Pistolets,
> That, more than cannon-shot, availes or lets,
> Which, negligently left unrounded, looke
> Like many-angled figures in the booke
> Of some greate Conjurer, which would enforce
> Nature, as these do Justice, from her course (29–35)

The word "pistolet" refers to "a Spanish gold escudo," especially the "double-escudo."[4] In 1537, Charles V (1500–58) decreed that gold coins were denominated in "escudos" and silver coins in "reales."[5] One gold escudo equaled two silver coins of eight reales. So the famous "*piece of eight* [reales] always refers to the largest silver—never gold—coin of everyday circulation," and the term "double-escudo" means "always gold, never silver."[6] The "piece of eight" was also called a "peso," a Spanish word that originally meant "weight" but later became "the name of the standard monetary unit of silver (and sometimes gold) in many Spanish American

---

[1] For general works on Renaissance literary representation of coinage see Sandra K. Fischer, *Econolingua: A Glossary of Coins and Economic Language in Renaissance Drama* (Newark: U of Delaware P, 1985); and Stephen Deng, *Coinage and State Formation in Early Modern English Literature* (New York: Palgrave, 2011).

[2] The quotes of Donne's verses are from *John Donne, The Elegies and the Songs and Sonnets*, ed. Helen Gardner (Oxford: Clarendon, 1965); John Donne, *The Divine Poems*, ed. Gardner, 2nd ed. (Oxford: Clarendon, 1978); John Donne, *The Satires, Epigrams and Verse Letters*, ed. Wesley Milgate (Oxford: Clarendon, 1967); and John Donne, *The Epithalamions, Anniversaries and Epicedes*, ed. Milgate (Oxford: Clarendon, 1978). All Donne's sermons come from *The Sermons of John Donne*, ed. George R. Potter and Evelyn M. Simpson, 10 vols. (Berkeley: U of California P, 1953–62). References to the sermons are cited parenthetically by volume and page number.

[3] For Donne's image of coins see "The Dreame," lines 3–5; "A Valediction: of Weeping," lines 3–4; "The Second Anniversary," lines 369–70; and 521–22.

[4] "Pistolet, n.2." 3rd ed. June 2006. *OED Online*. June 5, 2012.

[5] Timothy R. Walton, *The Spanish Treasure Fleets* (Florida: Pineapple, 1994), 20.

[6] Daniel Sedwick and Frank Sedwick, *The Practical Book of Cobs: Included an Expanded Guide to Shipwrecks*, 4th edn. (Winter Park, FL: Daniel Frank Sedwick, 2007), 2, 3. See also Shepard Pond, "The Spanish Dollar: The World's Most Famous Silver Coin," *Bulletin of the Business Historical Society* 15.1 (1941): 12–16.

countries."[7] In the Renaissance, a large amount of Spanish bullion flowed into England so much so that "it was Spanish Coin—the ubiquitous pistolets—which constituted the lion's share" in royal mints.[8] The Spanish background is thus crucial to understanding Donne's "unfil'd Pistolets," but most studies focus on their political and military connotations, and rightly so, given those wars and diplomatic negotiations financed by "Spanish Stamps."[9]

The worldwide flow of Spanish bullion in the early modern period, however, necessitates viewing its influence from a global rather than Eurocentric perspective. Dennis O. Flynn and Arturo Giráldez claim that "imperial Spain can be fully understood only within the context of an emerging, silver-centered *global* economy."[10] According to John J. TePaske:

> American silver was so ubiquitous that merchants from Boston to Havana, Seville to Antwerp, Murmansk to Alexandria, Constantinople to Coromandel, Macao to Canto, and Nagasaki to Manila all used the Spanish peso or piece of eight (*real*) as a standard medium of exchange; these same merchants even knew the relative fineness of the silver coins minted at Potosi, Lima, Mexico, and other sites in the Indies thousands of miles away.[11]

Given the "ubiquitous" presence of Spanish bullion, a regional or national approach to Donne's pistolet cannot do justice to its full implications. Timothy R. Walton observes that "silver pesos and galleons became potent symbols of how Europe was fastening its grip on the rest of the world."[12] Donne's pistolet proves to be one of those "potent symbols" that evoke at once the colonial ambitions of the Europeans and a global commercial network catalyzed by those ambitions. But few have noticed the global dimension of Donne's Spanish stamps. Though

---

[7] Sedwick and Sedwick, *Book of Cobs*, 2, 3.

[8] Christopher Challis, *The Tudor Coinage* (Manchester: Manchester UP, 1978), 193. For Spanish and English trade see Jason Eldred, "'The Just will Pay for the Sinners': English Merchants, the Trade with Spain, and Elizabethan Foreign Policy, 1563–1585," *Journal for Early Modern Cultural Studies* 10.1 (2010): 5–28.

[9] Marius Bewley, ed. *The Selected Poetry of Donne* (New York: Signet Classic, 1966), 127; Donne, *Satires, Epigrams and Verse Letters*, 131; and John T. Shawcross, ed. *The Complete Poetry of John Donne* (New York: Anchor Books, 1967), 44. Also see John Carey, "Donne and Coins," in *English Renaissance Studies Presented to Dame Helen Gardner in Honour of Her Seventieth Birthday*, ed. Carey and Helen Peters (Oxford: Clarendon, 1980), 151–63; and Albert C. Labriola, "Altered States in Donne's 'The Canonization': and Alchemy, Mintage, and Transmutation," *John Donne Journal* 27 (2008): 121–30.

[10] Flynn and Giráldez, "Spanish Profitability in the Pacific: The Philippines in the Sixteenth and Seventeenth Centuries," in *Pacific Centuries: Pacific and Pacific Rim History since the Sixteenth Century*, ed. Flynn, L. Frost and A. J. H. Latham (London: Routledge, 1999), 23–27, 26.

[11] John J. TePaske, "New World silver, Castile, and the Philippines, 1590–1800," in *Precious Metals in the Later Medieval and Early Modern Worlds*, ed. John F. Richards (Durham: North Carolina UP, 1983), 397–424, 425.

[12] Walton, *Treasure Fleets*, 42, 114.

Shankar Raman claims that "Spanish colonial gains do not remain confined to Spain's domains," he restricts their circulation only to "the political and religious body of Europe."[13] Coburn Freer holds that "Donne is one of the first English poets to sense the vast economic changes coming over Europe in general and England in particular,"[14] but he does not associate these changes with the early modern global trade set off by the discovery of American mines.

Situating Donne's pistolets within the worldwide flow of gold and silver and especially in relation to the Chinese market in the early modern period, I adopt the globalization framework to study Donne's image of Spanish coinage. For Flynn and Giráldez, only when Spanish "galleons" or "treasure fleets" started to cross the Pacific and head towards Manila did the world become truly global. In reality, "the only avenue available for Spanish participation in Asian trade was via Mexico, over the Pacific Ocean," because the direct "Europe-Asia trade" of American bullion was controlled by the Portuguese, the Dutch, and the English.[15] Since the so-called Manila Galleons connected the Atlantic and the Pacific for the first time in history, Flynn and Giráldez claim, the establishment of the Manila colony by the Spanish in 1571 marked the "birth" of early modern globalization. Drawing upon Flynn and Giráldez's theory, I propose that Donne's image of unfiled pistolets captures a global economy dominated by Ming China, the largest "demand-side" of American silver.[16] I will study how Donne's depiction of Spanish coinage draws in, through the rich associations of such metaphors as "veines" (38) and "unlick'd beare-whelps," the various strands that tied the European economies to a global market of precious metals.

In "The Bracelet," Donne represents a threefold loss caused, either directly or indirectly, by Spanish stamps—personal, national, and global. Above all, the deluge of Spanish pesos has augmented not only the business of trading uncoined metals but also the practice of melting coined money back into "bullion," that is, uncoined gold or silver in bars or ingots. For Donne's speaker, both customs

---

[13] Shankar Raman, "Can't Buy Me Love: Money, Gender, and Colonialism in Donne's Erotic Verse," *Criticism* 43.2 (2001): 135–68, 151–52.

[14] Coburn Freer, "John Donne and Elizabethan Economic Theory," *Criticism* 38.4 (1996): 497–520, 497.

[15] Flynn and Giráldez, "Arbitrage, China and World Trade in the Early Modern Period," in Flynn and Giráldez eds., *China and the Birth of Globalization*, 10. For early modern transpacific trade also see, William Lytle Schurz, *The Manila Galleon* (New York: E. P. Dutton, 1939); Hang-Sheng Chuan, "The Inflow of American Silver into China from the Late Ming to the Mid-Ch'ing Period," *Journal of the Institute of Chinese Studies of the Chinese University of Hong Kong* 2 (1969): 61–75; and Chuan, "Trade between China, the Philippines and the Americas during the Sixteenth and Seventeenth Centuries," in *Proceedings of the International Conference of Sinology: Selection on History and Archaeology* (Taipei: Acedemia Sinica, 1981), 849–54; Brian Moloughney and Wenzhong Xia, "Silver and the Fall of the Ming Dynasty: A Reassessment," *Papers on Far Eastern History* 40 (1989): 51–78; and William S. Atwell, "Another Look at Silver Imports into China, ca. 1635–1644," *Journal of World History* 16.4 (2005): 467–89.

[16] Flynn and Giráldez, "Silver Spoon," 207.

tend to cost the very subsistence of his life—"my guard, my ease, my food, and my all" (50). Beyond the personal loss, the robust "travailing" of Spanish coins also wreaks havoc upon national economy, debilitating "France" and "Scotland," and "mangle[ing]" the seventeen provinces of the Netherlands (40–41). Last but the least, in stating that the Spanish bullion "run[s] through th' earths every part, / Visit[s] all Countries" (18–19), Donne evokes its global circulation and impact. In this chapter, I aim to show that the economic crisis of the European countries Donne represents in his elegy is not an isolated event; rather, it is part of the chain effect of the debasement of silver in Ming China, a devaluation caused by none other than the global currency of the Spanish stamps.

Donne's "many-angled" pistolets elicit, above all, the larger context of Spain's discovery of gold and silver in American mines, the primary supply market in the early modern global trade. The sixteenth century witnessed Spain opening up a series of rich mines in Peru and Mexico, which yielded such staggering volumes of precious metals that "the official imports registered at Seville indicate that between 1500 and 1650 over a hundred and eighty tons of gold and sixteen thousand tons of silver were sent from the New World to Spain."[17] Mints close to local mines were built in Mexico in 1535 and in Peruvian Lima and Potosí between 1565 and 1574.[18] During the reign of Phillip II (1554–98), to expedite output, these colonial mints launched the so-called cob coinage.[19] "Cobs" are gold or silver coins struck "in hit-or-miss fashion on planchets (blanks) of irregular shape and uneven surface" in American mints.[20] "Unfiled pistolet" was a special form of these colonial cobs. Walton remarks, "Mint workers hammered the silver into a thin bar, cut off chunks roughly equivalent to the weight of the coins, and then trimmed and stamped the coins by hand."[21] Donne's adjectives such as "unfil'd," "unlick'd," "unrounded," and "many angled" graphically capture the most striking feature of American cobs—their "rough" and "irregular" forms. Both silver and gold cobs were impressed with "Spanish Stamps" and subsumed under the general term *bullion*.[22] As Donne notices, American cobs were purposefully or "negligently left unrounded." In fact, part of the popularity of colonial cobs came from their very irregularity. American mints produced "asymmetrical" rather than "rounded" coins because, Daniel Sedwick and Frank Sedwick explain, "most cobs were not struck primarily for circulation but as an expedient means for sending bullion in fixed quantities, easily divisible and accountable, back to the treasuries in Spain and ultimately to the melting pots of Europe."[23]

---

[17] Henry Kamen, *Empire: How Spain Became a World Power 1492–1763* (New York, Perennial: Harper, 2004), 287; also see Walton, *Treasure Fleets*, 82.

[18] For other Spanish colonial mints, see Sedwick and Sedwick, *Book of Cobs*, 51–56.

[19] Sedwick and Sedwick, *Book of Cobs*, 8. Walton holds that "initially ... gold coins were not manufactured in the colonial mints, and all gold was shipped to Europe as bullion." *Treasure Fleet*, 20.

[20] Sedwick and Sedwick, *Book of Cobs*, 8.

[21] Walton, *Treasure Fleets*, 41.

[22] Sedwick and Sedwick, *Book of Cobs*, 10, 11, 12.

[23] Sedwick and Sedwick, *Book of Cobs*, 10.

Alongside the Europe-New World nexus, Donne's pistolets also evoke the New World-China-Europe lap of the global commerce. It is now a consensus among revisionist historians that China played a predominant role in early modern global economy, especially through its dominance of the silver trade. Hobson calls China's primacy in early modern silver trade a "global system of arbitrage," "'global' because it took the form of a continuous loop that went from the Americas, across Eurasia to China and back westwards to Europe."[24] For Pomeranz, if China had not "absorb[ed] the staggering quantities of silver mined in the New World over three centuries," American mines "might have become unprofitable within a few decades."[25] The China trade connection of Donne's pistolets was crucial, though not immediately visible because it moved through such intermediaries as Spain and America. But the Chinese background sheds fresh light on Donne's monetary image, allowing us to understand the poet's unique response to the economic implications of early modern global trade that involved almost all known continents. I am not claiming Donne's direct or even explicit knowledge of the historical reality that large quantities of Spanish colonial silver ended up in China. But the various images and allusions in his poems and sermons do point to an awareness of the global commerce between East and West. As he himself puts it, "by the sea the most remote and distant Nations enjoy one another, by traffique and commerce, East and West becom[e] neighbours" (5:238).

The sources of Donne's image of China could be the same as Jonson's *Entertainment*, though the latter was specially commissioned by the Secretary of State to promote Chinese goods. They could be the Jesuits' accounts, travelers' reports, or even some fantastic tales from those enterprising merchants. But a most certain source of Donne's knowledge of the Eastern trade should be Hakluyt's *Principal Navigations*. Hakluyt presents an extensive account of the Northeast and Northwest passages project, a program launched by the English with the express purpose to seek Eastern gold and spices. Donne's various allusions to the polar passage ventures, his attention to "Easterne riches" in the "Pacifique Sea,"[26] his constant reference to American mines and the debasement of gold caused by the influx of Spanish bullion, as well as his personal participation in the famous Cardiz and Azores expeditions (1596–7) to intercept Spanish treasure fleets—all these bear upon his awareness of the "ubiquitous" travelling of colonial metals, its journey to Ming China in particular.

China and the Global Arbitrage of Silver and Gold

In order to understand Donne's imagery of gold and silver, we need to consider the global circulation of Spanish bullion and how it operated in the early modern period. As W. A. Raleigh notes, Eastern wealth, gold in particular, was a central inspiration for maritime explorations. In his *Travels*, Marco Polo, the Venetian

---

[24] Hobson, *Eastern Origins*, 67.
[25] Pomeranz, *Great Divergence*, 273.
[26] Donne, "Hymne to God My God, in my Sicknesse," lines 16–17.

traveler who stayed in the court of the Yuan emperor Kublai Khan (1214–94) for over two decades, records a tower built of gold measuring "a full finger's breadth in thickness."[27] The fourteenth-century English travel writer Sir John Mandeville depicted the imperial palaces of the Yuan Empire as supported by "twenty-four columns of fine gold."[28] It was chiefly by resorting to Polo and Mandeville's alluring pictures of the Eastern gold that Columbus won the support of the Spanish sovereigns for his 1492 voyage. Columbus was noted for his gold manifesto: "Gold is the most precious of all commodities; gold constitutes treasure, and he who possesses it has all he needs in this world, as also the means of rescuing souls from purgatory, and restoring them to the enjoyment of paradise" (PN 12:17,18). Columbus's gold rush established a model for later explorers. The queen's famous courtier Sir Walter Ralegh's (1554–1618) voyage to Guiana was made with the explicit purpose of seeking the mythical gold city of El Dorado. The English explorer Sir Martin Frobisher (c. 1535–94) brought home from his 1576 northwest venture "a piece of shining black stone, which the assayers of London tested and pronounced to be rich in gold," and it was mainly in search of this gold that he embarked on two other voyages (PN 12:27).

It is an irony of history that an adventure motivated by desire for Eastern riches ended up in the discovery of mines in America. But the East indeed possessed gold. In his "An Excellent Treatise of the Kingdom of China" (1590), the Jesuit missionary Duarte de Sande (1547–99) writes,

> This region [China] affordeth especially many sundry kinds of metals, of which the chiefe, both in excellencie & in abundance, is gold, whereof so many Pezoes are brought from China to India, and to our countrey of Japan, that I heard say, that in one and the same ship, this present yeerr, 2000 such pieces consisting of massie gold, as the Portugals commonly call golden loaves, were brought unto us for merchandise: and one of these loaves is worth almost 100 ducats. (PN 6:354)

This account agrees nicely with Polo and Mandeville's reports of Eastern gold. As Richard von Glahn notes, the Chinese "desired only one particular form of bullion—silver. Gold, a net import a century earlier, flowed out of China during the 'silver century.'"[29] Thus Chinese gold did ultimately flow to Europe, though unlike the colonial gold, it could not be discovered or freely appropriated by the Europeans: it had to be purchased with American silver.

William S. Atwell identifies three major routes through which the precious metals of the New World flowed to China. The first "ran directly across the Pacific from Acapulco on the west coast of modern Mexico to the Philippine Islands."[30]

---

[27] Polo, *Travels*, 188.
[28] Mandeville, *Travels*, 131.
[29] Richard von Glahn, *Fountain of Fortune: Money and Monetary Policy in China, 1000–1700* (Berkeley: U of California P, 1996), 132. For the different routes covered by gold and silver see also Flynn and Giráldez, "Silver Spoon," 207, 215.
[30] Atwell, "International Bullion Flows and the Chinese Economy, circa 1530–1650," in *Metals and Monies in an Emerging Global Economy*, ed. Flynn and Giráldez (Aldershot: Variorum, 1997), 141–63, 145.

Ships running on this Pacific pathway were famously called "Manila Galleons," which undertook "probably the most lucrative branch of international trade with the Orient."[31] Flynn and Giráldez hold that "throughout the seventeenth century, the Pacific galleons carried two million pesos in silver annually (i.e., more than 50 tons) from Acapulco to Manila, whereupon Chinese merchants quickly transshipped it to China."[32] Both the second and third routes passed from Europe around the Cape of Good Hope to the east. According to Atwell, "a second route for New World silver going to China began with the famous *flotas de plata*, the Spanish treasure fleets which carried bullion every year from Mexico and the Isthmus of Panama to Seville." A considerable amount of bullion carried via this route was "illegally" appropriated by the Portuguese and transported to Lisbon. From Lisbon the Portuguese reshipped the bullion they intercepted from the Spanish "around the Cape of Good Hope to Goa," through Malacca, and ultimately to Macao, where they "used this silver to purchase Chinese goods for the markets of Japan, India, the Middle East and western Europe." The third global circuit also started with the treasure fleets, "but in this case some of the bullion which arrived in Seville was shipped [thereafter], legally or illegally, to Amsterdam and London." The Dutch and English East India Companies undertook to transport part of this silver to Southeast Asia, where it was used to "purchase pepper, spices … Chinese luxury goods such as silk and porcelain."[33] In this way, Artur Attman says, "The precious metals which were re-exported from Spain and Portugal to the trading nations of Western Europe formed the basis of the growing bullion flow to the East."[34] But compared with the direct importation from American mines, shipment covered by the last two routes occupied a smaller percentage of the total silver output to China.[35]

Two key factors have rendered possible the Renaissance "global system of arbitrage" of gold and silver. First, in early modern Europe, gold, silver, and copper were separate monetary units with distinctive circulation routes. Accordingly, the

---

[31] Charles R. Boxer, *The Great Ships from Amacon: Annals of Macao and the Old Japan Trade, 1555–1640* (Lisbon: Centro de Estudos Historicos Ultramarinos, 1959), 170.

[32] Flynn and Giráldez, "Cycles of Silver: Global Economic Unity through the Mid-Eighteenth Century," *Journal of World History* 13.2 (2002): 391–427, 398.

[33] Atwell, "International Bullion Flows," 74–75. For the intermediary role played by the Dutch, see F. S. Gaastra, "The Exports of Precious Metal from Europe to Asia by the Dutch East India Company," in Richards ed., *Precious Metals*, 447–75.

[34] Artur Attman, *American Bullion in the European World Trade, 1600–1800* (Gb'teborg: Kungl: Vetenskaps-och Vitterhets-Samhallet, 1986), 31. Also see Ward Barrett, "World Bullion Flows: 1450–1800," in *The Rise of Merchant Empire: Long-Distance Trade in the Early Modern World, 1350–1750*, ed. James D. Tracy (New York: Cambridge UP, 1990), 224–54.

[35] According to Flynn and Giráldez, the annual transportation of New World silver via the Manila galleons "equals the combined quantity of silver shipped from Europe to Asia by the Portuguese *Estado da India*, the Dutch VOC, and the English East India Company combined during the seventeenth century." Flynn and Giráldez, "Cycles of Silver," 398, footnote 12.

movement of each metal should be conceptualized differently rather than subsumed under the umbrella concept of "money."[36] Second, there existed a profitable "bimetallic" ratio difference in the early modern Sino-European bullion trade. A "bimetallic system" means a "monetary system in which both gold and silver coins are legal tender." "Bimetallic flows" will be "set in motion when the disparity between the ratios [silver/gold] in two countries was particularly pronounced."[37] Chuan Hangsheng records that "from 1592 to the early seventeenth century gold was exchanged for silver in Canto at the rate of 1:5.5 to 1:7, while in Spain the exchange rate was 1:12.5 to 1:14, thus indicating that the value of silver was twice as high in China as in Spain."[38] Put another way, while in Spain 12.5 to 14 reales of silver were needed to buy 1 escudo of gold, in China, merely 5.5 to 7 reales of silver were required for the same amount. This great purchasing power of silver in Asia apparently made it very profitable for the Europeans to do gold business there. Pedro de Baeza, a Spanish official who had done business in Asia for almost three decades, remarked in 1609 that "bringing gold from China means a gain of more than seventy-five or eighty percent."[39]

One unavoidable outcome of these "bimetallic flows" was the ultimate decline in the purchasing power of both metals. Early modern European markets witnessed a glut of precious metals. Though a considerable part of American bullion wound its way to the Asian market, still a substantial portion went to Spain and circulated within Europe. Seville turned out to be a mere entrepôt that distributed New World bullion to other European countries or the Far East. Attman states that "a significant proportion of the American precious metals imported into the Iberian Peninsula were dispatched from there to the arteries of world trade, above all, in Holland, France, and England. This applies to Spain's precious metals, as well as Portugal's."[40] In 1571, the Spanish theologian and economist Tomás de Mercado (1525–75) deplored that "in Flanders, in Venice and Rome, there is so much money from Seville that the very roofs could be made of escudos, yet in Spain there is a lack of them. All the millions that come from our Indies, are taken by foreigners to their cities."[41] Meanwhile, new mines were discovered in eastern Europe. So the gold bought with silver from China, along with "the deluge of gold imports from America," as well as "the flow of gold" from eastern Europe, led ultimately to a

---

[36] Flynn and Giráldez, "Cycles of Silver," 397. For the necessity to distinguish silver and gold as separate monetary units, see also Kirti N. Chaudhuri, *The Trading World of Asia and the East India Company, 1660–1760* (New York: Cambridge UP, 1978), 156.

[37] J. D. Gould, *The Great Debasement: Currency and the Economy in Mid-Tudor England* (Oxford: Clarendon, 1970), 27.

[38] Chuan, "The Inflow of American Silver into China," quoted in Flynn and Giráldez, "Silver Spoon," 206.

[39] Quoted in Boxer, "*Plata es Sangre*: Sidelights on the Drain of Spanish-American Silver to the Far East, 1550–1700," *Philippine Studies* 38 (1970): 457–78, 461.

[40] Attman, *American Bullion*, 30.

[41] Tomás de Mercado, *Suma de Tratos y Contratos* or *Compilation of Deals and Contracts* (Seville, 1571), quoted in Kamen, *Empire*, 193.

surfeit of gold in western Europe.[42] This is why among the "four or five causes" of "the high prices we see today" identified by the French Universalist Jean Bodin (1530–96) in 1568, "the principal & almost only one [cause](which no one has referred to until now) is the abundance of gold & silver, which is today much greater in this Kingdom than it was four hundred years ago." In particular, Bodin says, "there have come from Peru since the year 1533, when it was conquered by the Spaniards, more than a hundred millions of gold, & twice as much silver."[43] The precious metals overflowing European markets naturally gave rise to price inflation.[44]

"Unlick'd beare-whelps": European-New World Implications of Donne's Pistolets

As is outlined above, Donne's unfiled pistolets reflect the global trade network enacted by Spanish bullion. This section focuses on the Europe–New World cycle of this network. Donne's poems display a particular attention to American mines and gold. In his elegy "To his Mistris Going to Bed," the speaker pleads for "License" for his "roving hands" to touch "my America, my new found lande, / My kingdome" and to embrace "My myne of precious stones, my Empiree" (25–29). Donne's amatory metaphor of "precious stones" here has a material base—it recalls both the American mines and the imperial desire to possess them. As is instanced by Sir Francis Drake's (1540–96) famous capture of Spanish treasure fleets in 1577 and Sir Walter Ralegh's two expeditions to the legendary gold city of Guiana (1596, 1616), what English explorers wished to appropriate for the Crown were those Indian mines that had immensely enriched the Spanish monarchs. American mines glitter in Donne's sermons as well. In a sermon preached at Lincolns Inn in May 1620, he observes that "hee that hath a plentifull fortune in Europe, cares not much though there be no land of perfumes in the East, nor of gold, in the West-Indies" (3:123). He asks in a sermon dated January 30, 1625, "Wouldest thou say and not be thought mad for saying so, God hath created a West Indies, therefore I cannot want Gold?" (6:208) For Donne, it is a preacher's duty to serve "as his [Christ's] Ophir, as his Indies, to derive his gold, his precious consolation upon the King himselfe" (7:135). In other words, the Gospel, when properly tapped, works like either the biblical Ophir or American mines, a resourceful goldmine for the English crown.

---

[42] For mines opened upon in Eastern Europe see Peter L. Bernstein, *The Power of Gold: The History of an Obsession* (New York: John Wiley & Sons, 2000), 152.

[43] Jean Bodin, *The Dearness of Things* (1568), in *Early Economic Thought: Selections from Economic Literature prior to Adam Smith*, ed. Arthur Eli Monroe (Cambridge, MA: Harvard UP, 1924), 127, 129.

[44] For inflation caused by the surfeit of American treasures, see Earl J. Hamilton, *American Treasure and the Price Revolution in Spain, 1501–1650* (Cambridge, MA: Harvard UP, 1934); and J. H. Parry, *The Spanish Seaborne Empire* (Berkeley: U of California P, 1990), 244.

The body proves a central metaphor in Donne's representation of the New World mines, and what distinguishes this body is its unguarded openness and remarkable fertility, attributes that render it an ideal site for imperial exploitation. Donne's image of American mines features a rich and unresisting female body that invites the willful exploration of Western planters. Under the touch of his "roving hands," the speaker in "To his Mistris" observes, "my America" becomes a body that can not only be touched but also produces, in large numbers, "precious stones." A similar corporeal metaphor appears in "The Bracelet" as well. The global circulation of Spanish pesos, the speaker here says, resembles the movement of "the soule" that "quickens head, feet, and heart, / As streames, like veines, run through th'earths every part" (37–38). This "soule," a symbol of the robust travelling of Spanish pistolets, should be the same spirit that at once animates the fertile womb of the "new found lande" and "quickens" the birth of those infant whelps. For fanciful planters like Donne's speakers, not only the motherland but also its offspring should belong to "My kingdome" and "my Empiree," terms that speak eloquently of England's colonial ambitions in America.

England's imperial dream in the New World, however, was not as promising as Donne's speaker wishes; rather, it met considerable setbacks in both North and South America. England's fortune in North America vividly registers in Donne's image of unlicked whelps. Bears famously lick their young whelps into shape. Likewise, those irregular pistolets, while working their way into "th'earths every part," would be cast into any shape that suited to local needs. Shortly after the Powhatan massacre, an Indian uprising against the English in the Virginia colony in March 1622, Donne resorts to the malleability of American bullion figured in unlicked whelps to counsel the planters and investors of the Company of Virginia on further actions. In a sermon preached to the Company dated November 13, 1622, eight months after the massacre, Donne says,

> [B]e not discouraged. Great Creatures ly long in the wombe; *Lyons* are littered perfit, but *Beare-whelpes* lick'd unto their shape; actions which Kings undertake, are cast in a mould; they have their perfection quickly; actions of private men, and private purses, require more hammering, and more filing to their perfection. (4:271)

The unlicked "beare-whelps" and unlittered "Lyons" in this passage readily recall those unfiled pistolets in "The Bracelet." Accordingly, the "wombe" that breeds "great Creatures" refers to none other than those productive colonial mines. For Donne, both "Kings" and "private men," that is, planters and investors in the Company, are midwives of baby bears and lions buried deep in those fertile wombs. But disapproving of the rash "actions" of the investors to force the issue and act independently of the state, he counsels patience and cooperation between the crown and private men. Since "Great Creatures ly long in the wombe; *Lyons* are littered perfit," he argues, the planters should, rather than force those metallic creatures into premature births, wait patiently for their natural ripening. Further, because metals mined by private persons "require more hammering, and more filling to their perfection" and those "lick'd unto their shape" by the king go "quickly" into circulation, the investors should coordinate their "actions" to those of the crown. The tender and supple nature of those infant creatures in the "wombe" of American mines, Donne intimates, definitely invites, despite the resistance from the natives, the delivering and shaping hands of the planters, a prospect that must have sounded especially inspiring amidst the gloom generated by the massacre.

In addition to the colonial enterprise in Virginia, Donne's metaphor of unlicked whelps also mirrors England's frustrated ambition in South America. In a verse letter to Mr. R. W., Donne writes, "Guyanaes harvest is nip'd in the spring, / I feare" (18–19), and if "these Spanish businesse" (23) "Eclipse [s] the light which Guyana would give" (25), "Almightie Vertue" might be "an India" (28). What is described here is England's competition with Spain for colonies in South America, especially Ralegh's futile attempts to turn Guiana in to "an India" for the English crown. Most tellingly, in Ralegh's gold expedition to Guiana in 1595, the ship invested by the state secretary Sir Robert Cecil was named none other than "the Lions whelpe." In his sermon to the Virginia Company, Donne separates the two images of bear and lion whelps, remarking that "*Lyons* are littered perfit, but *Beare-whelpes* lick'd unto their shape," a differentiation intended both to highlight the attraction of the New World gold and suggest effective ways of appropriating it. Though American gold appears an inexhaustible fountain, Donne suggests, the investors should be patient and strategic in tapping that fountain. Rather than the bear, the royal vessel opted for the lion, reputed king of the animal world, to express the state's resolve to lick into shape the New World whelps, that is, "the plates of gold" of Guiana, a term that recurs like a refrain in Ralegh's *The Discoverie of the Large, Rich, and Beautiful Empire of Guiana* (1595). *Lion* also recalls the idiom "lion's share," an association that brings out the English's prodigious greed for American wealth. This avarice to obtain a "lion's share" of the unfiled pistolets produced by American mines is made the more explicit by Ralegh in his multifarious references to "Mint," "trial," "refiner," "Assay-master," "comptroller of the Mint," the "scume of gold," "gold ... in grains," "massie gold," and "gold oare" in the preface to the *Empire of Guiana* (PN 10:343–45). The piling of images of precious metals and their mintage suggest the English determination to "assay" and get a hold on American gold. Whereas "Charles the 5 ... had the maidenhead of Peru" (PN 10:346), Ralegh was resolved to shape the whelps of Guiana gold into perfect lions, turning the empire of Guiana into "a better Indies for her Majestie [Queen Elizabeth] then the king of Spaine hath any" (PN 10:342). Simply stated, English planters wished to stamp the "massie gold" of Guiana with the image of their own Queen. But as Donne says, "Guyanaes harvest is nip'd in the spring." Though submissive to the touch of the Spanish, those unlicked bears and lions proved unyielding to the "roving hands" of the English explorers.

The failure to find another "India" in South America, however, did not prevent England from appropriating Spain's American wealth. As Challis points out, the English won Spanish bullion "through trade, war and diplomacy, piracy and privateering, and bi-metallic flows."[45] In his elegy "Loves Warre," Donne alludes to these various illegal means of usurping Spanish treasures. Though "Midas joyes our Spanish journeys give / Wee touch all gold," the speaker in this poem says, we could "find no foode to live" (17–18). The word "touch" here evokes, apart from the legend of Midas and its amatory associations, England's attempts to capture Spanish galleons loaded with precious metals. The phrase "Spanish journeys" brings to mind the whole history of England's imperial wars with Spain and the hijacking of the treasure fleets culminated in Drake and Ralegh's adventures, either in the Peruvian and Mexican waters or close to the Spanish homeland. A chief purpose of the Cardiz and Azores expeditions Donne famously attended was to intercept Spanish treasure fleets and to seize a base along the Iberian coast.[46]

Paradoxically, Spanish bullion, instead of enriching, impoverished England and other European countries once it was appropriated. As Donne succinctly puts it, though "wee touch all gold" in "our Spanish journeys," we could "find no foode to live." While the crown and his planters were bent on amassing American wealth abroad, colonial metals backfired at home. Above all, the moldable nature of those "unrounded" pistolets provided marvelous candidates for "clipping" and "sweating," illegal techniques used to obtain gold chips and crumbs filed off from irregular coins and thereby causing the devaluation of coined money.[47] It was easy to cast those rough-hewn metals into any shape that suited one's needs. Harry E. Cross observes that "when dealing with Spanish pesos ... a variance of plus or minus 5.0 percent in actual silver content should be allowed to account for the irregularities of mintage and clipping."[48] These fraudulent practices find their way into Donne's poems as well. Stephen Deng rightly states that Donne's French crowns are "'pale' from having a high content of base metal such as tin, and they are 'lame' and 'lean' from clipping, washing, sweating."[49]

Along with these counterfeiting undertakings was the more pernicious practice of melting already coined money back into tradable bullion. "The Bracelet" captures the prevalent anxiety over this custom, with the speaker fearing and unwilling to cast his gold coin into a necklace. In the Renaissance, gold and silver served as, in addition to hoarded wealth and monetary currency, commodities in exchange.

---

[45] Challis, *Tudor Coinage*, 150.

[46] For Elizabeth's organized pirating of Spanish treasures see Susan Ronald, *The Pirate Queen: Queen Elizabeth I, Her Pirate Adventures, and the Dawn of Empire* (New York: Harper, 2007).

[47] C. H. V. Sutherland, *English Coinage 600–1900* (London: Batsford, 1973), 66, 69; John Chown, *A History of Money from AD 800* (London: Routledge, 1994), 13; and Sedwick and Sedwick, *Book of Cobs*, 12.

[48] Harry E. Cross, "South American Bullion Production and Export 1550–1750," in Richards ed., *Precious Metals*, 397–424, 398–99.

[49] Deng, *Coinage and State Formation*, 176. For Donne's image of these counterfeiting skills, also see Coburn Freer, "John Donne and Elizabethan Economic Theory," *Criticism* 38.4 (1996): 497–520, 506. For the "sweating" of coins see "Satire 5": "The mony which you sweat, and sweare for, is gon / Into' other hands" (40–41).

According to the speaker in "Love's progress," the intrinsic worth of gold resides in its innate nature, but its commercial value arises from "our new nature," that is, "use," "the soul of trade" (11–16). But trade proved a double-edged mechanism: it enhanced the appeal of casting coined money into trading commodities, especially when gold or silver coins were debased, but this practice led to a great outflow of precious metals. R. B. Outhwaite holds that "the gold which was exported was not necessarily monetised gold; the undervaluation of gold would make it profitable to melt down gold plate, jewelry and other ornaments."[50] This tendency to commercialize coined money, Sir Walter Ralegh remarks in his advice to King James on "trade, commerce, and coin," has "drained" England of bullion. As he put it:

> While the current cash of this kingdom can be converted into bullion, and so made a trading commodity, it will either be conveyed to the best market or wrought into plate at home. It is evident, notwithstanding those great sums coined in the last two reigns, 'twas no sooner made than converted into trading commodity, which, if it happens again, the nation may be totally drained of it.[51]

In fact, the melting of gold and silver coins into tradable bullion had always been a concern for English sovereigns before the eighteenth century. The Elizabethan Proclamation on October 9, 1560, explicitly prescribed that "any person who broke or melted even one single coin, or exported more than he could take in his purse, should be guilty of felony and should be punished, not merely according to the existing laws, but with the 'greatest and most severe pain that may be devised.'"[52] But as is noted by Ralegh, such laws proved far from effective. In reality, this practice continued well into the seventeenth century. In 1637, the Star Chamber charged a dozen persons of "culling out the weightiest coins, for melting down His Majesty's money into bullion, and for giving above the prices of His Majesty's Mint for gold and silver."[53] Donne's "The Bracelet" vividly captures the contagious influence of this illegal practice. To compensate for her lost necklace, the speaker says, his love asks him to melt his gold coin bearing "twelve righteous angels" (9). But the speaker himself is apparently unwilling to turn his "current cash" into a "trading commodity." Coins impressed with "angels" were issued during the reign of Henry VII (1457–1509), and they proved reliable monetary units in early modern England. Unlike the silver penny whose weight was continuously in decline from 1526 to 1601, the gold angel had, ever since its first issuing, been

---

[50] R. B. Outhwaite, *Inflation in Tudor and Early Stuart England*, 2nd ed. (London: Macmillan, 1982), 56.

[51] Sir Walter Ralegh, *Select Observations relating to Trade, Commerce, and Coin*, quoted in W. A. Shaw, *The History of Currency* (London: Wilsons and Milne, 1895), 135.

[52] Sir Albert Feavearyear, *The Pound Sterling: A History of English Money*, 2nd ed. (Oxford: Clarendon, 1963), 81.

[53] John Rushworth, *Historical Collections* (London, 1659), quoted in Feavearyear, *Pound Sterling*, 91.

"progressively enhanced until 1551," and its value remained steady the rest of the sixteenth century.[54] Three possible meanings thus suggest themselves in Donne's adjective "righteous." First, it denotes the decent or right use of gold as a monetary currency. Second, the epithet indicates that gold angel is solid money that one can rely on. But this reliable currency, Donne's speaker suggests, is deteriorating as a result of fraudulent practices. Third, the term also veils a critique of turning coined money into a commodity.

Aside from commercial profit, the tendency to melt coined money into tradable commodities also arose from the popular fashion of fetishizing objects. The coins impressed with "angels" were made from those "ubiquitous pistolets" that constituted the "lion's share" in the royal mints. Rather than protecting "righteous Angels," those baby bears produced in American mines, once transported to an alien soil, grew into "bad Angels" (75) that wreaked havoc upon private lives. This transformation was inseparable from the practice of fetishizing objects. In his *The Anatomie of Abuses* (1583), Philip Stubbes (c. 1555–1610) draws attention to the poverty caused by idolizing objects, especially exotic goods. For Stubbes, it is the undue valuing of "trifling merchandizes" "beyond the seas" that "impoverish[ed] us." Stubbes attributes this overestimation of alien objects to "pride."[55] Donne shares Stubbes's view of the baneful effect of fetishizing. In "The Bracelet," the speaker "Mourne[s]" the disappearance of his love's "seavenfold chaine" not for his bad "luck" but for "the bitter cost" this loss has brought on him (7–8). His gold coin "should do good workes, and should provide / Necessities," the speaker complains, but it "now must nurse thy pride" by being cast into a necklace (73–74). Thus like Stubbes, Donne also blames the infatuation with trivial objects to vain "pride," and he represents the "bitter cost" caused by this vanity through contemplating on the relation of "form" and "being." According to Thomas Mun (1571–1641), the East India Company director, "that is not the denomination of our pounds, shillings and pence, which is respected, but the intrinsique value of our Coins."[56] For Donne, since "forme gives being" (76), the denomination or formal stamp and the inherent value are equally important. He turns to the theological meaning of "Angels" to express the close relation of matter and form. Theologically speaking, "Angels" are "commanded" by "heaven," the speaker says, to "provide / All things to me, and be my faithfull guide, / To gaine new friends, t' appease great enemies, / To comfort my soule" (13–16). While bearing the "forme" of "righteous Angels," his gold coin insures the "matter" of his life, that is, his basic subsistence, social relations, and the peace of his soul. But once "these twelve innocents" (17) "are burnt and tyed in chaines" (22) for vain pride, they become "bad Angels," a new

---

[54] Challis, *Tudor Coinage*, 166–67.
[55] Philip Stubbes, *The Anatomie of Abuses* (London, 1583), sig. Clr. For early modern fetishism of commodities, see Hawkes, *Idols of the Marketplace*.
[56] Thomas Mun, *Discovrse of Trade: from England vnto East-Indies: Answering to Diuerse Obiections Which are Usually Made Against the Same* (1621), in *Early English Tracts on Commerce*, ed. J. R. McCulloch (Cambridge: Cambridge UP, 1970), 149.

form or denomination that will cost the very "necessities" of his life, on two accounts. First, the transmutation deprives the gold of its "use" value, reducing it to a mere symbol of riches incapable of providing for his life. Second, when thus transformed, though the original being—gold "doth still remaine" (69), its old form—the good angels, vanish; with them is gone the insurance of his physical, social, and spiritual life. So what is cost in transmuting his gold into an object is not only money or "that seely old moralitie" (5) but also the basic rights symbolized by those good angels. It is this deprivation of his fundamental human rights that makes the "wretched Finder" (91) deserve "my most heavy curse" (94).

The havoc wrought by those "bad angels" coined from Spanish bullion extends beyond personal life to national economy. In fact, the Europeans themselves were quite aware of the subversive power of Spanish coinage. In the preface to his *Empire of Guiana*, Ralegh calls attention to the formidable power of Spanish pistolets. "It is his [King of Spain] Indian gold," Ralegh says, "that indangereth and disturbeth all the nations of Europe, it purchaseth intelligence, creepeth into counsels, and setteth bound loyaltie at libertie, in the greatest Monarchies of Europe ... to the general losse and impoverishment of the kingdome and common weale so reduced" (PN 10:347). Similarly, a friar remarked in 1630 that "Potosí lives in order to serve the imposing aspirations of Spain: it serves to chastise the Turk, humble the Moor, make Flanders tremble and terrify England."[57] Donne reproduces this invidious working of colonial metals in his poems. In "Satire 2," the speaker says, "Rammes, and slings now are seely battery, / Pistolets are the best Artillerie" (19–20). For the speaker in "The Bracelet," Spanish "pistolets" or "pistols" are weapons that are "more" destructive "then cannon-shot" (32). The unnatural power of these monetary arms is so great that they can, like those "figures" used by "some greate Conjurer," "enforce / Nature ... from her course." National economy proves most vulnerable to the unnatural power exerted by Spanish pesos. The vigorous travelling of Spanish coins, rather than boosting European economy, has "slily made / Gorgeous *France*, ruin'd, ragged and decay'd; / *Scotland*," and "mangled seventeen-headed *Belgia*" (39–42). Nor did England escape the general wreck. Though by 1561 Elizabeth had managed to stem the monetary deterioration caused by the "Great Debasement" in the 1540s, English coins were in jeopardy once again in the latter part of the sixteenth century.[58] Both Bodin and Thomas

---

[57] Enrique Otte, ed. *Cartas privadas de emigrantes a Indias, 1540–1616* or *Private Letters of the Emigrants to the Indies* (Seville, Jerez: Escuela de Estudios Hispanoamericanos, 1988), 525, quoted in Kamen, *Empire*, 286.

[58] Gould, *Great Debasement*. For Challis's criticism of Gould's work see his "Currency and the Economy in Mid-Tudor England," 2nd ser. *Economic History Review* 25 (1972): 313–22. Gould's responses appeared in his "The Great Debasement and the Supply of Money," *Austrian Economic History Review* 13 (1973): 177–89, and "Currency and Exchange Rate in Sixteenth-Century England," *Journal of European Economic History* 2(1973): 149–59. For a "deeper and more general depression in the years after 1586," see Berry E. Supple, *Commercial Crisis and Change in England 1600–1642: A Study in the Instability of a Mercantile Economy* (Cambridge: Cambridge UP, 1959), 24.

Smith (1513–77), Elizabeth's secretary of the state, blamed the "debasement and exchange depreciation" of coins to the importing of foreign, especially Spanish bullion.[59] The grave consequence of this devaluation resonates in Donne's monetary images too. We hear Donne asking why "the whole precious Gold" has changed "To such small copper coynes" in "The Second Anniversarie (429–30), and "had wee chang'd to gold / Their silver" in "The First Anniversarie." Likewise, in "The Lamentations of Jeremy," the speaker wonders "How is the gold become so dimme? How is / Purest and finest gold thus chang'd to this?" (269–70).

Circulatory "Veines": The Chinese Association of Donne's Spanish Coinage

Up to now, I have dealt chiefly with the English-Spanish-American commercial nexus implicit in Donne's unfiled pistolets. This section studies the global dimension of this image, especially its association with the Far East. Aside from the practices of clipping and fetishizing, "bi-metallic flows" of gold and silver also contributed to the ruining of European economies as dramatized in "The Bracelet." Like trade in general, the flows set in motion by the disparity in the gold-silver ratio proved double-edged as well: they could at once enrich domestic economy by attracting the inflow of foreign bullion and impoverish it by causing an outflow of precious metals. Outhwaite remarks that "if one metal was debased more than the other, there would be a tendency for bi-metallic flows to be encouraged, with the most debased metal entering the country and the least leaving it."[60] Simply stated, debased money engendered a vicious cycle that drove out good and drew in bad metals. In a letter to William Cecil in 1551, a London merchant called William Lane writes that the "lightness" of the silver coin caused both the exchange rate to fall and the merchants to export "a hundarthe thowsand powndes of gold" within a short time of only three months. Since "the pownd of gold ys Rychar than the pownd of whyte mony," Lane deplores, "shortely we shall be quite off all owre Ryche mony for a base quyne."[61]

Early modern bi-metallic flows were not a regional but a global phenomenon, and they were greatly facilitated by the various trading circuits running across the globe. The three transoceanic routes through which American bullion flowed to China exemplify such global highways. In "The Bracelet," Donne represents these global trading circuits in the image of "veines." It is via "streams" or "veines" (38), the speaker observes, that the "soule" of Spanish pistolets flowed to "th'earths every part." The word *vein* literally means a "tubular vesse[l] in which the blood is conveyed through the animal body" or a "small natural channel" within the earth through which "water trickles or flows." But *vein* also denotes "a deposit of metallic or earthy material having an extended or ramifying course under ground; a seam or lode; spec. a continuous crack or fissure filled with matter (esp.

---

[59] Outhwaite, *Inflation*, 23–44; 54–56.
[60] Outhwaite, *Inflation*, 55.
[61] Quoted in Outhwaite, *Inflation*, 56.

metallic ore)."⁶² In his *Decades of the New Worlde* or *West India by Peter Martyr* (1555), the English travel literature compiler Richard Eden (1521–76) equals "myne" with "veyne"—mines are subterranean veins that contain metallic ores.⁶³ Likewise, in his *Devotions upon Emergent Occasions* (1623), Donne makes the same connection when he imagines to "extend ... all the veins in our bodies ... to rivers, and all the sinews to veins of mines."⁶⁴ While mines are veins of the earth, oceans are arteries of the globe. So Donne's image of veins elicits at once the earthly "vessels" through which Spanish bullion wound its way to "th'earths every part," the metallic veins teemed with unlicked whelps, and the oceanic bodies that helped distribute those precious whelps throughout the globe.

The mines or veins that subjected America to colonial exploitation turned out to be the very agency that allowed it to participate in the early modern global commerce. As an isolated continent living largely in the state of nature, America appeared a helpless virgin that yielded passively to the "roving" hands of Western colonizers. Once linked with other continents via those fluid veins, however, whether subterranean mines or oceanic arteries, this maiden land became a formidable matrix that swayed the economies of countries visited by its metallic offspring. The global commercial network enacted by American mines represented in "The Bracelet" accords with Donne's general notion of the oneness of the world, as he puts it this oft-quoted passage: "No man is an island, entire of itself; every man is a piece of the continent, a part of the main ... any man's death diminishes me, because I am involved in mankind ... ."⁶⁵ An "island" is connected to and becomes "a piece of the continent" through none other than those watery throughways. Since *vein* also signifies "an inclination or desire, a tendency, towards something specified,"⁶⁶ those oceanic veins would incline the isolated land of America to expand and connect with other continents. "If all the veins in our bodies were extended to rivers, and all the sinews to veins of mines," Donne says, then the human body would coincide with the earthly body.⁶⁷ Likewise, if "the veins of mines" in America were "extended," they would merge with those oceanic veins to circulate around the globe.

What was carried by both earthly and watery veins constituted the lifeblood of the nations visited by Spanish pistolets. Like France, Belgia, and Scotland mentioned in "The Bracelet," China was numbered among such nations. A Spanish official expressly called the flow of bullion from the New World "the lifeblood of the kingdom [Spain]" and compared the sea lanes to "the very veins that give

---

⁶² "vein, n." 2nd edn. 1989. *OED Online*. June 5, 2012.

⁶³ Richard Eden, *Decades of the New Worlde or West India by Peter Martyr* (London, 1555), 211.

⁶⁴ See Donne, *Devotions upon Emergent Occasions and Death's Duel, with the life of Dr. John Donne by Izaak Walton*, ed. Andrew Motion (New York: Vintage, 1999), 19.

⁶⁵ Donne, *Devotions*, 103.

⁶⁶ "vein, n." 2nd edn. 1989. *OED Online*. June 5, 2012.

⁶⁷ Donne, *Devotions*, 19.

life to this great and vast body."[68] Since veins are primarily "vessels in which the blood is conveyed through the animal body," the "lifeblood" here speaks vividly of the crucial importance of American bullion to Spain, a "great and vast body" that, paradoxically, relied on those infant bears for survival. American bullion was "lifeblood" not merely to Spain; "silver" was "blood [*plata es sangre*]" for the "Great and Mighty Kingdom of China" as well.[69] In the 1570s, the Ming Empire promulgated the so-called "Single-Whip" taxation policy, which required taxes be paid in silver rather than in the previous paper money.[70] This "silverization" of taxation generated such a demand for American silver that it virtually became "blood" for Ming China.[71] One Spanish admiral remarked in 1638 that "the king of China could build a palace with the silver bars from Peru which have been carried to his country."[72] Frank Spooner observes that "the avidity of the Chinese for silver established a commercial epoch for the international economy." "Without this avidity," the Florentine merchant Filippo Sassetti said on January 20, 1586, "the [Spanish] reales would not have risen so much in value as they now are. The Chinese, among all the peoples of Asia, are wild about silver as everywhere men are about gold."[73]

Given the global circulation of Spanish stamps and the large absorption of silver by Ming China, the early modern European economic crisis as is noted by Bodin and Smith and represented in Donne's "The Bracelet" proved only part of the chain-effect caused by the American-China-Spain bullion trade. Flynn and Giráldez argue that sixteenth-century European price inflation was a global phenomenon, since it reflected the repercussions of the debasement of silver in China. Ming China, though drawing in most of the world's silver, did not spend it. J. P. Geiss notes that "in the late sixteenth century ... when silver from Mexico and Japan entered the Ming empire in great quantity, the value of silver began to decline and inflation set in, for as the metal became more abundant, its buying power diminished."[74] So the "silver sink" became ultimately a real "sink" that sank the Ming Empire into economic depressions. Chinese silver inflation played

---

[68] Charles H. Carter, *The Secret Diplomacy of the Hapsburgs, 1598–1625* (New York: Columbia UP, 1964), 56.

[69] Boxer, "*Plata es Sangre.*"

[70] For the "Single-whip" tax policy of Ming China, see Flynn and Giráldez, "Silver Spoon," 208; Fang-chung Liang, *The Single-Whip Method of Taxation in China*, trans. Wang Yü-ch'uan (Cambridge, MA: Harvard UP, 1956); and Ray Huang, *Taxation and Government Finance in Sixteenth-Century Ming China* (New York : Cambridge UP, 1974).

[71] The term "silverization" comes from Flynn and Giráldez, "Silver Spoon," 208.

[72] Hieronimo de Bañuelos y Carrillo, *Relation of the Filipinas Islands* (Mexico, 1638), in *The Philippine Islands 1493–1898, Explorations by Early Navigators, Descriptions of the Islands and their Peoples*, ed. Emma H. Blair and James A. Robertson, 59 vols. (Mandaluyong, Rizal: Cachos Hermanos, 1973), vol. 29. 71.

[73] Frank Spooner, *The International Economy and Monetary Movements in France, 1493–1725* (Cambridge, MA: Harvard UP, 1972), 77.

[74] J. P. Geiss, "Peking under the Ming, 1368–1644," Diss. Princeton U, 1979, 165.

a crucial part in the collapse of the Spanish Empire—"Spain vanished as a serious Western power as its silver basis eroded." This contagious influence caused by Chinese silver debasement was not confined to Spain; it "was responsible for a power shift within early modern Europe" as well.[75] Its royal mints relying heavily on Spanish bullion, England was necessarily implicated. "As an integral part of the sixteenth-century European economy," Challis claims, "England obeyed the forces which dominated that economy, amongst which was the influx of bullion from the New World."[76]

Apart from such graphic metaphors as veins and unlicked whelps, the Chinese resonance of Donne's pistolets also suggests itself in his general attention to the Far East. Donne was quite aware of the countries around the Pacific Ring newly revealed in the "race for the Far East." In "Hymne to God My God, in my Sicknesse," he speaks of locating a "home" in "the Pacifique Sea" or "The Eastern riches" (16–17). In a letter written in 1614 to his friend Tobie Matthew, he says, "Men go to China, both by the Straights, and by the Cape."[77] But Donne's interest in Eastern trade is most apparent in his constant reference to the Northeast and Northwest passages project.

It is by "the discovery of a passage through one of the innumerable inlets of the North," that is, the Northeast and Northwest routes to "the fabled realm of Cathay," that "the story of the English Voyages begins" (PN 12:10). Economic profit was the key driver behind England's polar ventures. The sixteenth century saw the English economy suffering from Spanish imperial hegemony and the flooding of foreign commodities. According to Hakluyt, by the 1550s it had become almost impossible for the English to trade with their European neighbors who requested only a "small" amount of their goods. Even the demand for commodities that had long enjoyed popularity was in decline. This formed a drastic contrast with the strong currency of "all foreign merchandises" whose prices were "wonderfully raised" (PN 2:239). It is at this moment that the Far East came into the picture for the English—the rich land of China looked like a savior that could not only revitalize but also enhance its competitive edge *vis-à-vis* the Iberian rivals. According to Hakluyt, the three factors of the intention to "remed[y]" the "mischiefe" besetting the English market, the envy of "the wealth of the Spaniards and Portingales" that was "marveilously increased" by "the discoverie and search of newe trades and countreys," as well as the supposition that "the same [seems] to be a course and meane for them also to obteine the like" combined to oblige "certaine grave Citizens of London" to strike alternative ways to deliver the English economy

---

[75] Flynn and Giráldez, "Silver Spoon," 212, 210. For the political implication of the eastern trade also see Jack A. Goldstone, "East and West in the Seventeenth Century: Political Crises in Stuart England, Ottoman Turkey, and Ming China," *Comparative Studies in Society and History* 30.1(1988): 103–42.

[76] Challis, *Tudor Coinage*, 198.

[77] Donne, "With a Kind of Labore'd Complement to a Friend of His" (1614), in *John Donne, Dean of St Paul's: Complete Poetry and Selected Prose*, ed. John Hayward (London: Nonesuch, 1967), 357–409, 467.

from its quandary. Ultimately, those wise heads "resolved upon" "a newe and strange Navigation," that is, to "open a way and passage for our men to travaile to newe and unknown kingdomes" (PN 2:239–40). This new resolution led to none other than the Northeast and Northwest passages program.

The key objective of the polar passages project was to gain Eastern riches and to "feed those heathen nations with our commodities" (PN 3:264). In the epistle dedication to Robert Cecil in the second edition of his *Principal Navigations* (1599), Hakluyt writes,

> because our chiefe desire to find out ample vent of our wollen cloth, the naturall commoditie of this our Relame, the fittest places, which in al my readings and observations I find for that purpose, are the manifold Islands of Japan, & the Northern parts of China, & the regions of the Tartars next ajoining. (PN 1: lxxii)

Likewise, in his *A Discourse of a Discoverie for a New Passage to Cataia* (1576), Sir Humphrey Gilbert argues that the Northwest Passage through America is "the onely way for our princes, to possesse the wealth of all the East parts (as they terme them) of the world, which is infinite" (PN 7:185). To motivate Englishmen to participate in the Eastern trade, Richard Willes, who is noted for his editing of Eden's travel literature, painted a rosy picture of countries plying trade in the Far East:

> The rude Indian Canoa halleth those seas, the Portingal, the Saracens, and Moores travaile continually up and downe that reach from Japan to China, from China to Malacca, from Malacca to the Moluccaes: and shall an Englishman, better appointed then any of them all … feare to sail in that Ocean? What seas at all doe want piracie? What Navigation is there voyde of perill? (PN 7:201) [78]

As is pointed out by Willes, though their continental and even Muslim neighbors had rushed to the East, profiting from its seemingly inexhaustible resources, Englishmen, for fear of "piracy" and "peril," had been lagging far behind in exploiting the Eastern market, a belatedness that would cost its economy dearly. The usual excuses of "piracy" and "peril" invented by Englishmen, Willes suggests, would only further exclude England from the profitable grid of trade in the Far East.

The picture Willes depicted in the 1570s must have inspired Donne's imagining of trading with the Far East. Donne refers to England's polar passages project a couple of times. In "Epithalamion I, The Time of Mariage," he speaks of the "the passage of the West or East" (111) around "the Northerne Pole" (114). In "Satire III," talking about the courage of those resolved to blaze a path in the north, the speaker observes, "Hast thou couragious fire to thaw the ice / Of frozen North discoveries?" (21–22) Though proceeding in full swing after its initiation in the

---

[78] Richard Willes edited and augmented Richard Eden's *The History of Trauayle in the West and East Indies* and published it in 1577.

1550s, the Arctic venture appeared an impossible dream for the English by the 1630s. However, in a sermon preached on April 5, 1629, Donne says,

> who ever amongst our Fathers, thought of any other way to the Moluccaes, or to China, then by the promontory of Good hope? yet another way opened it self to Magellan; a Straite; it is true; but yet a way thither; and who knows yet, whether there may not be a North-East, and a North-West way hither, besides? (8:371)

This statement shows not only a comprehensive knowledge of the various stages marking the discovery of China but also a cheerful optimism for the polar enterprise. There are many possible ways to circumvent the route around "Good hope" to reach the Spice Islands and China, Donne points out, but no Englishman had ever tried to seek those ways out before Magellan discovered the Southwest strait in 1519–22. The polar passage project might appear hopeless, but just as Magellan once turned the impossible into the possible, the English might eventually find "a North-East, and a North-West way." Thus although in his youth Donne showed anxiety about the global repercussions of the Eastern trade, in his old age, he sounded quite optimistic towards the commercial opportunities offered by the Far East. Given this sustained attention to English trade with the Far East, Donne could not have been ignorant of the "sink" that sank many unfiled pistolets.

Donne's representation of the global circulation of Spanish coinage is not an explicit expression of his cosmopolitanism towards cultural differences, but it does indicate his attention to trading partners or commercial others beyond the European borders. Put differently, Donne's cosmopolitan outlook in this chapter registers in his awareness of the global forces that involved almost all known continents, especially the Far East, in a commercial network, as well as his willingness to engage the implications of those forces. Most importantly, these earlier globalizing processes allow us to understand the economic base of early modern globalization, and Donne's poetic reproduction of these processes provides insight into the cultural superstructure shaped by that material base. As is shown by both Porter and Markley, the pattern of global trade emerging in Donne's "The Bracelet" resonated through the seventeenth to the eighteenth century, though the whole picture was transformed by the Dutch's intervention in the Eastern market, and the focus of exchange shifted from gold and silver to such staple Chinese goods as tea, silk, and porcelain.[79]

---

[79] Porter, *Ideographia*, Chapter 4; and Porter, "A Peculiar but Uninteresting Nation: China and the Discourse of Commerce in Eighteenth-Century England," *Eighteenth-Century Studies* 33 (2000): 181–99. Markley, *The Far East and the English Imagination*, chapter 1, 4, and 6; Markley, "Civility, Ceremony, and Desire at Beijing: Sensibility and the European Quest for 'Free Trade' with China in the Late Seventeenth Century," in *Passionate Encounters in a Time of Sensibility*, ed. Anne Mellor and Maximilian Novak (Newark: U of Delaware P, 2000), 60–88; and Markley, "Riches, Power, Trade, and Religion: The Far East and the English Imagination, 1600–1720," *Renaissance Studies* 17 (2003): 433–55. Also see Flynn and Giráldez, "Cycles of Silver."

Chapter 2
The Anyan Strait: Donne's Global Vision and Theological Cosmopolitanism

In the previous chapter, I examined how Donne's image of Spanish coins at once signals his awareness of the global trade of precious metals dominated by Ming China and reflects the economic base of East-West contact in the Renaissance. This chapter shifts from the material base to the superstructure and explores how maritime discoveries and geographical expansion to the Far East impacted early modern reconfigurations of the world and the conceptual adjustment to the emergence of a global horizon. Specifically, I examine how Donne's image of the "Anyan" strait in his "Hymne to God my God, in my Sicknesse" (1623) symbolizes his perception of the limitations of biblical discourse, and how this new vision impels him to accommodate the scriptural economy to a globalized world.

For early modern England, the strait of "Anyan" represents the impossible dream of reaching the fabled Cathay via the Arctic region. This sixteenth-century dream of encompassing the world through the polar routes has miraculously turned into reality in modern times. On September 16, 2009, two German ships, that is, the *Beluga Fraternity* and *Beluga Foresight*, successfully passed Novaya Zemlya, an island off Russia's north coast. This event signifies the opening of the legendary Northwest Passage. The hotly disputed global warming has unexpectedly opened up the Arctic sea-lane that was deemed impassable by early modern explorers after about half a century's ceaseless quest. This chapter will trace the genesis of the polar passage and its resonance in Donne's image of "Anyan" in his divine poem.

Hakluyt's extensive travel compendium that documents maritime explorations and discoveries proved pivotal to raising the English's consciousness of ongoing globalizing processes. Donne was numbered among those who responded nimbly to the siren call sounded from Hakluyt's multivolume compilations. Images of new geographical discoveries pervade Donne's works, particularly his "Hymne to God." Here the speaker remarks,

> Is the Pacifique Sea my home? Or are
> The Easterne riches? Is *Jerusalem*?
> *Anyan*, and *Magellan*, and *Gibraltare*,
> All streights, and none but streights, are wayes to them,
> Whether where *Japhet* dwelt, or *Cham*, or *Sem*. (16–20)

This stanza is marked by both the number of geographical references it contains and the coupling of biblical figures with newly discovered places. There are two general critical approaches to Donne's spatial imagery. One focuses on his physical places. Robert R. Owens claims that "since Donne's geography is mystical in intent, exact designation of places is unimportant."[1] But other scholars recognize the importance of "exact" locations to understand Donne's works. Donald Anderson associates Donne's images of the earth with medieval "T-in-O" maps.[2] While Robert Sharp traces them to sixteenth-century "Cordiform Maps," Claude Gandelman and Noam Flinker link them with "anthropomorphic" landscapes.[3] Second, some critics do recognize the relevance of Donne's "new geographic names," but for most of them, John Gillies says, the poet's new regions are "remorselessly typologised and sacralised, incongruously translated into the patristic geography in which all places point towards the ultimate place (the centric *omphalos* of Jerusalem) and in the sacred direction (east)."[4] In contrast, Gillies himself proposes to regard Donne's new places on in their own right.

Neglected in scholarship on Donne's geographical metaphors are their global dimensions and the part played by the "Far East" in shaping his universal perspective.[5] As the historian W. A. Raleigh observes, "Modern travel and geography owe their chief advances to the search for the fabled realm of Cathay [China]" (PN 12:10). Three of the six geographical images represented in "Hymne to God" refer to the Far East: the "Anyan" strait, the "Pacifique Sea," and the "Easterne" regions, a predominance that indicates the importance of the Far East in Renaissance imagination. It is through "the discovery of a passage through one of the innumerable inlets of the North," Raleigh says, that "the story of the English Voyages begins" (PN 12:10). The "passage" mentioned here refers both to the

---

[1] Robert R. Owens, "The Myth of Anian," *Journal of the History of Ideas* 36.1 (1975): 135–38, 135.

[2] Donald K. Anderson Jr., "Donne's 'Hymne to God my God, in my Sicknesse' and the T-in-O Maps," *South Atlantic Quarterly* 71 (1972): 465–72. Medieval "T-in-O" maps feature the letter "T" contained with an "O" circle. "O" represents the known universe, and "T" divides the world into three parts—Europe, Asia, and Africa. Jerusalem, the old world center, lies at the very intersection symbolized in the letter "T." The three branches of "T" represent respectively the Mediterranean, the Aegean and the Black Sea, and River Nile and the Red Sea, watery bodies that separates the three known continents. The first "T-in-O" map appeared in the *Etymologiae* (c. 636) of Isidore, bishop of Seville (c. 560–636).

[3] Robert L. Sharp, "Donne's 'Good Morrow' and Cordiform Maps," *Modern Language Notes* 69 (1954): 493–95; Claude Gandelman, "The Poem as Map: John Donne and the 'Anthropomorphic Landscape' Tradition," *Arcadia: Zeitschrift für Vergleichende Literaturwissenschaft* 19 (1984): 244–51; and Noam Flinker, "John Donne and the 'Anthropomorphic Map' Tradition," *Applied Semiotics / Sémiotique appliqué* 3.8 (1999): 207–15.

[4] John Gillies, *Shakespeare and the Geography of Difference* (Cambridge: Cambridge UP, 1994), 185. Such studies named by Gillies include Clay Hunt, *Donne's Poetry: Essays in Literary Analysis* (New Haven: Yale UP, 1954); and Louis B. Martz, *The Poem of the Mind: Essays on Poetry, English and American* (New York: Oxford UP, 1966).

[5] By "Far East," I mean the Pacific region west of America, which includes Cathay or China, Cipangu or Japan, Korea, and the Spicy Moluccas in Southeast Asia.

northeast pathway through Russia to China and the northwest route to "Easterne riches" via the Anyan strait in the Pacific.[6] So "Anyan" and the "Pacifique" in Donne's divine poem represent two pivotal landmarks in the Northwest Passage project, a program that led ultimately to the discovery of America. This chapter studies Donne's response to the Western discovery of the Far East in light of the polar passage project. Since America was "the fourth part of the world" (PN 7:160) western Europeans encountered in the "race for the Far East," I will examine Donne's reception of the Amerindians too. In fact, all three straits depicted in "Hymne to God"—"Anyan," "Gibraltare," and "Magellan"—recall maritime exploration of the Far East. Whereas Anyan registered England's march to the Pacific, Gibraltar marked the Mediterranean–Red Sea gateway to the Indian Ocean, and Magellan was killed during an assault on a village in the Philippines. Donne's three straits symbolize, therefore, the global circuits unsealed in "the race for the Far East."

The ostensible globalized world featured in "Hymne to God" renders globalization an apt framework to study the rich associations of Donne's place names. As a multidimensional concept, globalization can be defined in terms of various referents, one of which is geographical place. According to David Held and Anthony McGrew, "identifiable geographical referents" or specified "spatial referents for the global" are such important indexes of globalization that without them it is impossible to "distinguish the international and transnational from the global, or for that matter, processes of regionalization from processes of globalization."[7] "Anyan" proves a representative geographical indicator for sixteenth-century globalization. For Donne's readers, this strait, bridging the two continents of Asia and America and linking the Arctic and Pacific, evoked at once the Far East, the Northwest Passage, and the New World, places that signify none other than a globalized world.

Referring both to globalization theory and Hakluyt's account of the polar passage program, I examine how Donne's image of Anyan symbolizes his awareness of the early modern geographical and exploratory processes and how these globalizing forces helped shape his universal vision and cosmopolitan spirit. The theological adjustment to a globalized world represented in both "Hymne to God" and Donne's sermons, I argue, suggests a *theological cosmopolitanism*, by which I mean an attempt at once to resituate biblical discourse within a global context and to engage the cultural pluralism revealed by the global lens. Ivan Strenski remarks that one can find "original and explicitly theological justifications of early globalization" in "the writings and teachings of sixteenth-

---

[6] Helen Wallis, "England's Search for the Northern Passages in the Sixteenth and Early Seventeenth Centuries," *Arctic* 37.4 (1984): 453–72; and Marijke Spies, *Arctic Routes to Fabled Lands: Olivier Brunel and the Passage to China and Cathay in the Sixteenth Century* (Amsterdam: Amsterdam UP, 2002).

[7] David Held and Anthony McGrew, "The Great Globalization Debate: An Introduction," in *The Global Transformations Reader: An Introduction to the Globalization Debate*, ed. Held and McGrew (Cambridge: Polity, 2003), 1–50, 4.

and seventeenth-century Christian theologians and doctors of jurisprudence" such as Francisco de Vitoria and Hugo Grotius.[8] Donne's globalizing of the scriptural economy represents one of such "theological justifications of early globalization." In an undated sermon preached upon the Penitential Psalms, Donne says, "if I were to work upon Heathen men, Westerne Americans, or Easterne Chineses, for their conversion to Christ, I should scarce adventure to propose to them the histories of the Martyrs of the Primitive Church" (9:336). Donne's theological cosmopolitanism, I will show, is exemplified in his reception of the "Heathen men" represented by people on both divides of the Anyan strait, that is, "Westerne Americans" and "Easterne Chineses."

For early modern Europeans, Anyan was not a mere strait—it was closely associated with the "fabled realm of Cathay." H. J. C. Grierson and Clay Hunt identify Donne's Anyan with the Bering Strait.[9] Refuting Grierson and Hunt's view, Owens argues that Donne's Anyan is "not a place but an idea that was transformed into an image and for nearly two centuries masqued as a physical location," and that "Donne's important intention in the poem is not to identify places on the earth, but to assert a spiritual unity symbolized finally by Jerusalem, 'Christs Crosse and Adams tree'."[10] Though agreeing with Owens's claim of the fictional and spiritual associations of Donne's Anyan, I nevertheless focus on the relevance of its physicality to the poet's global imagination, but by this I mean a referent larger than the Bering Strait. Donne's Anyan brought to mind a geographical concept much broader than a mere gulf. Nor was this concept totally detached from physical moorings. In his *Principal Navigations*, Hakluyt writes that "Anian" refers both to the "people of, on the borders of America" and the "strait" central to the Northwest Passage project (PN 12:133). In fact, apart from the referents mentioned by Hakluyt, Anyan also elicited the vast regions encompassed under the umbrella epithet of the Far East, especially the Ming Empire that exercised an absolute sway over the eastern hemisphere. Anyan most likely originated from a Chinese province called "Ania."[11] Ania showed up in the Italian cartographer Giacomo Gastaldi's *Asiae Nova Descriptio* (1570) as a large province spanning the area between "Ganzu" (Gansu) and "Quinsai" (Hangzhou). In his *A New Passage to Cataia*, Sir Humphrey Gilbert (1539–83) speaks of "the people which inhabit Mangia, Anian, & Quinzay" (PN 7:165). "Mangia" can be traced to Marco Polo's *Travels*, which referred to the southern part of China in the Yuan Dynasty.[12] The rich and beautiful city of "Quinzay" (Kinsai or Quinsay)

---

[8] Ivan Strenski, "The Religion in Globalization," *Journal of American Academy of Religion* 72.3 (2004): 631–52, 633.

[9] H. J. C. Grierson, ed. *The Poems of John Donne*, 2 vols. (Oxford: Oxford UP, 1912), vol. 1. 249–50; Hunt, *Donne's Poetry*, 241; also see Harry M. Campbell, "Donne's 'Hymn to God, My God, in My Sickness,'" *College English* 5.4 (1944): 192–96, 194.

[10] Owens, "Myth of Anian," 135.

[11] "The Province of Aniu" appears in Polo's travels but it refers to present Yunnan province in the south of China, see Polo, *Travels*, 190.

[12] Polo, *Travels*, 164

appeared in almost all medieval and early modern travel literature. In juxtaposing Mangia, Anian, and Quinzay, Gilbert apparently considered Anian a Chinese province. John Dee (1527–1608/9), Elizabeth I's physician, mathematician, and cartographer, directly called Anyan "the province of Ania." In his advice to Arthur Pet and Charles Jackman about the "Northeasterne discoverie" in 1580, Dee remarked that if they "shall trend about the very Northerne and most Easterly point of all Asia, passing by the province of Ania," they "may enter into Quinsay haven, being the chiefe citie in the Northern China" (PN 3:263).

Aside from a land of "riches," Anyan also signified for the English the accessibility of the Pacific region. As Hakluyt points out, Anyan was frequently associated with the Northwest Passage, the Pacific entrance to the Far East. Gilbert defined the passage of "West and Northwest" as the route "on the North and Northwest part of America" through which "our Merchants may have course and recourse with their merchandize, from these our Northernmost parts of Europe, to those Orientall coasts of Asia, in much shorter time, and with greater benefite then any others" (PN 7:212). Anyan was a linchpin in this northwestern route—its physical existence determined the feasibility of the whole project. In his treatise "Certaine Other Reasons, or Arguments to Proove a Passage by the Northwest" (1576), the English travel literature writer Richard Willes (fl. 1558–76) expressly calls this gulf "the Northwesterne straight or Anian frette" (PN 7:202).

Donne's Anyan, as well the Far East, Northwest Passage, and the New World this strait elicited, bespeaks a global consciousness. The profusion of what Fred Spier calls "Earth icons" in Donne's works indicates a broad awareness of global processes that transcend national or European borders, an enlightenment that inevitably modifies and reshapes his perspectival ken. Donne's global consciousness registers centrally in the union of "East and West," an image that occurs like a refrain in his sermons.[13] This obsession with the unity of East and West is inseparable from Donne's recognition of how a "flat" earth was transformed into a "round" globe by those globalizing forces. Unsurprisingly, Donne constantly employs the flat-round topos to articulate the east-west motif. In a sermon preached on March 28, 1619, he writes, "take a flat Map, a Globe *in Plano*, and here is East, and there is West, as far asunder as two points can be put: but reduce this flat Map to roundnesse, which is the true form, and then East and West touch one another, and all are one" (2:199). The flat-round topos here is used to represent the "touch[ing]" of "East and West," a meeting that bears on the "one[ness]" of the world. The same rhetorical pattern and thematic concern also appear in a sermon preached upon the Penitentiall Psalmes dated 1623: "in a flat Map, there goes no more, to make West East, though they be distant in an extremity, but to paste that flat Map upon a round body, and then West and East are all one" (6:59). In other words, despite their discursive separation on a "flat" map,

---

[13] Since for Donne in "the round frame of the World, the farthest West is East, where the West ends, the East begins" (10:52), the "east" and "west" in his idiomatic phrase "east and west" should refer to "Far East" and "Far West."

"West and East" converge physically across a rounded globe. The flat-round topos is implicit in a sermon preached upon All-Saints Day dated about 1623 as well: in "the round frame of the World, the farthest West is East, where the West ends, the East begins" (10:52). As a northwestern gateway to the east, Anyan symbolized precisely the point at which the flat earth turns into a round globe or where "the West ends, the East begins," and was thereby crucial to bearing out the "true" or globalized "form" of the world.

The globalization approach allows us to see, above all, how Donne responds theologically to a globalized world. The global horizon epitomized in Anyan or the union of East and West compels Donne to resituate Christianity not in the old world center (Jerusalem) but in the newly available idea of the global. While knowledge of the Far East helps cultivate a global consciousness, this consciousness serves, in turn, to alert him to the limitations of biblical discourse whose symbolic jurisdiction had been confined to the old worlds. A globalized lens has apparently afforded Donne special insights into theological matters. As he describes in a sermon preached in 1622, "I can see round about me, even to the *Horizon*, and beyond it, I can see *both Hemispheres* at once, God in this, and God in the next world too … I can see him in all angles, in all postures" (4:175). What is depicted here is a universal outlook that allows one to see not only geographical but also theological unity. But a global perspective also helps highlight the limitations of the biblical economy conceptualized within the Ptolemaic framework. This perception is implicit in Donne's juxtaposition of old and new place names in "Hymne to God." According to Genesis 10, after the flood, Noah's three sons, Ham, Sem, and Japheth, scattered over the earth and settled down respectively in Africa, Asia, and Europe. In the passage cited in the beginning of this chapter, Donne juxtaposes the biblical world center "Jerusalem" with the new regions in the Pacific and the Far East, and couples the newly opened straits of Anyan and Magellan with the old continents divided between Noah's three sons. The tension suggested in this arrangement reflects the broader conflict between the Ptolemaic biblical cosmogony and the globalized world of the Renaissance. In the age of discovery, the world broadened out daily, and new regions kept on bursting upon the boundaries delimited by Ptolemy, as Toby Lester summarizes, "Thule in the north, the Fortunate Isles in the west, Cape Bojador in the south, Taprobane in the east, none was ultimate anymore. The ocean was unloosing its chains, and new worlds were coming into view."[14] Put another way, maritime explorations burst open the four extreme corners designated by Ptolemy, expanding the world beyond the European borders to new oceans and lands. With the collapsing of the old "ultimate" horizons, the scriptural cosmogony grounded in the Ptolemaic system started to collapse. The regional character of biblical locations appeared the more striking against a globalized world that had become a predominant motif in Renaissance cartographical and geographical discourses. Within a rounded globe, the old world appeared to shrink to smaller size and the old navel was irrevocably

---

[14] Lester, *Fourth Part*, 213.

dislocated. The authority of Scripture thus hung critically on its ability to address regions far beyond its initial jurisdiction. To reinstate the centrality of Christianity, the whole infrastructure of biblical discourse needed to be orientated towards not Jerusalem or any other specific locations, but the entire globalized world. Donne was not only aware of but also undertook to address the limitations of biblical discourse. But rather than "assimilating the new science into the old" as Jeanne Shami claims, he seeks to expand the scriptural framework to contain a rounded globe.[15] Specifically, he tries to globalize such cardinal biblical concepts as Jerusalem, Trinity, and the Gospel. The union of East and West proves a pertinent metaphor for Donne to represent the universality of the scriptural economy.

Donne's global consciousness reshapes, apart from his theology, his perception of the other. Donne's attempt to rearticulate the scriptural economy within a global framework indicates at once an apologetic will to justify Christianity and a cosmopolitan will to engage differences. Since Donne typically addresses cultural pluralism from a theologian's viewpoint, I call this approach to the other "theological cosmopolitanism"—the willingness to engage religious difference by expanding the symbolic scope of biblical jurisdiction. Enlightened by a global horizon, early modern Europeans showed an increasingly liberal cosmopolitanism towards the non-Western other.[16] Alison Games argues that Renaissance cosmopolitans distinguished by their pluralistic approach to those "unlike themselves." For instance, whereas merchants embraced cultural pluralism "with enthusiasm and curiosity," clerics accommodated to religious differences through "ecumenism," and the colonialists expressed their cosmopolitan will in "their willingness to adapt and to learn from the examples of rivals and predecessors."[17] Donne's theological cosmopolitanism partakes of this multivocal response to the foreign other, though in seeking to fit the scriptural framework to a globalized world, he expresses, like Vitoria and Grotius, a theologian's reaction.

The "sun" image that symbolized cosmopolitanism in both classical and medieval times nicely captures Donne's cosmopolitan spirit. Commenting on Seneca's idea of cosmopolitanism, the German theologian Nicholas de Cusa (1401–64) remarks,

---

[15] Jeanne Shami, "John Donne: Geography as Metaphor," *Geography and Literature: A Meeting of the Disciplines*, ed. William E. Mallory and Paul Simpson-Housley (Syracuse: Syracuse UP, 1987), 161–67, 162.

[16] On early modern cosmopolitans see, Pamela A. Brown, "'I care not, let naturals love nations': Cosmopolitan Clowning," *Shakespeare Studies* 35 (2007): 66–77; Alan B. Farmer, "Cosmopolitanism and Foreign Books in Early Modern England," *Shakespeare Studies* 35 (2007): 58–65; Crystal Bartolovich, "Utopian Cosmopolitanism," *Shakespeare Studies* 35 (2007): 47–57; and Alison Games, "England's Global Transition and the Cosmopolitans Who Made it Possible," *Shakespeare Studies* 35 (2007): 24–31. Also see Margaret Jacob, *Strangers Nowhere in the World: The Rise of Cosmopolitanism in Early Modern Europe* (Philadelphia: U of Pennsylvania P, 2006). Jacob focuses on the period around 1650 to 1800.

[17] Games, *Web of Empire*, 10.

[E]ach of us dwells in two communities—the local community of our birth, and the community of human argument and aspiration that is, in Seneca's words, 'truly great and truly common,' in which we look to neither this corner nor to that, but measure the boundary of our nation by the Sun.[18]

For Seneca as well as de Cusa, the Sun signifies the cosmopolitan "community" of "argument and aspiration." Donne expressly articulates the cosmopolitan sweep of his "thoughts" in terms of the Sun in his *Devotions*. "My thoughts" that "reach from east to west, from earth to heaven," he says, tend to go "with the sun, and beyond the sun." An imaginary cosmopolitan who, though trapped "in a close prison, in a sickbed," can nevertheless make cosmic journeys through his far-ranging "thoughts," is vividly conjured forth through the recurrent image of the Sun.[19]

Anyan and the Northeast and Northwest Passages Project

The northern passages appear a number of times in Donne's poems and sermons, which signals his awareness of contemporary exploratory processes that helped expand a Eurocentric outlook to a global horizon. In "Epithalamion I, The Time of Mariage," he expresses the hope that "the passage of the West or East would thaw, / And open wide their easie liquid jawe / To all our ships" around "the Northern Pole" (111–14). In "Satire III," speaking of the courage of those resolved to strike a path in the north, the speaker says, "Hast thou couragious fire to thaw the ice / Of frozen North discoveries?" (21–22) Also, in a sermon preached on April 5, 1629, Donne remarks,

> Who ever amongst our Fathers, thought of any other way to the Moluccaes, or to China, then by the Promontory of *Good hope*? Yet another way opened it self to *Magellan*; a Straite; it is true; but yet a way thither; and who knows yet, whether there may not be a North-East, and a North-West way hither, besides? (8:371)

This passage reveals a substantial acquaintance with the various stages in the Western discovery of the Far East. Though none of "our Fathers" had "ever" imagined "any other way" to the east except by the Cape of Good Hope, Donne says, the inconceivable did happen: Magellan opened up a southwest way. Nor is Magellan's strait the only alternative. There are many other possible ways to the Far East, and the "North-East" and "North-West" passages represent such very possibilities.

---

[18] Quoted in Martha Nussbaum, "Kant and Stoic Cosmopolitanism," *Journal of Political Philosophy* 5.1 (1997): 1–25, 6.
[19] Donne, *Devotions*, 19.

Donne's image of the polar route recapitulates a far-reaching national project that sought to encompass the world through the North Pole.[20] The possibility of reaching the Far East via the Arctic region was already imagined in 1527 by Robert Thorne, a London merchant long residing in Seville. In a letter to King Henry VIII (1491–1547), Thorne writes that "of the foure partes of the worlde, it seemeth three parts are discovered by other Princes." Since the Iberian sovereigns have "encompassed the world" through almost all other ways, for England, "there is left one way to discover, which is into the North" (PN 2:161). Thorne proposed three means of encircling the world through the Arctic area: northwest, north-south, and northeast. (PN 2:163) Though the blueprint Thorne outlined did not receive much enthusiasm from King Henry, the project was earnestly pursued during the reign of King Edward (1547–53).

The English showed considerable irresolution between a northeast or northwest approach to the Far East.[21] Though Gerard Mercator (1512–94), the famous Flemish cartographer who exhibited great interest in the English cause, ultimately favored a northeastern way, this decision was made after much vacillation. As Nicholas Crane notes, "On Mercator's first map [1538], there had been a northwest passage to the Indies, but no north-east passage, then on his globe [1541] there was a north-east passage but no north-west passage. On his new world map [1569], there was a north-east *and* a north-west passage."[22] The uncertainty exhibited by Mercator mirrored the hesitancy in practical explorations that relied much upon cartographical theorizations. When the polar project was resolved upon by "certaine grave citizens of London" in 1553 (PN 2:239), the English began with the eastward exploration, and then left it off to search for a western

---

[20] For ancient and medieval cartographical mapping of the routes to China and the Far East see, Charles R. Beazley, *The Dawn of Modern Geography*, 3 vols. (New York: Peter Smith, 1949), especially vol. 3.; Yule, ed., *Cathay and the Way Thither*; and Evelyn Edson, *The World Map, 1300–1492: The Persistence of Tradition and Transformation* (Baltimore: Johns Hopkins UP, 2007).

[21] The feasibility of the two passages was actually officially debated before the queen and the Privy Council in 1565 between Sir Humphrey Gilbert and Anthony Jenkinson (1529–c. 1610), the English explorer noted for his explorations of Muscovy [Russia]. For this debate see *New American World: A Documentary History of North America to 1612*, ed. David B. Quinn, 5 vols. (New York: Arno Press and Hector Bye, 1979), vol. 4. 179, 188–190. Like Jenkinson and Eden, John Dee also supported a northeast approach. See Eden, *Decades of the New Worlde*; Dee, *The Great Volume of Famous and Riche Discoveries* (London, 1577); E. G. R. Taylor, "John Dee and the Map of North-East Asia," *Imago Mundi* 12 (1955): 103–6; and Wallis, "England's Search for the Northern Passages," 456. Gilbert and Willes championed a northwestern approach. For Gilbert see *The Voyages and Colonising Enterprises of Sir Humphrey Gilbert*, ed. D. B. Quinn (London: Hakluyt Society, 1938).

[22] Nicholas Crane, *Mercator: The Man Who Mapped the Planet* (London: Phoenix, 2003), 233–34. For England's indebtedness to Mercator's cartography see Taylor, "A Letter Dated 1577 from Mercator to John Dee," *Imago Mundi* 13 (1956): 56–68; for Mercator's letter to Richard Hakluyt see PN 3:275–81.

route. The first north adventure undertaken by Sir Hugh Willoughby and Richard Chanceler in 1553 was directed eastwards. Later in 1580 Pet and Jackman also embarked on a northeast quest. But both voyages ended up in failure, which "cast grave doubts on the possibility of reaching Cathay by the North East." In effect, "The only incidental gain of the North Eastern voyages was the establishment of trading relations with Russia" (PN 12:23). By the 1570s, the Northwest Passage appeared the only way left for England to access the much fabled Cathay. In his "Arguments" for a Northwest passage, Willes speaks of "four famous wayes" of going to "those fruitfull and wealthie Islands, which wee doe usually call Moluccaes." These ways include, "the Southeasterne way round about Afrike by the Cape of Good hope" discovered by Vasco Da Gama in 1497; the "Southwest" way unsealed by Magellan in 1519–22; the "Northeast, beyond All Europe and Asia" that proved inaccessible by Willoughby; and the "Northwest," which "Sir Humphrey Gilbert ... discourseth at large" but was "not thoroughly known" then (PN 7:191,192). The work mentioned here refers to Gilbert's *A New Passage to Cataia* that undertakes to "prove a passage by the Northwest to Cathaia, and the East Indies" (PN 7:160). So by 1576 the only choice left for England to get to the Far East was the northwestern entrance.

The Anyan strait was central to the mapping of a northwestern passage. This Pacific door to the Far East was, Hakluyt says in the epistle dedication of his *Principal Navigations* (1600), of "exceeding great consequence" for England's oversees ventures. To illustrate this importance, Hakluyt specially "inserted the voyage of one Francis Gualle a Spaniard" who has travelled from Acapulco in the New Spain to the Philippines and Macao and then back through Japan to the West Indies. During this trans-Pacific journey, Gualle found what is "called in most mappes The Streight of Anian" (PN 1:lxxvii–viii). Anyan registers not only practical experimentation but also an earnest intellectual attempt to conceptualize an unprecedented endeavor.[23] Anyan sparked considerable "controversies of Geographie" (PN 7:203). The feasibility of a northwestern route hinged on two hypotheses: whether there was a navigable strait between Asia and America, and whether the American continent continued into the Arctic region or if there was a passage between them. However, sixteenth-century cartographers could not reach a consensus "concerning the divers situation and sundry limits of America" (PN 7:203). As Willes summarizes,

> Ortelius in his universall tables, in his particular Mappes of the West Indies, of all Asia, of the Northren kingdomes, of the East Indies, Mercator in some of his globes, and generall Mappes of the world, Moletius in his universall table of the Globe divided, in his sea Carde, and particuler tables of the East Indies, Zalterius, and Don Diego, with Ferdinando Bertely, and others, doe so much differ from Gemma Frisius and Cabota ... . (PN 7:203)

---

[23] See the Anian strait on the map in Hakluyt, PN 7:256.

With regard to the first hypothesis, the Flemish cartographer Franciscus Monachus (c. 1490–1565) joined America to Asia with a narrow waist of land in his 1526 world map, a claim supported by the Italian geographer Josephus Moletius (1531–88) and many others (PN 7:194). The Dutch mathematician Gemma Frisius (1508–55) rejected Monachus's postulate, arguing that although many "connect this part of the earth [America] with Asia and say that it is one single continent … their arguments are not valid."[24] In his terrestrial globe of 1536 [collaborated with Mercator], Gemma divides Asia and America with the "*Fretum arcticum sive Fretum trium fratrum*," that is, "the Arctic Strait or the Strait of the three Brothers," a proposition that was, according to Willes, corroborated by the northwest voyage of Sebastian Cabot in 1508–9 (PN 7:194). Also, the Italian cartographer Gastaldi depicts Asia and America as a single landmass in his 1548 world map, but in 1562 he gave up his previous theory, declaring in a small book that there was a strait separating the two continents and naming this strait "*Streto di Anian*." Anyan appears in the 1566 map of North America by the Venetian cartographer Bolognino Zaltieri as a narrow channel that divides Asia and America. The globe that first shows the passages north and south of America was an anonymous globe gores of about 1530 (issued c. 1550).[25] But the most affirmative cartographical evidence of a Northwest Passage came from Abraham Ortelius, the famous geographer to the King of Spain who, Gilbert says,

> doth coast out in his generall Mappe set out Anno 1569, all the countreys and Capes, on the Northwest side of America, from Hochelaga to Cape de Paramantia: describing likewise the sea coastes of Cataia and Gronland, towards any part of America, making both Gronland and America, Islands disjoyned by a great sea, from any part of Asia. (PN 7:163)

In addition, though initially insisting on the "continuance" of "the West Indies land" to "the North Pole," Mercator and Moletius later "opened a gulfe betwixt the West Indies and the extreame Northerne land" (PN 7:193).[26]

It was Gilbert who put forward the most sophisticated argument for the possibility of a Northwest Passage to the Far East. For Gilbert, it was possible to find an oceanic pathway to "Cataia, the Moluccae, India, and all other places in

---

[24] Gemma Frisius, *De principiis astronomiae* (Antwerp, 1530), quoted in Peter van der Krogt, *Globi Neerlandici: The Production of Globes in the Low Countries* (Utrecht: HES, 1993), 51.

[25] These gores are now in the New York Public Library; see its facsimile version in Wallis, "England's Search for the Northern Passages," 458. "Gore" means "one of the many triangular or lune-shaped pieces that form the surface of a celestial or terrestrial globe." "Globe gores" indicate printed maps designed to be cut into triangular segments to past over a globe. "gore, n.2." 2nd ed. 1989. *OED Online*. June 5, 2012.

[26] For a detailed discussion of sixteenth-century mapping of the north Pacific region see Wallis, "England's Search for the Northern Passages," 456–58; and L. Breitfuss, "Early Maps of North-Eastern Asia and of the Lands around the North Pacific Controversy between G. F. Müller and N Delisle," *Imago Mundi* 3 (1939): 87–99, 87.

the east" through "America by the Northwest" (PN 7:162,163), as he states in his *A New Passage to Cataia*:

> I found [America] to bee an Iland environed round about with Sea, having on the Southside of it the frete or straight of Magellan, on the West side Mar del Sur, which Sea runneth towards the North, separating it from the East parts of Asia, where the Dominions of the Cathaians are: On the East part our West Ocean, and on the North side the sea that severeth it from Groneland, thorow which Northren Seas the Passage lyeth, which I take now in hand to discover. (PN 7:160)

The "Passage" lying through the "Northren Seas" and which Gilbert "take[s] now in hand to discover" refers to none other than the Northwestern route. By "Mar de Sur," Gilbert means "the West Ocean beyond America ... knowen to be open at 40. degrees elevation from the Island Japan" (PN 7:194). Put differently, while "our West Ocean" indicates the Atlantic, "Mar del Sur" means the northern part of the Pacific. If America is "but a part of ye continent adjoyning to Asia," Gilbert argues, then "the people which inhabit Mangia, Anian, & Quinzay ... would before this time have made some road into it, hoping to have found some like commodities to their owne." But no evidence shows that the Asians have ever crossed the Pacific, nor has anyone "ever found entry from thence [America] by land to Cataia, or any part of Asia." The logical outcome is that, America is "one Island, and in no part ajoyning to Asia" and there should be a "Northren Seas and Passage" that continues with "Mar del Sur, by some fret that lyeth between America, Groneland and Cataia" (PN 7:165,166). Simply put, there should be both a pathway running between America and the polar region and "a navigable passage" that separates Asia from America (PN 7:172). This conclusion, Gilbert declares, is "verified by the opinions of all the best, both Antique, and Moderne Geographers, and plainely set out in the best and most allowed Mappes, Charts, Globes, Cosmographical tables & discourses of this our age" (PN 7:164).[27] Incited by Gilbert's argument, Sir Martin Frobisher (c. 1535–94) embarked on his famous northwest quests in 1576–78 (PN 7: 204–42; 284–367) and John Davis (1550–1605) continued the search in 1585–87 (PN 7:381–422).

"East and West are one": Donne's Globalizing of Biblical Discourse

In the Renaissance, the image of the globe has increasingly become a point of reference of theological contemplations. In 1570 Dee remarked that "some, for one purpose: and some, for another, liketh, loveth, getteth, and useth, Mappes, Chartes, and Geographicall Globes."[28] One reason of the popularity of globes resides in

---

[27] For the "best moderne Geographers" cited by Gilbert to support his Northwest Passage thesis see PN 7:162–63.

[28] Dee, "Preface," in Euclid, *The Elements of Geometry*, trans. Henry Billingsley (London, 1570), sig. A4. D.

their theological relevance. Featuring the meditation of a devout soul in the throes of high fever, "Hymne to God" explores this relevance through cosmographical imagery. Standing at the "dore" of death, the speaker thinks it urgent to "tune" (3–4) the soul to afterlife. To articulate this preparedness, he compares his doctors to "Cosmographers," and "I," the suffering patient, to "their mappe":

> Whilst my Physitians by their love are growne
> Cosmographers, and I their Mappe, who lie
> Flat on this bed, that by them may be showne
> That this is my South-west discoverie,
> *Per fretum febris*, by these streights to die (6–10)

The doctor-cosmographer analogy here anticipates the remarks of Sir Thomas Browne (1605–82), a doctor and theologian in his own right. In his *Religio Medici* (1643), Browne says, "The world that I regard is myselfe, it is the Microcosme of mine owne frame that I cast mine eye on; for the other, I use it but like my Globe, and turne it round sometimes for my recreation." Here Browne proves to be no less adept in playing imaginative games with the globe. In playing with the human body "like a globe" for his own "recreation," the doctor transforms himself into a cosmographer. Whereas Browne the player *himself* takes on the part of a doctor-cosmographer, Donne imagines his ailing body as a "mappe" subjected to the perusal of *his* doctor-cosmographer. For Browne, the doctor-cosmographer role allows him to see the "earth" as "a point not onely in respect of the heavens above us, but of that heavenly and celestiall part within us."[29] Likewise, in turning his doctor into a cosmographer and his ailing body into a map, Donne's speaker envisions a new relationship with God in afterlife. Since "All streights, and none but streights are ways," high fever is one of the "straights" that lead to God. Magellan died of "*febris*" [fever] when exploring South America, but he succeeded in discovering the Southwest passage [*fretum*]. Likewise, the fever might loosen his bonding with God, Donne's speaker says, but this relaxing can lead to "my South-west discoverie" (9), that is, other signs of divine grace.

The union of East and West serves as an archetypical metaphor for Donne's vision of a globalized world. In fact, he constantly evokes this cosmic image to meditate on the Resurrection at such critical moments as sickness and death. In the sermon preached on March 28, 1619, he remarks that the "one[ness]" represented by the touching of East and West coincides with the "circle" of life, that is, the meeting of "the womb and the grave," a coincidence he elicits to give comfort to King James who was "dangerously sick at New-Market" (2:199–200). Also, in the same sermon preached in 1623, he says, just as in a rounded globe "the farthest West is East, where the West ends, the East begins … so in thee, (who art a World too) thy West and thy East shall joyne, and when thy Sun, thy soule comes to set in thy deathbed, the Son of Grace shall suck it up into glory" (10:52). Here the

---

[29] *Sir Thomas Brown: The Major Works*, ed. C. A. Patrides (London: Penguin, 1977), 153.

merging of East and West offers an apt metaphor for the unity of life and death as well.

The speaker of "Hymne to God" also uses the East-West analogy to speculate on the Resurrection.[30] What marks Donne's use of this analogy in his divine poem is its association with Willes's theorization of the Anyan strait. Here we hear the speaker exclaiming:

> I joy, that in these straits, I see my West;
> For, though theire currants yeeld returne to none,
> What shall my West hurt me? As West and East
> In all flatt Maps (and I am one) are one,
> So death doth touch the Resurrection (11–15)

The journey and return via the "straits" featured in this stanza recalls Willes's rationalization of the importance of Anyan in joining the two halves of the world. Subscribing to Gilbert's Northwest Passage hypothesis, Willes claims that practical voyages of travelers who "have gone out of Europe into Mar del Zur, and returned thence at the Northwest, do most evidently conclude that way to be navigable, and that passage free" (PN 7:196). So, he argues,

> Our travailers neede not to seeke their returne by the Northeast, neither shall they be constrained, except they list, either to attempt Magellans straight at the Southwest, or to be in danger of the Portingals for the Southeast: they may returne by the Northwest, that same way they doe goe foorth, as experience hath shewed. (PN 7:201–2)

To "disprove" possible objections to this thesis, Willes contends that though "in Magellans straight wee are violently driven backe Westward," this does not mean that we are unable to "returne Eastward," "through the Northwesterne straight or Anian frette." It is the "want" of "sea roome" that "causeth all narrow passages generally to be most violent," he reasons, but according to the maps of Cabot, Gemma, and Tramezine, "the northwestern straight hath more sea roome at the least by one hundredth English myles, then Magellans frette hath." Thus it is possible that we can "returne Eastward" through the "Anian gulfe" (PN 7:202–3). Donne's speaker most likely has had Willes's theory in mind when exclaiming, "I joy, that in these straits, I see my West / For, though theire currants yeeld returne to none, / What shall my West hurt me?" What is alluded to here is the popular notion that "those currents yield return to none" mentioned by Willes—one cannot "returne Eastward" via the Anyan or Magellan straits. But in attempting to return to Europe through "these straits," whether Anyan or Magellan, the speaker argues, even if he would be "driven backe Westward" and thereby "see my West," he will still rejoice, for two reasons. First, if he cannot return eastward to Europe, he can nevertheless locate a "home" in the Pacific and reap "the Easterne riches."

---

[30] Joseph E. Duncan, "Resurrections in Donne's 'A Hymne to God the Father' and 'Hymne to God my God, in my Sicknesse,'" *John Donne Journal* 7.2 (1988): 183–96.

Second, "What shall my West hurt me?" Anyway, "West and East / In all flat maps ... are one" (10:52). So the sight of the Far East is simultaneously a beholding of the Far West. In his "Goodfriday, 1613. Riding Westward," the speaker states, "I am carryed towards the West / This day, when my Soules forme bends toward the East. / There I should see a Sunne, by rising set, / And by that setting endlesse day beget" (9–12). Jonathan Goldberg argues that in this poem Donne presents "the tensions occasioned between two journeys: the outward physical journey west, and the internal eastern journey," and ultimately these two journeys collapse into one: "the journey west that becomes the journey east."[31] The union of geographical and spiritual journeys also features in "Hymne to God." Here by delineating a trip east that is simultaneously a journey west, Donne represents the globalized nature of his spiritual "home." Even though dislocated from Jerusalem, the speaker suggests, he can still find a "home" through the Northwest Passage in the Pacific region.[32] The meeting of Far East and Far West fictionally experienced by the Speaker as a traveler perfectly expresses the "touching" of "death" and the Resurrection imagined by the believer lying sick in bed. Just as Far East joins Far West via the Anyan strait, the speaker observes, "death doth touch the resurrection" through the *fretum* [strait] unsealed by his *febris* [fever].

But earth images are double-edged metaphors—their global scope serves to sharpen the focus on the regional character of biblical *loci*. Renaissance Europe saw various apologetic attempts to accommodate the Ptolemaic scriptural cosmogony to an extended globe, and these endeavors threw into relief how much biblical signifiers relied on geographical referents for validity. For instance, noticing the questionable nature of the centrality of Jerusalem in an expanded world, the Venetian mapmaker Fra Mauro remarks in his *Mappamundi* of c. 1450,

> Jerusalem is in the middle of the inhabited world *according to* the latitude of the inhabited world, although *according to* longitude it is too far west. But because the western part, Europe, is more heavily populated, it is still in the middle *according to* longitude, not *considering* the physical space of the earth but the number of its inhabitants.[33]

Mauro describes here an attempt to adjust some old religious locations to an enlarged world. As is indicated in his repeated use of the prepositional phrase

---

[31] Jonathan Goldberg, "Donne's Journey East: Aspects of a Seventeenth-Century Trope," *Studies in Philology* 68.4 (1971): 470–83, 481, 471.

[32] The relative nature of such terms as east and west is succinctly articulated in Toscanelli's letter to Columbus in 1475: "Do not marvel at my calling 'west' the regions where the spices grow, although they are commonly called 'east'; because whoever sails westward will always find those lands in the west, while one who goes overland to the east will always find the same lands in the east." Quoted in *The Life of the Admiral Christopher Columbus by his Son Ferdinand*, trans. and ed. Benjamin Keen (London: Folio Society, 1960), 45.

[33] Quoted in Edson, *World Map*, 145, my own italics.

"according to," Mauro's apologetic strategy is to alter the conceptual parameter within which a particular place is signified. "Jerusalem" takes on different meaning when viewed according to the three different points of reference—the "latitude" and "longitude" of the inhabited world and "the number of its inhabitants." The local character of scriptural concepts proved also the concern of the Dutch scholar Isaac Vossius (1618–89). In his justification of the primacy of the Noachian flood, Vossius conceded that the whole world was not inhabited in the age of Noah, and the deluge most likely occurred only within "the borders of Syria and Mesopotamia." Like Mauro, Vossius also resorted to changing the framework within which biblical signifiers were initially conceptualized. Whereas Mauro argues for what David N. Livingstone calls a "demographic" rather than cartographic universality of Jerusalem, Vossius claims that though local in spatial terms, "the Deluge was universal in an oecumenical sense, since the destruction was universal and the whole inhabited world overwhelmed."[34]

Donne's "Hymne to God" features the same tension between the biblical geography and a globalized world. This tension is exemplified, above all, in the Anyan strait, a throughway that, by extending the world to the Pacific Rim, raised doubts about the centrality of Jerusalem. Donne does intend to "assert a spiritual unity" in the poem, but this unity is symbolized by, instead of Jerusalem as Owens argues, new geographical regions.[35] The historical context informing Donne and Vossius's world picture differed from that of Mauro's. Projected before Columbus and Magellan's epoch-making discoveries, Mauro's world map sought to integrate into a single cartographical grid the "three disparate traditions" prevalent by the 1450s, that is, Ptolemaic atlases, medieval mappaemundi, as well as the potlan charts.[36] By comparison, Donne and Vossius faced a totally changed world—those pioneer circumnavigators had transformed, as Donne calls it, the "flat" earth into a "round" globe. What Donne seeks to do in "Hymne to God" is to accommodate the biblical division of the world to this new configuration of the earth. Donne notices the inability of the scriptural economy to contain the new worlds, but rather than shifting the conceptual frameworks like Mauro and Vossius or superimposing the biblical picture upon the new geographical form as "T-in-O" map makers did, he presents the old and new place names as equals.[37] In the poem the speaker asks,

---

[34] David N. Livingstone, *Adam's Ancestors: Race, Religion, and the Politics of Human Origins* (Baltimore: Johns Hopkins UP, 2008), 38; Isaac Vossius, *Dissertatio de vera aetate mundi* (The Hague, 1659), quoted in Don C. Allen, *The Legend of Noah: Renaissance Rationalism in Art, Science, and Letters* (Urbana: U of Illinois P, 1963), 86–87.

[35] For other claims of the primacy of Jerusalem in "Hymne to God," see Hunt, *Donne's Poetry*, 96–117; and Gardner, *John Donne: The Divine Poems*; Gardner even equates "Eastern riches" with "Jerusalem" in geographical terms, 108.

[36] Edson, *World Map*, 140.

[37] Apart from the map of Isidore of Seville, the thirteenth-century Ebstorf Map also features the superimposing of the biblical view of the world upon the geographical grid in representing the image of the physical world as is encompassed by the head, hands, and feet of Christ.

"Is the Pacifique Sea my home? Or are / The Easterne riches? Is *Jerusalem*? / *Anyan*, and *Magellan*, and *Gibraltare*." Here the four spatial images—Jerusalem, the Far East represented by Anyan and the Pacific, South America registered in the Magellan strait, and the Mediterranean Sea embodied by Gibraltar—signify four reference points for the center of the world. The four italicized place names, their undifferentiated juxtaposition, and above all, the three emphatic question marks, indicate an evaluation of their equal candidacy for the world center. In effect, the repeated use of the question marks suggests at once an interrogation of the primacy of Jerusalem and the imagination of the Pacific region as the new world navel or spiritual "home."[38]

The merging of Far East and Far West both makes it necessary and affords an ideal framework for Donne to globalize the Trinity, another core concept in biblical discourse. For Donne, the Father is "the God of East and West, of all places" (5:325), since only the divine eye "can fixe it self upon East and West at once" (9:134). Further, in the same way "a Compasse" that "reaches over all our Map, over all our World, from our East to our West," the Holy Spirit whose "*Cloven tongue*" that "opens as a Compasse" spans "from our birth to our death, from our cradle to our grave" (7:435). Here the geographical image of the "compass" is used to signify the universal "voice" of the Holy Ghost. The global scope of the Son's redemptive power is pointedly articulated in a sermon preached in 1625: "the sins of all Nations, all the East and West, and all the North and South ... were at once upon Christ" (6:275).

Given the global feature of biblical discourse, scriptural cosmogony and the new geography represented in "Hymne to God" agree rather than clash with each other. Donne represents this congruence through the speaker's awareness of the unity of humankind embodied by the two Adams, as he puts it, "both *Adams* met in me" (23). Apart from the union of life and death or "*Paradise* and *Calvarie*" (21), the two Adams also symbolize the oneness of humankind. For the speaker, the world is "one" (14) according to both Mosaic and apostolic laws—whereas the first Adam bonds us in physical life, the second [Jesus Christ] unites us in the afterlife. It is through, once again, the east-west metaphor and the flat-round topos that Donne manages to translate the biblical notion of unity into the unity registered in the new geography. It is true that east and west remain separated when the speaker lies "flat" in bed and his "Cartographers" fail to detect the route to his sickness. But when the fever is gone and the flat map or the ailing patient gathers and "round[s]" up, east and west will join through him and in him. The speaker's simultaneous awareness of being a rounded map and of being an epitome of "both Adams" suggests, therefore, a conscious attempt to merge the biblical economy with the new configuration of the earth.

---

[38] Gillies also argues for the possibility of the Pacific ring as the new world center in the early modern world, Gillies, *Geography of Difference*, 187.

Donne's Theological Cosmopolitanism towards the Chinese and Amerindians

The global consciousness symbolized in Donne's image of Anyan and personified in the ailing patient in "Hymne to God" also informs his perception of the other in the new worlds. Put another way, Donne's theological cosmopolitanism is expressed as a will not only to globalize biblical discourse but also to engage the cultural diversities unleashed by those new regions. The strait of Anyan, as an emblem of the joining of Far East and Far West, represents the global scope of this cosmopolitan spirit—it extends to peoples residing along the Pacific Rim.

Donne's theological cosmopolitanism informs his response to people on both divides of the Anyan strait—the Chinese and Amerindians. According to David Hollinger, it is a "universal will to find common ground" and a "cosmopolitan will to engage human diversity."[39] Donne's reception of the other represented by the Chinese signals both the "universal will" and "cosmopolitan will" identified by Hollinger. In an undated sermon preached on Luke 23:24, Donne envisions a cosmopolitan neighborhood in the union of East and West, as he says, "as by the sea the most remote and distant Nations enjoy one another, by traffique and commerce, East and West becom[e] neighbours" (5:238). China was numbered among the Eastern neighbors in a global commercial network. Along with his theological accommodation to the Far East as represented in "Hymne to God," Donne also engages the Chinese in his sermons. In the undated sermon preached upon the Penitential Psalms, Donne presents "Easterne Chineses, or Westerne Americans" as representatives of "Heathen men" and thereby ideal candidates for the evangelical cause. (9:336) In coupling the Chinese with Americans and designating them as heathens, Donne shows recognition of both their affinity and the otherness they embody. But rather than barbarian and primitive pagans, Donne defines a "heathen man" as "a mere naturall man, uncatechized, uninstructed in the rudiments of the Christian Religion" (3:357) or one "without any knowledge of God" (4:149). This definition of heathens as "naturall" men uninitiated in the Christian doctrine indicates a "universal will" to identify common humanity. Also, in his theological treatise *Essayes in Divinity* (1614), Donne lists various accounts of the origin of history and nations, and he singles out Chinese chronicles, observing that "The Chinese vex us at this day, with irreconcilable accounts."[40] As is shown by his extensive exposition of Genesis and Exodus, the biblical account of time and history, Donne, instead of unreflectively dismissing Chinese chronology on the grounds of its heathen nature, seriously engages rival claims of antiquity. This attempt to fit the disconcerting Chinese chronicles into the biblical timetable bespeaks a "cosmopolitan will" to accommodate cultural diversity.

---

[39] David A. Hollinger, *Postethnic America: Beyond Multiculturalism* (New York: Harper, 1995), 84.
[40] Donne, *Essayes in Divinity*, 22.

Donne's theological cosmopolitanism is most apparent in his attempt to apply the apostolic economy to the West Indies. In a sermon preached to "the Honorable Company of the Virginia Plantation" dated November 13, 1622, he observes that "The *Gospell* must first be published among all Nations," but those "Heathen" Amerindians who worshipped idols or natural deities "surely ... had not heard of the *faith* and the *obedience* of the *Romanes*" (4:279). The term "all Nations" meant different things in the time when the Gospel was first pronounced and in the early modern period. By the seventeenth century, "all Nations" should refer not only to regions around Palestine and within European borders but also peoples throughout the world. Donne admits that when the Gospel was promulgated, the apostles had not

> Dream'd of this world [America] which hath been discover'd since, into which, wee dispute with perplexitie, and intricacy enough, how any men came at first ... for when *Augustus* his Decree went out, *That all the world should bee taxed*, the Decree and the Taxe went not certainly into the *West Indies*; when Saint *Paul* says, *That their Faith was spoken of throughout the whole world*, and that *their obedience was come abroad unto all men*, surely the *West Indies* had not heard of the *faith* and the *obedience* of the *Romanes*. (4:279)

Nevertheless, though not reaching "the West Indies" when first proclaimed, the evangelical message was meant to address the whole world,

> But as in *Moses* time, they call'd the *Mediterranean Sea*, the *great Sea*, because it was the greatest that those men had then seene, so in the *Apostles* time, they call'd that all the world, which was knowne and traded in then; and in all that, they preach'd the *Gospell*. So that as *Christ* when he said to the *Apostles*; *I am with you, unto the end of the World*, could not intend that of them in person, because they did not last to the ende of the world, but in a succession of Apostolike men, so when he says, the *Apostles* should preach him to all the world, it is of the *Succession* too. (4:279–80)

Three apologetic strategies are suggested in these two passages. First, like Mauro, Donne turns to indicators other than old geographical markers to argue his case. Just as the "Mediterranean Sea" signified the whole world in Moses's time, the "known" world was considered "all the world" by people in the Apostles' time. Put differently, just as the universe meant the known world for the Greeks and Romans, the whole world in Moses's and the Apostles' time indicated, in addition to physical places, the scope of people's knowledge of the world. Second, anticipating Vossius, Donne suggests that the Gospel is "universal" not in a physical but "an oecumenical sense." "Ecumenical" as a term that means "representing the whole (Christian) world, or the universal church" was first proposed by John Foxe in his *Actes and Monuments* (1563), and it started to denote "universal" or "worldwide" by 1607.[41] Physical boundaries might pose constraint upon knowledge, but

---

[41] "ecumenical | œcumenical, adj." 2nd ed., 1989. *OED Online*. June 5, 2012.

they cannot hinder the expansion of a spiritual church. So when Christ said "I am with you, unto the end of the World," he did not mean the physical world; rather, he referred to "a succession of apostolic men" devoted to the evangelical cause. Likewise, by "all the world," Christ signified a "succession of world" to be opened up with the spreading of the Gospel. So a "succession of world" means, apart from temporal unfolding, the successive revelation of the new worlds. The implicit message is that Christ had foreseen such discoveries and prepared his Gospel accordingly. Donne's third apologetic tactic consists in a subtle shifting of parameters of reference, both physical and conceptual. The transposition of "the world" to the apostolic men and the translation of "all the world" into a "succession" of worlds bespeak a deliberate manipulation of the symbolic range of the signifiers under discussion. Whereas the signified, that is, the physical world within which the Gospel was first articulated, remains unchanged, the signifiers are detached and expanded to address the new lands.

Beck defines cosmopolitanism at once as recognition of "differences" and "conflicts," the need to "redraw old boundaries," and an awareness of "interdependence" or "civilizational community of fate."[42] The cosmopolitan features identified by Beck show up in Donne's attitude towards the Amerindians. Unlike Spanish conquistadors who exploited, usually with military arms, the Americans under the banner of the apostolic mission, Donne advised the English planters to show cosmopolitan tolerance even to those natives who resorted to violence. In the same sermon preached to the Virginia Company, Donne attempts not only to globalize "the kingdome of the *Gospell*" (4:269) but also to accommodate the religious alterity of those uninitiated heathens. The sermon was preached on November 13, 1622, shortly after the Powhatan massacre that happened on March 22. Here Donne not only recognizes but also makes the best of the "conflicts" between the planters and the natives, as he states:

> Beloved, you are *Actors* upon the same Stage too: the uttermost part of the Earth are your *Scene*: act over the *Acts* of the *Apostles*; be you a light to the *Gentiles*, that sit in darknesse; be you content to carry him over these *Seas*, who dryed up one *Red Sea* for his first people, and hath powred out another *red Sea*, his owne bloud, for them and us. (4:265)

What is proposed here is a policy totally different from the one adopted by Captain John Smith and Governor Thomas Dale who, like the conquistadors, saw the indigenous people as a "military problem."[43] To avoid further conflicts with

---

[42] Beck, *Cosmopolitan Vision*, 7.
[43] Keith Glenn, "Captain John Smith and the Indians," *Virginia Magazine of History and Biography* 52 (1944): 228–48. On the Massacre, see also John Smith, *The Generall Historie of Virginia, New England, and the Summer Isles* (London, 1624); Alden T. Vaughan, "'Expulsion of the Savages': English Policy and the Virginia Massacre of 1622," *William and Mary Quarterly* 35.1 (1978): 57–84; and Benjamin Woolley, *Savage Kingdom: The True Story of Jamestown, 1607, and the Settlement of America* (New York: Harper, 2008).

the natives, Donne advises the settlers and their investors to take a different view of their roles. Rather than armed men or colonial planters, they should regard themselves as apostolic missionaries who undertake "to convay that name of *Christ Jesus*, and to propagate its *Gospell*" (4:265).[44] By practically performing the "*Acts* of the *Apostles*," the planters will become the "light" that guides the New World "Gentiles" out of their superstitious "darknesse." The evangelical role, Donne says, can turn the blood shed by the Amerindians into both the "Red Sea" that symbolizes the emancipation of those enslaved Jews and the "red Sea" that signifies the Savior's "owne bloud." Thus what Donne preaches here is a cosmopolitan spirit to tolerate and assimilate even a bloody other through the apostolic cause.

Donne's cosmopolitan spirit seeks not only to convert but also to turn a hostile other into a friendly "neighbor," an image that indicates recognition of the "interdependence" with the Amerindians. In a sermon preached on April 22, 1622, only one month after the Powhatan massacre, Donne appeals to the "civilizational community of fate" to express the intrinsic bonding between Christians and heathens. Declaring that "all are our Neighbours," Donne says:

> A man is thy Neighbor, by his Humanity, not by his Divinity; by his Nature, not by his Religion: a Virginian is thy Neighbor, as well as a Londoner; and all men are in every good mans Diocess, and Parish. (4:110)

Francis Bacon holds that the "difference" between the Europeans and the natives in the West Indies "comes not from soil, not from climate, not from race, but from the arts."[45] For Donne, "A man is thy Neighbor, by his Humanity, not by his Divinity; by his Nature, not by his Religion." Whereas Bacon gauges cultural difference by the level of civilization, Donne calibrates it by common "humanity," a criterion that differs qualitatively from "Divinity" and "Religion." By locating the universal neighborhood in common humanity rather than religious convictions or intellectual sophistication, Donne articulates a kind of cosmopolitanism grounded in the law of Nature. Thus it is the perception of the "civilizational community of fate" with the New World heathens that compels one to regard a "Virginian" and a "Londoner" as neighbors, though by a "Virginian" Donne might

---

[44] On the colonial approach see, Stanley Johnson, "John Donne and the Virginia Company," *English Literary History* 14.2 (1947): 127–38; R. V. Young, " 'My America, My New-found-land': Pornography and Imperial Politics in Donne's Elegies," *South Central Review* 4.2 (1987): 35–48; Paul W. Harland, "Donne and Virginia: The Ideology of Conquest," *John Donne Journal* 18 (1999): 127–52; Florence Sandler, "'The Gallery to the New World': Donne, Herbert, and Ferrar on the Virginia Project" *John Donne Journal* 19 (2000): 267–97; Jay Stubblefield, "'I Have Taken a Contrary Way': Identity and Ambiguity in John Donne's Sermon to the Virginia Company," *Renaissance Papers* (2001): 87–106; Stubblefield, "'Very Worthily Sett in Printe': Writing the Virginia Company of London," *Renaissance Papers* (2003): 167–87; and Tom Cain, "John Donne and the Ideology of Colonization," *English Literary Renaissance* 31.3 (2001): 440–76.

[45] Bacon, *New Organon*, 118.

have meant both the planters and indigenous Americans. Like the Sun, the image of "neighbor" is also significant in bearing out Donne's cosmopolitan will to not "laughest him [an idolater] to scorn" but to "assist him, direct him if thou canst" (4:110). A "neighbor" is "a person who occupies an adjoining or nearby house or dwelling." The contradictory ideas of distance and continuity with the other entailed in *neighbor* suggest the necessity of both drawing proper boundaries and maintaining peaceful intercourse. Moreover, in Scripture, neighbor signifies "a fellow human" or "teaching responsibility."[46] Donne's neighbor implies thus both the common ground upon which the old communicates with the new world and the cosmopolitan will to teach "a fellow human." With this cosmopolitan neighborhood in mind, Donne observes in the same sermon preached to the Virginia Company, the planters will augment Christendom by working on the continuity between the new and old worlds, as he states:

> You shall have made this *Iland*, which is but as the *Suburbs* of the old world, a Bridge, a Gallery to the new; to joyne all to that world that shall never grow old, the Kingdome of heaven, You shall add persons to the Kingdome, and to the Kingdome of heaven, and adde names to the Bookes of our Chronicles, and to the Booke of Life. (4:280–81)

The planters should regard the New World, Donne suggests in the quoted passage, instead of an isolated island, "suburbs of the old world." This idea of the interconnection between the old and new worlds is vividly telescoped in the image of the "bridge." By continuing to build and fortify this linking "bridge," Donne says, the planters can expand "the Kingdome of heaven" to include even those pagan "persons," adding heathen "names" both to "the Bookes of our Chronicles" and "the Booke of Life." Simply put, the Christian regime will be greatly augmented by embracing those "Heathen men" represented by the Chinese and Amerindians.

Donne's theological cosmopolitanism has qualifications—it extends to a heathen and even a bloody other but not to confessional enemies such as the Jesuits and Papists within Christendom. For Donne, the New World other can be converted by the apostolic message propagated by Protestant rather than Catholic missionaries. In his *Ignatius his Conclave*, he describes the Jesuit apostolic cause as being modeled upon that of Lucifer, a hellish enterprise that "obtrude[s] to those ignorant and barbarous people sometimes naturall things, sometimes artificiall, and counterfeit."[47] This critique of the Jesuitical mission reflects the rivalry between the Catholics and Protestants for converts in the New World. The extreme success of Jesuit missionaries in South America proved a great cause of distress and envy for Protestants and Puritans who had encountered repeated failures in

---

[46] "neighbour | neighbor, n. and adj." 3rd ed. September 2003. *OED Online*. June 5, 2012.

[47] Donne, *Ignatius his Conclave*, in Hayward ed., 393.

their attempts to convert the natives in the north.[48] Richard Eburne, a preacher and defender of the colonial cause in America, observed in 1624: "I would to God there were among us, us Protestants, that professe and have a better religion then they the Papists, one halfe of that zeale and desire to further and disperse our good and sound Religion, as seemes to be among them for furthering and dispersing theirs."[49] John White (1575–1648), another promoter of the New England colony, exclaimed, "What a scorne would it be to the Religion we professe that we should refuse to purchase the propagation of it at so easie a rate, when the Popish partie charge themselves with such excessive expense; for the advancement of idolatry and superstition?"[50] In his sermon to the Virginia Company, Donne pictures a prospect that reverses the comparative notion of the apostolic achievements of the Protestants and Catholics. It is not the Catholic Jesuits, Donne remarks, but a Company comprising enterprising and conscientious Protestants that had become "a marke for the Envy, and for the ambition of our Enemies." By "our Enemies," he refers pointedly to "our *Doctrinall*, not *Nationall* Enemies," that is, "the *Papists*" (4:272–73).

The strait of Anyan and the new peoples it represented allow us to capture Donne's distinctive reaction to England's participation in the "race for the Far East." Donne's conscious attempt to accommodate Christian theology to a globalized world through various adaptive strategies bespeaks both an enlightened view of cultural pluralism and an intellectual flexibility to adjust to changed historical and geographical conditions. Though more pronouncedly articulated in his attitude towards the Amerindians, Donne's theological cosmopolitanism suggests itself in his response to the Chinese as well—the people on the other divide of Anyan. The American and Far Eastern contexts thus shed new light on Donne's famous obsession with images of travels and voyages, a fascination at once originated from and enabled by his global vision and cosmopolitan spirit to know and embrace the other beyond the seas.[51]

---

[48] For the competition between Catholics and Protestants for converts in the New World, see Evans, *Milton's Imperial Epic*, 24–28.
[49] Richard Eburne, *A Plaine Pathway to Plantations* (London, 1624), 4.
[50] John White, *The Planters Plea* (London, 1630), 47.
[51] For Donne's obsession with voyage images see Anthony Parr, "John Donne, Travel Writer," *Huntington Library Quarterly* 70.1 (2007): 61–85; and Stephen Burt, "Donne the Sea Man," *John Donne Journal* 16 (1997): 137–84.

Chapter 3
Chinese Chronology and Donne's Apologetic Exegesis in *Essayes in Divinity*

As I have shown in the previous chapters, an increasingly globalized world revealed some problems intrinsic to a monotheistic and Eurocentric culture in the early modern period, problems that would not be visible within a nationalist, Orientalist, or colonial framework. Whereas the global flow of gold and silver challenged a national or Eurocentric economic pattern, the geographical expansion of the world to the Far East raised doubts about the alleged universality of the Christian religion. The challenge appears the more striking when a rapidly expanding world disclosed a different set of historical data that directly called into question the biblical conception of the beginning of the world, a cornerstone assumption of Western civilization. This chapter explores how Donne negotiates the anxiety and threat mounted by Chinese chronology to the biblical system of time in his divine treatise *Essayes in Divinity* (1614). Donne's prudent and deliberate exegesis of scriptural chronology in face of powerful rival claimants to antiquity provides a prime example of a liberal cosmopolitan's response to cultural conflicts.

For orthodox Christians in the Renaissance, "Pentateuch beginning with the first chapter of Genesis … constituted an infallible history of the origin and initial progress of the human race."[1] In his *Essayes*, Donne comments on the biblical account of the beginning of time and history as is represented in Genesis and Exodus. Donne's biblical commentary has an apparent apologetic agenda. The *Essayes* is *usually* read as an autobiography in which Donne justifies his being ordained as an Anglican priest in 1615.[2] Apart from the personal note, Donne's apologetic exegesis also arises from a desire to wage a "defensive warr"[3] against sectarian religions, for only when "the whole Catholick Church were reduced to such Unity and agreement," he remarks, can the Savior "allure and draw those to us, whom our dissentions, more then their own stubbornness with-hold from us."[4] One purpose of this "defensive warr," I shall show in this chapter, is to establish a unified front within Christendom against alternative accounts of time presented

---

[1] C. A. Patrides, *Milton and the Christian Tradition* (New York: Oxford UP, 1969), 28. "Pentateuch" refers to the first five books of the Old Testament, that is, Genesis, Exodus, Leviticus, Numbers, and Deuteronomy.

[2] Donne, *Essayes in Divinity*, Raspa ed., xxxix–xliv. All quotations about this treatise are from Raspa's edition. My work is greatly indebted to Raspa's extensive and illuminating comments on the *Essayes* in the endnotes.

[3] Donne, *Essayes*, 58.

[4] Donne, *Essayes*, 59.

by pagan annals, or as Donne puts it, to prove the "antiquity"[5] of Moses against "many strong oppositions."[6]

Chronological considerations obviously lie behind the apologetic agenda in Donne's *Essayes*. St. Augustine (354–430) holds that "If any, even the smallest, lie be admitted in the Scriptures, the whole authority of scripture is presently invalidated and destroyed."[7] Donne recognizes the subversive power of numbers in biblical commentary. As he puts it,

> And error in Numbring is *De substantialibus* … and sometimes annuls, ever vitiates any Instrument, so much, as it may not be corrected. Nothing therefore seems so much to indanger the Scriptures, and to submit and render them obnoxious to censure and calumniation, as the apparance of Error in Chronology, or other limbs and members of Arithmetick.[8]

Scripture is most prone to chronological lapses because, Donne explains, "the author hath erred … if any number be falsely delivered."[9] He uses a legal analogy to show the necessity of justifying scriptural chronology against "any profane Historie."[10] Just as a defendant in a court must give protestations that can be supported by evidence from his friends and neighbors, Donne says,

> when any profane Historie rises up against any place of Scripture, accusing it to Humane Reason, and understanding … it is not enough that one place justify it self to say true, but all other places produced as handling the same matter, must be of the same opinion, and of one harmony.[11]

Profane originally denotes "unholy," "heathen," or "pagan." But when used to describe history and literature, profane is a neutral term unrelated to "what is sacred or biblical." Thus *profane history* means "secular," "lay," or "civil," which distinguishes from sacred or ecclesiastical history.[12] Like evidence offered in a legal court, according to Donne, the integrity of Scripture resides in its overall doctrinal "harmony." Chronological errors tend to undermine this unity and thereby make Scripture susceptible to "accus[ations]" from "profane" histories, a vulnerability that accords a topical urgency to the exegesis of the biblical timeline as is depicted in the first two books of Moses.

---

[5] Donne, *Essayes*, 14,
[6] Donne, *Essayes*, 15.
[7] Quoted in William Whitaker, *A Disputation on Holy Scripture Against the Papists, Especially Bellarmine and Stapleton* (1595), trans. and ed. William Fitzgerald (Cambridge: Cambridge UP, reprinted 1849), 37.
[8] Donne, *Essayes*, 62.
[9] Donne, *Essayes*, 62.
[10] Donne, *Essayes*, 63.
[11] Donne, *Essayes*, 63.
[12] "Profane, adj. and n." *OED Online*. 3rd ed. June 15, 2012. In the *Essayes*, Donne uses the word "profane" to describe pagan peoples and nations, see 22, 50, 54, 63.

Chinese antiquity was numbered among Donne's profane histories that rose up against Scripture. Edwin J. Van Kley maintains that Chinese chronology did not "create problems" in Europe before the publication of the Jesuit missionary Martino Martini's *Sinicae historiae decas prima* (1658).[13] But as is shown in Donne's *Essayes*, Chinese antiquity had already raised problems by the 1610s. According to Donne, "That then this Beginning *was*, is a matter of *faith*, and so, infallible. *When* it was, is a matter of *reason*, and therefore various and perplex'd."[14] He cites eight authoritative accounts that claimed to address the "beginning" of the world through reason. From these eight records, he singles out the Eastern annals, observing that "The Chinese vex us at this day, with irreconcilable accounts."[15] Much has been written on Donne's exegesis in the *Essayes*, but few have associated it with the chronology polemic, especially the debates sparked by Chinese antiquity.[16] Anthony Raspa does draw attention to Donne's reference to Chinese history, but he confines his consideration of the Eastern background to some general remarks.[17]

[13] Edwin J. van Kley, "Europe's 'Discovery' of China and the Writing of World History," *American Historical Review* 76.2 (1971): 358–85.

[14] Donne, *Essayes*, 22.

[15] Donne, *Essayes*, 22.

[16] For Donne's biblical exegesis see Raspa ed., *Essayes in Divinity*, endnotes; Allen, *Legend of Noah*, 68–69; Helen Gardner, *The Limits of Literary Criticism*, Riddell Memorial Lectures, 28th ser. (London: Oxford UP, 1956), 40–55; William R. Mueller, *John Donne: Preacher* (Princeton: Princeton UP, 1962), 89–92; Dennis B. Quinn, "John Donne's Principles of Biblical Exegesis," *Journal of English and German Philology* 61 (1962): 313–29; Winfred Scheleiner, *The Imagery of John Donne's Sermons* (Providence: Brown UP, 1970), 185–200; Chanita Goodblatt, "From 'Tav' to the Cross: John Donne's Protestant Exegesis and Polemics," in *John Donne and the Protestant Reformation: New Perspectives*, ed. Mary A. Papazian (Detroit: Wayne State UP, 2003), 221–46; and Jeanne Shami, "'Speaking Openly and Speaking First': John Donne, the Synod of Dort, and the Early Stuart Church," in Papazian ed., *Donne and Protestant Reformation*, 48–51.

[17] Raspa ed., *Essayes*, xxxvii–xxxviii. Raspa identifies two sources of Donne's image of China. One is Gerard Mercator's *Historia Mundi: Containing his Cosmographicall Description ... of the World* (Seville, 1535). The other is Richard Willes's augmented edition of Richard Eden's translation of the Spanish historian Pietro Martire d'Anghiera's (1457–1526) accounts of Spanish discoveries under the title of *Decades of the New World* (1555).Willes's edition appeared under the title of *The History of Travayle in the West and East Indies* (London, 1577). (Raspa ed., 131). It should be noted that Raspa misplaced Eden and Willes chronologically: it is Willes who augmented Eden's work, not vice versa. I add to Donne's source of Chinese history Joseph Scaliger, *De emendatione temporum* (Paris, 1583); Rev. ed. (Leiden, 1598; Geneva, 1629), Scaliger, *Thesaurus temporum* (Leiden, 1606), and Juan González de Mendoza, *Historia de las cosas más notables ritos y costumbres del gran reyno de la China*, 8 vols. (Rome, 1585; Venice, 1588). Mendoza's work was translated into Latin by Joachim Brullius and published in Frankfurt (1589) and Antwerp (1655), 4 vols. It was rendered into French by Luc de Laporte (Paris, 1589), 8 vols. I quote from the English edition *History of Great and Mighty Kingdom of China* (1588) translated by Parke and edited by Staunton.

This chapter situates Donne's allusion to Chinese annals within the context of the chronological controversy ignited by González de Mendoza's *Mighty Kingdom of China* and Joseph Scaliger's engagement with Mendoza's account in his chronological theory.[18] Mendoza's treatise was "the key European authority on China until [Nicholas] Trigault's version of Matteo Ricci's fundamental history was published in 1615,"[19] and it presented, above all, a system of time that clashed with the biblical timeline. Synthesizing various reports on China, Mendoza represented Chinese dynastic history in the form of a catalogue of more than 200 monarchs, spanning from Vitey or Huangdi (2717–2599 BC) all the way to Emperor Wanli (1572–1620) of the Ming Empire.[20] Mendoza's work did not deal with Chinese chronology *per se*, but his chronicling of China's imperial lineage served to bring out its deep antiquity. The historical data Mendoza set forth proved difficult to integrate into scriptural chronology. The conflict between the Eastern and biblical timelines became more evident when Scaliger, founder of modern chronology, insisted on giving an equal weight to profane histories and used Mendoza as a source of Chinese history in constructing a universal temporal framework. In the working version of the first edition of his *De emendatione temporum* (1583), Scaliger resorted to Mendoza's account to speculate on Chinese chronology, and in the second edition (1598) he discredited outright Eastern antiquity.[21] Later in 1602, Scaliger came across the Byzantine historian George Syncellus's (d. 810) *Ekloge*

---

[18] Mendoza "was a member of an abortive Spanish embassy to China in 1584," and his work "is made up from a collation of the reports of various Augustine and Franciscan friars who had attempted to penetrate into China." Hudson, *Europe and China*, 242.

[19] Joan-Pau Rubiés, "The Spanish Contribution to the Ethnology of Asia in the Sixteenth and Seventeenth Centuries," in *Asian Travel in the Renaissance*, ed. Daniel Carey (Oxford: Blackwell, 2004), 93–123, 104.

[20] For Mendoza's account of Chinese history, see the *Mighty Kingdom of China*, Book III, chap. I., 69–76. For Mendoza's various sources see Rubiés, "Spanish Contribution," 104.

[21] Since Scaliger quoted from Mendoza in his chronology published in 1583, an earlier version of *Mighty Kingdom of China* should have appeared in the same year or earlier. My work is deeply indebted to Anthony Grafton's magisterial study of Scaliger and early modern chronology. See Grafton, *Joseph Scaliger*. This work is referred to henceforth by the title of its second volume, that is, *Historical Chronology*. Also see Grafton, "Joseph Scaliger and Historical Chronology: The Rise and Fall of a Discipline," *History and Theory* 14 (1975): 156–85; "From *De eie natali* to *De emendatione temporum*: The Origins and Setting of Scaliger's Chronology," *Journal of the Warburg and Courtauld Institutes* 45 (1985): 100–43; and "Dating History: The Renaissance and the Reformation of Chronology," *Daedalus* 132.2 *On Time* (2003): 74–85. In addition to Grafton's works, my study also draws upon Donald J. Wilcox, *The Measure of Times Past: Pre-Newtonian Chronologies and the Rhetoric of Relative Time* (Chicago: U of Chicago P, 1987); Don LePan, *The Cognitive Revolution in Western Culture* (London: Palgrave, 1989); C. A. Patrides, "Renaissance Estimates of the Year of Creation," *Huntington Library Quarterly* 26.4 (1963): 315–22; Michael T. Ryan, "Assimilating New World in the Sixteenth and Seventeenth Centuries," *Comparative Studies in Society and History* 23 (1981): 519–38; and Robert Markley, "A Brief History of Chronological Time," *Danish Yearbook of Philosophy* 44 (2009): 59–75.

chronographias or *Extract of Chronography*, which records Part I of Eusebius of Caesarea's (c. 263–339) *Chronicle*, a section omitted in St. Jerome's translation.[22] In this long-neglected part, Eusebius lists the ancient dynasties of Egypt as documented by the third-century Egyptian historian Manetho. In his *Thesaurus temporum* (1606), Scaliger posited *pre-Creation* "proleptic time" to address the Egyptian history that exceeded the scriptural timeframe. Although Scaliger discounted Chinese chronology before his encounter with Manetho's Egyptian history, his "proleptic time" nevertheless reflected back upon his previous theory, a reflection that tended to cede authority to Chinese antiquity as well.

Referring to Mendoza's account and Scaliger's problematic response, I argue that Chinese chronology, together with the Chaldean and Egyptian antiquities, played an indispensable part in motivating Donne's exegesis of Genesis and Exodus. As is shown in the works of Scaliger, the French universalist Jean Bodin, and the Dutch humanist J. Goropius Becanus (1519–72),[23] of the eight popular accounts of world history Donne cites, the problems raised by Chaldean and Egyptian chronicles were more or less resolved by the time the *Essayes* was composed. By contrast, the disturbing antiquity of the Chinese remained to be grappled with. The reign of Vitey (2717–2599 BC) called into doubt the biblical version of the world's origin. Since Exodus features the "miracle" of numbers— "what a small Number, in how short a time, how numerous a people, through how great pressures, and straits, were by him [God] propagated and established,"[24] this biblical account is vulnerable to the charge of chronological errors. To defend scriptural chronology against the challenges mounted by Chinese antiquity thus constitutes an important motive behind Donne's biblical commentary. Although Donne mentions China only once in the *Essayes*, this reference is nevertheless symptomatic of a thinker who was attempting to reconcile a different system of time with an accepted view of chronology, an orthodox timeline that was putatively supported by divine authority.

Donne's apologetic arsenal comes chiefly from the exegetical discourse. Since his images of profane histories are embedded within an extensive exposition of the first two books of Moses, apologetic exegesis is the predominant strategy he adopts to negotiate the chronology polemic. Donne subscribed to the traditional fourfold exegetical scheme that addressed the literal, allegorical, anagogical, and typological

---

[22] Eusebius's *Chronicle* consists of two parts. Part I "Annals" contains the unsettling accounts of Egyptian and Babylonian histories as is recorded by Manetho and Berossus. Part II "Chronological Canons" compiles, in tabular forms, synchronized dates from Assyrian, Hebrew, Egyptian, Greek, and Roman histories. See Grafton, "Dating History," 83; and *Historical Chronology*, 540–43.

[23] See J. Goropius Becanus, *Origines Antwerpianae* (Antwerp, 1569); and Jean Bodin, *Methodus ad facilem historiarum cognitionem* (Paris, 1566). I quote from the modern translation of the *Methodus*: *Method for the Easy Comprehension of History*, trans. Beatrice Reynolds (New York: Columbia UP, 1945). Donne mentions Scaliger and Johannes van Gorp or Goropius in the *Essayes*, 15.

[24] Donne, *Essayes*, 61.

senses of Scripture. Following Protestant and humanist hermeneutics, he advocated the primacy of the literal sense, representing it as a matrix from which other senses derive. But to refute charges on chronological grounds, he needed, above all, to establish the historicity of Scripture by representing it as a literal and historical document whose chronology could be counted on. Nevertheless, Donne notices that despite its historical status, Genesis cannot be adequately interpreted by a chronological methodology. None of the eight authoritative accounts of the world's history can "ease us, nor afford us line enough to fathom this bottom [the world's beginning]," he asserts in the *Essayes*, so "the last refuge uses to be, that prophane history cannot clear, but Scripture can."[25] But "since the world in her infancy did not speak to us at all (by any Authors;) and when she began to speak by Moses, she spake not plain, but diversly to divers understandings," he argues, the infant world can only be addressed by spiritual "faith."[26] Likewise, the chronology controversy also resonates in his exposition of the "numbers" and "names" in Exodus, two major sources of chronological errors. To counteract accusations based on numerical and nominal grounds, Donne links these two double-edged concepts together. When separate, numbers and names might bolster profane histories, but once combined, they bear out a "Miraculous History"[27] that has the capacity to enfold all peoples, together with their chronologies, into "One fold, and one shepherd."[28]

We should differentiate between Renaissance historical exegesis and the chronological methodology advanced by Scaliger. Though like the "metaphorical" or "anagogical," the "historical" is numbered among the "various applications and accommodations" of the literal sense,[29] historical exegesis aims to define Scripture as a verifiable document by examining some physical indicators of the Mosaic history. By comparison, the chronological framework uses dates and numbers to study the principle of time represented in *all* histories, whether sacred or profane, and thus prioritizes the numerical over other historical indexes. After Scaliger's epoch-making reform, the chronological model was widely used in historical studies, Hebrew history included. Thus whereas historical exegesis regards Scripture as a historical rather than allegorical text, chronological exposition focuses on the consistency of dates and numbers in the Mosaic books.

The anxiety Donne evinces over Chinese antiquity evokes the larger context of ancient and the early modern debates over chronology. As St. Augustine's negotiation with the Egyptian history in his *City of God* shows, the primacy of scriptural chronology was already a contested point for the early fathers.[30] To

---

[25] *Essayes*, 22.
[26] *Essayes*, 23.
[27] *Essayes*, 53.
[28] *Essayes*, 56.
[29] Whitaker, *Disputation*, 404.
[30] Arnaldo Momigliano, "Pagan and Christian Historiography in the Fourth Century AD," *The Conflict between Paganism and Christianity in the Fourth Century*, ed. Momigliano (Oxford: Clarendon, 1963), 79–99; and Momigliano, *On Pagans, Jews, and Christians* (Middletown, CT: Wesleyan UP, 1987), 11–57.

denounce the claims of an Egyptian history of "more than a hundred thousand years," Augustine writes, we should "place our reliance on the inspired history belonging to our religion and consequently have no hesitation in treating as utterly false anything which fails to conform to it."[31] Although Augustine's monotheistic approach to chronology was followed in the Renaissance, in his edition of *City of God*, the humanist Juan Luis Vives (1493–1540) nevertheless called attention to the Chaldean history of 47,000 and the Egyptian's of over 50,000 years.[32] Not only Egyptian and Chaldean dynasties but also the lately discovered Incan, Aztec, and Chinese empires presented a new set of data that clashed with the biblical timeline.[33] Don C. Allen remarks that "a controversial storm over the discrepancies in the universal calendar was roaring by the end of the sixteenth century."[34] Michael T. Ryan also notes that "what really interested sixteenth-and seventeenth-century observers about exotic peoples was their past, not their present. This was especially true for the so-called high civilizations in Mexico, Peru, India, and China."[35] Early modern thinkers responded differently to the new pagan histories. The famous classical scholar Isaac Casaubon (1559–1614) dismissively declared that "I don't see how these fantasies [alternative claims of antiquity] of foolish peoples are of much use for real history."[36] Similarly, Francis Bacon observes in his *The Advancement of Learning* that those "Heathen Antiquities" made up mostly of "fables and fragments" were undoubtedly "deficient."[37] In contrast, Christopher Marlowe (1564–93) and Giordano Bruno (1548–1600) seemed to look favorably on pagan chronicles. Bruno appeared to believe a Chinese history of "twenty thousand" years,[38] and Marlowe was accused of endorsing the doctrine that "the Indians and many Authors of antiquity haue assuredly writen of aboue 16 thousand yeares agone wheras Adam is proued to haue lived within 6 thousand years."[39]

---

[31] St. Augustine, *Concerning the City of God against the Pagans*, trans. Henry Bettenson (New York: Penguin, 2003), 815.

[32] See Juan Luis Vives, *St. Augustine's "City of God"* (Basle, 1522). Book XII, Chap. 10. Vives made the commentary on the advice of Erasmus, and it was translated into English by John Healey in 1610.

[33] On the Aztec chronology see Diego Durán, *The Ancient Calendar* (c. 1579), in *Book of the Gods and Rites and the Ancient Calendar*, trans. F. Horcasitas and D. Heyden (Norman: U of Oklahoma P, 1971), 395–96. Donne mentions in the *Essayes* the accounts of the Spanish Jesuits such as José de Acosta, Alphonsus Bracena, and Diego Torres-Bollo, 91–92. For Scaliger's account of the Mesoamerican calendar see *De emendation temporum* (1629), 224–26.

[34] Don C. Allen, *Mysteriously Meant: The Rediscovery of Pagan Symbolism and Allegorical Interpretation in the Renaissance* (Baltimore: John Hopkins UP, 1970), 63.

[35] Ryan, "Assimilating New World," 531.

[36] Quoted in Grafton, "Rise and Fall," 174.

[37] Bacon, *Advancement of Learning*, 180.

[38] Quoted in James S. Slotkin, ed. *Readings in Early Anthropology* (Chicago: Aldine, 1965), 43.

[39] Paul H. Kocher, *Christopher Marlowe: A Study of his Thought, Learning and Character* (New York: Russel & Russel, 1962), 34. On Renaissance chronological

The chronological data provided by the new worlds tended to corroborate the pre-Adamic doctrine that became popular in the latter part of the sixteenth century.[40] The antiquity of the new pagan annals seemed to place those newly discovered peoples within a non-Adamic lineage. The reputed alchemist and physician Paracelsus (1493–1541) claimed that "it cannot be believed that such newly found people in the islands are of Adam's blood," and they must have come from "a different Adam." Likewise, for Bruno, "the black race / Of the Ethiopians, and the yellow offspring of America … cannot be traced to the same descent, nor are they sprung / From the generative force of a single progenitor."[41] The French Calvinist Isaac de La Peyrère (1596–1676) was more outspoken, declaring pointedly the existence of pre-Adamites in his *Praea-Adamitae* (1655). In remarking that "an enormous pretending Wit of our nation and age undertook to frame such a language, herein exceeding *Adam*,"[42] Donne exhibits not only knowledge but also disapproval of the pre-Adamic thesis, a heretical doctrine that seemed espoused by "an enormous pretending Wit" in early modern Europe. Not surprisingly, Chinese antiquity that seemed to support such a radical theory was vexatious to Donne's devout sensibility.[43]

What was at stake in Renaissance controversy over chronology was the primacy both of the biblical timeline and the Adamic lineage, which gave most orthodox chronological studies an apologetic edge. Colin Kidd claims that the "study of universal chronology became one of the foremost disciplines of the early modern period. It tackled questions of fundamental importance to the identity of Christendom, and it attracted some of Europe's foremost minds."[44] Anthony Grafton holds that "from the late sixteenth century onward, in fact, religious dissidents regularly cited chronological evidence when they challenged the authority of the Bible."[45] For Arthur B. Ferguson, "what led protestant England to the study of chronology was, after all, not so much a disinterested desire to clarify the perspective of history as a compulsion to bring universal history into accord

---

controversy, also see Ernest A. Strathmann, *Sir Walter Raleigh: A Study in Elizabethan Skepticism* (New York: Columbia UP, 1951), 199–218; and Livingstone, *Adam's Ancestors*, 8–11.

[40] On the pre-Adamites see Livingstone, *Adam's Ancestors*; Richard H. Popkin, *Isaac La Peyrère (1596–1676): His Life, Work and Influence* (Leiden: E. J. Brill, 1987), 26–41; and William Poole, "Seventeenth-century Preadamism, and an Anonymous English Preadamist," *Seventeenth Century* 19 (2004): 1–35.

[41] Quoted in Slotkin ed., *Early Anthropology*, 43.

[42] *Essayes*, 27.

[43] For English Preadmites see Popkin, *Isaac La Peyrère*, 36, and Poole, "An Anonymous English Preadamist."

[44] Colin Kidd, *British Identities before Nationalism: Ethnicity and Nationhood in the Atlantic World, 1600–1800* (New York: Cambridge UP, 1999), 17.

[45] Grafton, "Dating History," 80.

with the biblical narrative."[46] The challenge to scriptural chronology appeared the more striking when considering the conflicting accounts of time set out in the Latin Vulgate and Greek Septuagint bibles. In his *A Disputation on Holy Scripture against the Papists* (1588), the English Calvinist William Whitaker (1547–95) notes that "there is the greatest difference between the Hebrew and Greek books in the account of dates and years," for "the Greek books reckon 2242 years from Adam in the beginning of the world to the flood, as we read in Augustine, Eusebius, and Nicephorus's Chronology. But in the Hebrew books we see that there were no more than 1656. Thus the Greek calculation exceeds the Hebrew by 586 years."[47] Given the contradiction in the biblical canons themselves, it is but natural that the temporal markers they represent such as the creation and Exodus were susceptible to charges from profane histories.

Universal History and the Chronological Discourse

In order to understand how the discovery of Chinese chronology affected Western thought, we need to examine how the West, especially the early modern thinkers, imagined human origins and how they conceived of time, which is summarily captured in the two discourses of history and chronology.[48] Bodin defines the "chronological principle" as "a system of universal time" that serves as "the guide for all histories."[49] "Time," according to René Descartes (1596–1650), is "only a mode of thinking" about "duration."[50] As a special form of thinking about time intervals, chronology is widely used to calculate and establish temporal frameworks for great events in biblical, national, and universal histories. History deals with the deployment of time as well, but time means different things in history and chronology, which became two distinctive disciplines at the turn of the seventeenth century. According to the French Jesuit theologian Dionysius Petavius

---

[46] Arthur B. Ferguson, *Utter Antiquity: Perceptions of Prehistory in Renaissance England* (Durham: Duke UP, 1993), 48.

[47] Whitaker, *Disputation*, 121.

[48] For "Renaissance search for Origins," see Allen, *Mysteriously Meant*, 21–82; Brian Croke, "The Origins of the Christian World Chronicle," in *History and Historians in Late Antiquity*, ed. Croke and A. Emmett (Sydney: Pergamon, 1983), 116–31; Momigliano, "Pagan and Christian Historiography," 107–26, and Grafton, *Defenders of the Text: The Traditions of Scholarship in an Age of Science, 1450–1800* (Cambridge, MA: Harvard UP, 1991), 76–103, esp. 80–81.

[49] Bodin, *Method*, 303, 337. See L. F. Dean, "Bodin's *Methodus* in England before 1625," *Studies in Philology* 39 (1942): 160–66; and Julian H. Franklin, *Jean Bodin and the Sixteenth-Century Revolution in the Methodology of Law and History* (New York: Columbia UP, 1963).

[50] René Descartes, *Principles of Philosophy* (1644–47), in *René Descartes: Philosophical Essays and Correspondence*, ed. Roger Ariew (Indianapolis: Hackett, 2000), 246.

(1583–1652), chronology is a "pure calculation of time" that differs qualitatively from "history," for

> History has as its own to possess fully the matter of deeds and to write down their order, usually with proofs, arguments, and witnesses, whence the order of individual years is established. Chronology indeed inquires after one thing, by what signs and marks each thing may be arranged in its years and times, and is nearly always content with that. It does not extend further than individual events.

In fact, for Petavius, chronology is "one of the four sciences [physics, astronomy, music, and civil divisions of time] which have do to with time."[51] However, despite their distinction, chronology and history are nevertheless closely connected. The German astronomer Erasmus Reinhold (1511–53) wonders: "What obscurity would there be in the past had there been no distinction of time? What chaos would there be in our present life if the sequence of years were unknown?"[52] In fact, chronological dates, together with geographical locations, are veritable indicators of historical narratives. It is on this account that Richard Hakluyt called geography and chronology "the Sunne and the Moone, the right eye and the left of all history" (PN 1: xxxix).

But historical and chronological studies had undergone different stages of development by the Renaissance. Compared with the robust growth of history, chronology appeared an atrophied discipline. The sixteenth century saw a marked development of chronology, however, since it was during this era that people became fully aware of the necessity of a linear and universal principle of time.[53] This intense "chronological awareness," that is, "a consciousness of dates and numbers,"[54] was enhanced by the universal history project flourishing in France, an intellectual movement that sought to establish a uniform timeline by reassessing the historical sources of such disciplines as theology, jurisdiction, and history. Bodin asserts that since "the most important part of the subject [universal history] depends upon the chronological principle ... a system of universal time is needed for this method of which we treat," because "those who think they can understand histories without chronology are as much in error as those who wish to escape the windings of a labyrinth without a guide."[55] Just as cartographers tried

---

[51] Dionysius Petavius, *Rationarium temporum* (Paris, 1633), Preface. *Rationarium* is a French translation and abridgement of Petavius's *Opus de doctrina temporum* (Paris, 1627). For Petavius's chronology, see Wilcox, *Measure of Times Past*, 205; and Elias J. Bickerman, *Chronology of the Ancient World*, 2nd ed. (London: Thames and Hudson, 1980), 9.

[52] Tatian, *Oratio ad Graecos*, 3; cited by Scaliger on the title page of his *De emendatione temporum* (1583), see Grafton, "Origins and Setting," 100.

[53] On Renaissance chronology see, in addition to Scaliger and Wilcox's works, Patrides, "Renaissance Estimates," and Almond, *Adam and Eve*, 82–86.

[54] LePan, *Cognitive Revolution*, 113, 122.

[55] Bodin, *Method*, 303. For primary works on universal history also see, Philipp Melanchthon, *Sententiae veterum aliquot patrum de caena domini* (Wittenberg, 1530);

to encompass the globe in a single grid, the Universalists attempted to comprehend the historical world within a unifying matrix. However, neither classical nor medieval chronological theories could provide the overarching temporal paradigm demanded by the universal history project. Donald J. Wilcox notes that ancient and medieval chronological theorizations tend to be "relative," "epochal," and "thematic," characteristics that render them insufficient to address the cosmic architecture of time imagined by the Universalists. The Christian chronological model represented in Eusebius's *Chronicle* also fell short of a universal scale. Since "Eusebius was more interested in a particular synchronization, that between the sacred history of the Hebrew and the profane history of the world's empires," Wilcox remarks, "the dates he chose for the synchronization were epochal and thematic rather than absolute."[56] Though medieval chronologers such as Otto of Freising (1114–58) and Matthew Paris (1200–59) displayed awareness of dates and numbers, chronology during this period still privileged multiple timelines and lacked a comprehensive framework. The Renaissance witnessed a broad chronological awakening, which can be glimpsed in the mushrooming of chronicles and the high prestige they enjoyed.[57] In a letter to Seth Calvisius dated December 3, 1605, Scaliger said that every year the Frankfurt book fair witnessed a new crop of chronologies.[58] In the same year, Bacon remarked that among the three parts of "Just and Perfect history," that is, "Chronicles," "Lives," and "Narrations or Relations," chronicles are "the most complete and absolute kind of history, and hath most estimation and glory."[59]

Two major factors lie behind the unprecedented flourishing of universal chronicles in the Renaissance. The contradictory interpretations of scriptural chronology and the discordant sources presented by both classical antiquity and new pagan annals combined to call forth the necessity of instituting an umbrella

---

Francois Baudouin, *De institutione historiae universae et ejus cum jurisprudentia conjunctione* (Paris, 1561); Melchior Cano, *De locis theologicis* (Salamanca, 1563); and Henry Isaacson, *Saturni Ephemerides: sive Tabula Historico-chronologica* (London, 1633).

[56] Wilcox, *Measure of Times Past*, 106. For Scaliger's critique of Eusebius, see *De Emendatione* (1583), 251.

[57] Major English chronicles include, Thomas Lanquet, *An Epitome of Chronicles* (1549); Lodowik Lloyd, *The Consent of Time* (1590); John More, *A Table from the Beginning of the World to this Day* (1593); Christian Helvetius, *Historical and Chronological Theatre* (1609); Anthony Munday, *Briefe Chronicle of the Successe of Times from Creation* (1611); and Sir Walter Ralegh, *History of the World* (1614).

[58] Scaliger to Calvisius, December 3, 1605, quoted in Grafton, *Historical Chronology*, 10. For major continental chronicles see, Hartmann Schedel, *Nürnberger Chronik* (Nürnberg, 1493); Sebastian Franck, *Chronica* (Strasbourg, 1531); Guillaume Postel, *Cosmographicae disciplinae compendium* (Basle, 1561); Gerald Mercator, *Chronologia* (Cologne, 1569); M. Beroaldus, *Chronicum Scripturae Sacrae* (Geneva, 1575); and F. Patrizi, *Mystica Aegyptiorum et Caldeorum* (Ferrara, 1591). For a synthesis of classical, medieval, and Renaissance universal chronicles, see Patrides, *Milton and the Christian Tradition*, 226–49.

[59] Bacon, *Advancement of Learning*, 179.

principle that could at once locate, chart, and reconcile all histories within a uniform chronological matrix. On the one hand, Renaissance exegetes could not reach a consensus concerning the scriptural timeline. C. A. Patrides lists 29 proposals of the Creation date from 108 early modern writers.[60] Iacobus Curio complained in 1557 that "you will find it easier to make the wolf agree with the lamb than to make all chronologers agree about the age of the world."[61] Likewise, the physician chronologer Thomas Allen (1608–73) observed in 1659 that there were "very many (and some great) differences amongst *Chronologers* and in the *Computation* of *Scripture-Chronologie*."[62] On the other hand, the apparent conflict between the new pagan annals and the biblical timeline cried out for explanation, for as Thomas Nashe (1567–1601) lamented, "impudently they persist in it that the late discouered Indians are able to shew antiquities thousands before *Adam*."[63] The inadequacy of classical and medieval chronological schemes both to address the divergent biblical commentaries and contain the new historical data impelled Renaissance chronologers to seek a universal timeline. Though acutely aware of such a necessity, Bodin did not propose a specific chronological model. It was Scaliger who undertook to construct the unifying temporal principle imagined by Bodin, establishing chronology as an independent discipline.

Donne's Knowledge of Chinese Antiquity and Scaliger's "Proleptic Time"

In the *Essayes*, Donne declares that "of such Authors as God preordained to survive all Philosophers, and all Tyrants, and all Heretics, and be the Canons of faith and manners to the worlds end, *Moses* had the primacy."[64] Donne's statement reflects the undisputed priority enjoyed by scriptural chronology in the Renaissance. As van Kley notes, most early modern thinkers tended to "[test] the ancient annals or records of any people by their conformity to" the biblical timeframe.[65] The Calvinist Matthaeus Beroaldus (d. 1576) claimed in 1575 that "we have everywhere followed the authority of Holy Scripture, which the Lord has granted us as a sure and indubitable foundation."[66] John More, the "apostle of Norwich," asserted unequivocally that profane histories must be brought "to that account which is set down in Scriptures, from the beginning of the worlde till the suffering of Christ, most exactly, and so labour to make the times of forreigne

---

[60] Patrides, "Renaissance Estimates," 316–17.
[61] Iacobus Curio, *Chronologicarum rerum* (Basle, 1557), lib. II, 8, quoted in Grafton, "Origins and Setting," 102.
[62] Thomas Allen, *A Chain of Scripture Chronology* (London, 1659), 5.
[63] Ronald B. McKerrow, ed. *The Works of Thomas Nashe*, 2nd ed. 5 vols. (Oxford: Blackwell, 1958), vol. 2., 116.
[64] Donne, *Essayes*, 15.
[65] Van Kley, "Europe's 'Discovery' of China," 360.
[66] Beroaldus, *Chronicum* (1575), quoted in Grafton, *Historical Chronology*, 167.

histories to agree with that account of the holy Scripture."[67] For Bodin, "if the sacred founts of the Hebrews and the revelations of divine law bear witness that the world had a precise beginning of creation ... to seek further would seem a crime—to doubt, seems wicked."[68]

Scaliger proved an exception in according an equal status to "profane" histories in a universal temporal framework. For Scaliger, chronology "aims not to find a moral order in the past, but simply to reconstruct that past; it employs not merely the one divinely-inspired source, but all sources."[69] In insisting on giving due weight to "all sources," Scaliger refused to regard scriptural timeline as the sole standard. Contrary to those who "babble that the authors whom they call profane did not know the events of their own time," he writes in *De emendatione*, "profane" writers do "have their own understanding of divine and human letters, and

> It is not surprising if they, to whom sacred history is one thing, and *profane* history, as they call it, another, come to conclusions different from ours ... Nor do we care about the fantasies of those who despise *profane* letters. No truth is *profane*. In the mouth of a *profane* man all truth is sacred.[70]

The bold statements that "no truth is *profane*" and "in the mouth of a *profane* man all truth is sacred" amount to a declaration of the independence of pagan histories. As possible carriers of "truth," Scaliger contends, profane and scriptural systems of time contribute equally to a universal timetable.

To accommodate profane histories to a single template, Scaliger invented a chronological model called the "Julian Period." In 525, to construct an Easter table for the years 532–626, Exiguus, inventor of the Anno Domini (AD) dating system, adopted the 532-year cycle (the 19-year lunar cycle times the 28-year solar cycle). Drawing upon Exiguus's Easter calendar, Scaliger managed to formulate a chronological principle by adding a third variant, that is, the "indication," a term that means "a civil cycle of fifteen years, at the end of which a census was to be taken for tax purposes." By multiplying 15 with Exiguus's 532-year cycle, Scaliger got a cycle of 7,980 years, a timeline he designated as the "Julian Period."[71] Wilcox summarizes the significance of Scaliger's Julian model as follows:

> By multiplying the three cycles Scaliger had created a chronology that would comprehend all the events of human and divine history and would run almost 1,700 years into the future. With this instrument he could integrate all the civil and religious calendars he had collected and studied, could correlate all previous

---

[67] More, *A Table* (1593), Preface.
[68] Bodin, *Method*, 303.
[69] Grafton, "Rise and Fall," 169–70.
[70] Scaliger, *De emendatione* (1583): 398–99, quoted in Grafton, "Rise and Fall," 168–69.
[71] For the "Julian period," see *De emendatione temporum* (1583), 198. For a detailed discussion of the Julian system see Wilcox, *Measure of Times Past,* 198–99; Grafton, "Rise and Fall," 162; and *Historical Chronology*, 249–50.

dating systems, and could locate any event or series of events completely and unambiguously on a single time line. He had devised an absolute dating system whose numbers were independent from any specific series of events.[72]

Thus for the first time in Western history, there appeared a linear and absolute temporal framework that was supposed to embrace all histories, whether sacred or profane. Scaliger's innovation received international acclaim; as the Italian philosopher Tommaso Campanella (1568–1639) put it, "the Germans admire Scaliger's chronology, and many of our countrymen follow it ... for he wished to correct the count of years from the eclipses and lunar cycles mentioned in the histories of older times."[73]

But there were disturbing exceptions that disrupted the Julian parameter. Egyptian dynastic history as is recorded by Manetho and preserved by Eusebius proved one of these exceptions—it could not be contained by the 7,980-year cycle. Scaliger's famous accommodation of this anomaly in his *Thesaurus temporum* exposed the limitations of the Julian system. In Manetho's record, Egyptian history goes back to 5285 BC, a period of time that evidently exceeds the creation date (3949 BC) or the Julian Period (4713 BC) set up by Scaliger.[74] To accommodate this difference, Scaliger posits "the first Julian Period of proleptic time," calling it "the postulated Julian Period." By "proleptic time," he means "that which is assumed before the Mosaic computation," which is distinct from "Historic time," that is, "that which is traced downwards from the Hebraic computation."[75] Scaliger's Julian period, which integrates the lunar, solar, and indication systems, was not novel, since it had been used by Byzantine historians.[76] But his "proleptic time" caused "the dismay of many of his Protestant friends and the delight of many of his Catholic critics" when *Thesaurus temporum* was published in 1606.[77] Even Scaliger himself was uneasy with a proleptic history beyond biblical creation, and "tried several times to justify his own compromise procedure."[78]

China also presented a set of historical data that exceeded Scaliger's Julian framework. Before his encounter with the Egyptian history in 1602, Scaliger had already expressed disbelief in Chinese chronology, but his engagement with Mendoza's account served to corroborate rather than discount Eastern antiquity

---

[72] Wilcox, *Measure of Times Past*, 199.
[73] Tommaso Campanella, *De libris propriis et recta ratione studendi syntagma* (Paris, 1642), in Hugo Grotius, *H. Grotii et aliorum dissertationes de studiis instituendis* (Amsterdam, 1645), 406, quoted in Grafton, "Origins and Setting," 121.
[74] Grafton, "Rise and Fall," 171.
[75] Scaliger, *Thesaurus temporum*, *Isagogici Canones*, 117, quoted in Grafton, "Rise and Fall," 172. For a detailed account of Scaliger's discovery of Egyptian antiquity, see Grafton, *Historical Chronology*, 540–43.
[76] Wilcox, *Measure of Times Past*, 208.
[77] Grafton, "Dating History," 84.
[78] The passages in question are Scaliger, *Thesaurus temporum*, *Isagogici Canones*, 117, 273, 274, 309–10, 312; Grafton, "Rise and Fall," 173.

and its heretical implications. On the margins of the working version of the first edition of *De emendatione* (1583), Scaliger jotted down Mendoza's catalogue of Chinese monarchs:

> The Sinese (whom the Spanish call Chinese, for reasons unfathomable to me) reckon 4,282 years from their ancient king Vitey to Honog, who ruled after the year of the Lord 1570. For they count 2,257 years from Vitey to Tzintzom, the last of the race of Vitey. He separated the Tartars from the Sinese by a continuous wall. From him to Honog, around the years of the Lord 1570, 1571, 1572, etc., they reckon 2,025 years. This sum amounts to 4,282 years, as we said before. Hence Vitey is far older than Abraham.[79]

Mendoza traced Chinese dynastic rule from Vitey to Boneg (Scaliger's Honog) or Emperor Longqing (1567–72). Longqing's successor Wanli was the reigning monarch when the *Mighty Kingdom of China* was published in Rome in 1585. "Tzintzom" refers to "Qin Yingzheng," that is, Emperor Qin Shihuang (221–210 BC) who united China for the first time in 221 BC and built the Great Wall to "[separate] the Tartars from the Sinese." "Vitey" should refer to the legendary Yellow Emperor "Huangdi." Scaliger put 4,282 years between Vitey and Honog, a calculation that agreed with Chinese chronology, since Huangdi is credited with having ruled in about 2717–2599 BC. Mendoza's Chinese source for Huangdi's reign was most likely the Shiji or *The Records of the Grand Historian* written by Sima Qian (c. 140–86 BC), the famous historian of the Han Dynasty who composed the first Chinese biographical annals.[80] There are two different traditions of representing Huangdi in ancient China. One is the legendary tradition represented by *Shan Hai Jing* or *Books on Mountains and Seas*, a pre-Qin text of unknown authorship. Since this work was full of mythological and unbelievable figures and monsters, it was not taken seriously even in ancient times.[81] The other is the historical tradition emerging from the works of the "One Hundred Schools" during the Spring and Autumn and Warring States period (770–221 BC) but formally established by Sima in *Shiji*. According to *Han Shu: Yi Wen Zhi* or *On Art and Culture* by another Han historian Bangu (AD 32–92), scholars in the "One Hundred Schools" presented about 47 different images of Huangdi. As Li-jen Lin points out, each of these schools adapted the story of Huangdi to suit their own doctrinal and political agendas in an age of constant warfare. A historical approach can be discerned from these multiple representations of ancient emperors, a methodology exemplified by *Chunqiu*, which is a historiographical work edited by Confucius for pedagogical purpose. In the preface to *Shiji*, Sima

---

[79] Grafton, *Historical Chronology*, 406.
[80] Sima Qian [司马迁], *Shiji* (史记) or *The Records of the Grand Historian*, c. 109–91 BC.
[81] For legendary images of Huangdi in *Shan Hai Jing*, see Li-Jen Lin, "The Intention to Begin from Huang-Ti in 'Shi-ji Biographic Sketches of Five Emperors,'" *Paper of Humanities and Social Sciences* (人文社會學報) 5 (March 2009): 39–67, 50–52.

declares pointedly that he is following the historical methodology Confucius set up in *Chunqiu*.[82] But unlike Confucius who began Chinese history with King Yao (c. 2377–2259 BC), in "Benji"—12-volume annals in *Shij* that chiefly deal with imperial biographies—Sima started Chinese history from Huangdi, dismissing other legendary figures such as Fuxi and Shennong.[83]

Mendoza's description of Huangdi largely conforms to Sima's account in *Shij*. According to Sima, after becoming the supreme commander in Zhongyuan, a region of both strategic and cultural importance for any imperial contestant, Huangdi united and inducted all tribes under his dominion into civilized life. To transform China from a nomadic, tribal culture into a civil society, Huangdi "reportedly asked his wife Leizu [嫘祖] to teach people to raise silkworms for clothing. He also ordained Cangjie to invent characters on the basis of practical signs common in use, Fengning to make ceramic earthenware, Yongfu to construct tools for grinding rice, and Gonggu and Huodi to build ships."[84] Some of these much-cited stories of invention and civilizing policies appear in Mendoza's work. Mendoza relates that Vitey "was the first that did reduce the kingdome to one empire gouernment," a fact of which "their [Chinese] histories … doo make particular mention." He refers to Vitey's inventions of both "the vse of garmentes" and the "making of shippes." Apart from organizing nomadic tribes into "cities, townes, and villages," another policy of "great consideration" mentioned by Mendoza is that Vitey ordained "no woman to be idle, but to worke, either in her husbands occupation, or in sowing or spinning. This was a law so generall amongst them, that the queene her selfe did obserue and keepe it."[85] The queen here refers to none other than Leizu who, for the first time in Chinese history, raised silkworms to clothe the people or "衣被天下."[86] Sima's work was authoritative throughout all the dynasties in imperial China, the Ming Empire included. When Mendoza wrote *Mighty Kingdom of China*, most Chinese, despite the legendary figure described in *Shan Hai Jing*, believed in the image of Huangdi as he is represented by Sima, an

---

[82] Lin, "Intention to Begin from Huang-Ti," 42–44; on Huangdi in pre-Qin text, see 54–58.

[83] For the historical image of Huangdi in *Shiji* see Lin, "Intention to Begin from Huang-Ti," 45–49.

[84] Handa Lin, et. al. eds., *Chinese History of Five Thousand Years from Antiquity to Modern Times* (上下五千年) (Shanghai: Children's Publisher, 2002), 8; my own translation. Lin's account of ancient emperors draws chiefly from Sima and Bangu's works. Though a book meant for children, *Chinese History of Five Thousand Years* is a reliable source. For Sima's account of Huangdi see *Twenty-four Histories of China* (二十四史), 63 vols. (Beijing, Zhong Hua Shu Ju [中华书局], 2000), vol. 1.

[85] Mendoza, *Mighty Kingdom of China*, vol.1. 70, 71.

[86] For Queen Leizu see Jiexiang Zheng (郑杰祥), *Huangdi and Leizu* (黄帝与嫘祖), and *Xinzheng, Huangdi's Hometown and Capital* (黄帝故里故都在新郑) (Zhengzhou: Zhongzhou Antiquity Publisher [中州古籍出版社], 2005).

image that was reinforced by the dominance of Confucian doctrine in state policy.[87] It is only in the 1920s that the historicity of Huangdi started to be questioned by the so-called Doubting Antiquity School during the New Culture Movement. One central task of this school was to interrogate the authenticity of pre-Qin texts, particularly those on ancient emperors.[88] However, as Joseph Needham has noted, modern archaeological discovery, especially the excavation of "oracle bones" in Anyang Yinxu (安阳殷墟), capital of the Shang Dynasty (1600–1050 BC), proves that Sima "did have fairly reliable materials at his disposal—a fact which underlines once more the deep historical-mindedness of the Chinese."[89] Thus Huangdi was a historical figure for Ming China, and presumably for Mendoza as well, who drew upon Ming historical works for his synopsis of Chinese history. Mendoza himself says that "all" of his sources are "taken out of the books and histories" of the Chinese, which "were brought vnto the citie of Manilla, printed and set forth in China, and were translated into the Spanish tongue, by interpreters of the saide nations." These "interpreters" were Chinese converts who "remaine as dwellers amongst vs in these islands [the Philippines]."[90]

Scaliger must have reacted strongly to the antiquity of Huangdi as is represented by Mendoza. His conclusion that "Vitey is far older than Abraham" had greater resonance when it was rearticulated in the second edition of *De emendatione* (1598). According to Grafton, "no passage in the second *De emendatione* would have a more powerful—or unexpected—impact than the discussion of Chinese chronology that Scaliger included as a counter-weight to his assemblage of pagan reports that agreed neatly with the Bible." "His [Scaliger's] disapproval is clear enough," Grafton observes, for he thinks the Chinese's claim of an antediluvian history showing themselves as "*veris monumentis historiae destitute*," and that their antiquity was invented because of their "*temporum inscitia*" and "*vetustatis affectatio*."[91] However, despite his disapproval, the heretical suggestion of

---

[87] For the fact that Huangdi was regarded as a historical figure before the 1920s, see K. C. Chang [张光直], *Art, Myth, and Ritual: The Path to Political Authority in Ancient China* (Cambridge, MA: Harvard UP, 1983), 2.

[88] The interrogation was initiated by Hu Shi (胡适) (1891–1962) and culminated in Hu's disciple Jiegang Gu's (顾颉刚) (1893–1980) who is noted for his seven-volume *Gu Shi Bian* (古史辨) or *Debates on Ancient History*. See Gu, "How Yao, Shun, and Yu are Related to Each Other," in *Gu Hhi Bian*, 7 vols. (Shanghai: Shanghai Guji, 1982 [first published 1926–41]), vol. 1. 127–32. On the doubting school see, Tze-Ki Hon, "Ethnic and Cultural Pluralism: Gu Jiegang's Vision of a New China in His Studies of Ancient History," *Modern China* 22.3 (1996): 315–39; and see doubts on Huangdi in Michael Puett, *The Ambivalence of Creation: Debates Concerning Innovation and Artifice in Early China* (Stanford: Stanford UP, 2001); 93.

[89] Joseph Needham, *Science and Civilization in China*: Volume 1, *Introductory Orientations*, reprint (Richmond: Kingprint, 1972), 88.

[90] Mendoza, *Mighty Kingdom of China*, vol.1. 20.

[91] Grafton, *Historical Chronology*, 405–6. For Scaliger's comments on Chinese history, see *De emendatione* (1629), 366.

Scaliger's response to Chinese chronology can nevertheless be interpolated from his handling of Egyptian antiquity. Grafton holds that "Scaliger certainly realized that he seemed to be calling the authority of the Bible into question," for

> The prominent place of his discussions of Egypt and proleptic time in the *Thesaurus* ensured that no careful reader could miss them. Scaliger's insistence on giving equal weight to the Bible and to the pagans could only lead to disaster in a case where they disagreed so unequivocally. But he refused either to abate the rigorousness of his method or to recognize the seriousness of the conflict between his sources. He neither attacked the Bible explicitly, nor made it clear that he was not attacking it.[92]

The radical message implied by both the prominence Scaliger gives to proletpic time and his ambiguity towards "his method" and "the conflict between his sources" was aptly captured by La Peyrère to make his "attack" on "the chronological authority of the Bible."[93] La Peyrère claimed that it was by resorting to, in addition to Egyptian, Chaldean, and Amerindian antiquities, Scaliger's theory of the "prodigious account of the Chinenesians" that he proposed the pre-Adamic thesis.[94]

La Peyrère's speculation was not ungrounded: it was supported by other numbers in Scaliger's chronological tables. In *De emendatione*, Scaliger puts the creation in 3949 BC, the flood in 2294 BC, Babel in 2177 BC, Abraham's migration in 1941 BC, and the Exodus in 1496 BC.[95] Mendoza dated the rule of the first Chinese monarch Vitey in 2717–2599 BC, a date that challenged several numbers in Scaliger's template. Chinese antiquity called into question, above all, Abraham's status as the father of all nations. Wilcox maintains that "Scaliger's use of nonbiblical sources raised doubts about the antiquity of the Kingdom of Israel and its precedence over the pagan empires," because "as scholars came to see a single continuous time in which the events from all empires occurred, the process of synchronization made the position of Israel seem incongruous to the pious."[96] The "nonbibical sources" of the Chinese posed a direct challenge to the "precedence" of "the Kingdom of Israel." Scaliger notices that by Mendoza's account there are 2,257 years from Vitey to Tzintzom and 2,025 years from Tzintzom to Honog, which makes a total of 4,282 years, a number that, Grafton says, proves "Vitey [c. 2717–2599 BC] is far older than Abraham [1941 BC]."[97] Not only Abraham but Noah's patriarchal status was also called into doubt, because the Chinese lived 303 years before the flood, a fact that came to Scaliger's mind in the second edition of

---

[92] Grafton, "Rise and Fall," 173.
[93] Grafton, *Historical Chronology*, 406.
[94] La Peyrère, *Men before Adam* (London, 1656), 177ff.
[95] Grafton, *Historical Chronology*, 277.
[96] Wilcox, *Measure of Times Past*, 209.
[97] Grafton, *Historical Chronology*, 405–6.

De emendatione: "*quare Vitey fuerit longe antiquior Abrahamo, cum ea summa longe epocham diluvii post se relinquat.*"[98]

The *Essayes* reproduces this contemporary chronological debate. Donne lists 58 alternative accounts of time in this treatise:

> In the Epistle of *Alexander the Great* to his Mother, remembered by *Cyprian* and *Augustin*, there is mention of 8000. years. The *Chaldeans* have delivered observations of 470000 years. And the Egyptians of 100000. The *Chineses* vex us at this day, with irreconcilable accounts. And to be sure, that none shall prevent them; some have call'd themselves Aborigenes. The poor remedy of Lunary and other planetary years, the silly and contemptible escape that some Authors speak of running years, some of years expired and perfected; or that the account of dayes and monthes are neglected.[99]

As is noted by Raspa, Donne identifies eight authoritative systems of time in the quoted passage, that is, Cyprian and Augustine's records of Alexander's epistle to his mother; the ancient histories of the Chaldeans, Egyptians, and Chinese; some aboriginal annals and the hypotheses both of "running years" and "Lunary and other planetary years."[100] Aside from these eight popular views, he mentions 50 others. The Dominican friar Sixtus Senensis (1520–69) "reckons almost thirty several supputations of the years between the Creation, and our blessed Saviour's birth, all of accepted authors, grounded upon the Scriptures," and the Spanish Jesuit theologian and exegete Benedictus Pererius (1535–1610) claims that "he might have increased the number by 20."[101] But Donne does not seem to think it necessary to engage Senensis's 30 "supputations" and the additional 20 added by Pererius.[102]

Three among the eight influential accounts of history Donne names proved especially unsettling in the Renaissance: the Chaldeans, Egyptians, and Chinese. The Egyptians claimed a history of 100,000 years; "the Chaldeans were the most ancient of all peoples, by the weighty testimony of not only Moses but also Herodotus, Ctesias, and Xenophon";[103] and the hitherto unresolved chronology of the Chinese continued to "vex us at this day." But the Chaldean and Egyptian antiquities had been more or less reconciled with scriptural chronology by the

---

[98] Scaliger, *De emendatione* (1629), 366.

[99] Donne, *Essayes*, 22.

[100] Raspa ed., *Essayes*, 130–32. Alexander's letter came down to us through the citations made by the bishop of Carthage St. Cyprian in his *Liber de idolorum vanitate* (AD 247) and Augustine's *City of God*. I follow Raspa's scheme in identifying Cyprian and Augustine as two separate sources. For Donne's seventh and eighth sources, see Raspa ed., *Essayes*, 131, 132.

[101] Donne, *Essayes,* 22.

[102] The authorities Sixtus Senensis named are in his *Bibliotheca Sancta* (1566), Book V. Benedictus Pererius's work means his *Commentariorum et Disputationum in Genesim* (Lyons, 1606). See Raspa ed., *Essayes*, 132.

[103] Bodin, *Method*, 337.

1610s. Bodin discounted both Herodotus's record of "a kingdom among the Egyptians for 13,000 years" and Cicero's account of the Chaldean history of 470,000 years, because the Hebrew writer Josephus (AD 37–100), with "a most definite system of chronology" based on Manetho and the Phoenicians, had "openly refuted the inane stories of the Egyptians and the Greeks by adding the ages of the kings of the Egyptians and of the Phoenicians."[104] Likewise, Scaliger thought Manetho's account "more worthy of belief" than those of Herodotus, who was but a foreigner.[105] Unlike Egyptian antiquity, for most Renaissance thinkers the Chaldean history agreed with rather than contradicted scriptural chronology. Western knowledge of Babylonian history came chiefly from the Greek historian Callisthenes (360–28 BC), Aristotle's disciple who went with Alexander on his eastern expedition. According to the Greek commentator Simplicius (AD 490–560), when requested by Aristotle "to collect the antiquities and records of the Chaldeans," Callisthenes "wrote back that he had diligently collected the Chaldean records and had found there the history of 1,903 years." "This number," Bodin observes, "fits the sacred history of Moses and Philo." In fact, for Bodin, both Callisthenes and Moses "drew the truth from the purest sources, agreed so far as concerns a universal system of time."[106] Goropius also holds that Callisthenes's report provides "remarkable evidences of agreement between the Chaldeans and those whose computations rest on the Bible."[107] Scaliger maintains that "the Chaldean computation deviates very little from the Mosaic" as well.[108]

Easy as it seems to accommodate the Chaldean and Egyptian antiquities to the biblical temporal system, Donne admits that "The Chineses vex us at this day, with irreconcilable accounts." This remark raises three points. First, the Eastern annals are not only singled out but also characterized by a strong verb, "vex." Second, whereas histories of other ancient civilizations are set down in exact numbers, Chinese chronicles are cast in a disconcerting phrase, that is, "irreconcilable accounts." While the verb "vex" connotes feelings of trouble and distress after a serious engagement with some disturbing problems, the adjective "irreconcilable" signals frustrated endeavors. Together, they suggest an unsuccessful negotiation with the chronology problematic. Moreover, "vex" also implies an acute awareness that without reconciling the "irreconcilable" Eastern antiquity, Scripture could not claim a universal jurisdiction. Third, the temporal phrase "at this day" indicates the topical urgency of the chronological issue around 1614 when the *Essayes* was written.

---

[104] Bodin, *Method*, 320.
[105] Scaliger, *Thesaurus temporum, Isagogici Canones*, 310, quoted in Grafton, "Rise and Fall," 172; also see *Historical Chronology*, 714.
[106] Bodin, *Method*, 320–21.
[107] Goropius, *Origines Antwerpianae* (1569), 434–35, quoted in Grafton, *Historical Chronology*, 267.
[108] Scaliger, *De emendatione* (1583), 202, quoted in Grafton, *Historical Chronology*, 264; for Renaissance attempts to synchronize the biblical and Babylonian timelines as is reported by Callisthenes see 262–67 of Grafton's *Historical Chronology*.

Donne's attention to the chronological polemic was corroborated by his knowledge of Scaliger's innovation. That Donne knew Scaliger's chronology is supported by the presence of the 1583 edition of *De emendatione* in his library and by his annotation on its fly-leaf in the form of a Latin epigram:

> To the Author.
>
> Times, laws, rewards, and punishments, thou 'art fain
> To improve, friend Joseph; sure, thou'lt strive in vain;
> The zealot crew has found the task too tough;
> Leave them no worse than they are, and that's enough.
>
> J. Donne.[109]

The tone expressed in this epigram is that of disapproval and friendly suggestion. The term "friend Joseph" indicates that the disagreement is directed at the work not the author. Indeed, Donne might have personally known Scaliger through his close friend Henry Wotton (1568–1639). Wotton once befriended Casaubon who kept up a lengthy correspondence with Scaliger from 1594 onwards. Donne thinks that "friend Joseph" has certainly "[striven] in vain," because he failed to "improve" "times, laws, rewards, and punishments" through, presumably, the effort to reform chronology. In addition to commenting on the general effect, Donne's Latin epigram also alludes to contemporary responses to Scaliger's chronological reformation—"the zealot crew has found the task too tough." A possible referent of "the zealot crew" might be those committed Christians who found it hard to stomach Scaliger's proleptic time. The last sentence is a caveat: it is "enough" for Scaliger to "leave them no worse than they are." The third-person pronouns here could refer either to "the zealot crew" or the chronologers whose works Scaliger had taken upon himself to reform. In addition to the direct pithy comment in the poetic form, Sir Geoffrey Keynes says, "there is plenty of evidence in Donne's copy of the book that he was interested in Scaliger's work."[110]

Chinese Chronology and Donne's Apologetic Exegesis in the *Essayes*

To understand Donne's engagement with the controversy over Chinese antiquity, we should take a look at his interpretation of the scriptural system of time as it is represented in Genesis and Exodus. A chief objective of Donne's biblical commentary is to prove that Scripture is "the last refuge" in establishing a universal timeline.[111] To achieve this aim, he needs to justify scriptural chronology against the 58 alternative claims of time, especially the "strong oppositions" from the eight authoritative accounts. Though neither the Chinese nor any other chronology

---

[109] The poem is taken from Sir Geoffrey Keynes, "Doctor Donne and Scaliger," *Times Literary Supplement* (February 21, 1958): 108.
[110] Keynes, "Donne and Scaliger," 108.
[111] *Essayes*, 22.

appears in Donne's actual exegesis, the challenges they pose nevertheless serve as the invisible but powerful background to which the interpreter unconsciously refers.

The biblical exegesis featured in the *Essayes* was typical of Renaissance hermeneutics that prioritized the literal sense of Scripture. Ancient and medieval commentators largely followed the fourfold exegetical scheme proposed by John Cassian (d. 435) who divided the "spiritual *scientia*" into "three genera," that is, "*tropologia, allegoria,* and *anagoge.*" These three "spiritual" senses, together with the "literal," constitute the fourfold expository framework.[112] Most early and medieval commentators privileged the "allegorical" sense, but Thomas Aquinas (1225–74) and Nicholas of Lyra (1279–1340) came to realize the importance of the "literal" meaning.[113] In the Renaissance, the literal sense was elevated to an unparalleled status by the Reformers and humanists.[114] Don C. Allen remarks that since "the Bible was the center of Luther's theology and the literal interpretation of the text was the beginning of all his thinking,"[115] "the literal exposition was widely approved as the basic exposition by most of the exegetes of the Renaissance."[116] The interpretive principle Whitaker proposed was representative of the Protestant hermeneutics, according to which "there is but one true, proper and genuine sense of scripture, arising from the words rightly understood, which we call the literal."[117] The literal sense was further promoted by the humanist "grammatical exegetes" such as Desiderius Erasmus (c. 1467–1536) who "applied the philological to the scriptural text to the exclusion of mysticism or spiritual apologetics," with "the exposition of accurate and literal meaning" as their typical "*modus operandi*" and "grammar and philology" as their "*apparatus criticus.*"[118]

---

[112] John Cassian, *De Collationes Patrum* or *The Conferences of the Fathers* (c.435), quoted in James S. Preus, *From Shadow to Promise: Old Testament Interpretation from Augustine to the Young Luther* (Cambridge, MA: Belknap-Harvard, 1969), 21. For early and medieval biblical exegesis, also see James D. Wood, *The Interpretation of the Bible* (London: Gerald Duckworth, 1958); and Beryl Smalley, *The Study of the Bible in the Middle Ages*, 2nd ed. (Notre Dame: U of Notre Dame P, 1964).

[113] Wood, *Interpretation of the Bible*, 76–84; Smalley, *Study of the Bible*, 83–106; and Preus, *From Shadow to Promise*, 27–66.

[114] For Renaissance biblical exegeses see Arnold Williams, *The Common Expositor: An Account of the Commentaries on Genesis 1527–1633* (Chapel Hill: U of North Carolina P, 1948); David C. Steinmetz, ed. *The Bible in the Sixteenth Century* (Durham: Duke UP, 1990); Christopher Hill, *The English Bible and the Seventeenth-Century Revolution* (London: Penguin, 1994); and Debora K. Shuger, *The Renaissance Bible: Scholarship, Sacrifice, and Subjectivity* (Waco: Baylor UP, 2010).

[115] Allen, *Legend of Noah*, 42–43.

[116] Allen, *Legend of Noah*, 68–69.

[117] Whitaker, *Disputation*, 404.

[118] George N. Conkin, *Biblical Criticism and Heresy in Milton* (New York: King's Crown, 1949), 17–18. For the philological approach also see, Gillian R. Evans, *The Language and Logic of the Bible: The Road to Reformation* (New York: Cambridge UP, 1985); Jerry H. Bentley, *Humanists and Holy Writ: New Testament Scholarship in the Renaissance* (Princeton: Princeton UP, 1983); and Erika Rummel, *Erasmus' Annotations*

Donne was quite aware of the exegetical tradition outlined above, and following the Reformers and humanists, he emphasized the primacy of the literal sense. Chanita Goodblatt rightly observes that "Donne's continuous citing of such an array of textual authority bespeaks his participation in 'a tradition of literal exposition originated in the Middle Ages and culminated in the great exegetical works of the Reformers'."[119] Donne claims that "the sense which should ground an assurance in Doctrinall things, should be the literall sense" (7:192), calling "the curious refining of the allegorical fathers" some "fine cobwebs to catch flies" or "strong cables by which we might anchor in all storms of disputation and persecution."[120] He states expressly in the *Essayes* that "we inherit the talents and travels of al Expositors,"[121] and when commenting on Genesis, he declares pointedly that he is following "the Example of our late learned Reformers."[122] Although he opposes the philological practices to "excerpt and tear shapeless and insignificant rags of a word or two, from whole sentences, and make them obey their purpose in discoursing," his extensive exegesis of names and numbers in the *Essayes* shows visible influence of the humanists.[123]

Donne does not privilege the literal at the expense of the metaphorical, though Dennis B. Quinn claims that "all Donne had in mind was the eschewing of nonliteral senses, with which allegory, tropology, and anagogy had become synonymous."[124] In reality, rather than "eschewing … nonliteral senses," Donne attempts to articulate an exegetical principle that at once prioritizes and reconciles the literal with all the other senses. Since "to divers understandings there might be divers literal senses," he says in the *Essayes*, to be "called literall is to distinguish it from the Morall, Allegoricall, and the other senses."[125] Put differently, the other senses are but different "understandings" of the literal, an interpretation that recalls both Whitaker's expository doctrine and Lyra's theory of *duplex sensus literalis*. Whitaker maintains that "allegories, tropologies, and anagoges are not various senses, but various collections from one sense, or various applications and accommodations of that one meaning [the literal]."[126] For Lyra, a "[letter] can apply to a [second] literal sense which is just as literal as the first. In light of this, one should consider that the same letter at times has a double sense."[127] By a

---

on the New Testament: From Philologist to Theologian, Erasmus Studies 8 (Toronto: U of Toronto P, 1986).

[119] Goodblatt, "From 'Tav' to the Cross," 223–24.
[120] *Essayes*, 46.
[121] *Essayes*, 30.
[122] *Essayes*, 21.
[123] *Essayes*, 46.
[124] Quinn, "Donne's Principles of Biblical Exegesis," 316.
[125] *Essayes*, 46.
[126] Whitaker, *Disputation*, 404.
[127] Nicholas of Lyra, *Postillae perpetuae in universam S. Scripturam* (Rome, 1471); quoted in Preus, *From Shadow to Promise*, 66. Donne speaks of Lyra's theory of double signification in the *Essayes*, 10.

second literal sense, Lyra means the various derivations of the first literal sense. Thus for Donne as well as Lyra and Whitaker, the literal is the primary matrix from which other senses derive.

In addition to reasserting the literal, Renaissance also witnessed an attempt to reconceptualize the "historical" sense of Scripture. Both early and medieval commentators tended to identify the historical with the mere literal or "grammatical" sense.[128] Historical exegesis assumed a new dimension in Protestant hermeneutics— it looked at biblical stories, not as allegorical and typological metaphors, but as real historical events. Debora K. Shuger remarks that when "Scaliger's *De emendatione temporum* came out in 1583, Casaubon's New Testament scholia in 1587—a new sensitivity to historical continuity developed, replacing the seamless fabric of typological time" and turning Scripture into "a historical document that both implies and elucidates late antique culture."[129] Donne noticed this "new sensitivity to historical continuity" in biblical scholarship. Patrides points out that in the Renaissance "the acceptance of the historicity of the Mosaic account of creation is attested by the widespread persuasion that the world was created, as William Perkins estimated late in the sixteenth century, 'between fiue thousand and sixe thousand yeres agoe'."[130] Donne subscribes to this "widespread persuasion," interpreting the literal sense as the "historicity" of Scripture as well. "Because we are utterly disprovided of any history of the World's Creation," he declares, "except we defend and maintain this Book of Moses to be Historical, and therefore literarrly to be interpreted."[131] To interpret Genesis "literally" is to regard it as a "historical" document.

To treat Scripture as a historical text necessarily subjects it to the scrutiny of the chronological methodology that emphasizes the consistency of numerical evidence. To counteract accusations of chronological errors in Scripture, Donne insists on the distinctive feature of the Mosaic history, that is, its allegorical signification, declaring that "there is then in Moses, both history and precept."[132] In other words, Scripture represents at once history and allegory—when literally interpreted, it features "history," and when allegorically approached, it conveys "precept." In effect, the literal sense is often expressed in precepts or "by allegories," Donne argues, so that "in many places of Scripture, a figurative sense is the literall sense" (6:62–63). Thus, he says in a sermon preached on 1 Corinthians 15:29, "We [Anglicans] have a Rule, by which that sense will be suspicious to us, which is, Not to admit figurative senses in interpretation of Scriptures, where the literall sense may well stand" (7:193). Given this necessity of the allegorical and its frequent coincidence with the literal sense, a chronological model that relies largely on numbers and dates cannot adequately account for the Mosaic

---

[128] Whitaker, *Disputation*, 404.
[129] Shuger, *Renaissance Bible*, 45, 23, 24.
[130] Patrides, *Milton and the Christian Tradition*, 28.
[131] *Essayes*, 21.
[132] *Essayes*, 21–22.

history. Things would be much simpler, he says in his *Pseudo-Martyr* (1610), "if the errour were onely in *Chronologie*, as to give Pope Nicholas a place in the Councell of *Carthage*, who was dead before; Or in *Arithmeticke*, as when purposely he enumerates all the *Councels*, to make the number lesse by foure."[133] But in truth, chronological lapses only indicate something superficial, and the deeper allegorical meaning goes beyond mere arithmetic calculations.

As a distinctive expression of the metaphorical sense, spiritual "faith" proves the ideal model to interpret the fathomless "bottom" of the creation.[134] For Donne, the exegetical principle that "a figurative sense is the literall sense" is especially pertinent to the study of Genesis. On the one hand, he suggests a literal approach, for in this book "there is danger in departing from the letter" (6:62). On the other hand, a mere literal exegesis proves inadequate because "the literall interpretation of successive days cannot subsist, where there are some dayes mention'd before the Creation of these Planets which made days."[135] But this pre-Creation time can nevertheless be interpreted allegorically and addressed by faith. Donne defines faith as, in contrast to rational reasoning out of "Logick" or "Rhetorique," a "Character, and Oridinance which God hath imprinted in me" (7:95). He argues for the primacy of this divine seal in commenting on such scriptural tenets as the Resurrection and Creation. To understand the Resurrection, "the roote and foundation thereof is in Faith; though Reason may chafe the wax, yet Faith imprints the seale," since "the Resurrection is not a conclusion out of actuall Reason, but it is an article of supernaturall faith" (7:95). In like manner, "it is an article of our belief, that the world began."[136] So when interpreting Genesis, "we are not under the insinuations and mollifyings of perswasion, and conveniency; nor under the reach and violence of Argument, or Demonstration, or Necessity," he argues; rather, we should subject its exegesis "under the Spirituall, and peaceable Tyranny, and easie yoke of sudden and present Faith."[137] The inscrutable nature of the Creation dictates that its account should go beyond both rational theorization and mathematical calculation—there is no way to imagine the world's origin; never mind calculate its exact date.

Though inapplicable to Genesis, the chronological model cannot be easily refuted when used to interpret Exodus, a book in which numbers figure prominently. Since "the miracle of propagating" represented in Exodus "consists in the Number,"[138] this book is easily challenged on chronological grounds. Faith can address prehistorical time, but it cannot account for events that happened in historical time and could be verified with physical evidence. Since the creation permits little room for our "reason" and "discourse" and "must be at once swallowed and devour'd by faith," Donne observes, it is not so "apt" to stimulate

---

[133] Donne, *Pseudo-Martyr*, ed. Anthony Raspa (Montreal: McGill-Queen's UP, 1993), 192.
[134] *Essayes*, 22.
[135] *Essayes*, 38–39.
[136] *Essayes*, 19.
[137] *Essayes*, 19.
[138] *Essayes*, 61.

us to great "Acts of Honour."[139] By comparison, we can be well affected by God's delivery of those captivated Israelites, because such "miracles" "are somewhat more submitted to reason, and exercise and entertain our disputation, and spiritual curiosity by the way."[140] Thus, "though in our supreme Court in such cases" as "when profane Historie rises up against any place of Scripture, accusing it to Humane Reason, and understanding," "the last Appeal" is "Faith," Donne says, "yet Reason is her Delegate."[141] So the numbers in Exodus cannot be lightly dismissed with a spiritual faith—it must be intellectually engaged with reason. St. Augustine holds that "an argument aroused by an adversary" sometimes "turns out to be an opportunity for instruction."[142] Donne responds with the same rationale to those who question the "variety in Numbring" in Exodus, arguing that by this "variety" God means

> his word should ensure and undergo the opinion of contradiction, or other infirmities, in the eyes of Pride (the Author of Heresie and Schism) that after all such dissections, & cribrations, and examinings of Hereticall adventures upon it, it might return from the furnace more refin'd, and gain luster and clearness by this vexation.[143]

Engagement with charges of numerical inconsistency thus ends up only adding more "luster and clearness" to Scripture.

In addition to numbers, names constitute another major source of chronological lapses, especially in histories composed of dynastic rules. Names are fundamental to maintaining the identity of a certain people, according to Bodin, so when they are "obliterated," confusion occurs unavoidably in their chronology. Reliable chronology should be constructed according to "certain epoch or initial point of time," Bodin asserts, and the very practice to " [define] time by the ages of kings is cause of chronological errors." For instance, because of the loss of the names of some of their monarchs, the chronological systems derived from "the kings of Assyrians, Persians, and Egyptians" remain problematic.[144] Though China did not appear in Bodin's list, its long dynastic history as is recorded by Mendoza must have been viewed in the same light by early modern Europeans.[145]

Donne's strategy to address the chronological confusion caused by numbers and names is to link them together. To counteract charges on nominal grounds, he seeks to establish the "certainty and constancy"[146] of the names occurring in Exodus by comparing them with those corruptible and easily perishable "ethnick"

---

[139] *Essayes*, 61.
[140] *Essayes*, 61.
[141] *Essayes*, 63.
[142] Augustine, *City of God*, 650.
[143] *Essayes*, 63–64.
[144] Bodin, *Method*, 324, 325–26.
[145] For Renaissance fascination with dynastic history, see Grafton, *Historical Chronology*, 70–71.
[146] *Essayes*, 54.

or "heathen" names.[147] God's concern with names is everywhere in Scripture, he writes, since "How often in the Scripture is the word *Name*, for *honour, fame, vertue*? How often doth God accurse with abolishing the Name?"[148] In particular, God shows special care with names in the book of exile. As he puts it, "in no language are Names so significant" as in Exodus, so much so that " if one consider diligently the senses of the Names register'd here, he will not so soon say, That the Names are in the History, as that the History is in the Names."[149] Consequently, "wheresoever these Names shall be mentioned, the Miraculous History shall be call'd to memory; And wheresoever the History is remembered, their Names shall be refreshed."[150] While "ethnick" or "heathen" names "putrifie and perish," Donne says, those "honour'd with a place in this book [Exodus] cannot perish, because the Book cannot."[151] He concedes that names in Exodus, just like numbers, "are diversely named" and "not always alike."[152] But he argues that although "error and variety in Names, may be pardonable in profane Histories, especially such as translated from Authors of other language," the "one Author of al[l] these books [of Scripture], the Holy Ghost" ensures the "certainty and constancy" of the names in Exodus.[153] By turning the tables, Donne strikes home the point that, unlike profane histories, nominal lapses are simply unpardonable in the Mosaic history. Paradoxically, the truth of names in Exodus comes from their close alliance with numbers. Since God "commands His [people] to be numbered, and to be numbered by name," Hebrew history closely follows "this Order, of being first Named, and then Numbred; or first Numbred, and then Named."[154] Donne's argument is that, when separate, numbers and names might support profane histories, but once combined, they symbolize a "Miraculous History" that has the capacity to enfold all peoples in "One fold, and one shepherd." Given this unity, the new pagans such as the Chinese and Amerindians should belong to the Adamic family; accordingly, their systems of time should conform to scriptural chronology.

As the words "vex" and "irreconcilable" suggest, despite his efforts, Donne's attempt to assimilate Chinese chronology into a scriptural timeframe proved to be unsuccessful. As is to be shown in the next chapter, Chinese antiquity continued to bother thinkers in the middle of the seventeenth century, with greater intensity due to an increasing knowledge of the Eastern country. Despite the insufficiency of Donne's solution, however, his serious engagement with the chronological issue in an extensive theological treatise attests to his awareness of its gravity. Most importantly, this engagement shows at once his intellectual openness to radical difference and his liberal cosmopolitanism to reconcile the non-Christian other to the biblical symbolic economy.

---

[147] *Essayes*, 51.
[148] *Essayes*, 50–51.
[149] *Essayes*, 51.
[150] *Essayes*, 53.
[151] *Essayes*, 50.
[152] *Essayes*, 54.
[153] *Essayes*, 54.
[154] *Essayes*, 60.

Chapter 4
The Resonance of Chinese Antiquity in Milton's *Paradise Lost*[1]

Not only Donne but also Milton was wrestling with the radical implications of the Chinese culture, implications that appeared the more disturbing as knowledge of the Eastern country expanded. Initially a new world to early modern Europe, China had become well known by the 1670s. In his *An Historical Essay ... the Language of the Empire of China is the Primitive Language* (1669), the first extensive European treatise on the Chinese language, the English architect and linguist John Webb declares, "Their [Chinese] discovery is generally completed; their Antiquity certainly known; Their Language plainly understood ... *Time* being to make known the rest."[2] In this chapter and the next, I will show that mid-seventeenth-century engagement with China, a negotiation based on more "certain" and "plain" knowledge of the Eastern country, also exhibits a liberal cosmopolitan spirit. Specifically, I will explore Milton's responses to Chinese history and language in *Paradise Lost*. While this chapter focuses on the resonance of the chronological debate in Milton's representations of Hebrew history and world histories, Chapter 5 deals with the contention between Webb's Chinese linguistic model and Milton's image of the primitive language in his epic poem.

If Donne's cosmopolitan spirit remained on the visionary plane, in his *Areopogitica* (1644), a treatise celebrated for its passionate defense of such liberal principles as free speech and expression, Milton articulated a practical cosmopolitan agenda in regards to state policy towards foreign knowledge. In the treatise, we hear the poet declaring that "our hearts are now more capacious, our thoughts more erected to the search and expectation of greatest and exactest things" (YP 2:559). The "capacious" hearts and "erected" thoughts signal none other than a lofty cosmopolitan vision, and one of the "greatest" things that came to Milton's broadminded purview is the cultures and histories of different lands and peoples. For Milton, it is politically imperative to get to know foreign cultures, because "to sequester out of the world into *Atlantick* and *Eutopian* politics, which never can be drawn into use, will not mend our condition" (YP 2:526). Likewise, the institution of effective moral and ethical systems also comes from an informed knowledge of the histories of other regions. As he puts it in his "Prolusion VII," "How great an additional pleasure of the mind it is to take our flight over all the history and

---

[1] All quotes about Milton's poetry come from *John Milton, Complete Poems and Major Works*, ed. Merritt Y. Hughes (Indianapolis: Hackett, 1957, Repr. 2003).

[2] John Webb, *An Historical Essay Endeavoring a Probability That the Language of the Empire of China is the Primitive Language*, London, 1669, 69.

regions of the world, to view the conditions and changes of kingdoms, nations, cities, and people—all with a view to improving our wisdom and our morals."[3] To study alien histories and cultures for the advancement of "our wisdom and our morals," Milton declares, is at once "the way to live in all the epochs of history" and "to be a contemporary of time itself."[4] What Milton attempts to express here is what David Porter calls "historical cosmopolitanism"— a cosmopolitan liberality both to recognize the value of and learn from all histories in the world, whether big or small, pagan or Christian.[5]

Liberal cosmopolitanism informs not only Milton's vision of world histories but also his attitude towards pagan or unorthodox knowledge. Resonating Bacon's metaphor of the "ships" of "letters," Milton calls attention to the fact that the newly opened global circuits were enacting worldwide circulation of knowledge. So no matter how "severely" "our Spanish licensing gags the English Press," he argues, "by which compendious way all the contagion that foreign books can infuse, will finde a passage to the people of farre easier and shorter then an Indian voyage, though it could be sail'd either by the North of *Cataio* Eastward, or of *Canada* Westward" (YP 2:518–19). Put differently, domestic censorship cannot arrest the "contagion" of "foreign books," which keep on pouring into England via such global sea routes as the "Indian voyage" or the Northeast or Northwest passage. Given the irrepressible global dissemination of knowledge, Milton contends, the best way to confront foreign books is to adopt a cosmopolitan attitude, because "a little generous prudence, a little forbearance of one another, and some grain of charity might win all these diligences to joyn, and unite into one generall and brotherly search after Truth" (YP 2:554). Words such as "generous prudence," "forbearance," and "charity" bear on a striking liberal cosmopolitanism not only to embrace alien cultures but also to join them in a concerted effort to "search after Truth."

Milton gives three rationales for his argument for a cosmopolitan tolerance of cultural pluralism. First, he considers cultural diversity a natural condition of human life, on the grounds that "the goodly and the graceful symmetry" of the world arises "out of many moderat varieties and brotherly dissimilitudes that are not vastly disproportionall" (YP 2: 555). Second, "if all cannot be of one mind," he reasons, it is "doubtless ... more wholesome, more prudent, and more Christian, that many be tolerated, rather than all compell'd" (YP 2:565). Third, he insists that "those neighboring differences, or rather indifferences ... need not interrupt *the unity of Spirit*." Instead, cultural pluralism can help form "*the bond of peace*" (YP 2:565).

---

[3] Milton, "Prolusion VII," "Learning makes men happier than does ignorance," in Hughes ed., 625.

[4] Milton, "Prolusion VII," "Learning," Hughes ed., 625.

[5] For the term "historical cosmopolitanism," see Porter, "Sinicizing Early Modernity: The Imperatives of Historical Cosmopolitanism," *Eighteenth-Century Studies* 43.3 (2010): 299–306, 299.

The liberal cosmopolitanism expressly articulated in *Areopogitica* calls into question Feisal G. Mohamed's well-received claim of Milton's parochialism.[6] As is shown above, even in 1644 when the treatise was written, a period deemed by critics as Milton's most nationalist moment, the poet displayed an astonishingly liberal cosmopolitanism towards foreign and pagan cultures. Later in the *Tenure of Kings and Magistrates* (1649), he contemplates a "brother-hood between man and man over all the world," a cosmopolitan community bonded together by a new kind of "Gospel" or "Law among equals" (YP 3:214–15). This global cosmopolitanism also finds a graphic articulation in *The Second Defence* (1654), in which he famously imagines "embark[ing] on a journey" and "surveying on high far-flung regions and territories across the sea, faces numberless and unknown." "From the Pillars of Hercules all the way to the farthest boundaries of India," he writes, "I seem to be leading home again everywhere in the world, after a vast space of time, Liberty herself" (YP 4:554–55). In concert with the "historical cosmopolitanism" expressed in "Prolusion VII," the geographical cosmopolitanism depicted in this passage bespeaks a stance far from parochial.

Despite his declared cosmopolitanism, however, Milton, true both to his Puritan upbringing and the religious temper of his age, upheld the universality of Hebrew history. This is evident both in his adjudication of the time schemes and his representation of world histories in *Paradise Lost*. Unable to transcend the monotheistic tradition he inherited, Milton frames the histories of almost all the known worlds within the prophetic purview of Adam, the biblical patriarch of humankind. As with Donne's attempt to globalize the biblical discourse, however, *theological* adjustment to a globalized world does not contradict the *intellectual* attempt to negotiate non-Christian cultures. As is shown in his *The Christian Doctrine* (1658–65) and *The Art of Logic* (1672), Milton was a mature and intelligent believer who sought to understand the basic concepts of Christianity through both philosophical inquiry and logical reasoning. In effect, he tried to reassess the relevance of Christian tenets in terms of not only philosophical and theological traditions but also the changed face of the earth. By the time *Paradise Lost* came to press, not only new lands but also new cultures were brought into clearer and more definite view of western Europe. As with Donne, Milton also realized that the new configuration of the earth renders it imperative to reconsider the geographical and temporal coverage of the Judeo-Christian history in the contexts both of global geography and world histories.

Milton's response to Chinese antiquity offers a speaking instance of the liberal cosmopolitanism he propounds in *Areopogitica* and other works. As in Donne's divine treatise, China shows but briefly in *Paradise Lost*, but this seemingly random reference is telling enough to bear out Milton's general attitude towards the Eastern country. In Adam's survey of world histories in book XI, "the Seat / Of mightiest Empire" and "the destin'd Walls / Of Cambalu, seat of Cathaian

---

[6] Feisal G. Mohamed, *Milton and the Post-Secular Present: Ethics, Politics, Terrorism* (Stanford: Stanford UP, 2011).

Can" (11.386–88) take the lead. The pride of place Milton accords to China, the superlative epithet "mightiest" he uses to describe the Far Eastern empires, and his so-called "two Chinas" represented respectively by "Cambalu" and "Paquin" (11.390), all indicate his recognition of the high antiquity and importance of the Eastern empire.[7]

Milton's image of China takes on an import larger than a mere place name when seen in light of the seventeenth-century chronological controversy. In 1658, the Jesuit historian Martino Martini published his *Sinicae historiae decas prima*, which rekindled in a flash the chronological debate ignited by Mendoza. In his correspondence with Henry Oldenburg (1619–77) dated 1656, Milton speaks of the great enthusiasm towards Martini's book manifested by many Oxford scholars. In this chapter, I propose that Milton's reference to China in his epic poem registers his response to the contemporary chronological controversy. Milton was quite aware of the challenge Chinese antiquity posed to biblical systems of time and the Adamic precedence. Though denying Milton's concern with the Eastern chronology, Robert Markley admits that "his rejection of Jesuit accounts of China's history implicitly testifies to his awareness of the problems they pose."[8] I would argue that Milton's chronological awareness plays a pivotal part in shaping the arrangement and nature of his treatment of human history in *Paradise Lost*. History appears in two general forms in the poem: an invisible comprehensive system of time and a synopsis of world histories. Milton represents both forms with the chronological polemic in mind. Markley rightly states that "The destin'd Walls / Of *Cambalu*" "serve a complex double function" for Milton: "they stand synecdochically for the riches that will help Europeans overcome the curses of sin and scarcity and they pose a formidable challenge to Eurocentric visions of history, politics, and theology."[9] But rather than "sidestep[ping] the implications of Chinese antiquity" as Markley argues,[10] Milton was numbered among those "foremost minds" who undertook to "[tackle] questions of fundamental importance to the identity of Christendom."[11] Instead of claiming Milton's direct engagement, however, I propose that Chinese antiquity resonates both in his overall deployment of biblical time and his synoptic representation of world histories.

Milton's attention to Chinese culture and chronology has not received the critical attention it deserves, and the interpretive models so far employed in Milton studies are insufficient to articulate the rich implications of his image of China.[12]

---

[7] Y. Z. Chang, "Why Did Milton Err on Two Chinas," *The Modern Language Review* 65.3 (1970): 493–98.

[8] Markley, "'The destin'd Walls/ Of Cambalu': Milton, China, and the Ambiguities of the Far East," in *Milton and the Imperial Vision*, ed. Balachandra Rajan and Elizabeth Sauer (Pittsburgh: Duquesne UP, 1999), 191–213, 197.

[9] Markley, *Far East and the English Imagination*, 71.

[10] Markley, "Destin'd Walls," in Rajan and Sauer eds., 198.

[11] Kidd, *British Identities*, 17.

[12] On Milton's image of China see, Allan H. Gilbert, "Milton's China," *Modern Language Notes* 26.6 (1911): 199–200; also Gilbert, *A Geographical Dictionary of Milton*

Markley's focus on mercantile trade neglects the cultural complexity of Milton's Chinese image, and Lim's Orientalist approach that presupposes the superiority of European cultural forms ignores the impact of the Eastern culture upon Renaissance Europe.[13] Nor can the nationalist and colonialist models prevailing in Milton studies adequately account for his references to China. David Loewenstein and Paul Stevens argue that the nationalist model is especially pertinent to "debates about the nature and definition of nationalism in Milton and his England," because it can effectively address "what Milton of *Areopagitica* might consider 'brotherly dissimilitudes' and 'neighboring difference'."[14] But as Milton himself points out in *Areopogitica*, it requires a "capacious" mind and cosmopolitan "charity" to turn these "dissimilitudes" and "difference" into "the bond of peace," an approach that apparently goes beyond the nationalist framework. Milton's portrayal of China modifies his alleged colonialism as well. Signifying "the conquest and control of other people's land and goods," colonialism, like orientalism, also assumes the superior force of western Europeans.[15] Pompa Banerjee and J. Martin Evans read colonial implications in Milton's representations of eastern and western Indians, but the colonial model is obviously unable to address his response to the unique challenges posed by the Far East, a region deemed by Milton himself "the Seat / Of mightiest Empire."[16]

Rather than the Orientalist, nationalist, or colonialist models, I use globalization theory to study Milton's image of China within the context of the chronological debate intensified by the publication of Martini's book. Julie S.

(New Haven: Yale UP, 1919); Frank L. Huntley, "Milton, Mendoza, and the Chinese Land-Ship," *Modern Language Notes* 69.6 (1954): 404–7; Huntley, *Essays in Persuasion: On Seventeenth-Century Literature* (Chicago: U of Chicago P, 1981), 133–41; and Sidney Gottlieb, "Milton's Land-Ships and John Wilkins," *Modern Philology* 84.1 (1986): 60–62.

[13] Markley holds that "Were it not for his conviction, shared by most educated Europeans, that the path to economic salvation led almost invariably to the 'destin'd Walls / Of Cambalu,'" "The Far east, in fact, might be dispensed with entirely." Markley, "Destin'd Walls," in Rajan and Sauer eds., 201. Lim, "Empire of Commerce in Milton's *Paradise Lost*," in Hayot et al. eds., *Sinographies*, 115–39; and Lim, "John Milton, Orientalism, and the Empires of the East in *Paradise Lost*," in Johanyak and Lim eds., *The English Renaissance*, 203–35.

[14] Loewenstein and Stevens, eds., *Early Modern Nationalism*, 12.

[15] Loombia, *Colonialism/ Postcolonialism*, 8.

[16] Pompa Banerjee, "Milton's India and *Paradise Lost*," *Milton Studies* 37 (1999): 142–65; and J. Martin Evans, *Milton's Imperial Epic: "Paradise Lost" and the Discourse of Colonialism* (Ithaca, NY: Cornell UP, 1996). On other works on Milton's colonialism see, Paul Stevens, "*Paradise Lost* and the Colonial Imperative," *Milton Studies* 34 (1997): 3–21; Jyotsna G. Singh, *Colonial Narratives/Cultural Dialogues: "Discoveries" of India in the Language of Colonialism* (London: Routledge, 1996); Balachandra Rajan, *Under Western Eyes: India from Milton to Macaulay* (Durham, NC: Duke UP, 1999); and Shankar Raman, *Framing "India": The Colonial Imaginary in Early Modern Culture* (Stanford: Stanford UP, 2002).

Peters also approaches *Paradise Lost* from a global perspective.[17] But whereas Peters focuses on Milton's conception of a global legal order, I examine his liberal cosmopolitanism towards radical cultural alterity. The Chinese context both provides new insight into the overall apologetic agenda in *Paradise Lost* and reveals Milton's liberal cosmopolitanism to find commonality and negotiate differences. On the one hand, at the outset of his epic poem, Milton pointedly declares that his purpose is to "assert Eternal Providence, / And justify the ways of God to men" (1.25–6). To defend the primacy of the biblical God, it is of paramount importance to incorporate an alternative system of time which, to use Oldenburg's words, threatens "the antiquity of the Mosaic and Adamite epoch" (YP 7:491). So as is with Donne's *Essayes*, the Chinese calendar serves as an invisible background to which Milton refers, albeit indirectly or unconsciously, in his dramatic exegesis of scriptural history.[18] On the other hand, the liberal cosmopolitan desire to "live in all the epochs of history" expressed in "Prolusion VII" finds a graphic dramatization in the synopsis of world histories and empires in book XI. Here Milton depicts how the temporal matrix represented by Hebrew history unfolds and incorporates histories of different lands and peoples by setting out an overview of "all Earth's Kingdoms and thir Glory" (11.384) through the "Visions of God" (11.377)—the perspectives both of the divine historian Michael and the first patriarch Adam. Corresponding to the cosmic scope of prehistorical time, historical time is showcased on a global stage featuring a host of geographical names, places that symbolize, as Peters says, "the whole expanse[s]" both of human history and geography.[19] To encompass a vast array of profane histories within Adam's prophetic vision shows that "alternative chronologies" are far from "superfluous" for Milton as William Poole claims.[20] Instead, this historical encompassing suggests both the indispensable place of "alternative chronologies" in a universal timeline and Milton's cosmopolitan urge to engage cultural pluralism.

Milton-Oldenburg Correspondence and the Rekindling of the Chronological Debate in the Mid-Seventeenth Century

The chronological debate over Chinese antiquity triggered by the publication of Mendoza's *Mighty Kingdom of China* in 1585 continued well into the middle of the

---

[17] Julie S. Peters, "A 'Bridge over Chaos': *De Jure Belli*, *Paradise Lost*, Terror, Sovereignty, Globalism, and the Modern Law of Nations," *Comparative Literature* 57.4 (2005): 273–93.

[18] On Milton and biblical exegesis see J. Martin Evans, *Paradise Lost and the Genesis Tradition* (Oxford: Clarendon, 1968); Patrides, *Milton and the Christian Tradition*; and Regina Schwartz, *Remembering and Repeating: Biblical Creation in Paradise Lost* (Cambridge: Cambridge UP, 1988).

[19] Peters, "A 'Bridge over Chaos,'" 278.

[20] William Poole, "Milton and Science: A Caveat," *Milton Quarterly* 38.1 (2004): 18–34, 22.

seventeenth century.[21] As I have shown in the previous chapter, Donne observed in 1614 that "the Chineses vex us at this day, with irreconcilable accounts."[22] In 1662, the Bishop of Worcester Edward Stillingfleet (1635–99) writes in his *Origines sacrae*, "The most popular pretenses of the Atheists of our Age, have been the irreconcilableness of the account of Times in Scriptures with that of the learned and ancient Heathen Nations."[23] One of these "learned and ancient Heathen Nations" was China, a powerful pagan empire once contemporaneous with Greece and Rome and which continued to exist alongside early modern Europe. That both Donne and Stillingfleet used the word "irreconcilable" to describe the clash between biblical and profane chronologies indicates that the issue that harassed thinkers in the 1610s remained unresolved in the 1670s. In his *Dissertatiode vera aetate mundi* (1659), a discourse of "those Nations, that are the greatest pretenders to Antiquity, as the *Hebrews, Samaritans, Chaldeans,* and *Aegyptians*," the Dutch scholar Isaac Vossius (1618–89) "brings up the *Chinois* in the rear."[24] In his "Histoire de la Chine," a fragment filed in his *Apology for the Christian Religion* (1670), the French philosopher Blaise Pascal (1623–62) puts the contention between Chinese and biblical chronologies bluntly, "which is the more credible of the two, Moses or China?"[25]

Milton's correspondence with Oldenburg indicates that he was well aware of the seventeenth-century debate centering on Chinese antiquity. In a letter to Milton dated June 1656, Oldenburg says,

> I believe that you have already read the reply which Maresius has made to the defender of the pre-Adamites, to whom a certain Martini, a fellow-countryman sent to Rome as agent of the Chinese mission, will shortly undertake a rejoinder. For this man reports, in a preface to a book which he has published about the tartar war, that he has brought back with him very old books of Chinese history and calendars leading with extraordinary accuracy from the very flood of Noah; and thence he promises to reconcile Chinese chronology with that which our sacred writings record, than which nothing could better protect the antiquity of the Mosaic and Adamite epoch. (YP 7:491)

The book about the "tartar war" Oldenburg mentions means Martini's *De Bello Tartarico Historia* (1654), and the treatise on "old books of Chinese history and

---

[21] Mendoza records Chinese history in book III, chapter I of his *Mighty Kingdom of China*, 69–76.
[22] Donne, *Essayes in Divinity*, 22.
[23] Edward Stillingfleet, *Origines sacrae*, Repr. (Oxford, 1797), xiv.
[24] Webb, *An Historical Essay*, 48; Isaac Vossius, *Dissertatio de vera aetate mundi* (The Hague, 1659), 44.
[25] Quoted in David Wetsel, "'Histoire de la Chine': Pascal and the Challenge to Biblical Time," *Journal of Religion* 69.2 (1989): 199–219, 199. For Pascal's three other references to Chinese antiquity see 201–2, note. 12. For Henri Gouhier, Pascal's work was written in response to Martini's *Sinicae historiae*. Gouhier, *Blaise Pascal: Commentaire* (Paris: Vrin, 1971), 228–29.

calendars" advertised in the preface to *Tartarico* refers to his *Sinicae historiae* that was to see print in 1658.[26] Martini also wrote *Novus Atlas Sinensis* (1659), a work that was published in Amsterdam by the Dutch cartographer Joan Blaeu (1596–1673) as volume VI of his *Atlas maior*.[27] In both *Tartarico* and *Atlas Sinensis*, Martini announced his plan to write a book on Chinese ancient history. This is why, as Oldenburg notes, even before its formal publication in 1658 in Munich, there had been much speculation about *Sinicae historiae*. The affirmative tone in Oldenburg's phrase, "I believe that you have already read," signals both the popularity of Martini's history and Oldenburg's knowledge of Milton's attention to the chronology issue.

Two interconnected polemics stand out in Oldenburg's epistle. The first is the chronological controversy noted in Martini's preface to *Tartarico*, that is, the conflict between Chinese chronology and "that which our scared writings record." According to Oldenburg, Martini "promise[d]," with his book on Chinese antiquity, to "reconcile" Eastern and scriptural chronologies and thereby "better protect the antiquity of the Mosaic and Adamite epoch." Hence lies the second polemic touched on by Oldenburg—the "pre-Adamites" doctrine proposed by the French theologian Isaac de la Peyrère in his *Prae-Adamitae* (1655), a radical thesis that directly challenged the "Adamite epoch."[28] La Peyrère's theory was so heretical that it attracted 19 refutations in 1656 alone, and the writer himself was forced to recant through conversion to Catholicism within one year after his work came to press.[29] Since Samuel Desmarets or Maresius (1599–1673), another notable French theologian, was "La Peyrère's strongest opponent," his *Refutatio fabulae praeadamiticae* (1656) should be numbered among those refutations.[30]

Chinese chronology appeared as a double-edged tool that could at once bolster and counteract La Peyrère's radical thesis. As Paul Cornelius notes, "conflicting

---

[26] Martini reached Macau in 1642 and left China for Rome in 1651 as the delegate of the Chinese Mission Superior to seek the pope's intervention in the "Rites controversy." *Sinicae historiae* was composed during his stay in Europe in 1655–58. There were two Latin editions of the work—Munich (1658) and Amsterdam (1659). My references come from the Munich edition.

[27] Martini's *Novus Atlas Sinensis* appeared later as part of Volume 10 of Blaeu's complete 11-volume *Atlas Major* (Amsterdam, 1662). See Johannes Keuning, "Blaeu's 'Atlas,'" *Imago Mundi* 14 (1959): 74–89, 86.

[28] La Peyrère's *Prae-Adamitae* (Amsterdam, 1655) or *Men before Adam* (London, 1656) was the first part of his *A Theological Systeme upon that Presupposition that Men were before Adam* (London, 1656). Queen Christina of Sweden paid for the publication of *Prae-Adamitae* in 1655. For La Peyrère's theory see Popkin, *Isaac La Peyrère*; 26–41; Poole, "An Anonymous English Preadamist"; and Philip Almond, "Adam, Pre-Adamites, and Extra-Terrestrial Beings in Early Modern Europe," *Journal of Religious History* 30.2 (2006): 163–74.

[29] For works issued in response to La Peyrère's thesis, see Allen, *Legend of Noah*, 136–37.

[30] Popkin, *Isaac La Peyrère*, 34.

sacred and profane chronologies gave evidence that the early dynasties of these countries [China included] had existed, and the early rulers of these countries had lived, in antediluvian times."[31] La Peyrère himself claimed the Chinese source of his pre-Adamic theory, arguing that Hebrew history "is wonderfully reconciled with all prophane Records whether ancient or new, to wit, those of the Caldeans, Egyptians, Sycthians, and Chinensians."[32] If scholars conceded Chinese antiquity, it was but a short step to accept the pre-Adamic thesis, which is why Martini believed that the Eastern chronology could be used to refute "the defender of the pre-Adamites." Martini, Oldenburg writes, "will shortly undertake a rejoinder" to Maresius's "reply" with evidence from Eastern history, a response that can "reconcile" Chinese and scriptural chronologies and thereby "protect the antiquity of the Mosaic and Adamite epoch."

As is shown in the word "reconcile," Milton and Oldenburg, resonating Donne and Stillingfleet, were also concerned with the "irreconcilableness" of the Chinese chronology. Milton's concern can be seen from his reply to Oldenburg dated June 25, 1656. In this letter, Milton confirms the "doubtless" eagerness a mere promise from the Jesuit historian has incited, especially among Oxford intellectuals, as he states:

> Meanwhile you yourself rightly observe that there are too many there [in Oxford] who by their empty quibbling contaminate both the divine and the human ... That ancient Chinese calendar, from the flood on, which you say is promised by the Jesuit Martini, is doubtless eagerly anticipated because of its novelty; but I do not see what authority or support it could add to the Mosaic books. (YP 7:492)

This response indicates certain knowledge of the chronology polemic. For Milton, it is simply out of "novelty" that people "eagerly anticipated" Martini's work, because he himself could not see "what authority or support" Chinese antiquity would "add to the Mosaic books." The doubt implied in the phrase "I do not see" is twofold: the skepticism is either directed at Oxford scholars or at Martini's promise of his book on Chinese antiquity. Oxford intellectuals are expecting to find in Martini's treatise evidence that can corroborate the Mosaic calendar. But Milton for his part cannot "see" the grounds for this hope, which might suggest that he considers the Chinese chronology either unreliable or a challenge to, rather than "support" for, the biblical timeline. But it is most likely that Milton discredits Chinese antiquity because of the credence it lent to the pre-Adamic doctrine, an association apparently much on Oldenburg's mind.[33] So Milton's comments

---

[31] Paul Cornelius, *Languages in Seventeenth and Early Eighteenth-Century Imaginary Voyages* (Geneva: Librarie Droz, 1965), 66.

[32] La Peyrère, *Theological Systeme* (1656), 18; and Popkin, *Isaac La Peyrère*, 47–48.

[33] Oldenburg's next extant letter (late 1656) tried to draw another response from Milton on the chronological issue, but Milton's reply did not survive. Poole, "Milton and Science," 22. Milton's disapproval of the pre-Adamic thesis could have something to do

show that he *did* reflect upon the chronological issue brought up by Oldenburg rather than that "he was not much interested in the matter" or that he considered "alternative chronologies" to be "branded as superfluous."[34] Even if Milton was skeptical about whether Chinese chronology could "add" any "authority or support" to the Mosaic books, he most likely felt obliged to justify his position against "too many" anticipants of Martini's work.

The Milton-Oldenburg correspondence thus captures two highly controversial and interconnected issues in the Renaissance: the pre-Adamic thesis and the chronological priority of the Chinese history. The debate sparked by Mendoza's chronicling of 243 Chinese kings and intensified by Scaliger's engagement with Mendoza's account in his *De emendatione temporum* (1583, 1598) was rekindled when Martini published his *Sinicae historiae* in 1658. Unlike Mendoza's brief relation and many misspellings, Martini's extensive account, with detailed facts, precise numbers, and accurate names, provides compelling evidence for Chinese antiquity. Martini himself admits that "there is hardly any nation in the whole World to be found comparable to the *Chinois* for their certainty in Chronology."[35] Vossius, who obviously read Martini's work, constantly used such superlative adjectives as "*accuratissima*" (most accurate) and "*certissima*" (most certain) to describe Chinese antiquity.[36]

Another main reason that Martini's *Sinicae historiae* inflamed the chronological controversy is that its record of Chinese history clashed with some major dates set down by Archbishop James Ussher (1581–1656) in his *Annales Veteris et Novi Testamenti* (1650–54), the most authoritative work on chronology in the seventeenth century. When summarizing Europe's century-long preoccupation with Chinese antiquity, the German philosopher Gottfried W. Leibniz (1646–1716) drew special attention to the discrepancy between Martini and Ussher's chronologies. Martini's work, Leibniz writes,

> contained a fair account of early imperial reigns the Chinese had established them ... [T]he chronology begins with Fuxi in 2952 BCE, which was troubling to many readers of Martini's work, because James Ussher's Biblical chronology

---

with Claudius Salmasius (1588–1653), his reputed adversary in the regicide debate. In his *De Armis Climactericis* (1648), Salmasius presents some astronomical and astrological materials that corroborate La Peyrère's thesis. La Peyrère wrote to thank Salmasius for researching on behalf of "*mes pre-Adamites.*" Mentioned by La Peyrère in his letter to De La Mare dated June 1660; quoted in Popkin, *Isaac La Peyrère*, 48.

[34] YP 7:491; and Poole, "Milton and Science," 22.

[35] Martini, *Sinicae historiae*, 10; and Webb, *Historical Essay*, 159. For Webb's endorsement of Chinese chronology and his eulogy of its sociopolitical system see, Rachel Ramsey, "China and the Ideal of Order in John Webb's *An Historical Essay ...*," *Journal of the History of Ideas* 62.3 (2001): 483–503; and Shou-yi Ch'en, "John Webb, a Forgotten Page in the Early History of Sinology in Europe," in Hsia ed., *The Vision of China in the English Literature*, 87–114.

[36] Vossius, *Dissertatio*, 44; and Webb, *Historical Essay*, 159.

had been published only a few years before and had persuaded many that creation had taken place in 4004 BCE, and the Noachian flood in 2349 BCE.[37]

Leibniz's use of "troubling" echoes Donne, Stillingfleet, and Oldenburg's "irreconcilable" and both adjectives capture the disturbances caused by the Chinese calendar. In his *Annales,* Ussher dated the creation in 4004 BC, the Noachian flood in 2349 BC, and the arrival of Abraham in Canaan in 2126 BC.[38] *Sinicae historiae* traces Chinese imperial lineage from King Fuxi (2952 BC) to Emperor Aidi (7–1 BC), and it relates a Chinese flood that occurred during the reign of the seventh emperor Yao or Jaus (2356–2255 BC).[39] As is pointed out by Mungello, Martini's chronological table largely agreed with that set down by the Chinese themselves then.[40] The historical data Martini revealed challenged both the flood and Abraham's rule dated by Ussher. Fuxi's reign preceded the biblical flood by about 600 years. Even admitting the legendary nature of Fuxi and dating from Yao or Yaus, a highly reputed wise king in Chinese recorded history, the Chinese were still an antediluvian people. As Webb put it, "*Martinius* and *Nieuhoff* by their late search find *Jaus* to have entred upon his Government over China sixty three years before the flood, though *Semedo* in his time will scarcely allow him twelve."[41] Further, the close proximity of the Chinese cataclysm (c. 2258–2207 BC) to the Noachian flood (2349 BC) suggests that the biblical deluge might be the Chinese flood, a conclusion actually drawn by Webb in his *An Historical Essay*. To corroborate this conclusion, Webb computes the Chinese chronology by the biblical temporal system. As he states:

> The Historical time therefore of the *Serians* begins two thousand and eight hundred forty seven years before CHRIST was born [2847 BC] … From the beginning therefore of the *Serian* Empire unto the end of this present year one thousand six hundred fifty eight after the birth of Christ [AD 1658], are numbered in the total four thousand five hundred five years [4,505]. Whereby appears, that according to the vulgar *Era*, which *Martinius* follows, and which makes from the Creation to the Flood of *Noah* one thousand six hundred fifty six years [1,656]; and from thence to the coming of CHRIST into the world

---

[37] Gottfried W. Leibniz, *Writings on China*, trans. and ed. Daniel J. Cook and Henry Rosemont Jr. (Chicago: Open Court, 1994), 15.

[38] The English biographer William Winstanley (c. 1628–98) noted that Ussher's work was "acknowledged by the learnedst Men of this Age for the admirable Method and Worth of it, not to have hitherto been parallel'd by any preceding writers." Winstanley, *England's Worthies* (London, 1660), 476–77. The orientalist Humphrey Prideaux (1648–1724) considered Ussher's *Annales* the "exactest and most perfect work of chronology that has been published." Prideaux, *The Old and New Testament Connected* (London, 1714–18), i.xxv.

[39] Martini, *Historiae sinicae*, 2–3, 26–27. For more on Martini's chronology see van Kley, "Europe's 'Discovery' of China"; and Mungello, *Curious Land*, 124–33.

[40] Mungello, *Curious Land*, 132.

[41] Webb, *Historical Essay*, 68.

two thousand two hundred ninety four years [2,294]; the Historical time of the *Chinois* begins several Ages, to wit, five hundred fifty three years [553] before the Universal Deluge, computing to the year one thousand six hundred fifty eight [AD 1658].[42]

All the dates in the quoted passage testify to the proximity between the Eastern and Western deluge. If the Chinese flood that happened during the reign of King Yao was the very biblical cataclysm, then the Eastern chronology necessarily "raised doubts about the antiquity of the Kingdom of Israel and its precedence over the pagan empires."[43] Simply stated, that both Fuxi and Yao ruled before the flood directly called into question Abraham's patriarchal status.

Since Ussher follows the temporal scheme of the Latin Vulgate, the discrepancy of the dates in the Vulgate and the Greek Septuagint renders Ussher's chronology all the more vulnerable to attack. The Septuagint puts the creation at 5200 BC and the flood at 2957 BC.[44] In his *A Disputation on Holy Scripture against the Papists*, Whitaker notes that the Greek calculation exceeds the Hebrew by 586 years," as "the Greek books reckon 2242 years from Adam in the beginning of the world to the flood," while "in the Hebrew books we see that there were no more than 1656."[45] The Vulgate timeline apparently cannot contain Chinese antiquity: Fuxi's rule [2952 BC] precedes the flood fixed by Ussher [2349 BC] by 603 years. Thus either there would be 2,259 (603 plus1656) years between Adam and Noah or Fuxi was numbered among those "long-lived pre-diluvian Patriarchs whose regularly recorded ages and generations provided accurate milestones back to the Creation."[46] Either case would directly challenge scriptural authority. Nor can the dates of the Septuagint provide convincing evidence against rival claims of antiquity. As Patrides notices, "to have accepted the Septuagint's chronology involved the inevitable conclusion that by the time of the Renaissance the world was, at the very least, 6500 years old—an obvious impossibility in view of the tradition that the world would end on or before its 6000th year."[47]

---

[42] Webb, *Historical Essay*, 52 By the first emperor, Webb means Fuxi, see 152–53. But Webb got Fuxi's reign wrong. According to Martini, Fuxi started to rule in about 2952 BC not 2847 BC as Webb states. By the "vulgar *Era* of CHRIST," Webb means the chronology of "the original *Hebrew* Text." Trigualt, Martini, Alvaro Semedo, and Jean Nieuhoff, all referred to the vulgar Era in their calculation of Chinese chronology. By comparison, Kircher and Vossius used the Greek Septuagint, which puts the Flood in 2256 BC. Webb, *Historical Essay*, 153–54. Ussher's date of the Noachian flood [2349 BC] is close to that in the Septuagint [2256]. Webb himself prefers the Vulgate to the Septuagint, *Historical Essay*, 156–57.

[43] Wilcox, *Measure of Times Past*, 209.

[44] See Jack Finegan, *Handbook of Biblical Chronology* (Princeton: Princeton UP, 1964), 191, 156, 184.

[45] Whitaker, *A Disputation*, 121.

[46] Hugh Trevor-Roper, *Catholics, Anglicans and Puritans* (London: Secker & Warburg, 1987), 157.

[47] Patrides, "Renaissance Estimates," 320.

Ussher's *Annales* adopts Scaliger's Julian system, so the conflict between the archbishop and Martini's dates also cast doubt upon the most advanced chronological theory in the Renaissance.[48] Scaliger's chronological system proved to be a double-edged framework. On the one hand, his invention of a pre-Creation "proleptic time" to accommodate the Egyptian history entails an implicit endorsement of its antiquity. On the other hand, if proleptic time could address the pre-Creation history of Egypt, it could surely assimilate the Chinese antediluvian chronology as well. This was actually the reading of La Peyrère. As Anthony Grafton notes, "His [Scaliger's] disapproval [of Chinese annals] is clear enough," but "one clever reader of his work, Isaac de la Peyrère would use the Chinese chronology Scaliger laid out, only slightly misquoted, as one of the bases for his own attack on the chronological authority of the Bible."[49] Given the equivocal nature of Scaliger's chronological theory, the authority of Ussher's chronicles appeared especially tenuous.

Martini's *Sinicae historiae* and Further Evidence of Milton's Awareness of the Chronological Debate

The broad consciousness of the conflict between Chinese and biblical chronologies raised by Mendoza's work accounts for the hot debate over Martini's *Sinicae historiae*.[50] To disentangle himself from a controversial issue, the Jesuit historian himself discredited the strict authenticity of Chinese antiquity.[51] But despite his disclaimer, most of Martini's contemporaries considered him a Chinese apologist or at least an objective ethnologist, for, David Wetsel says, "in the course of his exposition of the Chinese chronologies, Martini often comes off more as an ethnologist than as a Christian apologist." In fact, Wetsel observes, "Martini's real attitude toward the Chinese pretensions to great antiquity is difficult to assess. Often, he simply observes that, were the Chinese figures correct, it would be

---

[48] On Renaissance chronology see, Grafton, "Joseph Scaliger and Historical Chronology"; and "Dating History"; Patrides, "Renaissance Estimates of the Year of Creation"; Almond, *Adam and Eve in Seventeenth-Century Thought* (New York: Cambridge UP, 1999), 82–89; Paolo Rossi, *The Dark Abyss of Time: The History of the Earth and the History of Nations from Hooke to Vico*, trans. Lydia G. Cochrane (Chicago: U of Chicago P, 1984); Kenneth J. Knoespel, "Milton and the Hermeneutics of Time: Seventeenth Century Chronologies and the Science of History," *Studies in the Literary Imagination* 22 (1989); and Knoespel, "Newton in the School of Time: The Chronology of Ancient Kingdoms Amended and the Crisis of Seventeenth-Century Historiography," *The Eighteenth Century: Theory and Interpretation* 30 (1989): 19–41.

[49] Grafton, *Historical Chronology*, 405–6; see La Peyrere's own statement of his application of Scaliger's theory in *A Theological Systeme* (1656), 177ff. For La Peyrere's radical theory and its connection with the chronological issue see Wetsel, "Histoire de la Chine," 205–6.

[50] See more on this topic in Mungello, *Curious Land*, 124–27.

[51] Martini, *Sinicae historiae*, 26, 27.

necessary to revise radically the European version of history."[52] Wetsel's remarks are corroborated by Martini's own contemporaries. In his *Dissertatio*, Vossius writes, "the Interpreter [Martini] of the *Chinique* Chorography, a man that very well understood himself, writ far more moderately of the perfections of this people, than he thought."[53] Webb was more outspoken, asserting that if Martini who had "in a manner from his cradle to his grave studied their [Chinese] Antiquities ... written what he thought, and declar[ed] his mind plainly," there should have been less doubt about Eastern chronology.[54] The midcentury chronological disputation arose chiefly from this perception of the objectivity of Martini's work.

The middle of the seventeenth century witnessed various attempts to reconcile Chinese antiquity with scriptural chronology. In chapter 47 of his *Artificia Hominum, Admiranda Naturae in Sina et Europa* (1655), Adam Preyel deals with the incompatibility between "*Chronologia sinae*" and the Mosaic history.[55] Whereas Preyel claims the priority of Chinese history, Brian Walton (1600–61) seeks to "synchronize" Eastern and biblical timelines in his *Polyglot Bible* (1657).[56] Vossius was the most explicit Chinese apologist, for he expressly called the Chinese "a race of men by far the most skilled in letters of all the peoples than ever were," and who "preserve a continued History compiled from their monuments, and annual exploits of four thousand five hundred years [4,500]. Writers they have more antient than even *Moses* himself."[57] But despite this praise, Vossius nevertheless insisted on the primacy of Hebrew history, trying to accommodate Eastern antiquity by insisting on a Septuagint-based chronology in his *De septuaginta interpretibus* (1661). In addition, Vossius famously disputed with the Leiden historian Georg Horn (1620–70) over Chinese chronology.[58] Despite his initial disapproval, Horn ultimately admitted the authenticity of Martini's account in his *Arca Noae* (1666).[59]

Webb stood out as the most adamant defender of Martini's *Sinicae historiae*. For Webb, Martini "in his own thoughts, had an higher opinion of this people [the Chinese], than he deemed fitting to be vulgarly made known." Webb corroborates this high estimate by citing Martini's own discussion of his sources.[60] Martini himself writes that "the History of it by the *Chinois* themselves even from all Antiquity written, comprehendeth almost three thousand years before the birth of CHRIST, as more evidently by the Epitomy and Chronology out of their Annals

---

[52] Wetsel, "Histoire de la China," 207, 208.
[53] Vossius, *Dissertatio*, 45; and Webb, *Historical Essay*, 58.
[54] Webb, *Historical Essay*, 58.
[55] Adam Preyel, *Artificia Hominum, Admiranda Naturae in Sina et Europa* (Francofurti ad Moenum, 1655).
[56] Brian Walton, *Biblia Sacra Polyglotta* (London, 1657), Prolegomenon II, 9.
[57] Webb, *Historical Essay*, 48.
[58] For works yielded out of this controversy see van Kley, "Europe's 'Discovery' of China," 364, no. 18.
[59] Georg Horn, *Arca Noae sive historia imperiorum et regnorum* (Leiden, 1666).
[60] Webb, *Historical Essay*, 57–58.

appears."[61] Also, Martini declares that his work "epitomized their [Chinese] History from their Original Annals, and innumerable their other Books, yet extant even at this day amongst them from their first beginning to be a Nation."[62] Further, the Jesuit historian's description of the manner in which the Chinese composed their chronicles also suggests his trust in their authenticity. Martini notes that "it is unlawfull for any but the Historiographer Royal to intermeddle therewith, and criminal also, for the Writer of the succeeding times, to alter the preceding History."[63] This strict supervision over history compiling as described by Martini, Webb argues, is confirmed by Jean Nieuhoff (1618–72), steward to the 1655–57 Dutch embassy to Beijing. In his *An Embassy ... to the Grand Tartar Cham Emperour of China* (1669), Nieuhoff relates that "The Emperours of China"

> have evermore laboured to have the Annals of their Empire written by the most learned of all their philosophers, whom they chuse and oblige to that end, which makes this people glory, that there is nothing that surpasseth the truth of their Histories, and particularly those which are written from the two thousand, two hundred, and seventh year before the birth of Christ [2207 BC].[64]

This rigorous surveillance over historical writing ensures the unparalleled "certainty" of Chinese antiquity.[65] Given the authenticity of Chinese history as it is verified by both Martini and Nieuhoff, Webb claims, we should "make great use of Martinius his Authority."[66]

In addition to his correspondence with Oldenburg, Milton's awareness of the contemporary chronological debate can also be conjectured from his unusual attention to chronology at around the same time he discussed the Chinese calendar in his correspondences with Oldenburg dated June 1656. Oldenburg's epistle apparently set Milton considering more seriously the chronology problematic or to refresh an old concern with the subject. Nine months after receiving Oldenburg's letter, Milton wrote to Emeric Bigot on March 24, 1657, requesting his addressee to buy him some works by "Byzantine Historians" (YP 7:498). Among the seven historians mentioned by Milton, four signal his interest in the chronological issue at this particular point of his life.[67] Constantine Manasses's (d. 1187) *Epitome of History* is a metrical chronicle of the world from the creation to AD 1081,

---

[61] Webb, *Historical Essay*, 47.
[62] Webb, *Historical Essay*, 50; see Martini, *Sinicae historiae*, "Ad Lectorem."
[63] Webb, *Historical Essay*, 158; for Martini's own statement see *Sinicae historiae*, "Ad Lectorem," and 10.
[64] Webb, *Historical Essay*, 158.
[65] Martini, *Sinicae historiae*, 10.
[66] Webb, *Historical Essay*, 50.
[67] Around the time Milton wrote to Bigot, King Louis XIV of France (1643–1715) sponsored the publication of the first collective edition of Byzantine historians in Paris. The whole collection started in 1645 and completed until 1711. See David Masson, *The Life of John Milton: Narrative in Connextion with the Political, Ecclesiastical, and Literary History of his Time*, 7 vols., vol. 5. 1654–60 (London: MacMillan, 1877), 285–86.

and Michael Glycas's (c. 1118–1200) *Annals* starts from the Creation to the death of Alexiss I Commenus (1118). The third chronological treatise requested by Milton was St. Theophanes's *Chronography* (810–15), a work that deals with the accession of Diocletian (284) down to Michael I (813). St. Theophanes's work is a continuation of his friend George Syncellus's *Extract of Chronography*, which documents events from the Creation to 284. The Syncellus-Theophanes's combination, as the last and the most extensive chronology in Greek, represents, as Cyril Mango says, the "greatest achievement of Byzantine historical scholarship."[68] In 873–75 the papal librarian Anastasius Bibiliothecarius (c. 810–78), the fourth chronologer referred to by Milton in the Bigot letter, produced a Latin chronology out of the writings of Theophanes, Syncellus, and Nicephorus, which helped spread the Syncellus-Theophanes's synthesis to western Europe. Syncellus-Theophanes's chronology proved of vital importance to Scaliger's radical theory and the early modern chronological controversy in particular. Milton may have hoped that a careful perusal of the original sources might lead to findings that could refute Scaliger's proleptic time.[69]

Milton's concern with Chinese antiquity suggests itself in his interest in Eastern geography as well.[70] This interest can be surmised from his letter to Peter Heimbach dated November 8, 1656, written five months after he received Oldenburg's epistle on Martini's *Historia sinicae* and eight months after he wrote to Bigot on Byzantine historians. The proximity of these dates indicates their possible connection with the chronological issue. In this letter to Heimbach, Milton repeats his former request about the purchase of some atlases. After directing his correspondent to "find out the lowest price of the book," he says,

> I beg you to do me the further favor to find out, so that you can tell me when you return, how many volumes there are in the whole work and which of the two editions, Blaeu's or Jansen's, is the fuller and more accurate. This I hope to hear from you personally on your speedy return, rather than by another letter. (YP 7:495)

The urgency and earnestness expressed in his final line shows the impact of the chronological polemic upon Milton's mind.[71] "Blaeu" refers both to Willem

---

[68] Quoted in *The Chronography of George Synkellos: A Byzantine Chronicle of Universal History from the Creation*, trans. William Adler and Paul Tuffin (Oxford: Oxford UP, 2002), xxix.

[69] Salmasius might have played, again, a part in Milton's interest in Scaliger's innovation. Salmasius took the professorship formerly held by Scaliger at Leiden in 1631 and was on intimate terms with Isaac Casaubon, Scaliger's close correspondent. In addition, Milton discusses Scaliger's doctrine of "number" in his *Art of Logic* (1672), though interest in number does not necessarily indicate an equal interest in chronology (YP 8:233).

[70] For Milton and geography, see Gilbert, *A Geographical Dictionary of Milton*; and Robert R. Cawley, *Milton and the Literature of Travel* (Princeton: Princeton UP, 1951).

[71] Boleslaw Szcześniak, "The Seventeenth Century Maps of China: An Inquiry into the Compilations of European Cartographers," *Imago Mundi* 13 (1956): 116–36.

Janszoon Blaeu (1571–1638), who founded one of Europe's greatest cartographic publishing firms in 1599, and his son Johannes Blaeu (1596–1673), who inherited his father's business and became the official cartographer of the Dutch East India Company. The Blaeus had two chief competitors: Henricus Hondius (1563–1612) and Jan Jansen or Jansson (1588–1664)—Jansen joined and took over Hondius's map-making business in 1630. The "Jansen" in Milton's letter means this very rival of the Blaeus.[72] One salient feature that distinguishes the Blaeus' atlas is its incorporation of Martini's *Atlas Sinensis* in the 11-volume *Atlas Maior* (1662). In the Preface to volume V of his *Atlas* (1654), Blaeu announced the title of the sixth volume, that is, *Novus Atlas Sinensis* (1655), as he remarks:

> But look, while I was occupied herewith (i.e., with the Ancient Geography of Ptolemy), the Reverend Father Martinus Martinius comes from India, and brings with him the figurations and descriptions of the Empire of China. He insists that I print and publish these. Therefore I leave off all other things for the time being, in order to push forward this work.[73]

Including a general map of China and 15 maps of individual Chinese provinces, the Blaeu-Martini atlas "gives the most complete description of China of the time" possessed by the West.[74] In his earnest resolve to purchase the best atlases he could lay hand on, Milton was informed enough to know the authority of the Blaeu-Martini atlas in studying the Eastern country. Jansen's *China Veteribus Sinarum Regio nunc Incolis Tame dicta* (1636) was almost identical to Blaeu's, which might explain why Milton wanted to know which atlas (presumably of the Far East), "Blaeu's or Jansen's, is the fuller and more accurate."

The Chronological Polemic in Milton's Image of Prehistorical Time

What bothers Milton, Oldenburg, and other Oxford scholars is the ethnocentric, rather than legendary, feature of the Chinese history as is recorded in Martini's *Sinicae historiae*. Markley denies Milton's concern with Chinese chronology chiefly because of its affiliation with "Euhemerism," an approach to history originated from the Greek historian Euhemerus (330–260 BC) who interpreted gods and demigods as humans deified for some symbolic purposes. For Markley, Martini's work belongs to the euhemeristic historiography represented by Sir Walter Ralegh, Henry Issacson, and Isaac Newton, a tradition that "was pressed into the service of shoring up arguments for the historical and conceptual primacy of Mosaic history against the threat posed by China." In other words, the euhemeristic historiographical methodology was exploited by early modern

---

[72] C. Koeman, "Life and Works of Willem Janszoon Blaeu: New Contributions to the Study of Blaeu, Made during the Last Hundred Years," *Imago Mundi* 26 (1972): 9–16.
[73] Keuning, "Blaeu's 'Atlas'," 86.
[74] Keuning, "Blaeu's 'Atlas'," 87.

thinkers, Martini included, to assert the "historical and conceptual primacy of Mosaic history" over Chinese antiquity. Since the euhemeristic tradition is "both theologically and politically suspect," Markley argues, "Milton stands willfully outside" of it.[75] Markley rightly recognizes the political and theological implications of euhemerism, but what is problematic about his argument is that he aligns Martini's work with the euhemeristic tradition and denies Milton's interest in Chinese history on the grounds of this alignment. As is shown in his skepticism towards euhemerism in his *The History of Britain* (1670) (YP 5:4–5, 8–9), Milton did distance himself from the euhemeristic discourse, but not because of its apologetic implications as Markley claims; instead, it is on the grounds of its legendary nature that Milton discredits this methodology. Nor did Martini's work belong to the euhemeristic apologetic tradition represented by Ralegh, Issacson, and Newton. Rather, Martini was, as most contemporaries viewed him, a Chinese apologist. Far from a euhemeristic work, *Sinicae historiae* draws upon verifiable historical records, most of which were either noted or verified by the early modern reporters of China. Martini's work features, instead of gods or demigods, sage kings of flesh and blood, such as Fuxi, Yao, Shun, and Yu, wise men whose reigns and achievements were documented as physical and historical facts. In their *Journals*, Ricci and Trigault draw special attention to the ethnocentric feature of the Chinese history. As they put it,

> their [Chinese] history of more than four thousand years ... really is a record of good deeds done on behalf of their country and for the common good. The same conclusion might also be drawn from the books of rare wisdom of their ancient philosophers. These books are still extant and are filled with most salutary advice on training men to be virtuous.[76]

For instance, King Fuxi was famous for both his creation of Chinese pictorial characters and the composition of *Yijing* or the *Book of Changes*, a work that seeks to explain the creation and change of the world through divination and mathematical principles. The much-applauded feats of King Yao in channeling the Chinese flood found its way into Martini and Webb's works.[77]

Like most of his contemporaries who viewed Martini as a Chinese rather than Christian apologist, Milton considered *sinicae historiae* a historical rather than euhemeristic work. As Webb notices, despite his own disclaimer, Martini repeatedly emphasizes the objective and historical aspect of the Chinese history. The awareness of the irrefutable historicity of non-Christian histories like Chinese antiquity, I would suggest, obliged Milton to accentuate the literal and historical instead of euhemeristic or apocalyptic dimensions of Hebrew history.[78] On the

---

[75] Markely, *The Far East*, 72.
[76] Ricci-Trigault, *Journals*, 93.
[77] Martini, *Sinicae historiae*, 39–40, and Webb, *Historical Essay*, 60.
[78] For Milton's apocalyptic and millenarian thoughts see the collection of articles in Juliet Cummins, ed., *Milton and the Ends of Time* (Cambridge: Cambridge UP, 2003).

one hand, to regard Hebrew history in terms of euhemeristic myth or apocalyptic prophecy is far from a sound strategy to negotiate the antiquity of Chinese history or any other history catalogued in Adam's overview. When Hebrew history appears side by side with a host of histories composed of battles and empires no less famous than those biblical ones, it would be a more effective apologetic tactic to tone down rather than highlight its mythical or prophetic implications. On the other hand, Milton is too sophisticated a thinker to classify as mythical such a clearly defined cultural and geographical place as China, to regard Martini's patently ethnographical work as euhemeristic, or to appeal to a "theologically and politically suspect" framework to confront a controversial problem that has aroused the curiosity of, as he says, "too many" Oxford scholars. So Milton, recalling his contemporaries, saw Chinese chronology as ethnographically factual, a perception implied rather than explicitly articulated in *Paradise Lost*.

A cosmopolitan engagement with alternative systems of time, however, does not contradict the millenarian purpose apparently marking Milton and La Peyrère's conception of history.[79] Cosmopolitanism and millenarianism signify two different conceptual categories. Whereas cosmopolitanism indicates intellectual flexibility and ethical generosity, millenarianism is a spiritual belief in the Christian prophecy of the end of the world. Also, while millenarianism focuses on the future, seventeenth-century chronological debate fixates upon the past—it is not the future but the beginning of the world proposed by other histories that unsettled committed Christians like Donne and Milton.

To "assert Eternal Providence / And justify the ways of God to men," Milton undertakes, above all, to establish the priority of biblical chronology, an attempt consistent with his general conviction of the primacy of the scriptural economy. In his *The Christian Doctrine*, Milton expressly asserts the universal humanity represented by Adam, "for Adam, the parent and head of all men, either stood or fell as a representative of the whole human race" (YP 6:384). For Milton, the second Adam is a universal signifier too, because the communion of the members of Christ "need not be subject to spatial considerations: it includes people from many remote countries, and from all ages since the creation of the world" (YP 6:500). Since Christ is the head of the Church, he observes in *The Likeliest Means to Remove Hirelings out of the Church* (1659), "the Christian Church is universal; not ti'd to nation, dioces or parish, but consisting of many particular churches complete in themselves" (YP 7:292).

The chronological background brings to light Milton's image of a unifying temporal framework based on scriptural chronology. Much has been written on the time scheme in *Paradise Lost*, but rather than a systematic timeline, critics tend to either deny a temporal paradigm at all or focus on "small-scale readings

---

[79] Thomas Amorose, "Milton the Apocalyptic Historian: Competing Genres in *Paradise Lost*, Books XI–XII," *Milton Studies* 17 (1983): 141–62.

of chronology."[80] Grant MacColley's 31-day, Galbraith M. Crump's 28-day, and Alastair Fowler and Gunnar Qvarnström's 33-day timelines, though aiming at a uniform paradigm, speak to Milton's microcosmic rather his macrocosmic architecture of time.[81] Anthony K. Welch explicitly claims that "Milton rejects a single overarching chronology in favor of several" or "a set of small-scale chronological templates."[82] In fact, what Milton attempts to set up in his epic poem, instead of local time frames or several timelines, is an abstract unifying framework. Ussher dates human history from the creation of the world (4004 BC) to the destruction of Jerusalem (70 AD). In contrast, Milton's epic poem traces history from an abysmal eternity to an apocalyptic future, because, as Peter Sterry puts it, "in this light of eternity alone, is the Works of God seen aright, in the entire piece, in the whole design, from the beginning to the end."[83] George W. Whiting notes that "Milton was not interested in such detail" as "the exact date of the creation of the world and the number of years in each period."[84] Milton's privileging of general over particular time, I suggest, arises from apologetic considerations, one of which is the chronological issue. An overarching framework allows him both to establish the universality of scriptural chronology and to incorporate alternative accounts of time.

The comprehensive timeline Milton represents in his epic poem is marked by two distinctive yet interconnected epochs: the Creation and the Fall.[85] Whereas the Creation distinguishes between *pre-Creation* and *post-Creation* time, the Fall differentiates *prehistorical* from *historical* time that marks the birth of

---

[80] Anthony K. Welch, "Reconsidering Chronology in *Paradise Lost*," *Milton Studies* 41 (2002): 1–17, 4. For critics who deny a timeframe in *Paradise Lost* see Isabel G. MacCaffrey, *"Paradise Lost" as "Myth"* (Cambridge, MA: Harvard UP, 1959), 45; and Anne D. Ferry, *Milton's Epic Voice: The Narrator in "Paradise Lost"* (Cambridge, MA: Harvard UP, 1963), 47.

[81] On critics who seek to identify a temporal framework in *Paradise Lost* see, Welch, "Reconsidering Chronology"; Grant MacColley, *Paradise Lost: An Account of Its Growth and Major Origins, with a Discussion of Milton's Use of Sources and Literary Patterns* (Chicago: U of Chicago P, 1940), 16–17; Gunnar Qvarnstrom, *The Enchanted Palace: Some Structural Aspects of Paradise Lost* (Stockholm: Almqvist & Wiksell, 1967); *The Poems of John Milton*, ed. John Carey and Alastair Fowler (London: Longmans, 1968), 443–46; Galbraith M. Crump, *The Mystical Design of "Paradise Lost"* (Lewisburg, PA: Bucknell UP, 1975), 163–72; Douglas A. Northrop, "The Double Structure of *Paradise Lost*," *Milton Studies* 12 (1978): 75–90; Sherry L. Zivley, "The Thirty-Three Days of *Paradise Lost*," *Milton Quarterly* 34:4 (2000): 117–27; and Knoespel, "Milton and the Hermeneutics of Time."

[82] Welch, "Reconsidering Chronology," 14, 15.

[83] Peter Sterry, *A Discourse of the Freedom of the Will* (London, 1675), 166.

[84] George W. Whiting, *Milton and This Pedant World* (Austin: U of Texas P, 1958), 183.

[85] The Noachian flood was also a hotly contested point in seventeenth-century chronological controversy, but since it is a complex topic that merits a separate treatment, this study focuses only on the Creation and the Fall.

human history. *Prehistorical* time consists of three subcategories— pre-Creation, heavenly, and paradisiacal time. *Pre-Creation* time means the unfathomable period before the Creation, an epoch represented by Milton in the exaltation of the Son, the heavenly war, and the fall of the rebellious angels. Both *heavenly time* and the *paradisiacal time* indicate the time Adam and Eve enjoyed in the prelapsarian Eden. Accordingly, *post-Creation* time refers to what happens after the creation of Adam and Eve, and it includes both *paradisiacal* and *historical* time. Most scholars tend to confine Milton's temporal image to post-Creation time, neglecting his extensive account of the pre-Creation epoch.[86] Although some do touch on "the long Paradisal time," they do not associate it with the chronological issue.[87]

What distinguishes Milton's representation of scriptural chronology is his identification of prehistorical, especially pre-Creation time, an apologetic strategy that enables him at once to assert the primacy of the biblical timeline and to refute Scaliger's "proleptic" time that seemed to support Egyptian and Chinese antiquities. Milton's point is clear: since profane histories start to date from historical time, the prehistorical time unique to Hebrew history can assimilate any system of time. To illustrate the certainty of prehistorical time, Milton adopts three apologetic tactics. First, he uses the epic genre and the principle of causality to accord biblical chronology with both a universal scope and a consistent timeline. Second, he employs the narrative technique of multiple points of view to convey the certainty of the creation and thereby pre-Creation time. Third, he takes an analogous approach to the supernatural heavenly time, and uses Adam and Eve's recollections to describe the historicity of paradisiacal time.

Milton employs the epic genre and the causal principle it entails to draw out the universality of the biblical timeline. Given Martini's powerful presentation of Chinese history, a mere literal exegesis or a catalogue of the biblical timetable as is represented in Ussher's *Annales* appeared a feeble apologetic tactic. Compared with abstract chronological doctrine or those "useless records of either uncertaine, or unsound antiquity" (YP 1:624), an epic dramatization seems a more potent means to "assert Eternal Providence," since the genre itself gives the subject matter a cosmic amplitude. Milton might have derived the idea of representing the Mosaic history within a dramatic framework from Hugo Grotius's (1583–1645) *Adamus Exul* (1601) and Guillaume de Salluste Du Bartas's (1544–90) *La Sepmaine ou Creation du monde* (1578), as well as its sequel *La Seconde Semaine ou enfance du monde* (1584) as is translated by Joshua Sylvester.[88] But

---

[86] On Milton's representation of history and time see, Achsah Guibbory, *The Map of Time: Seventeenth-Century English Literature and Ideas of Pattern in History* (Urbana: U of Illinois P, 1986), 169–211; and Marshall Grossman, *"Authors to Themselves": Milton and the Revelation of History* (Cambridge: Cambridge UP, 1987).

[87] Welch, "Reconsidering Chronology," 8; and Helen Gardner, *A Reading of "Paradise Lost"* (Oxford: Clarendon, 1965), 39.

[88] For Milton's indebtedness to Hugo Grotius's *Adamus Exul* see, Evans, *Paradise Lost and the Genesis Tradition*, 207–16; for Milton's source from Du Bartas see Whiting, *Pedant World*, 186–89.

the universal history dramatized in *Paradise Lost* proves most compelling, for here, as Patrides says, "we have the most successful attempt in poetry to fuse the essential aspects of Christian view of history into a magnificent whole" and "we have the universalistic and Christocentric view of history."[89] Moreover, the universal dimension registered in the epic genre is reinforced by the causal principle Milton attributes to Hebrew history. In chapter 23 of his *Poetics*, Aristotle claims that unlike epic poetry, history lacks a causal plot because it deals with episodic events.[90] But in *Paradise Lost*, Milton dramatizes what happens before, during, and after the fall by fusing together the historical and epic conventions, a rhetorical maneuver that enables him to ascribe a causal unity to Hebrew history. In truth, the epic genre itself encodes the cause-effect dynamic. Unlike tabular chronicles marked by discontinuous gaps and blanks, an epic dramatization, by thrusting into the middle of the events at the outset, aims at bringing into sharper focus the function of the middle to join the beginning and the end into a causal whole. An imaginative narrative plot that encodes causal necessity and probability, and an epic form that integrates rather than fragments those epochal biblical events into an organic whole, combine to generate a universal template that has the capacity to accommodate all histories.

Creation was the point by which biblical time was reckoned. Milton identifies pre-Creation time in both his prose work and epic poem. The imagination of an inscrutable pre-Creation epoch was a staple feature of Renaissance chronological thinking. Scaliger's "proleptic time" addressed the time "assumed before the Mosaic computation." For Donne, since "we are utterly disprovided of any history of the Worlds Creation," we should "defend and maintain this Book of *Moses* to be Historical, and therefore literally to be interpreted."[91] But we should, Donne suggests, allegorically interpret those "dayes mention'd before the Creation of these Planets which made days."[92] Milton also believed in pre-Creation time, as he observes in *The Christian Doctrine*, "there is certainly no reason why we should conform to the popular belief that motion and time, which is the measure of motion, could not, according to our concepts of 'before' and 'after,' have existed before this world was made" (YP 6:313–14). But for Milton pre-Creation "eternity" means none other than "antiquity." As he puts it, "all the words which the scriptures use to mean eternity often mean only earthly times, or antiquity" (YP 6:143). By equating "eternity" with "antiquity," he at once affirms the historical status of the Mosaic books and endlessly prolongs biblical time. In addition, Milton also expresses the Creation's epochal status through memory, an image that gives a fundamentally allegorical or mythical story a temporal cast. After Raphael finishes

---

[89] Patrides, *Milton and the Christian Tradition*, 259.

[90] See Leon Golden and O. B. Hardison Jr., *Aristotle's Poetics: A Translation and Commentary for Students of Literature* (Tallahassee: UP of Florida, 1981); and Eric MacPhail, "The Plot of History from Antiquity to the Renaissance," *Journal of the History of Ideas* 62.1 (2001): 1–16.

[91] Donne, *Essayes in Divinity*, 21.

[92] Donne, *Essayes*, 38–39.

relating the heavenly war, Adam "desire[s] to know" "how this World … first began" "before his memory" (7.61–66). In response to Raphael's account, Adam offers to "[relate] what was done / Ere my remembrance" (8.203–04). Here human memory serves as the criterion that marks "this transient world, the race of time" from timeless eternity.

To demystify the biblical creation story and thereby prove the certainty of pre-Creation time, Milton turns to the narrative technique of multiple points of view. He puts the oppositional view in the mouth of Satan. For the fallen angel, the Creation is a "strange point and new," for, he interrogates, "who saw / When this creation was? Remember'st thou / Thy making, while the Maker gave thee being?" (5.855–59) To refute Satan's heretical view, Milton presents five alternative accounts of the Creation given respectively by Eve (4.449–91), Adam (8.203–16), the royal guard Uriel (3.709–35), the loyal Abdiel (5.823–25), and Raphael (7.174–557) the "Divine Interpreter" (7.72). So five witnesses who have either seen or heard about God's creation of the world are enlisted to reinforce the certainty of the Creation, a certainty that, in turn, lends credence to events that took place in pre-Creation time. The implicit message is that, there is no need to posit a "proleptic" time as Scaliger did; the pre-Creation abyss in scriptural chronology is eternal enough to contain any profane histories, Egyptian and Chinese antiquities included.

While pre-Creation time allows Milton to counter Scaliger's proleptic time that tended to bolster Egyptian and Chinese chronologies, supernatural *heavenly time* has the miraculous power to incorporate any system of time. Rather than a fictitious category, however, Milton's heavenly time or "Heav'n's great Year" (5.583) can be analogously understood. Milton's "great Year" derives but differs from the "Great Year" described by Plato in *Timaeus*. Whereas the Platonic Great Year is a temporal system based on the cyclic movement of heavenly bodies, Milton's is an analytical concept used to describe divine time.[93] Milton defines time as that which "applied / To motion, measures all things durable / By present, past, and future" (5.580–82). But divine motion cannot be described in temporal time, since "the speed of Gods / Time count not" (10.90–91) and "Immediate are the Acts of God, more swift / Than time or motion" (7.176–77). The uncountable nature of time in heaven is symbolized in "a Cave / Within the Mount of God, fast by this Throne, / Where light and darkness in perpetual round / Lodge and dislodge by turns." This "perpetual" cycle of light and darkness "makes through Heav'n / Grateful vicissitude, like Day and Night" (6.4–8). "Heaven's great Year" is proposed by Milton precisely to address this unique species of time. To preempt charges of inventing a mythical category, Milton tries to show that heavenly time, though uncountable and unutterable, can nevertheless be comprehended analogously, an approach summarily articulated by Raphael. To explicate "what surmounts the reach / Of human sense," Raphael says, "I shall delineate so, / By

---

[93] Plato, *Timaeus*, trans. R. G. Bury, The Loeb Classical Library (London: William Heinemann, 1929), 75–83; for the association between Platonic and Miltonic Great Year see Albert R. Cirillo, "Noon-Midnight and the Temporal Structure of *Paradise Lost*," *English Literary History* 29.4 (1962): 372–95, 373.

lik'ning spiritual to corporeal forms, / As may express them best" (5.571–74). Raphael himself describes heaven's "Grateful vicissitude, like Day and Night." Similarly, God remarks that "two days are past, / Two days, as we compute the days of Heav'n" (6.684–85). The comparative prepositions "like" and "as" indicate the analogous approach to divine time.

Like pre-Creation and heavenly time, *paradisiacal time* is peculiar to Hebrew history and signals the amplitude of biblical chronology to contain profane histories. To convey the certainty of this special species of prehistorical time, Milton articulates it in terms of human experience. In book IV, Eve tells Adam what has happened on her first wakening up to her being (4.449–91), a story cast in the form of recollection. Likewise, when conversing with Raphael, Adam recalls a series of events that occurred after his first coming into being (8.253–71): the dream of his own creation (8.286–91), the guidance by the "Heav'nly vision" (8.356) to paradise (8.319–21), God's prohibition about the Tree of Knowledge (8.323–33), his expostulation with God about a fit society (8.403–11), as well as his envisioning of Eve's creation (8.495–99). Thus rather than an abstract concept, paradisiacal time is depicted as a series of real events recollected by the first pair, lived experiences that attest to its physicality and therefore authenticity.

The "Seat / Of mightiest Empire": Milton's Negotiation with Chinese Antiquity

The Fall, another distinctive epochal moment in scriptural chronology, symbolizes the starting-point of *historical time*. Whereas *pre-Creation* time is corroborated by five narrators and *prelapsarian time* vividly registers in Adam and Eve's lived experiences, *postlapsarian history* finds an eloquent articulation in Adam's survey of world histories. A key objective of the historical revelation featured in book XI is to bring out the universal dimension of Hebrew history, a universality physically expressed in the global sweep of Adam's prophetic "visions." Standing on the "highest" hilltop in Paradise, Adam obtains a "clearest Ken" of "The Hemisphere of Earth," which "Stretcht out to the amplest reach of prospect lay" (11:377–80).

China and the Far East figure prominently in the global picture outlined in Adam's overview. Under Michael's guidance, Adam perceives,

> ... the Seat
> Of mightiest Empire, from the destin'd Walls
> Of *Cambalu*, seat of *Cathaian Can*
> And *Samarchand* by *Oxus*, *Temir's* Throne,
> To *Paquin* of *Sinaean* Kings, and thence
> To *Agra* and *Lahor* of great *Mogul*
> Down to the golden *Chersonese*, or where
> The *Persian* in *Ecbatan* sat ... (11.386–93)

The long list of place names in this passage graphically conjures a panoramic view of the whole known world. Standing on the "highest" hilltop in Paradise and looking towards where the Sun rises, Adam marks out, above all, the Great Wall of China that divides "Cambalu, seat of Cathaian Can" and "Paquin of Sinaean Kings." Shifting his eyes from the Far East southwards, he catches sight of India and the golden Chersonese; northward the Russian capital *"Mosco"* (11.395) comes into view. In Eurasia, he perceives "Temir's" Throne in "Samarchand," and "Ecbatan," the royal seat of the Persian shah. Along the eastern coast of Africa, he sees *"Ercoco," "Mombaza,* and *Quiloa,* and *Melinda* / And *Sofala"* (11.398–400). African cities along the Mediterranean Sea such as *"Morocco* and *Algiers,* and *Tremisen"* (11.404) are also captured by Adam's sweeping glance. The westward survey rests but briefly upon *"Rome,"* a formidable city that "was to sway / The World" (11.405–6). Moreover, though his eyes cannot reach the world across the oceans, Adam zooms into focus "in spirit" the rich cities of *"Peru," "Mexico," "Guiana,"* and *"El Dorado"* in western India (11.407–11). This string of place names sets forth a grand picture of a globalized world.

The literary model of Adam's global trip could be Ruggiero's cosmic journey in Ludovico Ariosto's *Orlando Furioso* (1516).[94] After escaping Alcina's court and deciding "to complete the circle he had started, so as to girdle the earth, like the sun," Ruggiero "chose to take a different way back" to the west. China is the starting point of this return trip: "On his journey he saw Cathay to one side and to the other Mangiana, as he passed over great Quinsai [Hangzhou]."[95] Thus the far-ranging journeys depicted by both Ariosto and Milton feature the emergence of a globalized world and the prominence of the Far East in this world.

Adam's prophetic survey in Book XI encapsulates both global geography and world histories. To illustrate the global scope of Adam's cosmic survey, Milton uses the coordinates of history and geography, a topos made popular by the "universal history" project. Flourishing in France in the sixteenth century, the universal history program was an intellectual movement that sought to reassess the historical sources of theology, jurisdiction, and history against a uniform chronological standard.[96] Cartographers who attempted to encompass the world within a single grid provided a conceptual model for the Universalists to comprehend all histories within a unifying template. Jean Bodin's *Method for the Easy Comprehension of History* (1566) marks the high water of this project. For Bodin, "the arrangement of history" is more easily understood via an "analogy to cosmography," for "like a man who wishes to understand cosmography, the historian must devote some study to a representation of the whole universe in

---

[94] Milton reread Sir John Harrington's translation of *Orlando Furioso* in 1642; see J. Milton French, ed. *The Life Records of John Milton*, 5 vols. (New Brunswick, NJ: Rutgers UP, 1949–58), vol. 2, 78–69.

[95] Ariosto, *Orlando Furioso*, 100, 101.

[96] For Renaissance works on universal history see Francois Baudouin, *De institutione historiae universae et eius cum jurisprudentia conjunctione* (Paris, 1561); Melchior Cano, *De locis theologicis* (Salamanca, 1563); and Jean Bodin, *Methodus* (Paris, 1566) or its English translation *Method for the Easy Comprehension of History*.

a small map."⁹⁷ By coordinating history and geography in the same template, Bodin says, one can "join to observations of the past reflections for the future and compare the causes of obscure things, studying the efficient causes and the ends of each as if they were placed beneath their eyes."⁹⁸ In the preface to his *Principal Navigations*, Hakluyt explicitly calls "Geographie and chronologie" "the Sunne and the Monne, the right eye and the left of all history" (PN 1: xxxix). Milton subscribed to the same view. He observes in *The History of Britain* (1670) that without recording one's history, one would "be ever Children in the Knowledge of Times and Ages" (YP 5:2). In *Of Education* (1644) he urges his students to learn to use "the Globes, and all the maps first with the old names; and then with the new" (YP 2:189), a geographical pedagogy that emphasizes historical comparison. Since, as Peters argues, Adam's overview encompasses the whole expanses of human history and geography, to catalogue geographical places is to enumerate the histories and empires symbolized by those places.

The histories and cultures included in Adam's global overview signify at once their irreducible place in a universal chronology and Milton's cosmopolitan effort to engage cultural differences. Paul Stevens claims that Milton shows "Leviticus thinking" regarding cultural diversities, according to which, England, like the elected nation of Israel, forms its national identity in denigrating other peoples and cultures.⁹⁹ For Walter S. H. Lim, "Milton may celebrate the fraternity of shared experience based on commonality of political vision," but "he generally holds a distrust of cultural mingling."¹⁰⁰ Milton's "mingling" of profane histories and empires in Adam's prophetic overview compels us to reconsider his response to cultural diversities. In fact, rather than an exclusionary or distrustful attitude, Milton's inclusion of a host of profane histories within the "visions" of the biblical patriarch exhibits a liberal cosmopolitanism to engage cultural alterity.

Milton's liberal cosmopolitanism towards alternative accounts of time was not singular. Most of those who sought to construct a universal chronology displayed a cosmopolitan tolerance of profane histories. Bodin remarks that "I call that history universal which embraces the affairs of all, or of the most famous peoples, or of those whose deeds in war and in peace have been handed down to us from an early stage of their national growth."¹⁰¹ Likewise, Scaliger observes that scriptural chronology can justify itself only by referring to significant events in secular and non-Christian histories. As he puts it:

---

[97] Bodin, *Method*, 25.
[98] Bodin, *Method*, 9–10.
[99] Paul Stevens, "'Leviticus Thinking' and the Rhetoric of Early Modern Colonialism," *Criticism* 35 (1993): 441–61.
[100] Lim, "Empires of the East in *Paradise Lost*," in Johanyak and Lim eds., 217. Instead of colonialism, Stevens and Rahul Sapra deal with Milton's reference to Akbar's tolerance, "Akbar's Dream: Moghul Toleration and English/British Orientalism," *Modern Philology* 104:3 (2007): 379–411. For general work on Milton and toleration see Sharon Achinstein and Elizabeth Sauer, ed. *Milton and Toleration* (Oxford: Oxford UP, 2007).
[101] Bodin, *Method*, 21.

> Suppose some great expert in the sacred history—one, that is, who has a complete knowledge of the most important historical intervals, as established by certain computation from Moses and the other books of the Bible—cannot connect any part of it to a fixed epoch in Greek or Roman history. Efforts of this kind can be of no use either to him or to students of the ancient world.

Scaliger cites the "learning of the Jews" as a case in point. The Jews "have made so much progress in computing the intervals in sacred history as to be very close to the truth," but as "they have no knowledge—or only a corrupt one—of events outside their tradition, they go badly wrong when they try to deal with sacred history without the help of foreign history."[102] Markley denies Milton's indebtedness to the universal history project, on the grounds that this program "demean(s) the Mosaic account by suggesting that the Old Testament's chronological and moral coherence requires buttressing from pagan sources."[103] I would propose that the undifferentiated mingling of a broad array of profane histories in Adam's global survey shows recognition of their necessary place in a universal timetable: the scriptural timeline cannot justifiably assume universality unless it is, in fact, "buttress[ed]" by "pagan sources." Porter calls the juxtaposition of histories "across national and cultural boundaries" "historical cosmopolitanism," a framework that "requires reciprocity in the construction of comparative frameworks, insisting on a multiplicity of perspectives to unsettle the complacency of univocal teleologies."[104] In juxtaposing a vast array of widely differing histories and cultures, Milton conveys precisely a "historical cosmopolitanism" that emphasizes the contribution of multiple perspectives to the representation of world history. But rather than to "unsettle the complacency of univocal teleologies," Milton intends to reassert the primacy of Hebrew history.

Given his six years' self-directed study in almost all the branches of the humanities upon graduating from Christ's College, Milton's "historical cosmopolitanism" should come from a comprehensive understanding of the various histories and cultures encompassed by Adam's overview.[105] In particular, his image of China draws on the rich sources of Western reports on the Eastern country. In calling "Cambalu" or "Paquin" "The Seat / Of mightiest Empire," Milton evinces recognition of the eminence of the Far East in world history, a status acknowledged by most medieval and Renaissance observers. In his "On Experience," Montaigne calls China "a kingdom whose polity and sciences surpass our own exemplars

---

[102] Scaliger, *De emendatione temporum* (1583), 2; quoted in Grafton, *Historical Chronology*, 262–63.

[103] Markley, "Destin'd Walls," 194. Also see Markley, "Newton, Corruption, and the Tradition of Universal History," in *Newton and Religion: Context, Nature, and Influence*, ed. James E. Force and Richard H. Popkin (Dordrecht: Kluwer, 1999), 123–46.

[104] Porter, "Sinicizing Early Modernity," 299.

[105] For Milton's historical vision, see David Loewenstein, *Milton and the Drama of History: Historical Vision, Iconoclasm and the Literary Imagination* (Cambridge: Cambridge UP, 1990).

in many kinds of excellence" and "whose history teaches me that the world is more abundant and diverse than either the ancients or we realized."[106] For Bacon, the three inventions of China, that is, "printing, gunpowder and the magnet," "have changed the whole face and state of things throughout the world; the first in literature; the second in warfare; the third in navigation."[107] China boasted not only an edifying history and unparalleled scientific accomplishments but also mighty monarchs and great riches. In his *Travels*, Polo states that "all the world's great potentates put together have not such riches as belong to the Great Khan alone."[108] For Mandeville, "the kingdom of Cathay is the largest kingdom there is in the world and the Great Chan is the strongest emperor there is under the firmament."[109] In his *Mighty Kingdom of China*, Mendoza declares pointedly that Ming China is "the mightiest and biggest" kingdom that thrives with "need of none other nation," because "they haue sufficient of all things necessarie to the maintaining of humane life."[110] Athanasius Kircher (1602–80), Martini's mentor at the Collegio Romano, refers to the Qing Empire as the "richest and most powerful nation in the world" in his *China Illustrata* (1667).[111] In calling the Far East the "seat" of the "mightiest Empire," Milton evokes this very sinological tradition of glorifying the Middle Kingdom.

Whereas the superlative epithet "mightiest" signals Milton's awareness of the formidable Eastern empires, his coupling of "Cambalu" and "Paquin," two cities that mean the same place, indicates more sophisticated knowledge of Chinese history than hitherto has been realized. Both "Cambalu," the Capital of the Yuan Empire (1271–1368) built by the Mongol Tartars, and "Paquin," the imperial seat of the Ming and Qing dynasties (1368–1911), refer to present-day Beijing. Allan H. Gilbert maintains that Milton's alignment of "Cambalu" and "Paquin" exposes his ignorance,[112] and for Y. Z. Chang this coupling indicates that Milton "err[ed] concerning Cathay and China, by which he meant "two countries." However, Chang argues, "his error was not the result of ignorance; it was the honest and excusable mistake of a sound and cautious scholar, unwilling to embrace a facile identification based on what he thought was flimsy and dubious evidence."[113] Chang traces Milton's "two Chinas" to the Portuguese Jesuit Benedict Goes's travel account (1615) and the French geographer Pierre d'Avity's *Les Estats, Empires, et Principautez du Monde* (1614). Milton did draw upon Goes's narrative, but as Henry Yule notes, Goes, instead of impressing the idea of "two Chinas," made "CATHAY … finally disappear from view, leaving CHINA only in the

---

[106] Montaigne, "On Experience," 1215.
[107] Bacon, *New Organon*, 118.
[108] Polo, *Travels*, 149.
[109] Mandeville, 139.
[110] Mendoza, *Mighty Kingdom of China*, vol. 1, 81, 93.
[111] Athanasius Kircher, *China Illustrata* (Amsterdam, 1667), 166.
[112] Gilbert, *Geographical Dictionary*, 65, 77–78.
[113] Chang, "Why Did Milton Err on Two Chinas," 497.

mouths and minds of men."[114] Though d'Avity considered Cathay and China as two separate nations in his *Les Estats*, his conclusion was soon superseded by later accounts.[115] In his *Hakluytus Posthumus*, Purchas observes that neither those who "confound Cathay with China" nor those who "wholly separate them" should be followed, since "the present kingdome of China comprehends the best part of Cathay, besides the ancient Chinian limits, by Polo called Mangi."[116] Purchas's "present kingdome of China" means the Ming Empire, which did incorporate most of "Cathay," the northern part of China in the Yuan dynasty, and "Mangi," a derogatory epithet given by the Mongol rulers to the Han Chinese in the southern part of the empire. Webb also draws attention to the various appellations of China, as he writes in *An Historical Essay*, "That this outmost Region of the known World, which *Martinius* calls the extreme part of *Asia*, is by some called *Serica*, *Sina*, or *China* by others, by the *Tartars Cathay* and *Mangin* ... But the *Chinois* call their Empire *Chunghoa*, and *Chunghue*."[117] "Chunghoa" or "Chunghue" [Zhonghua] means none other than "the Middle Kingdom." In fact, Ricci and Trigault had already clarified the relations of almost all the terms mentioned by Purchas and Webb in their *Journals* published in 1615.[118] Goes, even before leaving for China in 1603 with the special mission to investigate "whether the name of an empire coterminous with China might have been extended also to the latter [Cathay]," according to Yule, "had heard indeed, by extracts of Father Matthew's [Ricci] letters from the capital of China, that Cathay was but another name for the Chinese empire."[119] So by the 1650s "the Middle Kingdom" meant specifically the Qing Empire erected by the Manchu Tartars upon the ruin of the Ming dynasty in 1644, an empire that encompassed within its vast boundaries the regions designated by all the names in Purchas and Webb's remarks. Accordingly, by the time Milton composed *Paradise Lost*, China has already become a clearly defined geographical and cultural space. Given the definite contour of China in the middle of the seventeenth century, Markley claims that "Milton's doubling of Cambalu and Beijing, Cathay and China" is "sonorously anachronistic."[120]

I propose that Milton's "two Chinas" bears out both his recognition and awareness of the challenge posed by Chinese antiquity to the universality of biblical temporal system. Instead of "error" or "ignorance" as Chang or Gilbert claim, or an "anachronistic" mistake that "underscores his [Milton's] and his contemporaries' continuing fascination with the Chinese" as Markley argues, Milton juxtaposes

[114] Yule, ed., *Cathay and the Way Thither*, vol. 4, 171.
[115] See d'Avity's differentiation between China and Cathay in *Les Estats, Empires, et Principautez du Monde* (Paris, 1619), 830, 848. For Milton's use of d'Avity see Allan H. Gilbert, "Pierre Davity: His Geography and Its Use by Milton," *Geographical Review* 7 (1919): 322–38.
[116] Purchas, *Hakluytus Posthumus*, vol. 1, 465.
[117] Webb, *Historical Essay*, 49.
[118] Ricci-Trigualt, *Journals*, 5, 7.
[119] Yule, ed., *Cathay and the Way Thither*, vol. 4, 200.
[120] Markley, *Far East and the English Imagin*ation, 70.

"Cambalu" and "Paquin" for an apologetic purpose. To incorporate, in a prophetic vision, the "mightiest Empire" and its deep antiquity, testifies to, more than anything else, the universality of the scriptural timeline. Whereas the epithet "mightiest" shows tribute to the Eastern empires, Milton's "two Chinas" indicates his perception of what "Cambalu" and "Paquin" symbolize, an awareness that signals a substantial knowledge of Eastern history. As the capital seat of three long dynasties (Yuan, Ming, and Qing), "Cambalu" and "Paquin" call to mind different historical events and dynastic rules, which is precisely what Milton intends to bring out in coupling two names that mean the same place. For Milton, whether called "Cambalu" or "Paquin," the empires this capital city represents are the "mightiest." The crucial questions raised by these archetypical symbols of China are: what is the place of the "seat" of these "mightiest empires" in the Mosaic history? Does it belong to a separate pre-Adamic or the Adamic lineage?

Milton's concern with the position of Chinese history *vis-à-vis* the Adamic culture can be glimpsed from his representation of Adam's historical overview. To reveal the future history of Adam's offspring, Michael guides Adam onto the highest hilltop in Paradise so that "His eye might there command wherever stood / City of old or modern Fame" (11.385–86). The word "command" is significant in bearing out the universal dimension of the biblical timeline. "To command" is "to have authority over, to be master of, to hold in control or subjection."[121] In commanding "City of old or modern Fame," Adam mentally masters and dominates cities of all over the world. That Adam's gaze falls first upon the "destin'd Walls" of China, a synecdoche of Chinese civilization, indicates the necessary enfolding and primary importance of the Far East in a universal template. The adjective "destin'd" vividly evokes the succession of dynastic empires in the Fast East and the endless battles fought between the Han Chinese and its barbarian neighbors across the fated "Walls" that mark civilized from uncivilized societies.[122] For Milton, Adam's prophetic "visions" can "command" even the "mightiest Empire" in the world and, presumably, its deep antiquity as well. The assimilating strategy he deploys here is very simple: to subsume the two exemplary synecdochical symbols of China— Beijing and the Great Wall—within Adam's historical survey. This ideological commanding is represented as both a historical and geographical incorporation. When Adam directs his eyes under Michael's guidance eastwards, both divine and human visions capture China. The three place names, "Cambalu," "Paquin," and the "destin'd Walls," indicate that Adam's visual comprehension is simultaneously a geographical assimilation. Further, given that China is encompassed within Adam's vision and that the history revealed by Michael registers the experiences of Adam's descendants, it is a logical inference that the Chinese also sprang from the loins of the first biblical patriarch. The "seat" of the "mightiest Empire" is thus

---

[121] "Command, v." 2nd ed. 1989. *OED Online*. June 5, 2012.

[122] Milton must have learned the Tartarian invasion across the Great Wall into the Ming empire from Martini's *Tartarico*, which gives a detailed account of the Manchu-Ming warfare.

not only historically but also territorially and genetically contained in the biblical symbolic system. Though all the histories listed in Adam's cosmographical table enjoy equal status in the universal chronology represented by Hebrew history, Chinese history is exemplary in that its antiquity directly challenges the chronological authority of such fundamental scriptural tenets as the Creation, the Flood, and Abraham's patriarchy.

Skeptics might question the chronological implications of Milton's images of biblical chronology and world histories in *Paradise Lost*, on three accounts. First, Milton does not even allude to the chronological issue in his representation of the biblical timeline. Second, though a global vision undergirds Adam's historical survey, Milton's cosmopolitan leaning towards Chinese antiquity can only be conjectured from the names and adjectives he uses to describe the Eastern country. Third, except for those names and adjectives, there is hardly any other evidence that shows that Milton distinguishes China from other parts of the world catalogued in Adam's overview. Milton's three references to America have given rise to much scholarship on the poet's engagement with the New World—rightly so, considering the larger backdrop of maritime discoveries and colonial enterprises.[123] Likewise, given England's nearly half a century's quest for the mythical Cathay, and given the widespread stir caused by the discovery of the "Great and Mighty" Middle Kingdom, its high civility and antiquity in particular, Milton's scanty allusions to China deserve more critical studies than hitherto bestowed upon them. These references, as I argue in this chapter, not only evoke broader intellectual trends but also shed fresh light on Milton's overall attitude towards cultural differences. It is true that Milton did not directly refer to the chronological issue in his account of Hebrew history. But the fact that he went all the way to reproduce an all-too-familiar history in an epic poem does indicate an attempt to respond to the question predominating the midcentury intellectual platform—"Which is the more credible of the two, Moses or China?" Moreover, the liberal cosmopolitanism marking Milton's engagement with Chinese history is consistent with his general attitude towards cultural diversities as expressed in his "Prolusion VII," *Areopogitica*, and *The Second Defence*.

Like Donne, Milton might also have been unaware of the subtle implications of his image of China or the cosmopolitanism this image encodes. But it is clear that a liberal cosmopolitanism unwittingly underlies both authors' negotiations with the radical and powerful other embodied by China. This veiled cosmopolitan generosity signals an instinctive though not fully articulated perception of the limitations of a Eurocentric and monotheistic framework. When this subconscious imaginary emerged as a full-bodied discourse in eighteenth-century Chinoiserie, it cast reflexive light upon, and thereby brought out more distinctly the cosmopolitan dimension of the earlier phase of East-West contact.

---

[123] For Milton's references to America, see YP 1:585; 1:881; 1:802.

Chapter 5
Webb's Chinese Linguistic Model and the Primitive Language in Milton's *Paradise Lost*

Not only Chinese chronology but also its pictorial language proved a controversial site of contention in Renaissance intellectual forum. The middle decades of the seventeenth century saw the publication of a series of book-length treatises on China, such as Alvaro Semedo's (1586–1658) *The History of that Great and Renowned Monarchy of China* (1655), Martini's *Sinicae historiae decas prima* (1658), Athanasius Kircher's (1602–80) *China Illustrata* (1667), and Webb's *An Historical Essay ... the Language of the Empire of China is the Primitive Language* (1669). So it is no wonder that the Eastern language found itself implicated within at least three mutually informing strands of intellectual development in early modern Europe.

First, the Chinese language was inextricably tied to seventeenth-century chronological controversy. As is shown in the pre-Adamic doctrine advanced by Paracelsus and elaborated by La Peyrère, the dispute over chronological antiquity was inseparably bound up with debates over linguistic priority. The pre-Adamites proposed the existence of both histories and languages prior to the Adamic age. Since language, even in its oral form, carries the history of the people who speak it, linguistic antiquity bears irrefutable witness to the beginning of history. According to Bodin, since "the primary origin of all races ought to be attributed to the people from whom the idioms flow," a central "proof of origins" lies in "the old roots in language" or "linguistic traces."[1] In regards to China, if the "origins" of Chinese history could find evidence in its linguistic "roots," then its chronological antiquity would admit no doubt. This is actually what Webb claims in *An Historical Essay*. Given the "apparent" "certainty" of Chinese "Annals &Chronology," Webb argues, it is but a logical step to "enquire after" the "certainty" of the primitive status of "their Language and Letters."[2] The celebrated thesis of "real" characters Bacon proposed in his *The Advancement of Learning* tended to lend a theoretical support to the linguistic testimonial to Chinese antiquity. For Bacon, the Chinese pictorial characters not only address the "real" nature of things but also serve as a kind of universal script among different linguistic communities in the Far East, two features unique to the primitive language.[3]

---

[1] Bodin, *Method*, 337–38, 340.
[2] Webb, *Historical Essay*, 161.
[3] Bacon, *Advancement of Learning*, 230.

The second intellectual development in which the Chinese characters figure prominently concerns the growing perception of the limitations of the dominant linguistic system. Whereas the chronologies from the newly discovered worlds called into question the scriptural timeline, the languages by which those chronologies were represented tended to challenge the biblical story of the origin and dispersion of the *lingua humana*. According to Genesis 11:9, God confounded at Babel the primitive tongue Adam and Eve spoke in Eden, which gave rise to 70 or 72 languages.[4] But in reality, the English linguistic reformer John Wilkins (1614–72) notes in his *An Essay towards a Real Character and a Philosophical Language* (1668), "the several Languages that are used in the world do farre exceed this number." Put differently, the scriptural linguistic framework could not contain the various languages discovered in such new worlds as China, Peru, or Mexico.[5] The issue raised here is, how did early modern Europe respond to the languages that that exceed the biblical symbolic order, particularly the Chinese language whose antiquity and authenticity seemed to be supported by its ancient history?

The third intellectual strand that involved the Chinese language is closely linked with the second one, that is, linguistic innovations introduced to address the very limitations of the current linguistic system. Renaissance linguistic reform features two distinctive approaches to language—the universal and primitive language projects, both of which drew upon Bacon's theory of "real" characters.[6] Whereas Universalist linguists such as Wilkins and George Dalgarno (1626–87) interpreted Bacon's real characters as ideal components of a "universal language," the Primitivists like the German mystic Jacob Boehme (1575–1624) and the English physician John Webster (1610–82) read them as necessary elements of a "natural language." In his *A Real Character*, Wilkins adds "universal" to Bacon's "real" character, and defines a "universal real character" as a language that does not "signifie *words*, but *things* and *notions*, and consequently might be legible by

---

[4] St. Augustine holds that 72 nations were created at the Babel out of Noah's offspring, and each nation was given a different language: for instance, Assyrian for Assur, Hebrew for Heber, and so on. Augustine, *City of God*, 16: 9–11. For more see Hermann J. Weigand, "The Two and Seventy Languages of the World," *Germanic Review* 17 (1942): 241–60.

[5] John Wilkins, *An Essay towards a Real Character and a Philosophical Language* (London, 1668), 2–3.

[6] For the primitive and universal linguistic projects see Murray Cohen, *Sensible Words: Linguistic Practice in England 1640–1785* (Baltimore: Johns Hopkins UP, 1977), 21; Robert Stillman, *The New Philosophy and Universal Languages in Seventeenth-Century England: Bacon, Hobbes, and Wilkins* (Lewisburg: Bucknell UP, 1995), 40–41. Kristen Poole uses "perfect language" as an umbrella concept that "encompass[es] universal and philosophical language schemes as well as attempts to discover the actual language of Eden." Kristen Poole, "Naming, *Paradise Lost*, and the Gendered Discourse of Perfect Language Schemes," *English Literary Renaissance* 38.3 (2008): 535–60, 538. I differentiate between the Universalists and the Primitivists by the different linguistic agendas they pursued.

any Nation in their own Tongue."[7] In contrast, in his *Mysterium Magnum* (1654), Boehme states that Adam "*gave names to all creatures* from their essence, forme and property. He understood the Language of nature, viz. the manifested & formed Word in every ones Essence, for thence the *Name of every Creature* is arisen."[8] As is shown in the famous "Webster-Ward-Wilkins" debate, "the Language of nature" or natural language that addresses the "Essence" of things constitutes a moot point between the Primitivists and Universalists.[9] While the Primitivists identified natural language with the tongue Adam and Eve spoke in Eden, the Universalists considered it an artificial *lingua franca*.

In this chapter, I examine the Renaissance response to the linguistic diversity represented by Chinese characters in light of the three interrelated intellectual developments outlined above. Except for Paul Cornelius's foundational study of the Chinese context of Renaissance linguistic reform and David Porter's milestone work on the early modern attempts to decipher "the Chinese cipher," there has been little extensive critical engagement on this topic.[10] My study follows the lines of inquiry set down by Cornelius and Porter, with a view to providing some additional insights on the impact of the Chinese language upon Renaissance European culture. In his *Ideographia: The Chinese Cipher in Early*

---

[7] Wilkins, *Real Character*, 12–13. Wilkins used both "universal" and "philosophical" to describe a common lexicon. Since *philosophical* means to bear out a fundamental characteristic of a universal repertoire, I use "universal" to signify seventeenth-century linguistic reform. For Paolo Rossi, "perfect," "philosophical," or "universal" are interchangeable. Rossi opts for "perfect," defining a perfect language as an "artificial … system of signs which will be communicable and comprehensible—and hence applicable to either written or spoken language—regardless of the 'natural' language spoken by the reader." Rossi, *Logic and the Art of Memory: The Quest for a Universal Language*, trans. Stephen Clucas (Chicago: U of Chicago P, 2000), 156. Umberto Eco distinguishes between "perfect" and "universal" language, regarding the former as "a language capable of mirroring the true nature of objects," and the latter a linguistic system "which everyone might, or ought to, speak." Eco, *The Search for the Perfect Language*, trans. James Fentress (Oxford: Blackwell, 1995, rpt. 2006), 73. Benjamin DeMott identifies two stages in Renaissance imagination of a universal language, "a real character" in stage I and "a philosophical language" in stage II. DeMott, "The Sources and Development of John Wilkins' Philosophical Language," *Journal of English and Germanic Philology* 57 (1958): 1–13, 10.

[8] Jacob Boehme, *Mysterium Magnum; or An Exposition of the First Book of Moses Called Genesis*, trans. John Sparrow (London, 1654), 86.

[9] Ward refers to Seth Ward (1617–89), the Oxford professor of astronomy. For the debate see Thomas C. Singer, "Hieroglyphs, Real Characters, and the Idea of Natural Language in English Seventeenth-Century Thought," *Journal of the History of Ideas* 50 (1989): 49–70, 58–62; and Allen Debus ed., *Science and Education in the Seventeenth Century: The Webster-Ward Debate* (London: Macdonald, 1970).

[10] Porter, *Ideographia*; Cornelius, *Languages in Seventeenth and Early Eighteenth-Century Imaginary Voyages*.

Modern Europe, Porter proposes an "ideographical" approach to the early modern reception of Chinese characters. As he puts it,

> I will approach the response to the Chinese language ... as a foundational case of ideography, understood as the domestication of the foreign sign, the process by which the unintelligible is rendered legible and interpreted within a more familiar matrix of meanings, and contributes, in turn, to shaping it.[11]

This chapter offers a case study of the ideographical framework proposed by Porter. Whereas Porter deals with how such ideological imperatives as "linguistic crisis" and concerns with "material evidence of the possibility of legitimacy in representation" help shape Western responses to the Chinese script, I focus on the apologetic and polemical implications of Milton's particular reaction to the debate centering on that script.[12] Situating Milton's linguistic images within the broader context of seventeenth-century linguistic reform, I propose that Chinese real characters, like its chronology, lie behind the apologetic agenda in *Paradise Lost*. While Milton's representations of the Mosaic and world histories intend to incorporate competing systems of time, his decoding of "the Chinese cipher" bears out, albeit indirectly, his apologetic tactic to assimilate a disruptive "foreign sign" within the "familiar matrix" of biblical discourse. Milton's attempt to cope with the anxiety caused by the Chinese language helps, in turn, shape his imagining of an alternative linguistic paradigm to those advanced by the Primitivists and Universalists.

Critics tend to emphasize Milton's unusual "silence" to contemporary linguistic movement because of the rare references in his prose works.[13] Don C. Allen and Kristen Poole stand out as rare exceptions. For Allen, Milton "was quite aware of the general linguistic theories of his age." But since "a scientific study of the Original Language and of the evolution of the matrix language is an unwarranted intrusion on the mysteries of theology," Allen says, all Milton's "direct statements" about the primitive tongue are marked by "a tentative quality."[14] Poole argues that given the scale of the quest for a perfect language and Milton's own "intellectual fascination and engagement" with the theological, political, and scientific debates raised by these quests, Milton's "silence" "seems willful and calculated."[15] By studying the gender deployment in Milton's first tongue, Poole claims his engagement with contemporary linguistic controversy.

---

[11] Porter, *Ideographia*, 20.

[12] Porter, *Ideographia*, 20, 21.

[13] Milton rarely mentions the Adamic language in his prose works except for two cursory references in *Of Christian Doctrine* and *Tetrachordon* (YP 6:324; 2:602), but this very neglect makes its dramatization in *Paradise Lost* the more revealing.

[14] Don C. Allen, "Some Theories of the Growth and Origin of Language in Milton's Age," Philological Quarterly 28 (1949): 5–16, 6.7.

[15] Poole, "Naming," 540.

Referring to Allen and Poole's studies, I argue that Milton does present a language scheme in his *Paradise Lost*, and this scheme at once responds to and partakes of Renaissance linguistic innovation. In representing God's institution of language in a prelapsarian world, Milton apparently belonged among those Primitivists who sought the primitive tongue in the names Adam assigned to creatures. But in depicting the Edenic language as the *lingua humana*—the tongue of "Our primitive great sire" (5.350) and "Mother of human race" (4.475), Milton also aligned himself with the Universalists. Milton was, however, neither a pure Primitivist nor Universalist. The primitive language represented in *Paradise Lost* differs from the various models proposed by the Primitivists, for, as John Leonard points out, nowhere in his works did Milton identify the matrix tongue with the Hebrew or any other particular language.[16] Nor does Milton's *lingua humana* resemble the artificial linguistic system constructed by the Universalists, since he deems such ambitious projects as "vain design[s]" of building "New Babels" (3.467–68).

Since Webb's *An Historical Essay* represents a synthesis of Renaissance engagement with the Eastern script, I use it as a particular reference framework to study the Chinese resonance in Milton's images of language.[17] Allen notices that alongside "the amazing theories that grew out of the orthodox notion that all languages stemmed from the Hebrew," there are "some variant doctrines that were so heterodox in conception that one can easily understand why Milton was ready to accept the facts of revelation for certain and conduct no original investigation of his own." Webb's Chinese linguistic model is numbered among those "heterodox" theories.[18] Webb, like Milton, put forward an alternative linguistic model to contend with the language agendas of the Universalists and other Primtivists. He evinced undisguised disapproval of those zealous quests for a "Philosophical Language,"[19] and rejected pointedly such languages as Dutch, Hebrew, and Samaritan as candidates for the original *lingua humana*.[20] Rachel Ramsey argues that "Webb's political career allows us to read *An Historical Essay* as a politico-theological justification of or a reasoned critique of the patronage system which Webb held accountable for his thwarted career ambitions."[21] For

---

[16] John Leonard, *Naming in Paradise: Milton and the Language of Adam and Eve* (Oxford: Clarendon, 1990); 16.

[17] On Webb's *Historical Essay*, see Shou-yi Ch'en, "John Webb"; Ramsey, "Webb's *An Historical Essay*"; and John Bold, "John Webb: Composite Capitals and the Chinese Language," *Oxford Art Journal* 4.1 *Tradition* (1981): 9–17.

[18] Allen, "Language in Milton's Age," 12–13. Allen gives an elaborate account of Webb's "novel conceit." Such heterodox doctrines also include Nicholas Serarius's proposition of "Samaritan," Adrianus Schriekius of the "Celtic," and Goropius of the "Dutch" or "Low German" as the original language.

[19] Webb, *Historical Essay*, 145–46. For Webb's criticism of the philosophical language also see 164. But Webb seemed to approve Wilkins "real character," 187.

[20] Webb, *Historical Essay*, 42, 43.

[21] Ramsey, "China and the Ideal of Order," 484.

Ch'en Shou-yi, "The problem which John Webb attempted to solve in the *Essay* was rather Biblico-historical than linguistic."[22] Drawing upon scholarship on both Webb and Milton, I propose that in addition to its political and theological implications, Webb's apologetic scheme is pitted against rival linguistic theories as well. I argue that Webb's radical thesis that had already been implicit in the multiple heterodox sources epitomized in *An Historical Essay* has compelled Milton to conduct an "original investigation" of the language polemic in *Paradise Lost*. Simply stated, Webb's Chinese model was advanced to contend with, apart from other contemporary language projects, the linguistic paradigm or what I call the Edenic framework set out in Milton's epic poem.

Viewed in light of early modern primitive and universal linguistic programs, particularly that proposed in Webb's *An Historical Essay*, Milton's images of language take on two new dimensions. Both Milton and Webb use the Edenic image of the "figtree" to describe the primitive nature of the *lingua humana*. But Webb's Chinese model distinguishes from Milton's Edenic paradigm in two key aspects. First, while Webb relies on postlapsarian moral discourse to represent the primitive status of the Chinese, Milton turns to a prelapsarian world "unmediated" (5.149) by the knowledge of right and evil to describe the unique, irretrievable, and irreplaceable feature of the original tongue. Second, whereas Webb uses the idea of "radix" to bear out the natural source of the Chinese script, Milton resorts to rational discourse that differentiates between "Discursive" and "Intuitive" reason (5.492) to address the origin of knowledge encoded in Adam and Eve's speeches. The points of contact in Webb and Milton's linguistic models at once shed light on their apologetic agendas and allow us to see the moral and cultural allegories invested in linguistic signifiers.

Renaissance Reports and Theorization of the Chinese Language

It is the Augustine Friar Mendoza and the pioneers of the Chinese mission Ricci and Trigualt who first introduced Chinese characters to western Europe. Mendoza's *Mighty Kingdom of China* provides the earliest extensive account of the Chinese language.[23] Mendoza notes that the Chinese "write by figures" and "almost every word hath his character." Like Hebrew, Chinese is "better understood in writing than in speaking," since it has "certain distinction of points that is in every character differing one from the other, which in speaking cannot be distinguished so easily." Nevertheless, "although in the pronouncing there is difference in the vowels," Mendoza observes, "one figure or character unto them doth signify one thing." It is true that the Chinese "do speake manyie languages, the one differing from

---

[22] Ch'en, "John Webb," 95.

[23] Mendoza's work drew upon the Dominican Friar Gaspar da Cruz's *Tractado em que se côtam muito por estêso as cousas da China* (Evora, 1569), presumably the earliest account of Chinese Character. See James Knowlson, *Universal Language Schemes in England and France, 1600–1800* (Toronto: U of Toronto P, 1975), 24.

the other," but "generallie in writing they doo vnderstand one the other, and in speaking not." This universal written script, Mendoza remarks, allows the Chinese to communicate with "the Japones, Lechios, those of Samatra, and those of the kingdome of Quanchinchina and other borderers vnto them," countries or peoples with different "speech or language."[24]

Ricci and Trigault gave a similar report in *The Journals of Matthew Ricci* (1615). The two Jesuit missionaries also notice that the Chinese "draw figures of the things signified by words, and use as many figures as they do words." Like Mendoza, they draw attention to the fact that the Eastern script was used not only within "the fifteen provinces of the kingdom" but it "would also be understood by the Japanese, the Koreans, the inhabitants of Cochin China, the Leuchians, and even by peoples of other countries, who would be able to read it as well as the Chinese." The reason is that, they explain, "While the spoken languages of these different races are as unlike as can be imagined, they can understand written Chinese because each written character in Chinese writing represents an individual thing." "If this were universally true," they suggest, "we should be able to transmit our ideas to peoples of other countries in writing, though we would not be able to speak to them."[25]

Two salient features of Chinese stand out in Mendoza and Ricci and Trigault's accounts. The first is the correspondence between names and natures: "one figure or character unto them doth signify one thing" or "each written character in Chinese writing represents an individual thing." Unlike alphabetic representations based on arbitrary relations of the signifier and the signified, Chinese pictographic characters written in "figures" seem to capture the "real" nature of things. The second feature consists in the distinction between "spoken" and "written" Chinese and the remarkable communicative capacity of the latter. The equivalence between "word" and "character" makes the Eastern language more effective in "writing" than "speaking," a "universal" attribute that accounts for its wide application among different communities and countries. The "real" and "universal" attributes demonstrated by Chinese characters proved to be the very elements desired by Renaissance linguistic reformers. Further, according to Webb, "the certainty of Language consists not so much in the speaking and pronouncing, as in the reading and writing: not in the words but Letters."[26] Put another way, the communicative capacity of Chinese written characters testifies to its "certainty."

The real and universal characteristic of the Chinese script appeared the more striking in the reports of the mid-seventeenth century. Rather than general descriptions, accounts of this period offered concrete instances to illustrate these attributes, a practice epitomized in the famous pictographic paradigm composed of such characters as 十 (ten), 土 (earth), 王 (king), and 玉 (jade). What is illustrated by this oft-quoted paradigm is that, Webb says, "by adding, diminishing, or turning of

---

[24] Mendoza, *Great and Mighty Kingdom*, vol. 1, 121–22.
[25] Ricci-Trigualt, *Journals*, 131.
[26] Webb, *Historical Essay*, 188.

a stroke, they make other new and different ones, and of different significations."[27] Since all these new "significations" are closely associated with the root character [十] from which the other three derive, one can easily surmise the meaning of any character in the list from both its physical shape and affinity with the root. Thus even not knowing their pronunciation, people could understand and communicate effectively with these structurally similar and semantically connected signs. This graphic model appeared in most midcentury sinological works, such as Martini's *Sinicae historiae* and the Portuguese Jesuit Alvaro Semedo's *The Great and Renowned Monarchy of China*.[28] The pattern also showed up in Webb's *An Historical Essay* and the *De re literaria sinensium commentaries* (1660) of the German sinologist Gottlieb Spitzel (1639–91).[29] Kircher added two more words to this popular pattern: 生 (live) and 主 (master) in his *China Illustrata*.[30]

Bacon was the first to theorize the Chinese language. Like most of his scientific programs, Bacon's linguistic theory illuminates his natural philosophy that prioritizes practical observations over speculative contemplations.[31] So to understand Bacon's real characters, one needs to know his central philosophical tenet advanced in *The New Organon* (1620), that is, the "inductive method," a scientific "key" that can improve "the relation between the mind and nature" and "govern and direct" the mind "in ways that are most suitable to all things." "The whole secret" of his method, Bacon declares, is "never to let the mind's eyes stray from things themselves, and to take in images exactly as they are." Since epistemological inquiry "takes its origin not only from *the nature of the mind* but from *the nature of things*," he says, an inductive method can "clarify the part played by the nature of things and the part played by the nature of the mind," and thereby achieves an effective "marriage of the mind and the universe." This ideal "marriage" requires that the mind, when forming its own notions, should not "insert and mingle its own nature with the nature of things" but reflect "the true rays of things."[32] However, in reality, the mind is unavoidably ensnared by four illusions, one of which is the "idols of the marketplace," "the biggest nuisance of

---

[27] Webb, *Historical Essay*, 174.

[28] Martini, *Sinicae historiae*, 12; Alvarez Semedo, *Imperio de la China*. 1642. *The History of that Great and Renowned Monarchy of China*, trans. Thomas Henshaw (London, 1655), 31–34.

[29] Gottlieb Spitzel (Theophilus Spizelius), *De re literaria sinensium commentarius* or *Commentary on the Chinese Literature* (Leiden, 1660); see Mungello, *Curious Land*, 153, footnote. Spizel's *literaria sinensium* was based on Trigault's *De christiana expeditione apud Sinas* (1615).

[30] Kircher, *China Illustrata*, 233–35. Kircher's work also distinguishes by the "sixteen" types of Chinese characters he lists in accordance with the things from which they are derived, a table reproduced by Webb in *An Historical Essay*. Kircher, *China Illustrata*, 228; Webb, *Historical Essay*, 170.

[31] For the congruence between Bacon's philosophical and linguistic theories see Porter, *Ideographia*, 22; and Knowlson, *Universal Language*, 36.

[32] Bacon, *New Organon*, 109–10, 98, 52, 11, 2, 100, 19.

all" because "they have stolen into the understanding from the covenant on words and names." Though "Men believe that their reason control words," when "the covenant on words and names" breaks, Bacon remarks, "words retort and turn their force back upon the understanding, and this has rendered philosophy and the sciences sophistic and unproductive." Put differently, when words "retort," the order of nature they represent is distorted, which naturally gives rise to unnatural words, a chief source of "sophistic and unproductive" reasoning. Bacon identifies two kinds of such unnatural words:

> They are either names of things that do not exist (for as there are things that lack names because they have not been observed, so that are also names that lack things because they have been imaginatively assumed) or they are the names of things which exist but are confused and badly defined, being abstracted from things rashly and unevenly.[33]

What is violated by the misuses of words stated in this passage is the very order of Nature. Since names should "take in images exactly as they are," the misalliance between words and things would naturally lead to conceptual problems. For Bacon, instead of sophistic or unnatural names, a language that observes the orders of both the mind and Nature provides the best lexicon for deductive reasoning. Chinese characters that feature a close correspondence between words and things seemed to be an ideal candidate for Bacon.

To follow the order of the mind is to find suitable means to express it. It is when discussing the various means of expressing the mind that Bacon proposed his "real" characters thesis. Since "whatsoever is capable of sufficient differences, and those perceptible by the sense, is in nature competent to express cogitations," Bacon remarks, one's thoughts are not necessarily "expressed by the medium of words." The Chinese language is evoked to illustrate this point. As Bacon says,

> It is the use of China, and the kings of the high Levant [Far East], to write in *characters real*, which express neither letters or words in gross, but things or notions; insomuch as countries and provinces, which understand no one another's language, can nevertheless read one another's writings, because the characters are accepted more generally than the languages do extend; and therefore they have a vast multitudes of characters, as many, I suppose, as radical words.[34]

Just like the deaf who convey ideas through physical signs or gestures, Chinese "real" characters that represent "things or notions" rather than "letters or words" also provide an effective medium of communication. It is this "real" nature, according to Bacon, that accounts for the wide application of the Chinese script among "countries and provinces" with their own languages and dialects.

---

[33] Bacon, *New Organon*, 48–49.
[34] Bacon, *Advancement of Learning*, 230.

Chinese Inspiration of Renaissance Linguistic Reform and Webb's Chinese Model

Despite their disputation over natural language, both the Universalists and Primitivists tended to accept the biblical assumptions that there was a primitive language universal to all humanity and that this matrix tongue was lost at Babel. Hebrew had been the alleged primitive tongue by the early modern period. Whitaker states that both Scripture and the Fathers testify to the fact that Hebrew is "the most ancient of all languages, and was that which alone prevailed in the world before the deluge and the erection of the Tower of Babel."[35] Bodin asserts the priority of Hebrew because "before any semblance of the Greek and the Latin languages existed, peoples and regions used the Jewish names."[36] Hebrew's primitive status, however, was increasingly challenged in the Renaissance. Margreta de Grazia remarks that "Once thought to be the language God spoken at Creation and bequeathed to Adam, Hebrew is in the estimation of some seventeenth-century writers no better or worse than other tongues."[37] Sidonie Clauss notes that quite a few early modern linguists "had abandoned the quest for the language of Eden" by "denying the specialty of the Hebrew as exempt from the curse of Babel."[38] In their attempts to seek or construct other candidates for the original language, the Primitivist and Universalist reformers were numbered among those critics of the Hebrew. To ascertain which was the primitive tongue mixed with the multiple languages produced at Babel, Joseph Scaliger and Isaac Vossius, figures that played a leading role in the chronological polemic as well, undertook to compare etymologies by compiling word lists in different languages.[39] Other Primitivists such as Webb and the Dutch linguist Johannes Goropius Becanus (1519–72) proposed some nationalistic languages as possible candidates for the first letters.[40] In contrast, the Universalists, deeming it impossible to restore the primitive language, sought to construct an artificial universal character.

---

[35] Whitaker, *Disputation on Holy Scriptures*, 112.

[36] Bodin, *Method*, 338.

[37] Margreta de Grazia, "The Secularization of Language in the Seventeenth Century," *Journal of the History of Ideas* 41.2 (1980): 319–29, 328.

[38] Sidonie Clauss, "John Wilkins' *Essay toward a Real Character*: Its place in the seventeenth-century episteme," in *John Wilkins and 17th-Century British Linguistics*, ed. Joseph L. Subbiondo (Amsterdam: J. Benjamins, 1992), 45–67, 48, 49.

[39] For such compilers See Allen, "Language in Milton's Age," 8–9. On those who sought to restore Hebrew see, Guillaume Postel's *Linguarum duodecim characteribus differentium alphabetum* (1538), Conrad Gessner's *Mithridates* (1555), and Mercurius van Helmont's *Alphabeti verè naturalis Hebraici brevissima delineation* (1667). See Eco, *Search for the Perfect Language*, 74–85.

[40] For nationalist languages proposers see, Goropius, *Origines Antwerpiane* (1569); and Webb, *Historical Essay*. Also see David S. Katz, "The Language of Adam in Seventeenth-Century England," in *History and Imagination: Essays in Honour of H. R. Trevor-Roper*, ed. Hugh Lloyd-Jones, Valerie Pearl, and Blair Worden (London: Duckworth, 1981), 132–45; and Almond, *Adam and Eve in Seventeenth-Century Thought*.

Linguists of both schools, however, dreamed of a common lexicon that resembles the primitive *lingua humana*. They agreed that a general character was necessary, especially at a time when Latin had ceased to be an international language due to the confessional splits caused by the Reformation, when the universality of the Adamic tongue was threatened by those newly discovered languages, and when communication across national borders was hindered by the ascendency of vernacular languages. On the global stage, an increasingly globalized world needed a universal repertoire to conduct transoceanic exchanges, whether commercial or cultural. If the chronological issue was largely a cultural thing, language was of immediate practical relevance in early modern globalization.

One striking aspect of the Renaissance search for a primitive or universal real character was the Chinese inspiration.[41] The trading opportunities held forth by Eastern wealth immensely enhanced the appeal of the Chinese language, not to mention its intrinsic value as a real and universal character and the rich cultural implications it carries. Both the Primitivists and Universalists drew upon Bacon's real characters, looking up at the Chinese script as a model for a universal lexicon.[42] Cornelius notes that "almost every English universal language projector of the mid-seventeenth century acknowledged Bacon as a predecessor."[43] James Knowlson observes that it has become an "intellectual commonplace in the seventeenth-century world of learning" to evoke the Eastern language, because "Chinese character-writing rendered the whole idea of a common writing eminently feasible to European scholars."[44] Porter also draws attention to the fact that some

---

[41] On Chinese characters and Renaissance linguistic reform also see, Knowlson, *Universal Language Schemes*, 24–27; Knud Lundbaek, "Imaginary Ancient Chinese Characters," *China Mission Studies (1550–1800) Bulletin V* (1983): 5–23; Jonathan Cohen, "On the Project of a Universal Character," in Subbiondo ed., 237–51, 239; and *George Dalgarno on Universal Language: The Art of Signs* (1661), *The Deaf and Dumb Man's Tutor* (1680), *and the Unpublished Papers*, ed. and trans. David Cram and Jaap Maat (Oxford: Oxford UP, 2001), 4–5. On general studies see, Russell A. Fraser, *The Language of Adam* (New York: Columbia UP, 1977); Vivian Salmon, *The Study of Language in Seventeenth Century England* (Amsterdam: John Benjamins, 1988); Robert Markley, *Fallen Languages: Crises of Representation in Newtonian England, 1660–1740* (Ithaca: Cornell UP, 1993); William Poole, "The Divine and the Grammarian: Theological Disputes in the 17th-Century Universal Language Movement," *Historiographica linguistica* 30 (2003): 273–300; and Jaap Maat, *Philosophical Languages in the Seventeenth Century: Dalgarno, Wilkins, Leibniz* (Dordrecht: Academic Publishers, 2004).

[42] For the Universalists' reference to Bacon's real characters see Wilkins, *Mercury, or The secret and swift messenger* (London, 1641), 10–11; Henry Edmundson, *Lingua Linguarum* (London, 1655), "To the Reader"; and Cave Beck, *The Universal Character* (London, 1657), "Au Lecteur." For the Primitivists' reference to Bacon also see Gerhard Vossius, *De Arte Grammatica Libri Septem* (Amsterdam, 1635); and Herman Hugo, *De prima scribendi origine et universa rei literariae antiquitate* (Antwerp, 1617).

[43] Cornelius, *Imaginary Voyages*, 31.

[44] Knowlson, *Universal Language Schemes*, 25. Apart from Chinese, the picture language of the Mexicans and Incans, "Arabic numerals as well as astronomical and chemical symbols were invoked as examples of universal language" too. Cram and Maat eds. *Dalgarno*, 5.

"particular universal language schemes" of the period "modeled themselves on varying combinations of the perceived attributes of Chinese."[45]

Indeed, despite its apparent "regional universality," Renaissance linguistic projectors nevertheless relied on the interpretive key offered by Bacon, regarding the Chinese script as an "eminently feasible" model for a general lexicon.[46] Most of these constructors privileged the "Chinese example" over other claimants to a primitive or universal language such as Egyptian hieroglyphs and the picture writings of the Mexicans. In his *Proposal to the King for a Universal Script* (1627), the French linguist Jean Douet considered Chinese "a universal script," and Spitzel attributed the invention of the first letters to the Chinese in his *Literaria sinensium commentaries*.[47] In his *The Way of Light*, a work dedicated to the Royal Society in 1668, the Czech educator John A. Comenius observes that "the symbolic character used by the Chinese" can "help men of different languages to understand one another." If the Chinese model "seems to be advantageous," he suggests, we should "devote ourselves studiously to the discovery of a Real Language: to the discovery not only of a language but of thought, and what is more, to the truth of things themselves at the same time."[48] Similarly, in his *Ars signorum* (1661) Dalgarno claims the superiority of Chinese and Egyptian "hieroglyphical" characters over vocal letters. The object-oriented attributes of Chinese characters obviously helped to shape Dalgarno's idea of a "philosophical language" based on 20 basic letters or genera.[49] For Wilkins, neither Egyptian hieroglyphs nor the "*Mexican* way of writing by Picture" but Chinese represents a "universal real character."[50] What impressed Wilkins most about the Chinese script is its seeming universality. In his *Mercury or The Secret and Swift Messenger* (1641), he observes that "though those of *China* and *Japan* doe as much differ in their Language," they can nevertheless "by this help of a common character, as well understand the books and letters of the others, as if they were only their own."[51] Later, in *A Real Character* he remarks again that the Chinese "do now, and have for many ages, used a general character, by which the inhabitants of that large kingdom, many of them of different tongues, do communicate with one another, everyone understanding this common character and reading it in his own language."[52]

In reality, the Eastern language had so much grasped Renaissance imagination that the Royal Society appointed a special committee in 1668 to check its efficacy as a universal repertoire. Among the members of this *ad hoc* committee were such notable thinkers as Robert Boyle, Christopher Wren, John Wallis, and Robert

---

[45] Porter, "Writing China," 103.
[46] For the idea of "regional universality," see Porter, *Ideographia*, 18.
[47] Spitzel, *sinensium commentarius*, Sec. III.21ff.
[48] Comenius, *The Way of Light*, Cap XIX, sections 16 and 19, 186, 189.
[49] George Dalgarno, *Ars signorum* (London, 1661), 2; see also 27–28.
[50] Wilkins, *Real Character*, 12–13.
[51] Wilkins, *Mercury*, 106–7.
[52] Wilkins, *Real Character*, 12–13.

Hooke.⁵³ The findings of the committee can be glimpsed from the remarks Hooke made in 1686: "I fear the Relations I have hitherto met with concerning it [Chinese language], were written by such as did not well understand it,"⁵⁴ and "I conceive the present *Chinese* Language to have no affinity with the Character, the true primitive, of first language, or pronunciation of it, having been lost."⁵⁵ Though disclosing the illusive nature of the Chinese model, Hooke's observations cannot deny almost a century's enthusiasm to emulate this Eastern *lingua franca*.

Webb's *An Historical Essay* is the only extensive treatise that deals exclusively with the Chinese language in the Renaissance, and as is shown in his vigorous defense of the authenticity of Martini's *sinicae historiae*, his linguistic theory is based on recognition of the priority of Chinese chronology. In this treatise, Webb unreservedly proclaims that "the language of the Empire of CHINA, is, the Primitive Tongue, which was common to the whole world before the flood."⁵⁶ For Webb, unlike the rather corrupted alphabetical and hieroglyphic characters, the Chinese language has retained its original purity and clarity. In proposing Chinese as the primitive language, Webb showed his affiliation with the Primitivists. Webb admits that "the language spoken by our first Parents" is the *Lingua humana*, which remained "the common and general speech" until the confusion at Babel."⁵⁷ But rather than Hebrew or other nationalistic languages, he argues, the Chinese language used by various countries in the Far East is the primitive tongue, for, he explains,

> *Nieuhoff*, *Vossius*, and others have assured us, that the *Chinois* can and will in maintenance of the truth of *Theirs* produce faithful witnesses, Antient Records written from Age to Age in not Alphabetary, but significative Characters, such, as the World in the Infancy and Nonage thereof had in use, & such as *Martinius*, *Semedo*, & our *Chinique* authors have generally affirmed, are the same at this very day; as when primitively they were invented: which eminently convinceth that their Language remains as pure and uncorrupt at this present in those Characters, as when they first began to have a Language.⁵⁸

Given the "faithful witnesses" provided by "Chinique authors" themselves and the antiquity of the Chinese script as confirmed by Nieuhoff, Vossius, Martini, and Semedo, Webb says, "we may safely conclude that the MOTHER or NATURAL

---

⁵³ Entry in *Journal* Book of the Royal Society, under May 14 (1668), quoted in Cohen, "On the Project of a Universal Character," in Subbiondo ed., 247.

⁵⁴ Robert Hooke, "Some Observations and Conjectures Concerning Chinese Characters," *Philosophical Transactions of the Royal Society* 16 (March–April, 1686): 63–78, 69.

⁵⁵ Hooke, "Some Observations," 73.

⁵⁶ Webb, *Historical Essay*, 77.

⁵⁷ Webb, *Historical Essay*, 16. The Father here refers to Trigault who brought Ricci's journal to Europe and had it published under the title of *De christiana expeditione apud Sinas* in 1615.

⁵⁸ Webb, *Historical Essay*, 188.

Language of the Empire of *China*, perdures in its Antient purity without any change or alteration."[59] It is Noah who brought the primitive tongue to China, shortly after he descended from the Ark that rested in "Ararat," a ledge of mountains that run across the Great Wall of China and continues "through *Corea* until it encounters with the East Sea there."[60] Since when Nimrod, Noah's great grandson, went to Shinaar to build the Tower of Babel, China had already been "planted" by Noah, Webb reasons, Chinese "could not be concerned in the *Confusion* there, nor come within the curse of *confounded Languages*; but retained the PRIMITIVE Tongue, as having received it from *Noah*."[61] This explains why the Eastern language "remains as pure and uncorrupt at this present."

Echoing Dalgarno and Wilkins, Webb upholds the priority of Chinese at the expense of alphabetical and hieroglyphic letters. He agrees that "the first Characters, that were ever framed to language were of his [Adam's] invention,"[62] but he thinks it "in vain" to "search for the PRIMITIVE Language to remain with those Nations whose Languages consist in Alphabets," because "Alphabetary Letters … are aptly disposed to alteration and corruption."[63] Nor can one seek the original tongue in Egyptian "Hieroglyphicks" that involved "aenigmatically entire *Ideal* conceptions" and was invented only "to conceale their Arcana from the people." In contrast, the Chinese "framed the Characters to communicate their concepts to the people" by "declaring precisely the conceptions of single words, and names only."[64] Webb justifies his claim by turning to the "six principal guides" identified by "those who have written of the PRIMITIVE Tongue," that is, "Antiquity, Simplicity, Generality, Modesty of expression, Utility, and Brevity."[65] Since Chinese possesses all these attributes, he argues, it is the very "PRIMITIVE language."[66] He expatiates, in greater length, on the "antiquity" of Chinese. Refuting Kircher's view that Chinese characters derived from Egyptian hieroglyphs, he claims that among "those Nations, that are the greatest pretenders to Antiquity, as the *Hebrews*, *Samaritans*, *Chaldeans*, and *Aegyptians*," Vossius "brings up the *Chinois* in the rear."[67] Likewise, among the "pretenders" to linguistic antiquity such as "the *Aegyptians* or *Phoenicians*," the Chinese language boasts of longer usage, a fact reaffirmed by Ralegh, Semedo, Vossius, Martini, and even Kircher himself. Chinese is not only prior to other ancient languages but also "excells all other parts of *Asia*." Most importantly, the Chinese "invented" their characters "some Centuries of years before the dispersion at *Babel*."[68]

---

[59] Webb, *Historical Essay*, 190.
[60] Webb, *Historical Essay*, 78.
[61] Webb, *Historical Essay*, 32.
[62] Webb, *Historical Essay*, 147.
[63] Webb, *Historical Essay*, 150.
[64] Webb, *Historical Essay*, 152.
[65] Webb, *Historical Essay*, 162.
[66] Webb, *Historical Essay*, 209.
[67] Webb, *Historical Essay*, 48.
[68] Webb, *Historical Essay*, 48.

The linguistic model mapped by Webb in *An Historical Essay* offers an ideal framework to study the Chinese context of Milton's primitive tongue, for three reasons. First, both Webb's Chinese and Milton's Edenic models present a revisionist reading of the biblical story of the origin of language, and both represent distinctive developments of Bacon's real characters thesis. Whereas Webb regards "real" as a central marker of the primitive status of the Chinese script, Milton locates "real" characters in, rather than Hebrew, Adam and Eve's prelapsarian speeches. Second, published within the short span of two years and at the very peak of the universal language movement, both Webb and Milton's linguistic frameworks were, to use Porter's words, "rooted in contemporary discussions of more general linguistic ideals."[69] Third, apart from the language movement, Webb and Milton's linguistic schemes also drew upon Renaissance sinological discourse. The sources Webb jotted down on the margins of *An Historical Essay* indicate that his treatise was shaped by, and embedded within, the sinological tradition represented by Mendoza, Ricci, Trigault, Ralegh, Purchas, Vossius, Peter Heylin, Semedo, Martini, Kircher, and Niuehoff, all of whom are repeatedly quoted by Webb.[70] Webb's thesis is a summary of the multiple radical strands in the sinological works published before *Paradise Lost*. The host of evidence Webb cited suggests that his claim was not ungrounded or unprecedented—the priority of Chinese chronology and language had been either explicitly stated or implicit in most Renaissance writings on the Far East. What Webb did is merely to tease out those radical strands and recast them into a coherent argument.[71] Even if *Paradise Lost* came to press two years earlier (1667), Milton, when planning to represent the first tongue, had most likely had in mind the wide range of Chinese influences converged in *An Historical Essay*.

It is true that Milton did not directly engage the Chinese language, but in concert with his perception of the alliance between Chinese annals and the pre-Adamic thesis, his representation of the primitive tongue at a time when the linguistic reform reached its apogee signals an awareness of this widespread movement.[72] The popularity of seventeenth-century linguistic innovation that involved some of Milton's notable associates could not have escaped his attention. Wilkins noted that "there is scarce any subject that hath been more thoroughly

---

[69] Porter, *Ideographia*, 44.

[70] Ricci's map of China was inserted immediately after the dedication in Webb's *Historical Essay*. Webb quoted extensively from Trigault, Ralegh, Heylyn, Martini, Semedo, and Kircher. For his reference to Mendoza see 73, 165, 180, 181. For a more detailed discussion of Webb's sources, see Ch'en, "John Webb," 92–94.

[71] Ralegh and Heylyn held radical views about both the location of Ararat, the scriptural location where the Ark rested, and the first settlement of Noah after he came out of the Ark. Both views are cited by Webb to prove that Noah settled in China and did not go with Nimrod, his great grandson, to Shinar. See Webb, *Historical Essay*, 18–28, 35.

[72] For the various motivations behind the widespread, profound, and sustained interest in the universal language in the Renaissance see Clauss, "Wilkins' *Essay*," in Subbiondo ed.,46; Knowlson, *Universal Language Schemes*, 9–15; and 27–43.

scanned and debated amongst learned men than the *Original* of *Languages* and *Letters*."[73] Similarly, in the preface to his *The Universal Character* (1657), the schoolmaster linguist Cave Beck (1623–1706) says, "This last century of years, much hath been the discourse and expectation of learned men, concerning the finding out of a universal character."[74] The middle of the seventeenth century witnessed an upsurge of the linguistic enterprise, which came to a flowering by the end of the 1660s in Wilkins's *A Real Character* (1668), the English polyhistor Kircher's *China Illustrata* (1667), Comenius's *The Way of Light* (1668), and Webb's *An Historical Essay* (1669).[75] The successive publication of these great works on universal character in the last four years of the sixties, most of which speculated on the relevance of the Chinese model to a general lexicon, indicates both the pressing urgency and top priority enjoyed by the universal language project among "learned men." These "learned men" included Milton's associates Comenius, Samuel Hartlib (1600–62), and Theodore Haak (1605–90) who first translated *Paradise Lost* into German. Comenius proved pivotal to initiating England's linguistic reform, and it is Hartlib who propagated Comenius's work in England.[76] Hartlib also helped publish Francis Lodwick's (1619–94) *A Common Writing* (1647) and Dalgarno's *Character Universalis* (1657). Haak personally encouraged Wilkins in his pursuit of a universal language.[77] Also, we learned from Haak that Milton intended to write an "Epitome of all Purchas Volumes," a travel compendium that contains most medieval and early modern reports of China,

---

[73] Wilkins, *Real Character*, 2.

[74] Beck, *The Universal Character* (1657), quoted in Cohen, "Project of a Universal Character," in Subbiondo ed., 241.

[75] For works in mid-seventeenth century also see, Francis Lodwick, *A Common Writing* (London, 1647), Lodwick, *The Ground-Work or Foundation Laid for the Framing of a New Perfect Language* (London, 1652); Johann J. Becher, *Character pro Notitia Linguarum Universali* (Frankfurt, 1661); Dalgarno, *Universal Character and A New Rational Language* (1657) and *Ars signorum* (1661); and Kircher, *Polygraphia or A New and Universal writing in Many Languages Revealed by the Combinatory Art* (London, 1663). On secondary works see Vivian Salmon, *The Works of Francis Lodwick: A Study of His Writings in the Intellectual Context of the Seventeenth Century* (London: Longman, 1972); and George E. McCracken, "Athanasius Kircher's Universal Polygraphy," *Isis* 39 (1948): 215–29.

[76] Demott, "Comenius and the Real Character," in Subbiondo ed., 158; also see Rossi, *Art of Memory*, 152–54. Comenius entrusted his *The Way of Light* to Hartlib after he left England; see G. H. Turnbull, *Hartlib, Dury and Comenius: Gleanings from Hartlib's Papers* (London: Liverpool UP, 1947), 367. On Comenius's relation with Hartlib see Turnbull, *Gleanings from Hartlib's Papers*, 342, 377–88. For Hartlib's involvement in the language project see Demott, "Comenius and the Real Character," 158, note11; Turnbull, *Gleanings from Hartlib's Papers*, 59–61; and Knowlson, *Universal Language Schemes*, 270. On the relations of Wilkins, Comenius, Haak, Hooke, and Lodowyck, also see Dorothy L. Stimson, "Comenius and the Invisible College," *Isis* 23(1953): 383–88.

[77] Pamela R. Barnett, *Theodore Haak, F.R.S. (1605–1690): The First German Translator of Paradise Lost* (The Hague: Mouton, 1962).

including Ricci and Trigault's accounts of the Chinese language.[78] Considering his dedication of *Of Education* (1644) to Hartlib and his association with Haak, his substantial knowledge of Purchas's work, as well as his general concern with language and education, it is unlikely that Milton could have turned a deaf ear to contemporary linguistic reformation.

The Resonance of Webb's Chinese Model in Milton's Primitive Language

In *Paradise Lost*, Milton represents the original language through Adam and Eve's consciousness of their linguistic facility and agency. The pair's speeches and dialogues of their language experiences are cast in four memorable scenes. When Satan speaks "with Serpent Tongue / Organic" (9.529–30), Eve wonders why "Language of Man pronounc't / By Tongue of Brute, and human sense exprest," because she knows that language was "deni'd / To Beasts, whom God on their Creation-Day / Created mute to all articulate sound" (9.552–56). Here Eve displays knowledge of God's fundamental criterion in the institution of language—language is a special gift for rational humans but "deni'd" to "mute" brutes. Later, when told by Michael of their departure from Eden, she cries over parting from the "flow'rs" "which I bred up with tender hand / From the first op'ning bud, and gave ye Names" (11.276–77). Eve's deploring reveals a hitherto concealed event: it is she who has named the flowers in Eden. If Eve's linguistic capacity shows but indirectly and reflexively, Adam exhibits a more conscious perception of and is therefore more articulate about his language facility, as he addresses Raphael:

> But who I was, or where, or from what cause,
> Knew not; to speak I tri'd, and forthwith spake,
> My Tongue obey'd and readily could name
> Whate'er I saw. (8.270–73)

In this stanza, the first person pronouns "I" and "my" signal conscious subjectivity, while adverbs such as "forthwith" and "readily" indicates the unforced spontaneity of Adam's naming and speaking. Adam's innate capacity for language shows more distinctly when God brings "each Bird and Beast" "to receive / From thee thir Names" (8.342–43), as Adam himself describes,

> … each Bird stoop'd on his wing.
> I nam'd them, as they pass'd, and understood
> Their Nature, with such knowledge God endu'd
> My sudden apprehension … . (8.351–54)

---

[78] Purchas himself speaks of languages in both the new and old worlds and the controversy over the first letters in "A Discourse on the Diversity of Letters." *Hakluytus Posthumus*, vol. 1. 485–505.

Here awareness of personal agency registers, once again, in the first person pronouns, and the adjective "sudden" shows the simultaneity of the two processes of naming and understanding.

Before proceeding to a detailed discussion of Milton's linguistic model, it is necessary to set out the central conceptual terms to be used in this section. Leonard adopts the term "natural language" as "an interpretive key" to study the "prelapsarian and postlapsarian language" as is "reflected in his [Adam's] employment of names."[79] I use both the concepts of *natural language* and *universal language* suggested in Bacon's real characters theory to examine, in addition to Adam and Eve's "employment of names," the institution of language symbolized by their naming and speaking. Further, instead of "prelapsarian and postlapsarian language," I propose three other analytical categories to approach Milton's images of language. First, I use *original tongue* or *names* to describe Adam and Eve's naming—their assigning of names to creatures fresh from the womb of the Creation. Second, I use *Edenic language* to refer to the language the pair spoke in the prelapsarian Eden. Whereas *original names* bears on the "Intuitive" reason of the name-givers to grasp at the essences of things, the Edenic language Adam and Eve used to converse with each other, Satan, Raphael, and Michael bespeaks "Discursive" reason—logical reasoning made possible by employment of those original names. Since both original names and the Edenic tongue address a pristine world unmediated by any preexistent symbolic system, they are collectively called *primitive* or *matrix language*. Third, I also distinguish between *prelapsarian names* that reflect an unmediated world and *postlapsarian words* that address a world differentiated by knowledge of right and evil. Prelapsarian differs from postlapsarian discursive reasoning in that whereas the former employs original names, the latter uses arbitrary words.

The four linguistic episodes or variations on Milton's theory of language dramatized in *Paradise Lost* have received much critical comment.[80] The epistemological origin of Adam and Eve's naming proves the central point of contention.[81] Though concurring with the knowledge encoded in Adam and Eve's naming, critics differ in regards to the origin of this knowledge. Stanley Fish claims that "Adam's knowledge is infused into him directly by God, and the

---

[79] Leonard, *Naming in Paradise*, 20.

[80] Mary Nyquist, "The Genesis of Gendered Subjectivity in the Divorce Tracts and in *Paradise Lost*," *Re-Membering Milton: Essays on the Texts and Traditions*, ed. Nyquist and Margaret W. Ferguson (New York: Methuen, 1988), 99–127, 100; Robert L. Entzminger, *Divine Word: Milton and the Redemption of Language* (Pittsburgh: Duquesne UP, 1985); Catherine Belsey, *John Milton: Language, Gender, Power* (Oxford: Basil Blackwell, 1988); Leonard, *Naming in Paradise*; Poole, "Naming"; and Christopher Eagle, "'Thou Serpent That Name Best': On Adamic Language and Obscurity in *Paradise Lost*," *Milton Quarterly* 41 (2007): 183–94.

[81] On knowledge informing Adam's naming see Eagle, "Adamic Language," 184–86; Eco, *The Search for the Perfect Language*, 8.

names he imposes, like God's, are accurate, intensively and extensively."[82] For Cheryl Thrash, "While the definer [God] comprehends (in both meanings of the word) all language in its fullest, eternal meaning, time-bound creatures necessarily experience language in a progressive fashion." So Adam's knowledge, Thrash contends, is "discursive" and "fundamentally cumulative rather than definitive."[83] Both Christopher Eagle and John Leonard turn to the Hermogenes-Cratylus model set out in Plato's *Cratylus*. Plato's Hermogenes maintains that "there is no name given to anything by nature; all is convention and habit of the users" (384c–d). In contrast, Cratylus argues that "words should as far as possible resemble things" and "the perfect state of language" consists in the appropriateness and similarity between things and their "expressions" (435c).[84] For Eagle, "Milton does not definitively endorse the assertion that the rightness of Adam's names is predicated on his priori knowledge." What is at issue is, Eagle observes, "whether Milton's Adam is a Cratylist knower of essences, imbued with a priori knowledge, or a Hermogenist name-maker, imbued with authority over consensus."[85] Rejecting Fish's claim that God endows "Adam and Eve with an accurate knowledge," Leonard argues that Milton's God "endow[s] Adam and Eve with the reason to form an accurate language for themselves"; otherwise, Adam would be "a meer artificall Adam" (YP 2:527).[86] The Cratylist/ Hermogenist paradigm thus proves central to scholarship on Milton's images of language. But what is neglected in this source-oriented or purely epistemological approach is its association with the larger context of Renaissance linguistic movement and its Chinese inspiration.

Webb's Chinese model provides a pertinent framework to probe into the Chinese implications of Milton's linguistic paradigm. The linguistic system Milton outlines in *Paradise Lost* also follows the "six principal guides" used by most seventeenth-century linguistic reformers. But in addition to antiquity, purity, and simplicity, characteristics common to other primitive language claimants, Milton's original tongue is distinguished by two other features. To convey the certainty of Adam and Eve's speeches, Milton invents some special episodes to allow the first pair to talk about their own experiences with language. From Adam and Eve's monologues and conversations, we can discern two core features characterizing their language. First, the matrix tongue came into being in a prelapsarian world unmediated by the moral knowledge of good and evil. Second, the original language was, rather than totally inspired by God, deeply informed by "Intuitive" and "Discursive" reason. Both characteristics resonate in Webb's Chinese model.

The epic genre allows Milton to use dramatic devices to represent Adam and Eve as both enunciators of and witnesses to the institution of language.

---

[82] Stanley Fish, *Surprised by Sin: The Reader in Paradise Lost*, 2nd ed. (Cambridge: Harvard UP, 1997), 114.
[83] Cheryl Thrash, "'How cam'st thou speakable of mute?': Learning Words in Milton's Paradise," *Milton Quarterly* 31 (1997): 42–61, 47.
[84] *The Dialogue of Plato*, trans. Benjamin Jowett, 4 vols. (1871), vol. 3, 43.
[85] Eagle, "Adamic Language," 186.
[86] Leonard, *Naming in Paradise*, 12.

Though agreeing to Adam's linguistic agency, critics disagree over that of Eve.[87] Poole distinguishes between Adam's "rational, central, and dialogic" and Eve's "affective, marginal, and self-reflexive" modes of naming, a distinction that, he claims, "reveal[s] two very different conceptions of paradisiacal language, one tracing a genealogy to Bacon, the other to Boehme."[88] I suggest that Adam and Eve's speeches point to, instead of two distinct traditions, a single consistent linguistic framework. Rather than prioritizing Eve's linguistic agency, I propose that Eve and Adam share an equal rather than gendered role in Milton's linguistic scheme. Genesis presents a simple and straightforward account of the primitive tongue: "And out of the ground the LORD God formed every beast of the field, and every fowl of the air; and brought *them* unto Adam to see what he would call them: and whatever Adam called every living creature, that was the name thereof" (2:19). Instead of reproducing the Adam-centered story from Genesis, Milton invents a four-way dialogue between Eve, Satan, Adam, and Raphael to bring out both Adam and Eve's linguistic agency and conscious reflection of their language facility, a rhetorical device that highlights multiple mutually reinforcing approaches to the first letters. It is when conversing with Raphael that Adam speaks of his linguistic facility, and it is when talking to Satan that Eve raises doubts about the standard by which God institutes language. In both conversations, Adam and Eve take initiatives to reflect upon the language issue, a reflection that turns them into not only speakers but also commentators on the institution of language.

Once establishing the certainty of Adam and Eve's speech through the technique of multiple points of view, Milton needs to show that this speech is the very primitive tongue. Prelapsarian Edenic imagery offers an ideal repertoire to depict the purity and antiquity of the original language. What makes Webb's *An Historical Essay* immediately relevant to Milton's matrix tongue is its adoption of what Porter calls the "Edenic metaphors" to describe the simplicity of the Chinese language.[89] As Webb states,

---

[87] Nyquist holds that "Eve's 'naming' becomes associated not with rational insight and dominion but rather with the act of lyrical utterance," and as such it "seems never to have had the precise status of an event." Nyquist, "Gendered Subjectivity," in Nyquist and Ferguson, eds., 100. By comparison, Diane McColley defends Eve's naming, claiming that Milton's Eve "stands in radiant contrast to the sly or naive temptresses who bore her name in the works of Milton's predecessors and contemporaries." Diane McColley, *Milton's Eve* (Urbana: U of Illinois P, 1983), 3–4; for McColley's defense of Eve's naming see 113. Leonard argues that unlike those who "regard the giving of names as Adam's privilege alone," "Milton's Eve has both understanding and responsibility. She also has remarkable knowledge," and "in naming the flowers Eve shares in Adam's understanding of and lordship over Creation." Leonard, *Naming in Paradise*, 47. Likewise, Poole also admits that "Milton gave his Eve the authority to name. In so doing, he deviated from the story in Genesis, in which Adam alone conferred names upon the animals." Poole, "Naming," 539.

[88] Poole, "Naming," 550–51.

[89] Porter, *Ideograhia*, 45. For Webb's use of Edenic images see *Ideographia*, 45–48.

in the remote and hitherto unknown *China*, are now at last found out, the true *Indigenes*, that ever since the flood of *Noah*, being born and bred or within their own Countrey, never permitted or admitted conversation with forein people. But living contentedly at home, in all abundant prosperity, under their own vines, and under their own fig-trees ... .[90]

The language of these "true *Indigenes*," Webb declares, was "a perfectly natural speech," since it "was at first infused or inspired, as the PRIMITIVE Language was into our first Parents."[91] As a natural language, Chinese reflects "the true, genuine, and original sense of things" and is thereby "fitted" to "the Infancy and Simplicity of Time."[92] Webb's terms such as "original," "infancy," "simplicity," and "natural" evoke strongly Milton's prelapsarian language. Like Webb, Milton turns to such pristine images as "Undeckt" (5.379), "naked" (5.44), and "love unlibidinous" (5.448–49) to represent the "simplicity and spotless innocence" (4.318–19) of the original tongue. The Chinese who live "under their own fig-trees" readily recall the first pair innocently sporting in Milton's Eden. Just as the natives in the Far East retain the "Ancient purity" of their speeches "without any change or alteration," Adam and Eve's roles as "Patriarch of mankind" (5.505) and "Mother of human race" bespeak the antiquity of their language. What language could claim a more ancient status when Adam and Eve, the patriarch and matriarch of humankind, talk about their own linguistic consciousness and experiences?

The image of "figtree" is especially revealing about the resonance of Milton's Edenic model in Webb's Chinese paradigm. Webb claims that the Chinese are "true *Indigenes*" "living contentedly at home ... under their own fig-trees."[93] In *Paradise Lost*, Adam and Eve use "figtree leaves" (9.1101) to cover their private parts after the Fall. Critics tend to read literally the origin of Milton's figtree in his statement that "The Figtree, not that kind for Fruit renown'd, / But such as at this day to *Indians* known / In *Malabar* or *Decan* spreads her Armes" (9.1101–3).[94] In fact, in the Renaissance, "figtree" was also a metaphor for the threshold of the Fall—it marks at once the loss of the prelapsarian purity and the beginning of the postlapsarian moral world. Webb and Milton's figtree image elicits, above all, the different settings within which the first tongue was articulated. Webb's figtree, though put in a prelapsarian context, is signified through postlapsarian knowledge of morality. For Webb, the spotless infancy of Chinese characters registers chiefly in its moral chastity. Chinese "poems," he says,

---

[90] Webb, *Historical Essay*, 142.
[91] Webb, *Historical Essay*, 167–68.
[92] Webb, *Historical Essay*, 192.
[93] Webb, *Historical Essay*, 142.
[94] See such a typical reading in Balachandra Rajan, "Banyan Trees and Fig Leaves: Some Thoughts on Milton's India," in *Of Poetry and Politics: New Essays on Milton and His World*, ed. P. G. Stanwood (Binghamton, NY: Medieval & Renaissance Texts & Studies, 1995): 213–28.

treat of Love, not with so much levity nevertheless, as ours, but in such chaste Language, as not an undecent and offensive word to the most chaste ear is to be found in them. And which is more, they have no Letters whereby to express the *Privy parts*, nor are they to be found written in any part of all their Books, which cannot be said of any Language under the concave of Heaven, besides.[95]

As is signaled by "poems" and "Books," two archetypical symbols of discursive constructions, Webb turns to the moral discourse or a postlapsarian symbolic framework to represent the pristine purity of the Chinese language. In contrast, Milton articulates the matrix tongue in a world undifferentiated by any signifying system. It is in the unfallen Eden that the first parents bestow names on creatures and flowers fresh from the "brooding wings of the Spirit of God" (7.235). What distinguishes the prelapsarian world is its unmediated state, as "no place" in Eden "Is yet distinct by name" (7.535–36), and everything is in a state of "liquid lapse" (2.163), reflecting, passively and innocently, the way of Nature. Nature itself "Wanton'd as in her prime, and play'd at will / Her Virgin Fancies, pouring forth more sweet, / Wild above Rule or Art" (5.294–97). In other words, the wantonness and wildness of Nature in Eden goes beyond any discursive or artistic rules. Since "Spring and Autumn ... Danc'd hand in hand" (5.394–95), seasons remain undifferentiated as well. Also, rather than resorting to any preexistent symbolic system, Adam and Eve make sense of the world by merely living in "the regard of Heaven on all his ways" (4.620). In a world unmediated by any symbolic order and where both man and creatures emit unhindered their pristine beams, it is but natural for the "rays of things" to coincide with those of the mind.

Compared with Webb's moral paradise in the Far East, Milton's unmediated Eden allows him to provide a more convincing portrait of the *lingua humana* and its subsequent degeneration into arbitrary words. To argue for the purity of a primitive language in a postlapsarian world, Webb has to prove its immunity from corruptions caused by time, conquests, and commerce, which is a hard case to make. By comparison, an undifferentiated prelapsarian world offers Milton a vantage point from which to represent the uniqueness of the Edenic tongue—the pre-symbolic context allows him to bring out the *irreplaceable* and *irretrievable* nature of the first letters. Webb maintains that only those languages carried by Nimrod to Shinaar were confounded, and that the Chinese language that escaped the Confusion at Babel retains its ancient purity. For Milton, as a unique gift of Adam and Eve and a distinctive product of a prelapsarian world, the original language was lost with the Fall rather than at Babel. As Christopher Ricks famously puts it, "with the Fall of Man, language falls too."[96] To expound the full significance of the Fall, God commissions Michael to reveal the history to be evolved out of Adam's offspring. So to fall is to fall into history. Since history is a discursive construction out of arbitrary words, to fall into history is to fall into words—to be clothed with signs no longer consonant with naked natures. Thus the figtree

---

[95] Webb, *Historical Essay*, 99.
[96] Christopher Ricks, *Milton's Grand Style* (Oxford: Oxford UP, 1963), 109.

leaves Adam and Eve use to cover their private parts also symbolize discursive mantles clothed upon things. The putting on of clothing, whether on men or things, signifies the beginning of civilization that relies on fallen words for signification. The first tongue lost its purity when used to articulate, instead of undifferentiated seasons or beamy bodies, arbitrary words and moral principles. Since one could no longer go back to the prelapsarian Eden, the primitive language, once lost, is irretrievable and irreplaceable by any candidate or artificial system designed by the Primitivists and Universalists.

That the original tongue falls with the Fall suggests that postlapsarian antediluvian languages, if they had ever existed, are not as chaste as Webb claims; rather, they are as corrupted as their fallen speakers. For Webb, the figtree signifies both linguistic and moral purity, because the Chinese language is "nakedly" free from not only such "superfluous guides" as grammatical and logical rules but also the taint of "[un]chaste" characters.[97] So Webb evokes the figtree image to show the innocence and chastity of Chinese, or as Porter puts it, to "restage the scene of prelapsarian purity" in the Far East.[98] Milton's figtree symbolizes two different kinds of nakedness. While prelapsarian nakedness or "that first naked glory" (9.1115) signifies "honour," "faith," and "purity" (9.1074–75), postlapsarian nudity indicates shame and guilt, and by implication, the birth of a world structured by the knowledge of good and evil. It is the immoral ways of this postlapsarian world that directly triggered the Noachian Flood. Milton believed in antediluvian peoples and languages. In his *History of Britain* (1670), he writes, "That the whole Earth was inhabited before the Flood, and to the utmost point of habitable ground, from those effectual words of *God* in the Creation, may be more then conjectur'd" (YP 5:4–5). Antediluvian races also appear in Satan's speech to Belial in *Paradise Regained*: "Before the Flood thou with thy lusty Crew, / False tilt'd Sons of God, roaming the Earth / Cast wanton eyes on the daughters of men, / And coupl'd with them, and begot a race" (PR 2.178–81). Belial's "lusty Crew" echoes the rioters in the age of Noah described in *Paradise Lost*. In Webb's account of the Chinese language, speakers of the primitive language belong to a virtuous people who had already existed before the Flood in the Far East. But the riotous races in the ages of Belial and Noah represented in Milton's epic poems demonstrate that antediluvian peoples are far from perfect as Webb asserts, and thereby the least candidates for the primitive language speakers. Here lies the ethical significance of Milton's image of the Flood—it is a moral purging that ushers in "the second source of Men" (12.13).

Both Webb and Milton contemplate on a world order mediated by the *Lingua humana*. Whereas Webb's primitive language signifies civilized peace and prosperity, Milton's original tongue registers pre–civil unrest. For Milton, while the Flood is unleashed by God to raise a new "source" of men, the Fall heralds the rising of a new world order—an order fitted for humans rather than

---

[97] Webb, *Historical Essay*, 167–68.
[98] Porter, *Ideograhia*, 47.

gods. In Webb's idyllic and moral Eden, a language made of real characters is sufficient to articulate human desires and regulate civilized life. But for Milton, the human world should be ordered by the language of morality rather than that of Nature. In an Eden unmediated by any symbolic system, the matrix language and the "ignorance" it represents apparently cannot sustain a world destined for fallible humans. As Satan sharply points out, Adam and Eve simply cannot "onely stand / By Ignorance" and they cannot be "happie" with "obedience" and "faith" unenlightened by moral knowledge (4.518–20). So the Fall signifies at once the downfall of a world regulated by a linguistic system composed merely of essences and the rise of a world structured by a language informed by moral knowledge. Put another way, the pure primitive language is incapable of expressing human desires and aspirations, and the Fall serves both to liberate the passions suppressed by the forbidden tree and to introduce principles of morality to order them.

As Milton's modern critics point out, no linguistic models could bypass the problem of the epistemological origin of the primitive language. The "Webster-Ward-Wilkins" debate over the "dative" and "inventive" nature of natural language well illustrates the controversial nature of this problem in the Renaissance. In his *Academiarum Examen* (1654), Webster argues that to "[repair] the ruins of *Babell*," it is necessary to discover "universal characters" that are "real, not nominal, expressing neither letters or words, but things and notions" (25) and in which "one note serves for one notion to all nations" (26). Like Wilkins, Webster also couples "real" with "universal" but he identifies "a real universal character" as the "pure language of Nature" and locates it in the "*Paradistical*" tongue (27). For Webster, as a natural language, this "Paradistical" tongue is "so innate and implanate in him [Adam], and not inventive or acquisitive, but meerly dative from the father of light" (29). Webster's thesis met strong opposition from Wilkins and Ward, for whom neither the Baconian real character nor the "pure language of Nature" is natural; rather, both are artificial constructs. In his *Vindiciae Academiarum* (1654), a work written in direct response to Webster's *Academiarum Examen*, Ward admits the primitive nature of the Adamic tongue, but refuses to call it "a natural language." As he puts it:

> Such a language as this (where every word were a definition and contained the nature of the thing) might not injustly be termed a natural language, and would afford that which the *Cabalists* and *Rosycrucians* have vainely sought for in the Hebrew, And in the names assigned by *Adam*, which M. *Webster* ... would bring under ... [grammatical] laws.[99]

For Ward, the "natural language" people sought futilely either in "Hebrew" or "the names assigned by Adam" is not, as Webster says, "dative from the father of light." Like any other artificial language, Ward argues, the language of Nature is "inventive

---

[99] Debus ed., *Webster-Ward Debate*, 22. Both Webster's *Academiarum Examen* and Ward's *Vindiciae Academiarum* are reproduced in facsimile by Debus in *Science and Education*.

or acquisitive," and thereby "might soone receive a mighty advantage" "by the helpe of Logick and Mathematicks." Ward calls this logical and mathematical analysis of natural language a "philosophical" approach to a real character."[100] In his *A Real Character*, Wilkins also traces the matrix language to the Adamic tongue, stating that "'tis evident enough that the first language was co-created with our first Parents, they immediately understanding the voice of God speaking to them in the Garden."[101] But like Ward, he also rejects the equation of "the first language" with natural language, for, he argues, it is equally "evident enough that no one Language is natural to mankind, because the knowledge which is Natural would generally remain amongst men, notwithstanding the superinduction of any other particular Tongue, wherein they might be by Art."[102]

Webb and Milton responded differently to the Webster-Ward-Wilkins controversy by offering alternative models to the "dative" and "inventive" paradigms. To illuminate the primitive status of the Chinese characters, Webb also uses the idea of natural language, but he defines this concept differently. Whereas Ward and Wilkins promote the "mighty advantage" afforded "by the helpe of Logick and Mathematicks," Webb celebrates Chinese for being free from "all those troublesome aides that are brought in to the assistance of Art," that is, "Rules either for Grammar, Logick, or Rhetorick."[103] Echoing Webster, Webb observes that since the Chinese "hav[e] no other Rules in use, than what the light of Nature hath dictated unto them ... their Language is plain, easie, and simple, as NATURAL speech ought to be."[104] In this "natural" language, "every single Character importeth a single word or name, whereby they had need of as many Characters, as there are things, by which they would deliver the conceptions of their minds."[105] However, instead of being "meerly dative from the father of light" as Webster claims, the Chinese language is "natural" in the true sense of the word—rather than directly "infused and inspired" by God, it was "taught" by "Nature from God."[106] Simply put, if God is the first cause, then Nature is the immediate efficient cause of the Eastern language.

To distinguish a language immediately informed by Nature from that directly infused by God, Webb turns to the idea of "radix," a term that denotes "the base or point of origin" or "an original word or form from which other words are derived."[107] In his *A Real Character*, Wilkins observes that "Of all other Languages, the *Greek* is looked upon to be one of the most copious; the Radixes of which are esteemed

---

[100] Debus ed., *Webster-Ward Debate*, 21.
[101] Wilkins, *Real Character*, 1.1.2.
[102] Wilkins, *Real Character*, 1.
[103] Webb, *Historical Essay*, 167.
[104] Webb, *Historical Essay*, 192–93.
[105] Webb, *Historical Essay*, 164.
[106] Webb, *Historical Essay*, 146, 167–68.
[107] "radix, n." *OED Online*. December 2012. Oxford UP. January 22, 2013. <http://www.oed.com.myaccess.library.utoronto.ca/view/Entry/157352?redirectedFrom=radix>.

to be about 3244."[108] Webb locates the origin or "radix" of the Chinese language in things and characters themselves, a move that directly challenges those who claim either exclusive divine source or conventional consensus for the original tongue. Resonating with Webster, Milton's Adam remarks that he "understood" the "nature" of the birds as he "nam'd" them, "with such knowledge God endu'd / My sudden apprehension." The Cratylist/Hermogenist scholars are right in pointing out that, in allowing Adam and Eve to talk about their first language experiences, Milton is engaging the thorny issue why they can name things "sudden[ly]" and "rightly" (8.439). As one of those earliest readers of Milton, Webb might have the Cratylist/Hermogenist interpretation in mind when proposing his "radix" thesis. According to Webb,

> the *Chinois* are never put to that irkesome vexation of searching out a *Radix* for the derivation of any of their words, as generally all other Nations are; but the *Radix* is the word, and the word the *Radix*, and the syllable the same also ... the true, genuine, and original sense of things seems to remain with them.[109]

Whereas Milton is alleged to place the fountain of Adam and Eve's knowledge in established conventions or divine inspiration, Webb puts the origin of knowledge that informs the Chinese script in characters or things themselves: "the *Radix* is the word, and the word the *Radix*." Since "Radix" shares the same root with "radius," a term that means "a ray or beam of light,"[110] that "the *Radix* is the word" indicates the natural emission of the rays of things. Accordingly, the claim that "the word [is]the *Radix*" suggests the coincidence of the rays of things with those of the mind. For Webb, even if Paradise is irrevocably lost, the Chinese script still addresses natures and essences—"significative" of their own accord, Chinese characters are things themselves.

In addition to the Cratylist/Hermogenist approach, Webb's radix model might have also responded to a different interpretation of Milton's language scheme. It is possible that Adam or Eve is neither a "Cratylist knower of essences" nor a "Hermogenist name-maker" as Eagle claims.[111] Rather, Milton's first pair are, like most early modern philosophers enlightened by Bacon's experimental philosophy, rationalists who prioritize "reason" or the light of the mind over the light of both Nature and the Father. Put differently, whereas Webb locates the epistemological origin of the matrix tongue in the source or radix itself, Milton places it in rational reason; as Leonard rightly argues, he "endow[s] Adam and Eve with the reason to form an accurate language for themselves." While Webb's radix highlights the coincidence of the beams of things and the mind, Milton's reason puts a special emphasis on the rays of the mind. But this does not mean that Milton ignores the

---

[108] Wilkins, *A Real Character*, 453.
[109] Webb, *Historical Essay*, 192.
[110] "radius, n." *OED Online*. December 2012. Oxford UP. January 22, 2013 <http://www.oed.com.myaccess.library.utoronto.ca/view/Entry/157350?redirectedFrom=radii>.
[111] Eagle, "Thou Serpent," 186.

primacy of things; rather, it means that he approaches the source problem through the particular angle of a rational mind. Like most Renaissance natural philosophers, Milton did privilege "things" over "names." In the *First Defence of the English People* (1652), he says that "names are subordinate to things, not things to names" (YP 4:456) and that since "names give precedence to facts ... it is not our business to worry about names when we have done away with the reality" (YP 4:454–55). But he thinks that reason is crucial to the formation of the original language—"things" would be more adequately represented if illuminated by the rational light of the mind. Also consistent with his rational philosophy, Milton holds that reason, as the cardinal marker between man and animal, is the foundational tenet upon which God institutes language. This cornerstone assumption suggests itself strongly in his repeated emphasis on the distinction between humans and beasts. Raphael remarks that the "Master work" of God's creation is "a Creature who not prone / And Brute as other Creatures, but endu'd / With Sanctity of Reason" (7.505–8). Similarly, Adam argues that "But God left free the Will, for what obeys / Reason, is free, and Reason he made right" (9.351–52). When Satan talks in "Tongue / Organic," Eve doubts whether the rational faculty is really "deni'd" to brutes as God made them to understand, since she sees "in thir looks / Much reason, and in thir actions oft appears" (9.558–59). Likewise, rational reason constitutes the core argument of Adam's discourse on true society: "Of fellowship I speak / Such as I seek, fit to participate / All rational delight, wherein the brute / cannot be human consort" (8.388–91). God approves of Adam's reasoning based on the demarcation between "rational delight" and the pleasure of brutes, as he says, "I was pleas'd" to "find thee knowing not of Beasts along, / Which thou has rightly nam'd, but of thyself" (8.436–38).

Instead of using reason as an umbrella concept, Milton differentiates between "Intuitive" and "Discursive" reason. That Adam and Eve named things by virtue of intuitive and discursive reason rather than *a priori* knowledge or established conventions constitutes a unique feature of Miltonic primitive tongue. What distinguishes Milton's prelapsarian reasoning is that it employs not words informed by moral discourse but original names unmediated by any symbolic system. It is through the mouth of Raphael that Milton expresses the intuitive and discursive reason entailed in the matrix tongue. When conversing with Adam, Raphael speaks of the "gradual" sublimation of vegetative and animal "spirits" to the intellectual "Soul," as he puts it,

> ... flow'rs and thir fruit
> Man's nourishment, by gradual scale sublim'd
> To vital spirits aspire, to animal,
> To intellectual, give both life and sense,
> Fancy and understanding, whence the Soul
> Reason receives, and reason is her being,
> Discursive, or Intuitive; discourse
> Is oftest yours, the latter most is ours,
> Differing but in degree, of kind the same. (5.482–90)

For Milton, "reason" is the "being" of the intellectual "Soul," and this rational "being" consists of two parts that "[differ] but in degree"—intuition and discourse. Whereas *intuitive reason* stresses direct access to the nature of things, *discursive reason* emphasizes the acquisition of knowledge through logical reasoning and learned experience. According to the *OED*, *intuition* denotes, apart from "immediate perception ascribed to angelic and spiritual beings," a "sight or vision" that "consists in direct and immediate looking upon an object, and sees it as it is." Thus what is captured by an intuitive vision is "knowledge or mental perception" that "consists in immediate apprehension, without the intervention of any reasoning process." Opposite to *intuition*, *discursive reason* means the "passing from premises to conclusions; proceeding by reasoning or argument." In his *Observations upon Cæsars Commentaries* (1604), Clement Edmondes says that "the soule of man is endued with a power of discourse, whereby it concludeth either according to the certainetie of reason, or the learning of experience."[112] So while intuitive reason allows immediate access to the nature of things, discursive reason needs the mediation of both reasoning and experience. What is involved in Adam and Eve's naming is intuitive reason; and what they employed in the prelapsarian conversations is discursive reason.

Milton uses two particular narrative devices to bear out the intuitive knowledge governing Adam and Eve's prelapsarian speeches. First, he dramatizes their ignorance of the origin of their being, a state that signifies an equal ignorance of any preexistent signifying system. Eve is "much wond'ring where / And what I was" when "first" awakening (4.450–52) to her being; Adam does not know "who I was, or where, or from what cause" when first aware of his existence. Second, Milton redefines the act of naming to bring out the intuitive nature of Adam's knowledge. Raphael's statement that "And thou thir Natures know'st, and gav'st them Names" (7.492) means that the three processes of knowing, understanding, and naming occur at one and the same time. Instinctively, Adam is also aware of the simultaneity of the various cognitive processes involved in his naming. When animals come to "receive" "thir names," he remarks, "I nam'd them ... and understood / Thir Nature" with "sudden apprehension." The word "sudden" shows a spontaneous and almost unmediated articulation of what is on the mind, which indicates the synchronization of naming, knowing, and understanding. This undifferentiated naming process is represented as an ability to extemporize by Milton in his *The Christian Doctrine*. As he puts it, "Adam could not have given names to the animals in that extempore way, without very great intelligence" (YP 6:324).

As Milton pointedly declares, Adam's intuitive knowledge is informed by "very great intelligence" or the "prime Wisdom" (8.195) to know the proper measure of human knowledge. According to St. Augustine, the intellectual image of God expresses itself in the three faculties of the soul—will, memory,

---

[112] Clement Edmondes, *Observations upon Caesars Commentaries* (London, 1604), 39.

and understanding.[113] While figuring the "will" of the intellectual soul as rational "reason," Milton articulates its "understanding" capacity in Adam's "sudden apprehension." He uses the word "apprehend" in *Tetrachordon* to describe the rational base of Adam's naming, as he says:

> *Adam* who had the wisdom giv'n him to know all creatures, and to name them according to their properties, no doubt but had the gift to discern perfectly, that which concern'd him much more; and to apprehend at first sight the true fitness of that consort which God provided him, And therefore spake in reference to those words which God pronounc't before. (YP 2:602)

Adam's rational capacity to "form an accurate language" suggests itself here. Adam's ability to "name" things "according to their properties," Milton says, comes from the "wisdom ... to know all creatures." By "wisdom," he means "the gift to discern perfectly" or the ability to judge the "true fitness" of things. Leonard's interpretation of Milton's "apprehension" as "grasping with intellect" provides a fresh insight into Adam's linguistic facility.[114] But by "apprehend" Milton also means "comprehend," a word that signifies a higher intellectual order. To *comprehend* is to situate what is apprehended within a larger scope of significance—to comprehend it within a broader context of meaning. Raphael uses "comprehend" to talk about the proper measure of Adam's knowledge, as he says, "Meanwhile enjoy / Your fill what happiness this happy state / Can comprehend, incapable of more" (5.503–5). Here *comprehend* connotes perception of the boundary of human knowledge, an implication further reinforced when Raphael advises Adam to "be lowly wise / Think only what concerns thee and thy being, / Dream not of other Worlds" (8.173–75). Adam's response that "That not to know at large of things remote / From use, obscure and subtle, but to know / That which before us lies in daily life / Is prime Wisdom" (8.191–95) shows his recognition of such a limit. To "discern" is to compare and identify something from a larger framework, a meaning cognate with what is denoted by the word *comprehend*. This recognition of the proper measure of knowledge allows Adam not only to keep to his position and duty but also to know "thir [creatures] language and thir ways" (8.371–72) and judge the "fitness" of his "consort."

Limitations and Implications of the Chinese Model

The tension suggested in Webb and Milton's images of the primitive language reflects not only enthusiasm but also skepticism towards the Chinese model. The exemplary status of the Chinese language as a universal script came increasingly under attack as the seventeenth century progressed. Cornelius effectively

---

[113] For more on the intellectual image of God see Almond, *Adam and Eve in Seventeenth-Century Thought*, 11–13.

[114] Leonard, *Naming in Paradise*, 12.

summarizes the ambivalent reception of the Chinese script in the Renaissance: "optimism and pessimism mingled in the minds of Europeans who speculated on these universal characters of the Orient."[115] Even before the investigation committee was formed in 1668, the illusory nature of the Chinese model had already been noticed by its very advocates. For most reformers, a major defect that hinders the Eastern script from becoming a productive model resides in the sheer number of its characters.[116] Though admiring the Chinese example in his *Mercury*, Wilkins evinces doubt in *A Real Character*: "There are many considerable faults" in "the China Character and language, so much talked of in the world," he says, "which make it come far short of the advantage which may be in such a philosophical language as is here designed." Wilkins identifies three such "faults": the monstrous number of Chinese characters (80,000 ideograms); their "difficulty and perplexedness"; and their lack of "analogy betwixt the shapes of the characters and the things represented by them."[117] For Comenius, "the discovery of a Real Language would call for far less labor than those monstrous six thousand characters of the Chinese and would yield infinitely more fruit."[118]

But the value of the Chinese model for Renaissance linguistic innovators consists not so much in its fruitfulness as in the intellectual debates it fermented. It is in the attempts to interpret and assimilate an alien cipher that early modern Europeans came to reflect upon their own linguistic and theological assumptions, a reflection that helped, in turn, generate a host of competing and constructive frameworks. Linguistic experiments inspired by the Chinese example before the 1670s have yielded, as Porter has persuasively demonstrated, more sustained and productive discussions in the latter part of the seventeenth and the early decades of the eighteenth centuries.

Apart from the moral and theological implications, the comparison of Webb and Milton's linguistic schemes also sheds light upon the cultural allegories they entail. Chinese primitive language is symptomatic of its renowned cultural and political accomplishments. For Webb, not only was Chinese the very primitive language but also Chinese cultural and political systems served as exemplars for the West. Ramsay holds that Webb's linguistic model shows that "China's exemplary status is a result of its possession of the primitive language and its socio-political virtues are the consequence of its Noachian origins." Webb's revision of the biblical language story, Ramsay continues, "offered a politically-safe way for him to criticize the restored English monarchy by contrasting it to an idealized account of China's social and political state."[119] Indeed, while accommodating an alien cipher, Webb introduces an almost perfect monarchy in which "their Kings may be said to

---

[115] Cornelius, *Imaginary Voyage*, 37.
[116] For the Jesuit missionaries' reports of the number of Chinese characters see Webb, *Historical Essay*, 173.
[117] Wilkins, *A Real Character*, 450, 451; also see 452.
[118] Comenius, *The Way of Light*, 186–87.
[119] Ramsey, "China and the Ideal of Order," 483–84.

be Philosophers, and their Philosophers, Kings." The Eastern "philosopher king" provides an ideal exemplar for Western princes who were constantly entangled in religious wars and territorial disputes. As Webb puts it, "if ever any Monarchy in the world was constituted according to political principles, and dictates of right reason, it may be boldly said that of the Chinois is."[120] Markley claims that "Milton's ironclad commitment to a voluntarist theology and republican politics lead him to distance himself from sixteenth and seventeenth century accounts that celebrated China's wealth, socioeconomic stability, good government, and presumed nontheistic religion."[121] Though keeping reservations about Milton's "distanc[ing]" from contemporary reports on China, I nevertheless agree that the ideal monarchy depicted in these reports must have been especially unsettling to Milton, a declared enemy of monarchial rules. Against the "the Seat / Of mightiest Empire" (11.386–87), an England that had been torn apart by tyrannical kings and whose civil wounds remained unhealed by an abortive Republic must have sounded like the very epitome of a fallen world.

The Chinese presence not only provides new insight into Milton's response to linguistic diversity but also brings his language model into the global cultural platform engineered by Comenius, Hartlib, as well as John Dury (1596–1680), the English reformer and educator who translated in 1652 Milton's *Eikonoklastes* into French. The universal scope of the Renaissance linguistic movement can be seen from its overarching aim to enact a worldwide reform. Comenius calls the intellectual reformation he envisaged a "Panorthosia or Universal Reform."[122] For Comenius, the Universalists' "new [linguistic] schemes" aimed precisely to create such a "pansophic language" or "a polyglot speech" that could be "the universal carrier of light."[123] "When an Universal Language has been achieved," he declared, "all men will become as it were one race, one people, one household, one School of God."[124] Thus the linguistic enterprise was, rather than an isolated event, an integral part of "the broader program of an evangelical philosophy whose goal was world reformation."[125] Comenius's universal project found enthusiastic support from Hartlib and Dury, who joined him in 1642 with the explicit purpose of "promot[ing] ecclesiastical peace, to educate Christian youth to a reform and the

---

[120] Webb, *Historical Essay*, 92–93. The idea of Chinese "philosopher-kings" is also mentioned by Ricci-Trigault, *Journals*, 26, 55, 337.

[121] Markley, "Destin'd Walls," 192.

[122] Comenius, *Panorthosia or Universal Reform: Chapters 19 to 26*, trans. A. M. O. Dobbie (Sheffield: Sheffield Academic, 1993).

[123] Comenius, *The Way of Light*, 8. Quoted in Demott, "Comenius and the Real Character," in Subbiondo ed., 160.

[124] Comenius, *The Way of Light*, 198.

[125] Stillman, *New Philosophy*, 49. On the Universal significance of Renaissance linguistic reform, see *Samuel Hartlib and Universal Reformation: Studies in Intellectual Communication*, ed. Michael Leslie, Timothy Raylor, and Mark Greengrass (New York: Cambridge UP, 1994).

study of true wisdom,"[126] a religious and educational blueprint most likely shared by Milton. This "evangelical universalism" that aimed at "world reformation" based upon language and education signals not only a cosmopolitan outlook but a visionary cosmopolitan agenda.[127] Milton participates in this broad-minded agenda imagined by his close associates through not only the educational program he mapped in *Of Education* but also the linguistic scheme outlined in *Paradise Lost*.

Seventeenth-century linguistic innovation partakes of the large-scale "universal" movements in early modern Europe, intellectual reforms that displayed a truly remarkable liberal cosmopolitan spirit to engage the new historical data revealed by the recently discovered worlds. The universal claims of Renaissance linguistic reformers evoke the modern globalization theory of "universalism." Both the globalists and poststructuralists regard the concept of universalism as an ideological construct freighted with colonial, Eurocentric, and ethnic connotations. Whereas the globalists find fault with its insufficiency to address non-European cultures, the poststructuralists draw attention to its ideological and imperialist implications, criticizing its incapacity to articulate the postcolonial conditions of difference and hybridity. But Renaissance universalism, whether in the fields of history, chronology, or language, though inevitably implicated in a Eurocentric and monotheistic framework, show signs that transcend such categories as difference and hybridity. The universal history projects championed by Bodin, the universal chronological principle proposed by Scaliger, and the primitive language and universal character advocated by Webb and Wilkins—all these represent a cosmopolitan liberalism, a collective desire to reach out to connect with the new lands and to comprehend the whole globe within the compass of human knowledge. For Bodin, a universal history should address all nations and peoples; and for Scaliger, a universal chronological principle should be based on all histories. The universal language projects claim that it is not Hebrew nor any nationalistic languages but an artificial framework expressing the correspondence between the signifiers and the signified that counts as a common repertoire. The fundamental assumption behind such a universal signifier is, instead of racial or national difference, the transcendental principle of rational reason, for, as Wilkin remarks, "as men generally agree in the same principle of Reason, so do they likewise agree in the same Internal Notion or apprehension of Things."[128] Since reason is common to all humanity, Milton's emphasis on the rational dimension of the primitive language signifies, therefore, his universal will to seek common ground and cosmopolitan will to engage linguistic diversity.

---

[126] Turnbull, *Gleanings from Hartlib's Papers*, 363.

[127] Demott used the term "evangelical universalism," "Comenius and the Real Character," in Subbiondo ed., 16.

[128] Wilkins, *A Real Character*, 20.

Chapter 6
The Mongol Tartars' World Imperialism and Milton's Vision of Global Governance

Milton's images of Chinese history and language exemplify the liberal cosmopolitanism he expounds in *Areopagitica*. But as to be shown in this chapter, his representation of the Mongols' imperial model seems to demonstrate the limitations of his cosmopolitan tolerance. Milton's envisioning of a political settlement in the rule of the Son in his epic poems derives from a rejection of the imperial governance represented by the Mongol Empire, a rejection that appears to modify the liberal cosmopolitanism he propounds in *Areopagitica* and suggested in his responses to Chinese history and language. This modification does not, however, negate his intellectual openness to alien political models. For Milton, the global imperialism embodied by the Mongol Empire serves as both a testing stone for England's political experiment and a warning sign for its imperial outreach. So rather than compromising his cosmopolitanism, Milton's reception of the Mongol imperial model indicates a discerning cosmopolitanism that seeks to extract useful political lessons through cultural comparison and critical assessment.

In Adam's historical survey in book XI of *Paradise Lost*, Milton explicitly calls the capital city, "Cambalu, seat of Cathaian Can" and "Paquin of Sinaean Kings," "seat / Of the mightiest Empire" (11.386–90). Both "Cambalu" and "Paquin" mean present-day Beijing. "Cambalu" was the capital city of the Yuan Empire (1271–1368) built by Genghis Khan's grandson Kublai Khan (1215–94), and it changed its name into "Paquin" when it became the capital of the Ming Empire (1368–1644). After the Qing Dynasty (1644–1911) replaced Ming, Paquin continued to be the imperial seat. In calling Beijing "seat / Of the mightiest Empire," Milton evokes not only Chinese history and language but also the imperial monarchy in the Far East. This chapter investigates the cultural memory of the Mongols' world empire in Milton's conception of imperial rule and global governance by studying his images of the Tartar in his epic poem.

The image of empire features prominently in Milton's epic poems. As is shown in Satan's offer of Parthia and Rome, the "temptation of empire" is a major theme of *Paradise Regained*.[1] Similarly, in *Paradise Lost* a chief aim of Satan's venture to Eden is to "[Divide] Empire with Heav'n's King" (4.111).[2] Miltonic empire is a controversial image that has absorbed much critical energy. As Sharon Achinstein

---
[1] Balachandra Rajan, "The Imperial Temptation," in Rajan and Sauer eds., *Milton and the Imperial Vision*, 294–314.
[2] Robert M. Fallon, *Divided Empire: Milton's Political Imagery* (University Park: Pennsylvania State UP, 1995).

notes, most critics focus on identifying Milton's anti-or pro-empire tendencies, studying "whether, and at what time, and in what ways, Milton opposed empire."[3] Robert Fallon denies Milton's endorsement of imperialism before the Restoration, but he concedes that "the image of empire may well have suggested to the poet a paradigm for the political framework of his great epics," in which "the spiritual struggle between good and evil for the human soul is described as the clash of two great nations contending for control of a distant possession of one of them."[4] Bruce McLeod maintains that England's absence and Rome's fleeting appearance in Adam's historical survey in book XI indicate that Milton locates the "Lordly eye" in England and "is (re)producing the space of empire from an imperial view point."[5] In contrast, David Quint holds that Milton's epic poem presents "an indictment of European expansion and colonialism that includes his own countrymen."[6] Similarly, David Armitage argues that though Milton "produce[d] an epic whose secondary narrative was of Satan's exploration and colonization of a new world," the poet's "continuing commitment to the political program of English humanism ensured that this would be a consciously anti-imperial epic."[7]

A major problem with this scholarship is that critics tend to use the umbrella concept "imperial" to describe Milton's image of empire. In fact, Milton differentiates between the empire as it is represented by Satan and Chaos and the spiritual empire registered in the rule of the Son or Jesus Christ.[8] Whereas Satan and Chaos aspire to imperial expansion and conquest, the Son symbolizes a kind

---

[3] Sharon Achinstein, "Imperial Dialectic: Milton and Conquered Peoples," in Rajan and Sauer eds., 67–89, 69.

[4] Fallon, "Cromwell, Milton, and the Western Design," in Rajan and Sauer eds., 133–54, 153.

[5] Bruce McLeod, "The 'Lordly eye': Milton and the Strategic Geography of Empire," in Rajan and Sauer eds., 48–66, 57, 63. For the imperial approach also see Evans, *Milton's Imperial Epic*; Andrew Hadfield, "The English and Other Peoples," in *A Companion to Milton*, ed. Thomas N. Corns (Oxford: Blackwell, 2001), 174–90; and Willy Maley, *Nation, State, and Empire in English Renaissance Literature: Shakespeare to Milton* (New York: Palgrave, 2003).

[6] David Quint, *Epic and Empire: Politics and Generic Form from Virgil to Milton* (Princeton: Princeton UP, 1993), 265.

[7] David Armitage, "Literature and Empire," in *The Oxford History of the British Empire*, ed. Roger Louis, vol. 1. *The Origins of Empire: British Overseas Enterprise to the Close of the Seventeenth Century*, ed. Nicholas Canny and Alaine Low (Oxford: Oxford UP, 1998), 99–123, 120–21; also see Armitage, "John Milton: Poet against Empire," in *Milton and Republicanism*, ed. Armitage, Armand Himy, and Quentin Skinner (Cambridge: Cambridge UP, 1995), 206–26. For the anti-imperial approach also see J. P. Conlan, "'Paradise Lost': Milton's Anti-Imperial Epic," *Pacific Coast Philology* 33.1 (1998): 31–43.

[8] Since *Paradise Regained* signposts several times the identity of the "Son" with "Jesus," I use these two terms as synonyms. For instance, "The Father's voice / From heaven pronounced him his beloved son" (PR 1.31–2); "Thy father is the eternal King" (PR 1.236).

of spiritual and ethical rule. Since the two forms of sovereignty represented in Milton's epic poems aim at universal rather than regional or national governance, I use the framework of globalization/cosmopolitan theory to study Milton's conception of empire.[9]

Modern globalization theory contrasts "empire" with "cosmopolis." According to the OED, the word *empire* means both "imperial rule" and "an extensive territory (esp. an aggregate of many separate states) under the sway of an emperor or supreme ruler." Originating from the Roman *imperium*, the adjective *imperial* denotes literally what pertains to an empire, and figuratively the supreme authority to rule and command subject territories. *Cosmopolis* comes from *cosmopolite*, a word that indicates a "citizen of the world" or "one who regards or treats the whole world as his country."[10] Barry Gills argues that though both cosmopolis and empire express "an idea of human unity and community," they nevertheless "represent two antithetical conceptions and practices of world-consciousness and world order." Whereas *empire* means "the naked pursuit of power and wealth," Gill says, *cosmopolis* signifies "our spiritual side and our quest for harmony, moral order, and community."[11] Fred Dallmayr also compares cosmopolis with empire, arguing that the "juncture of radical state autonomy and globalization" "gives rise to two opposing tendencies":

> on the one hand, the ambitions of empire where globalization is subjected to global sovereignty (a global Leviathan); on the other side, a democratic cosmopolis (global commonwealth) achieved through the subordination of sovereignty to global interdependence.

Dallmayr defines "a global Leviathan" as "the extension of political and military power beyond the scope of the metropolitan homeland, that is, the wielding of dominion over foreign territories inhabited by non-citizen populations."[12] By comparison, "a global commonwealth" is an institution that "embrac[es]different cultures and societies and [is] held together not by a central Leviathan but by lateral connections and bonds of cultural and political interdependence."[13]

But empire and cosmopolis are not "antithetical" for those who seek to define empire in terms of cosmopolitanism, that is, as a juridical and ethical rather than imperial concept. Adam Watson maintains that "ethnic and civic loyalties

---

[9] For a globalization approach to Milton's imagination of an international legal order, see Peters, "Bridge over Chaos."

[10] "imperial, adj. and n." 2nd ed. 1989. *OED Online*. June 17, 2012; "cosmopolite, n. and adj." 2nd ed. 1989. *OED Online*. June 17, 2012.

[11] Barry K. Gills, "'Empire' versus 'Cosmopolis': The Clash of Globalization," *Globalizations* 2.1 (2005): 5–13, 5, 6.9.

[12] Fred Dallmayr, "'Empire or Cosmopolis: Civilization at the Crossroads," *Globalizations* 2.1 (2005): 14–30, 15, 16.

[13] Dallmayr, "'Empire or Cosmopolis," 26.

increasingly found their place within an imperial political and cultural horizon."[14] In their controversial work *Empire*, Michael Hardt and Antonio Negri also claim that "the classical concept of empire united juridical categories and universal ethical values, making them work together as an organic whole."[15] In a globalized world, Hardt and Negri argue, "sovereignty has taken on a new form, composed of a series of national and supranational organisms united under a single logic of rule." The two authors give this "new global form of sovereignty" the name of "empire," defining it as a "global concept under the direction of a single conductor, a unitary power that maintains the social peace and produces its ethical truths." The reason they choose "empire" to designate the new authority in a global age is that, Hardt and Negri explain, though "every juridical system is in some way a crystallization of a specific set of values," empire "pushes the coincidence and universality of the ethical and juridical to the extreme."[16] Andrew Jones calls Hardt and Negri's new governance structure "globalization-as-empire,"[17] but I will call it a *cosmopolitan empire* on account of the emphasis they put on its social and ethical capacities, attributes that signal a "cosmopolitan will" to "engage human diversity."[18] The two aspects of empire, that is, its imperial and cosmopolitan implications, are exemplified in the rule of Rome—the Roman Empire not only dominated but also showed considerable tolerance towards the cultural diversities it contained. In truth, as is argued by Amy Chua, in their rise to "global hegemony," almost all empires in history were noted for their remarkable "tolerance" of various religions and nationals subsumed under the imperial rules.[19]

This chapter adopts at once an anti-and pro-empire position. Drawing upon both the "imperial" and "cosmopolitan" definitions of empire in globalization theory, I argue that Milton conceives both a "global Leviathan" and a "global commonwealth" in his epic poems. According to Julie S. Peters:

> From the Hill of Paradise Michael not only gives Adam a vision of the whole expanse of human history, with its lessons about *failed empire*, but also shows him the whole expanse of human geography—the great 'Hemisphere of earth ... / Strecht out to the amplest reach' (11.379–80), with its promise of *happy empire*.[20]

---

[14] Adam Watson, *The Evolution of International Society: A Comparative Historical Analysis*, intro. Barry Buzan and Richard Little (London: Routledge, 2009), 102.

[15] Michael Hardt and Antonio Negri, *Empire* (Cambridge, MA: Harvard UP, 2000), 10.

[16] Hardt and Negri, *Empire*, xi, xii, 10.

[17] Andrew Jones, *Globalization: Key Thinkers* (Cambridge: Polity, 2010), 206.

[18] Hollinger, *Postethnic America*, 84.

[19] Amy Chua, *How Hyperpowers Rise to Global Dominance—and Why They Fall* (New York: Doubleday, 2007), xxi.

[20] Peters, "Bridge over Chaos," 278, my own italics.

Whereas the "failed empire" described by Peters reflects the "Global Leviathan," the "happy empire" is manifested in the "global commonwealth" symbolized in the Son's rule. Specifically, while representing the "global Leviathan" in the imperial ambitions of Satan, Chaos, and God, Milton imagines the "global commonwealth" in the rule of the Son. What Milton opposes is the "imperial" empire, and what he champions is a "cosmopolitan" empire. On the one hand, what is fought for between God, Satan, and Chaos is imperial hegemony or a "global leviathan." God is determined to defend his "ancient … claim / of Deity or Empire" (5.723–24) against the "rebellious crew" (4.952), and after the heavenly war he seeks to "over Hell extend / His Empire" (2.325–26). Satan also targets "Imperial Sov'ranty" (2.446). Not satisfied with "build[ing]" a "growing Empire" in Hell (2.315), Satan aspires to "[divide] Empire with Heav'n's King." Chaos participates in the imperial rivalry by allying himself with Satan, accepting Satan's offer to help "reduce" the created world to "her original darkness" and "once more / Erect the Standard there of *ancient Night*" (2.983–86). All these endeavors evince an imperial ambition for universal lordship, attempts that are deemed by Milton as "Hatching vain Empires" (2.378).

One prototype for Milton's idea of a "global Leviathan" is the empire built by the Mongol Tartars. Milton associates both Satan and his crew and Chaos with the figure of the Tartar in *Paradise Lost*. Satan, when making his way to Eden, is likened to "the roving *Tartar* … dislodging from a Region scarce of prey" (3.432–33). Book X speaks of the wandering of the fallen angels as the "retir[ing]" of "the *Tartar* from his Russian Foe" (10.431–33). The inassimilable chaos amidst God's creation is compared to "The black tartareous cold Infernal dregs / Adverse to life" (7.238–39), and it is the gunpowder made of "Tartarean Sulphur" (2.69) that enables the rebellious angels to achieve a decisive balance with the heavenly army and to premeditate further wars against God in the "great consult" (1.798). Most critics link Milton's Tartars with Muslim sultans in the Middle and Near East.[21] Eric Song proves to be an exception in tracing the origin of Milton's Tartarian image to the Tartary under the Mongols' rule.[22] For Song, Milton "deploy[s] the

---

[21] *Paradise Lost*, ed. Alastair Fowler (London: Longman, 1998), 563; Stevie Davies, *Images of Kingship in Paradise Lost: Milton's Politics and Christian Liberty* (Columbia: U of Missouri P, 1983), 51–88.

[22] Eric B. Song, "Nation, Empire, and the Strange Fire of the Tartars in Milton's Poetry and Prose," *Milton Studies* 47 (2008): 119–44. For Milton's Tartars also see Michael Bryson, "'His Tyranny Who Begins': The Biblical Roots of Divine Kingship and Milton's Rejection of Heaven's King," *Milton Studies* 43(2004): 111–44. "Tartary" means the vast area under the Mongol rule. As Richard W. Cogley notes, for early modern England, "Tartary was generally seen as running from the northern and eastern banks of the Caspian Sea (or even more capaciously, from the northeast of the Black Sea) all the way to the land or strait of Anian. Cathay (northern China) was often included within Tartary, but Han China (China proper) was usually placed outside it." Cogley, "'The Most Vile and Barbarous Nation of all the World': Giles Fletcher the Elder's *The Tartars Or, Ten Tribes* (ca.1610)," *Renaissance Quarterly* 58.3 (2005): 781–814; 796–97.

figure of the Tartar both to question the stability of political order based upon exclusion and conquest and to advance a critique of expansionist ambitions underwritten by any sense of national ascendency."[23] I argue for the Tartarian source of Satan and Chaos as well, but whereas Song focuses on its significance to Milton's conception of national politics and culture, I study its relevance to his imagination of global governance. Milton's Tartars most powerfully evoke, I shall show, the whole Mongol Empire founded by Genghis Khan (1162–1227) and his descendants, a world empire that encompassed within its vast boundaries not only the Middle and Near East but also the Far East and part of Europe.[24]

For early modern Europeans, the word "Tartar" called to mind at once the Mongols and Manchus, two distinct yet interconnected nomadic tribes in the Eurasian steppe that not only overthrew two powerful Chinese dynasties but also built their own empires upon their ruin.[25] As the English chronicler Matthew Paris (1200–59) noted, "they [the Mongols] are called Tartars, from a river called Tartar, which runs through their mountains."[26] The Mongols were known to western Europe through the far-ranging campaigns they waged against both the Muslims and Christians in 1218–60.[27] By conquering the Song Dynasty (960–1279) in China, Moscow and the regions around the Volga-Don Steppes, a large part of the Islamic world, and above all, a host of nations in Christendom, the Mongols established a world empire that stretched from the Pacific to the banks of Danube and from the Volga to the Ganges, the largest continuous land empire the world had ever seen. This vast empire forged by the "Cathaian Can," together with formidable monarchy built by "Sinaean Kings," that is, the Ming Empire, takes lead in the catalogue of the geographical regions Adam surveys in his overview of "all Earth's Kingdoms and thir Glory" (11.384) in book XI of *Paradise Lost*. Further, as is shown in the various place names mentioned together with the Tartars, Milton reproduces not only the Mongol Empire but also its western campaigns

---

[23] Song, "Strange Fire of the Tartars," 120.

[24] For the Mongols see Donald Ostrowski, *Muscovy and the Mongols: Cross-Cultural Influences on the Steppe Frontier, 1304–1589* (Cambridge: Cambridge UP, 2002); Jack Weatherford, *Genghis Khan and the Making of the Modern World* (New York: Three Rivers, 2004); and Morgan, *The Mongols*.

[25] For Western knowledge of the Mongols and Manchus see Cogley, "Fletcher the Elder's *The Tartars*," 797; and Edwin J. van Kley, "News from China: Seventeenth-Century European Notices of the Manchu Conquest," *Journal of Modern History* 45.4 (1973): 561–82.

[26] Matthew Paris, *Matthew Paris's English History from the Year 1235 to 1273*, trans. J. A. Giles, 3 vols. (London: Henry G. Bohn, 1852), vol. 1, 314. All quotes about Paris are from vol. 1.

[27] For the Mongols' western expedition see Hudson, *Europe and China*, 134–68; James Chambers, *The Devil's Horsemen: The Mongol Invasion of Europe* (Edison, NJ: Castle Books, 2003); and Herbert Franke and Denis Twitchett, ed. *The Cambridge History of China*. vol. 6, *Alien Regimes and Border States, 907–1368* (Cambridge: Cambridge UP, 1994).

in his epic poem, a reproduction that, I shall show, echoes his discussion of the Mongol-Muscovia relation in *A Brief History of Moscovia* (1682).

The study of Milton's image of empire in light of the Mongols' world conquest provides new insight into the heavenly war and the global warfare triggered by Satan's subversion of Eden. If the heavenly war is fought within the territorial borders of Heaven, Satan's conquest of Paradise involves all major power centers, that is, Heaven, Hell, Chaos, and Earth in a global war. The "global leviathan" Satan undertakes to forge definitely draws upon the formidable empires built by the Romans, Charlemagne, the Hapsburgs, the Spanish, and the Ottoman Turks. But the Tartarian association of both Satan and Chaos also suggests the inspiration of the Mongol Empire. The imperial model represented by the Mongols proves especially pertinent to study Milton's idea of "global leviathan," on three accounts. First, Miltonic Satan shares with the Mongol khans the title of the "Prince of Hell," a heathen sovereign who dares to raise military standards against the Christian God and his regime. Satan is frequently called "Prince of Hell" (2.313; 4.871; 10.621) in Milton's epic poem, and medieval princes such as Emperor Frederick II (1194–1250) and King Louis IX of France (1214–70) explicitly accorded this title to the Mongol khans.[28] Whereas Milton's Satan attempts to challenge the supremacy of God, Guyuk Khan (1206–48), in his letter to Pope Innocent IV (1243–54) dated 1246, demands "the great Pope, together with all the Princes" to "come in person to serve us."[29] Further, though worshipping some natural deity called God or the Eternal Sky, the Mongols were fundamentally atheists who showed a remarkable tolerance of the various religious groups under their rule, which distinguished them from the monotheistic Turks and Persians.[30] Similarly, Satan is called "Th' Apostate" (6.100), and his rebellious army designated as a "cursed" (6.806), "Godless" (6.811), and "Atheist crew" (6.370). What the "Godless" crew attempt to build is a "*heathenish* government" (YP 7:424) like that of the Mongols.

Second, compared with the conquests of other empires like Rome and the Habsburgs, which were largely confined to the Mediterranean ring and the European continent, the Mongol Empire aspired to global hegemony. The global enterprise of the Spanish Empire might also be a source of the Satanic empire in *Paradise Lost*. But Mammon's proposal to dig "Gems and Gold" in the "Desert soil" of Hell (2.270–71), a proposal that recalls Spain's exploitation of American mines, is vetoed by the "great consult" in Pandemonium. In effect, it is not a commercial but a political empire that is on the minds of Satan and Beelzebub, the "Pillar of State" whose "*Atlantean* shoulders" are "fit to bear / The weight of mightiest Monarchies" (300–306). Directed by Satan, Beelzebub imposes

---

[28] Paris, 312, 341, 346.

[29] Dawson ed., 85.

[30] For the Mongols' religion, see Polo, *Travels*, 160–61; and Mendoza, *Mighty Kingdom of China*, 54. For the Mongols' tolerance of various religions see Dawson ed., 237. The Mongols were not atheists in the modern sense, since they believed in the existence of an almighty deity. But their remarkable tolerance of various religions made them look like atheists to medieval and early modern Europeans.

upon the "infernal States" (2.387) the imperial plan to "possess" (2.365) Eden so that "this nether Empire" "might rise / By policy" (2.296–97). The "mightiest" monarchy Satan and Beelzebub aspire to forge echoes the "mightiest" empires towering in "Cambalu" or "Paquin." The global sovereignty of the Mongols is expressly declared by Guyuk Khan in the same letter to the pope: "from the rising of the sun to its setting, all the lands have been made subject to me. Who could do this contrary, to the command of God?"[31] Like Satan, the Mongol khans made it a state policy to build a world empire through imperial conquests, an ambition trumpeted to the world not only through military expeditions but also royal decrees and seals. Genghis Khan made it a royal command to "bring all nations into subjection if possible" so that "they alone shall rule the world.[32] Guyuk called himself "The strength of God, the Emperor of all men," impressing upon his royal seal the inscription that "God in heaven and Guyuc Chan on earth, the strength of God, the seal of the Emperor of all men."[33]

Last but most importantly, the figure of the Tartar allows Milton to represent not only imperial "over-reach" (10.879) but also the limitations of this far-reaching endeavor. As "the Parent of many Nations," the Mongol Empire disintegrated after reaching its zenith, a disintegration that gave rise to a host of new regions and nations in Eurasia.[34] Genghis Khan's eldest son Jochi came into possession of the Khanate of Kipchak or the Golden Horde in 1227, which was later inherited by Jochi's own son Batu. Genghis Khan's second son Chaghadai founded the Khanate in Transoxiania in central Asia in 1242. In Mongolia, headquarter of the Mongol rule, Ogodei and his son Guyuk ruled as great khans successively until 1251. The Mongol founder's youngest son Tolui ruled as regent during 1227–29, and Tolui's three sons carved the largest share of the empire between them. Tolui's eldest son Mongke became the great khan in 1251, and Mongke's brother Kubilai, after succeeding him in 1260, erected the Yuan Empire in 1271. Mongke's other brother Hulegu built the Ilkhanate in Persia in 1258.[35] However, though issuing from the same ancestor, the four khanates involved themselves in endless wars and rivalries for territorial dominion. As Peter Jackson notes, the confederation between the Mamluks in Egypt and the Khanate of Kipchak against the Persian

---

[31] Dawson ed., 86.
[32] Dawson ed., 38, 39, 25.
[33] Dawson ed., 86.
[34] Martini, *Tartarico* or *Invasion of the Tartars*. *Tartarico* was reprinted over 20 times between 1654 and 1706, and translated into nine languages. Martini calls the Tartars "the Parent of many nations," *Invasion of the Tartars*, 255.
[35] For the scattering of Khanates from the Mongol political center, see Polo, *Travels*, 152, 313; and Mandeville, 147–48. The Islamic world split into three empires after Hulegu sacked Baghdad in 1258, the center of Abbasid Persia (750–1258). These three new Islamic empires coexisting alongside early modern Europe were the Turkish Ottoman Empire (1299–1683), the Persian Safavid (1501–1722), and the Indian Mughal Empire (1526–1707).

Ilkhanate around 1260 marks the "dissolution" of the Mongol Empire.[36] Likewise, though originating from "one Almighty" (5.469) and "sons of one great Sire" (6.95), "Angel[s] should with Angel[s] war" (6.92) in heaven. The futility of the imperial rivalry between the great power centers in *Paradise Lost* recalls the collapsing of the Mongol Empire.

The limitations of an imperial project suggested in the Tartarian association of Satan and Chaos, together with Jesus's rejection of the Roman and Parthian empires in *Paradise Regained*, are intended by Milton to bear out the necessity of instituting a new sovereignty in the Son. This new authority, I claim, captures the idea of "global commonwealth" described by Dallmayr. In *A Readie and Easie Way* (1660), Milton writes, "a free commonwealth" is

> Not only held by wisest men in all ages the noblest, the manliest, the equallest, the justest government, the most agreeable to all due libertie and proportioned equalitie, both human, civil, and Christian, most cherishing to virtue and true religion, but also (I may say it with greatest probabilitie) planely commended, or rather enjoined by our Saviour himself, to all Christians, not without remarkable disallowance, and the brand of *gentilism* upon kingship. (YP 7:424)

What characterizes Milton's "commonwealth" is its ability to address "libertie," "equalitie," "virtue," and "true religion," ideas that speak evidently of its spiritual and ethical capacities. The national institutional form Milton envisaged in his political treatise was represented as the infrastructure of the Son's universal rule in his epic poems. Since the Son intends to "guide nations in the way of truth / By saving doctrine" (PR 3.473–4), his rule aims at an ethical, spiritual, and juridical governance that goes beyond territorial borders. For Hardt and Negri, empire symbolizes not "a historical regime originating in conquest" but "an order that effectively suspends history and thereby fixes the existing state of affairs for eternity." The global commonwealth Milton imagines in the Son's rule is not a real historical institution either; instead, it is a "spirituall architecture" (YP 2:555) that seeks to "define a project of international order,"[37] an order that can refocus the religious and ethical loyalties once harnessed within the framework of the nation state.

A globalization approach to Milton's image of empire naturally challenges his alleged nationalism.[38] A nationalist model refers both to claims of "national outlook" and "methodological nationalism" that presuppose that "the nation-state creates and controls the 'container' of society."[39] In modern globalization theory

---

[36] Peter Jackson, "The Dissolution of the Mongol Empire," *Central Asiatic Journal* 22 (1978): 186–244; also see Jackson, "The Crisis in the Holy Land in 1260," *English Historical Review* 95 (1980): 481–513; and Morgan, *The Mongols*, 139.

[37] Hardt and Negri, *Empire*, 14.

[38] The nationalist approach to Milton is crystallized in Loewenstein and Stevens eds., *Early Modern Nationalism and Milton's England*.

[39] Beck, *Cosmopolitan Vision*, 2.

the empire/cosmopolis conceptual paradigm is often proposed in opposition to the state system. David Held and Anthony McGrew suggest that "the roles and functions of states" be "rearticulated, reconstituted and re-embedded at the intersection of regionalizing and globalizing networks and systems."[40] Ulrich Beck uses the ideas of "cosmopolitanism" to reconcile the conflict between the global and national models, on the grounds that in a globalized world "cultural ties, loyalties and identities have expanded beyond national borders and systems of control."[41] For Herfried Munkler, "the failure of states, and especially their collapse, is more likely to prompt the intervention or creation of empires."[42] The early modern state, as a political unity that replaced medieval feudal lord-vassal system and the Holy Roman Empire, was instituted as a legitimate form of organizing national life in the Westphalia conference (1648). But this state system, especially when ruled by monarchs, showed limitations in addressing religious and ethical issues that cut across national borders.[43]

It is both the perception of the insufficiency of the monarchical system to articulate his liberal principles and the awareness of the limitations of imperial outreach, I argue, that compelled Milton to seek alternative world governance in a cosmopolitan empire.[44] George Dunne holds that nationalism "consists in a narrow and arrogant assumption of the finality of national cultural forms. To these forms it attaches absolute value and is thus incapable of recognizing the values inherent in other cultures."[45] After the Restoration, the "national cultural forms" embodied by the English monarchy could no longer represent "absolute value." Milton expressly states that "*Christ* apparently forbids his disciples to admit of any such *heathenish* government" (YP 7:424) as the monarchy to be restored in England. Put another way, after being yoked once again to monarchy, the English nationalism Milton vehemently championed in earlier years ceased to be a reference point to conceptualize "human, civil, and religious" liberty (YP 3:215). The nationalist model cannot address the various forces that go beyond territorial control in

---

[40] Held and McGrew, ed. *Globalization /Anti-Globalization: Beyond the Great Divide*, 2nd ed. (Cambridge: Polity, 2007), 211.

[41] Beck, *Cosmopolitan Vision*, 7.

[42] Herfried Munkler, *The Logic of World Domination from Ancient Rome to the United States*, trans. Patrick Camiller (Cambridge: Polity, 2007), ix.

[43] On the limitations of nation states and the importance of the Westphalia settlement of 1648 see Peters, "Bridge over Chaos," 280; Stephen Krasner, "Compromising Westphalia," *International Security* 20.3 (1995/96): 115–51; Martin van Creveld, *The Rise and Decline of the State* (New York: Cambridge UP, 1999); Charles W. Kegley Jr. and Gregory A. Raymond, *Exorcising the Ghost of Westphalia: Building World Order in the New Millennium* (Upper Saddle River, NJ: Prentice Hall, 2002); and Benno Teschke, *The Myth of 1648: Class, Geopolitics, and the Making of Modern International Relations* (London: Verso, 2003).

[44] For Milton's critique of monarchy, see his *Eikonoklastes* (1649) and *The Tenure of Kings and Magistrates* (1650).

[45] Dunne, *Generation of Giants*, 18.

Paradise Lost either. The imperial contenders cause a "universal ruin" (6.797) exceeding the power of national sovereignty. God's monarchial rule proves unable to prevent the revolt of the rebellious angels; nor can it contain the "tartareous" residue amidst his creation. What Satan embarks on is a global and transterritorial enterprise; and Chaos is ever ready to thrust the whole created world back into anarchy. In his attempt to build an "Empire tyrannous," Nimrod, the "mighty Hunter" "Before the Lord" (12.32–34), engenders linguistic diversities that cannot be articulated by a single national language. These globalizing tendencies have apparently gone beyond the jurisdiction of a territorial state and involved all in a global community. Thus it is but natural that the "saving doctrine" proposed by the Son targets a global institution beyond the national state. The new authority Milton invests in the Son aims at a rule in which "All Nations" can be entrusted (12.328–29).

Milton's Representation of the Mongols' Warfare and Sources for the Tartars

To understand the source for Milton's knowledge of the Tartars, we need to know first how the West came to its knowledge of the Mongols.[46] It was Mongol warfare that disclosed the Far East to the medieval West, bringing it onto the center stage of global affairs. To achieve world dominion, the Mongols launched a three-pronged imperial project: to subdue the Song Empire in the south, the Islamic world in middle and southwest Asia, and Christian Europe in the west. In 1218 the Mongols, led by Genghis Khan himself, rode into the Khwarizmi Empire (1077–1231) and sacked its capital Samarquand (Samarkand). Meanwhile, Genghis Khan dispatched his eldest son Jochi and his two generals Jebe and Subotei into Caucasus and the Kipchak Steppe in 1221. This special squad conquered in quick succession the Georgians, the Kipchak (also called Kuman Turks) residing on the Volga-Don Steppes, and the Russians on the Dnieper. In 1241, Ogodei Khan (1186–1241) started a second military movement. After destroying Moscow and Kiev, the Mongols, commanded by Jochi's son Batu, marched further west, defeating the confederated armies of the Germans, Poles, and Hungarians and stationing their equestrians at, as Emperor Frederick II said, "the door of Christendom."[47] As is noted by the Armenia historian Hetoum or Hayton in his *La fleur des histoires de la terre d'Orient*, while Batu scored victories in eastern Europe, his father Jochi "conquered the kingdom of Turkestan and lesser Persia, extending his lordship to

---

[46] Morgan identifies four major "sources" of the Mongols: the only surviving Mongols source, that is, *The Secret History of the Mongols* (c. 1240); the Chinese Official *Yuanshi* or *History of the Yuan Dynasty* (1370); the Persian records; and European sources represented by Paris's account. See Morgan, *The Mongols*, 8–25. See *The Secret History of the Mongols: The Life and Times of Chinggis Khan*, trans. and ed. Urgunge Onon (London: Routledge, 2001).

[47] Paris, 346.

the Phison River."[48] On the Far Eastern front in 1271, Kubilai Khan overthrew the Song dynasty and built the Yuan Empire. In the southwest in 1258, Hulegu subdued Baghdad, took Aleppo and Damascus, and built the Ilkhanate. Before the abrupt appearance of multitudes of Tartarian equestrians, the Far East, though mentioned by the ancients, was largely concealed from the West. For Paris, the Tartars "came with the force of lightening into the territories of the Christians," because "never till this time [1241] has there been any mode of access to them [the Tartars]; nor have they themselves come forth, so as to allow any knowledge of their customs or persons to be gained through common intercourse with other men."[49] In his *Purchas his Pilgrimage* (1617), Samuel Purchas also remarks that the "armies" and "Marchants" of the "Carthaginians, Macedonians, and Romanes" had once "discouered" the East, but that knowledge was "drowne(d)" over by "flouds of barbarous people." It is the "terrible thunder-clap, with the lightening and noyse of their Armies" that declared, once again, the Far East to the West.[50]

Most tellingly, the Mongols' western campaigns show up, though chiefly as place names, in *Paradise Lost*. In Book XI, under Michael's guidance, Adam perceives,

> ... .the Seat
> Of mightiest Empire, from the destin'd Walls
> Of *Cambalu*, seat of *Cathaian Can*
> And *Samarchand* by *Oxus*, *Temir's* Throne,
> To *Paquin* of *Sinaean* Kings, and thence
> To *Agra* and *Lahor* of great *Mogul*
> Down to the golden *Chersonese*, or where
> The *Persian* in *Ecbatan* sat, or since
> In *Hispahan*, or where the *Russian Ksar*
> In *Mosco*, or the Sultan in *Bizance*,
> *Turkestan*-born ... (11.386–96)

Here, by virtue of a series of place names, Milton presents an outline of the world order shaped by the Mongol invasions. The Khwarizmi Empire, the first kingdom collapsed under the Mongols' attack, ruled over a large part of present Persia, Turkey, and India in the thirteenth century. So most of the capital seats enumerated in this passage, such as "Samarchand," "Cambalu" and "Paquin" (present Beijing), and "Ecbatan" were once subjugated under the Tartarian rule. "Mosco" and the cities around it were the second to yield to the iron hooves of the

---

[48] Hetoum or Hayton, *The Flower of the Histories of the East*, book 3, chap. 20. http://rbedrosian.com/hetum3.htm. Accessed May 21, 2012. *Phishon* is one of the four rivers arising within the Garden of Eden mentioned in Genesis. The first century Jewish historian Flavius Josephus identified "Pishon" with the Ganges in book I, chapter I, and section 3 of his *Antiquities of the Jews*: "And Phison, which denotes a multitude, running into India, makes its exit into the sea, and is by the Greeks called Ganges."

[49] Paris, 313.

[50] Purchas, *Purchas His Pilgrimage* (1617), vol. 1, 463.

Mongol equestrians. "The roving Tartar" in book III who are bent on the "*Indian streams*" (3.436) might refer to Genghis Khan or his brave sons who, scaling the "snowy ridge" of "Imaus" (3.431), a mountain in the Himalayan range that reaches the Ganges, marched towards the Islamic world. In book X, Milton writes,

> As when the *Tartar* from his *Russian Foe*
> By Astracan over the Snowy Plains
> Retires, or *Bactrian* sophi from the horns
> Of *Turkish* Crescent, leaves all waste beyond
> The Realm of *Aladule*, in his retreat
> To *Tauris* or *Casbeen*. (10.431–36)

"Sophi" meant Persian shah for early modern Europe. The "retreat" of the Persian king "to Tauris or Casbeen" refers most likely to Shah Alā al-Dīn Muhammad II (1200–20) of the Khwarizmi Empire, who fled and died on an island in the Caspian Sea after the Mongols occupied Samarkand. After the death of his father, Prince Jalāl al-Dīn set up his capital at Tabriz ("Tauris") in 1225. The "waste" left by the royal fugitive represented in Milton's epic poem recalls thus the immense ruin and desolation inflicted by the Mongols.[51] The "Russian Foe" and "Astrakhan" or "Astracan" where once resided "Tartars of Mangat" (YP 8:484–85) elicit the Mongols' conquest of Moscovia, a historical fact that finds a more detailed account in his *History of Moscovia*.[52] Here Milton relates that George, son of the Duke of Moscovia, "was slain in battail by the *Tartar* Prince *Bathy* [Batu], who subdu'd *Muscovia* and made it a tributary" in 1237. "This *Bathy*, say the *Russians*," Milton writes, "was the Father of *Tamerlan*, whom they call *Temirkutla*" (YP 8:512–13). Batu was Genghis Khan's grandson who inherited the Khanate of the Golden Horde. Tamerlane (1336–1405) was the tragic hero of Christopher Marlowe's *Tamburlaine the Great* (1587–88). Western historians tended to regard Genghis Khan as "Tamerline or one of his successors," an identification that, the Jesuit missionary Nicholas Trigault says, "seems to me with good reason."[53] However, in his *De Bello Tartarico Historia* (1654), Martino Martini discredited the legend that "Tamberlain" had "subdued" China.[54] Martini is right. Tamerlane was neither Genghis Khan as Trigault thought nor his grandson Batu who subdued Moscovia, as Milton mentioned. Tamerlane came into power a century after Genghis Khan, though he himself claimed genealogy from the Mongol founder.[55] Tamerlane did plan to make a conquest of China, but he died

---

[51] For Jalāl al-Dīn's fleeing from the Mongols see Peter Jackson, "Jalāl al-Dīn, the Mongols, and the Khwarazmian Conquest of the Panjāb and Sind," *Iran* 28 (1990): 45–54.

[52] R. D. Bedford, "Milton's Journeys North: *A Brief History of Moscovia* and *Paradise Lost*," *Renaissance Studies* 7.1 (1993):71–85. For a detailed discussion of medieval Mongol-Russian relation see Charles J. Halperin, "Russia and the Mongols," in Kasinec and Polushin eds., *Expanding Empires*, 197–207.

[53] Ricci-Trigault, *Journals*, 42.

[54] Martini, *Invasion of the Tartars*, 255.

[55] For more on Tamerlane see Morgan, *The Mongols*, 174–77.

when marching his army there in 1405. Nevertheless, the popularity of the legend itself indicates the Renaissance tendency to misidentify Tamerlane with Genghis Khan or Kubilai Khan who actually conquered China. In just stating what the Russians "say," Milton showed a noncommittal attitude towards the Tamerlane legend. Apart from the Tartarian conquest of Moscovia, Milton also displayed knowledge of the Mongols' invasion of Europe when remarking that "the Tartars wasted also *Polonia, Silesia*, and *Hungaria*, till Pope *Innocent* the Fourth obtain'd peace of them for 5 years" (YP 8:512–13).

We can with certainty identify five major sources of Milton's Tartarian image: Paris's chronicle of English History; the *Of the Russe Common Wealth* (1591) of Giles Fletcher the Elder (c.1548–1611), the English ambassador to Moscow in 1588;[56] Purchas's travel collections; Martini's *Tartarico*; and the Western literary tradition of representing the Mongol Tartars.[57] Milton not only knew about Paris but also considered him "the best of our historians" (YP 3:218). In a letter to Milton dated June 1656, Henry Oldenburg spoke of Martini's *Tartarico* and the Jesuit historian's "promise" to publish his *Sinicae historiae decas prima* (1658) (YP 7:491), which suggests Milton's possible acquaintance with both works on Chinese history. Though dealing mainly with the Manchu Tartars and their war with the Ming Empire, Martini's *Tartarico* nevertheless draws attention to the historical connection between the two branches of the Tartarian family, that is, the Mongols and the Manchus who dominated the northern steppe in the thirteenth and sixteenth centuries respectively. Theodore Haak (1605–90) told Samuel Hartlib (1600–62), the famous educator to whom Milton dedicated his *Of Education* (1644), that "Milton is not only writing a Univ. History of Engl. But also an Epitome of all Purchas Volumes."[58] The work mentioned here refers to Purchas's *Hakluytus Posthumus or Purchas His Pilgrimes* (1625), an augmented compilation of Richard Hakluyt's posthumous travel collections. Milton himself confessed in his own notes that all of the material in his *History of Moscovia* came from Hakluyt and Purchas's travel accounts.[59] Both Hakluyt and Purchas adapted

---

[56] Giles Fletcher, the Elder, *Of the Russe Common Wealth* (London, 1591), in *The English Works of Giles Fletcher, the Elder*, ed. Lloyd E. Berry (Madison: U of Wisconsin P, 1964), 169–306.

[57] On Milton's various sources of the Tartars see Cawley, *Milton and the Literature of Travel*, 52–54.

[58] French ed., *Life Records of John Milton*, vol. 2, 214–15; also see Turnbull, *Hartlib, Dury and Comenius*, 40–41.

[59] Milton drew chiefly on Hakluyt's *Principal Navigations* (1598), vol. 1, 221–514; and Purchas, *Hakluytus Posthumus*, vol. 3, 413–567. See George B. Parks, "The Occasion of Milton's 'Moscovia'," *Studies in Philology* 40.3 (1943): 399–404, 400. Milton might have also drawn upon the royalist cosmographer Peter Heylyn's (1599–1662) description of China and the Far East in his *Cosmographie* (London, 1652). On Heylyn's account of the Far East, see Markley, *Far East and the English Imagination*, 57–63.

in their works Fletcher's *Russe Commonwealth*, which presents an elaborate account of the Russian-Mongol relations.[60]

Most medieval narratives of the Tartars appeared in Purchas's comprehensive travel compendium.[61] Marco Polo's *Travels*, though focusing largely on the Yuan Empire, nevertheless gives "an unvarnished account of the usage and customs" of "the genuine Tartars."[62] The chief concern of John of Plano Carpini (1182–1252) and William of Rubruck (1210–c. 1270), the two medieval pontifical legates to the Mongol court, was the Mongol Empire before its conquest of the Han Chinese. A leading figure of the Franciscan order, Carpini was dispatched by Pope Innocent IV on an embassy to the Mongol court in 1245–47. Carpini's *History of the Mongols* (1247) enjoyed great popularity in Europe, chiefly because it was incorporated into the Dominican friar Vincent of Beauvais's (c. 1190–1264) *Speculum Historiale*, the most widely disseminated part of his encyclopedic *Speculum Maius*. Rather than a diplomat like Carpini, Rubruck was sent by the King of France in 1253 as a missionary entrusted with the special mission to convert the Tartars. *The Journey of William Rubruck* (1253–55) is comparable to Polo's *Travels* in both its geographical and anthropological breadth. After his return, Rubruck met in Paris the English philosopher Roger Bacon (c. 1214–94), who took so great an interest in his Mongol account as to redact it into his famous *Opus Majus* (1267). It is largely through the enthusiasm excited by Bacon in England that Rubruck's work was well preserved and transmitted.[63]

The literary prototypes of Milton's image of the Tartars came from Geoffrey Chaucer's (c. 1340–1400) "The Squire's Tale" and Ludovico Ariosto's *Orlando Furioso* (1516).[64] Chaucer's tale tells the story of Cambuskan, a Tartarian king who is celebrating a royal birthday with Princess Canace and the two princes Algarsyf and Cambalus. During the feast, a knight rides in, holding four gifts from the king of Arabia and India—a brass steed, a magic mirror, a ring that can make its bearer understand birds' language, and a sword that can cure any wound it inflicts. The knight gives the ring and mirror to Canace. The magical ring enables the Tartarian princess to learn the story of a falcon betrayed by her lover. At this juncture, the narrator declares that he will tell the adventures of Cambuskan, Cambalus, and Algarsif. So ends the poem. Both Edmund Spenser and Milton famously expressed the wish to complete Chaucer's unfinished tale. While Spenser continued the story in book 4 of his *Faerie Queene*, Milton engaged it in both his prose work and

---

[60] Fletcher relates the Tartars in chapter 19 of *The Russe Common Wealth*; see Berry ed., *Works of Giles Fletcher*, 246–58. For Milton and Fletcher see Berry, "Giles Fletcher, the Elder, and Milton's *A Brief History of Moscovia*," *Review of English Studies* 11.42 (1960):150–56.

[61] These include the works of Polo, Mandeville, William of Rubruque, Nicolo di conti, Gaspar da Cruz, Mendoza, Benedict Goes, Giles Fletcher the Elder, Ricci, and Trigault. See Purchas, *Hakluytus Posthumus*, vols. 11, 12.

[62] Polo, *Travels*, 102, 101.

[63] I'm indebted to Dawson's *Mongol Mission* for these bibliographical sources.

[64] Geoffrey Chaucer, *The Canterbury Tales* (Oxford: Oxford UP, 1998).

poems. In "Il Penseroso" Milton evokes the "sad Virgin" (103) whose power could "call up him that left half told,"

> The story of *Cambuscan* bold,
> Of *Camball*, and of *Algarsife*,
> And who had *Canace* to wife,
> That owned the virtuous Ring and Glass,
> And of the wondrous Horse of Brass,
> On which the *Tartar* King did ride. (109–15)

Here Milton does not bother to continue the Chaucer's unfinished story, but as is shown in his repeated reference to the Tartar in *Paradise Lost* and his rehearsal of the love story between the "Tartar King" and a Cathayan princess in *Paradise Regained*, two major characters in Ariosto's *Orlando Furioso*, Milton was carrying on the Chaucerian saga of the Far East. In *Orlando Furioso*, Tartary is one of the Eastern countries visited by Orlando, who falls deeply in love with Angelica, a native of Cathay. In *Paradise Regained*, Milton, referring to Ariosto, relates how Angelica's lover "Agrican," king of Tartary, "with all his Northern powers / Besieg'd Albraca," the fortress of "Gallaphrone," Angelica's father and king of Cathay (PR 3.338–42).

Satan, Chaos, and the Tartars: Global Imperialists

Herfried Munkler differentiates between "empire" and "imperial" projects in terms of "center" and "periphery." Whereas imperialism "fixes its gaze on the goals of a few players in the center" and "downplay[s]" the periphery, Munkler argues, "theories of empire" "keep center and periphery equally in view."[65] Milton draws attention both to the center and the periphery in his representation of empire, but he puts special emphasis on the subordinate powers embodied by Satan and Chaos. The Satanic empire features as a subversive power in both of Milton's epic poems. Though references to the "misrule / of *Chaos*" (7.271–72) are sporadic in *Paradise Lost*, when gathered together, they allow us to see a picture of "subaltern" rebellion no less powerful than that represented by Satan.[66]

Paradise Lost stages two Satanic "revolt[s]" (6.262): the heavenly war and the sabotage of Eden. These two rebellions operate on different terrains. The war in heaven, though of a global dimension, is a civil strife or "Intestine War" (6.259). Satan's revolt, a peripheral rebellion against the center, or a subaltern insurgence against an oppressive overlord, is condemned by God as "Treason" (3.207) "Against the high Supremacy of Heav'n" (3.205). In fact, Satan is only one of the many heavenly princes who are, though endowed with certain authority, subordinate to God who "reigns / Monarch in Heav'n" (1.637–38). The monarchy

---
[65] Munkler, *World Domination*, 27.
[66] For the elite-subaltern theory, see Loomba, *Colonialism/Postcolonialism*, 166.

of heaven comprises a number of princely rules, with the power center located in God and the Son and the periphery delegated to "Scepter'd angels," as the speaker says,

> In Heav'n by many a Tow'red structure high,
> Where Scepter'd Angels held thir residence,
> And sat as Princes, whom the supreme King
> Exalted to such power, and gave to rule,
> Each in his Hierarchy, the Orders bright. (1.733–37)

In such a strictly hierarchical regime, Satan, like other heavenly "Princes," governs a designated number of angels with a "Royal seat" (5.756) on "The Mountain of the Congregation" (5.766) in the "The Quarters of the North" (5.689). It is only after the Fall that the rebellious angels, once "Throne and Imperial Powers, off-spring of heav'n," "chang[ed] style" and were "call'd / Princes of hell" (2.310–13). But for Satan, such "magnific Titles" as "Thrones, Dominations, Princedoms, Virtues, and Powers" are "merely titular" (5.772–74). Whatever power with which he is invested, he is a subordinate who has to pay "Knee-tribute" (5.782) not only to God but also to the newly "anointed" Son (5. 605). Gabriel sharply points out Satan's "servile" status: "who more than thou / Once fawned, and cringed, and servilely adored / Heaven's awful monarch?" (4.958–59) But Satan insists that "those Imperial Titles" "assert / Our being ordain'd to govern, not to serve" (5.801–2). Thus it is both an acute sense of "injur'd merit" (1.98) and the resolve to "move" "the great Hierarchical Standard" (5.701) in heaven that initiate the subaltern revolt.

The civil war in Heaven is but a prelude to the global war waged between Hell, Earth, Chaos, and Heaven. Satan "Stand[ing] on the brink of Hell" and "Pondering his Voyage" (2.918–19) into Chaos resembles Julius Caesar overlooking the banks of the Rubicon in 49 BC. This is an "imperial moment" for both Caesar and Satan: a step backward meant to be an absolute sovereign of a peripheral state like Hell or Gaul; a step forward presaged a war of empire that might lead to universal dominance.[67] Whereas Caesar's crossing of the Rubicon ended the Republic and ushered in the era of Roman Empire, Satan's plunging into Chaos disturbed the balance of power intended by God in creating the new world, and directly triggered global warfare. Both imperial adventurers threw the former regime into

---

[67] For Armitage, "The imperial moment of the English republic extends from the peace settlement which concluded the first Anglo-Dutch War in 1654 to the second Protectoral Parliament of 1656, and it comprehends Cromwell's Western Design, the beginnings of the Anglo-Spanish War, the growing opposition to Protectoral rule culminating in the exclusion of members from the 1656 parliament, and the publication of Harrington's *Oceana*." Armitage, "The Cromwellian Protectorate and the Language of Empire," *Historical Journal* 35.3 (1992): 531–55, 533. I argue that Milton reproduces this "imperial moment" in Satan's plunging into Chaos.

anarchy, which made it imperative to establish a new form of sovereign power.[68] Though lacking the grandeur of the heavenly war, Satan's subversion of Eden, a mere colony that "lie[s] expos'd / The utmost border of his [God's] Kingdom" (2.360–61), is a global project that involves almost all major power centers in a war of empire: Eden the object of competition, Hell the initiator, Chaos that agrees to form an alliance and facilitate Satan's passage and is therefore complicit in the Satanic imperial project, God the chief rival, and Sin and Death who are in "League" (4.375) with Satan. Simply put, the global war is waged between the God-Son alliance and the Satan-Chaos-Sin/death confederation. Both the divine and hellish monarchs put their expansionist plans into practice. God creates "another World" (2.347) as "Th' addition of his Empire" (7.555) and undertakes to "over Hell extend / His empire." The Satanic crew not only "sit in darkness here / Hatching vain Empires" (2.377–78) but also seek to bring that "hatching" to fruition through Satan's expedition. By comparison, Chaos and Sin and Death participate in the war of empire by reaping profits from the rivalry of the chief contenders. Chaos urges Satan, "go and speed / Havoc and spoil and ruin are my gain" (2.1009). Sin and Death not only share the "Trophies" (10.355) Satan gained from the downfall of mankind but also are "Create[d] / Plenipotent on Earth" (10.404) by Satan.

Figuratively speaking, the global warfare engineered by Satan necessarily infringes upon the integrity of territorial states. Satan's cosmic journey to Eden unfolds a continual transgressing of territorial borders. After issuing from "Th' infernal doors" (2.881), the prince of Hell delves into the "hoary deep" (2.891) of Chaos. Emerging from the realm of Chaos, Satan steps onto "the lower stair / That Scal'd by steps of Gold to Heaven Gate" (3.540–41). At Satan's "bold entrance on this place [Eden]," Gabriel rebukes him for having "broke[n] the bounds prescrib'd / To thy transgressions, and disturb'd the charge / Of others" (4.877–82). All these images—"doors," "stair," "Gate," "entrance," and "bounds"—mark the frontiers of territorial states. The fact that sovereign borders are repeatedly "transgress[ed]" (4.880) and "violate[d]" (4.883) by an adventurer bent on "havoc and "ruin" indicates at once their vulnerability and the imperial nature of Satan's enterprise.

Whether in the civil war in heaven or the global war featured in Satan's sabotage of Eden, what is at stake is divine "Omnipotence" (5.722), that is, God's spiritual and temporal sovereignty. God explicitly states that what is endangered by the Satanic rebellion is his "omnipotence" as is registered in his "ancient" "claim / of deity or Empire" (5.723–24). In attempting to divide empire with God, Satan seeks precisely to challenge God's spiritual and imperial hegemony. In the "great consult," Satan justifies his expedition into Eden with claims of "public reasons just, / Honor and Empire with revenge enlarg'd" (4.389–90). Here Satan

---

[68] For the imperial moment of Caesar, see Arthur M. Eckstein, "Rome and the Hellenistic World: Masculinity and Militarism, Monarchy and Republic," in *Enduring Empire: Ancient Lessons for Global Politics*, ed. David E. Tabachnick and Toivo Koivukoski (Toronto: U of Toronto P, 2009), 114–26.

unambiguously pronounces an imperial project: "Public reasons," "just / Honor," and above all, the imperative to build an "Empire," these three necessities "compel" (4.391) him to wreak "revenge" upon the newly created man. Satan's ambition to usurp God's authority is explicitly pointed out by the heavenly chorus. In rebelling against God, the Chorus says, Satan has sought to "impair" the "Mighty King" of Heaven, "bound / Thy empire," and "diminish" his "worshipers" (7.608–13). Though failing in this imperial attempt, Satan has nevertheless succeeded in "draw[ing] after him the third part of Heav'n's Host" (5.710).

The Satanic rule represents an "equal" royalty to the divine throne, or as God puts it, his "foe" "intends to erect his Throne / Equal to ours" (5.725–26). The deistic and imperial primacy he asserts by "ancien[t] … claim" (5.723), God realizes, is "now" (5.721) grievously challenged by an "equal" "Throne." Satan's ambition to establish an "equal" sovereignty is mentioned a number of times in *Paradise Lost*. The Satanic crew "Towards him bend / With awful reverence prone; and as a God / Extol him equal to the highest in Heav'n" (2.477–79). Gabriel perceives Satan's "hope / To dispossess" "Heav'n's awful Monarch" and "reign" by himself (4.959–60). Equality proves the central point of contention between Satan and the loyal Abdiel. Satan justifies his rebellion on the grounds of the "unjust[ness]" for "equal[s]" to "Reign" "over equals" (5.819–20). Even if "to grant it thee unjust, / That equal over equals Monarch Reign," Abdiel retorts, Satan is not so "great and glorious" as he "count[s]" himself (5.831–33). Despite this scathing taunt, Satan and his crew are resolved to prove by "our own right hand" "Who is our equal" (5.864–66). In fact, God himself admits that his "armed saints" (6.47) commanded by Michael and Gabriel are "Equal in number to that Godless crew / Rebellious" (6.49–50). God's repetitive use of the royal first-person possessive pronoun "our" evinces a broad awareness of the danger posed to "our high place, our sanctuary, our hill" (5.732).

Satan's imperial "over-reach" to be "equal" to God resonates with the global ambition of the Tartars. Satan's Tartarian association allows Milton to represent both the radical nature of the subaltern insurgence and the damage caused by the imperial contention. Pointedly identified as God's "foe," Miltonic Satan was "mighty Paramount" and "seem'd / Alone th' Antagonist of Heav'n" (2.508–9). What the Satanic crew aspire is to "prevail / Against God and *Messiah*" (6.795–96). Likewise, in claiming to fight for God's cause and raising military standards against Christendom, the Mongols proved a formidable enemy of the Christian God as well. In his *History of the Mongols*, Carpini observes that the Mongols "raised the standards of proceeding against the Church of God and the Roman Empire, and against all Christian kingdoms and nations of the West."[69] Paris remarked that the Tartars inflicted an "injury" at once "to Christ, to the Catholic Church, and all Christendom."[70] For Emperor Frederick, the Tartars intended to "subdu[e] the whole of the West … ruining and uprooting the faith and name of

---

[69] Dawson ed., 43–44.
[70] Paris, 473.

Christ."⁷¹ The Emperor's fear was not ungrounded. In the royal emissary delivered by Rubruck to the King of France, the Tartarian monarch declares openly, "This is the decree of the eternal God. In heaven there is but one eternal God, on earth there is but one Lord Chingis Chan, the son of God."⁷² The Mongol Khan's arrogation of the name of "the Son of God" and his equalization of God's "decree" with his own edict directly challenged the omnipotence of the Christian God. Most remarkably, the self-styled God in the East demanded "the great Pope, together with all the Princes" to "come in person to serve us." Thus unlike the "puny" Indian king,⁷³ the "great Commander" of Hell (1.358) recalls strongly the Mongol khans in his imperial outreach and boldness to wage wars against God's regime. Like the Tartarian khans who erected the "mightiest Empire," Miltonic Satan is "Fit to decide the Empire of great Heav'n" (6.303).

For the medieval West, the Mongol khans belonged to "the race of Satan" " residing in "Tartarus" or "Hell," sharing with Satan the title of the "Prince of Hell." Milton's Satan declares that he "glor[ies] in the name" of "the Race / Of Satan," because the title means "Antagonist of Heav'n's Almighty King" (10.385–87). God commands Michael to "drive" the rebellious angels "into their place of punishment, the Gulf / of *Tartarus*, which ready opens wide / His fiery *Chaos* to receive thir fall" (6.52–55). "Tartarus," a cognate of "Tartary," was the Greek and Roman term for the "underworld" or "Hell." In book 6 of his *Aeneid*, the Roman poet Virgil uses "*Tartarei*" (295) to signify the underworld punishment for evil doers. In his *The Tartars or Ten Tribes* (c. 1610), Fletcher remarks that "Tartaros" means "the place of the damned souls, and Hell it self, in resemblance, as may be thought, of like disorder and confusion of both the places."⁷⁴ To maintain order in heaven, the satanic race must be "scourage[d] ... back to Hell" (4.914). In like manner, to preserve the peace of Christendom, the Tartars must be "thrust" back into Tartarus, that is, Tartary. Medieval observers explicitly associated the Mongol khans with the race residing in Tartarus or Hell. For Paris, the Mongols "are well called Tartars, as it were inhabitants of Tartarus,"⁷⁵ and he called them "an immense horde of that *detestable race of Satan*" who "rushed forth, like demons loosed from Tartarus."⁷⁶ The king of France also observed that "if these people, whom we call Tartars, should come upon us, either we will thrust them back into the regions of Tartarus, whence they emanated, or else they shall send all of us to heaven."⁷⁷ In his letter to the English king Henry III (1207–72), Emperor Frederick writes, the Tartars "who have burst forth from the abodes of Tartarus,

---

⁷¹ Paris, 346.
⁷² Dawson ed., 202.
⁷³ Banerjee, "Milton's India," 154.
⁷⁴ Giles Fletcher the Elder, *That the Tartars are the Ten Tribes, who were Carried Captives, and Transplanted by the Assyrians* (c. 1610), in Berry ed., *Works of Giles Fletcher*, 318–31, 321.
⁷⁵ Paris, 312.
⁷⁶ Paris, 312, my own italics.
⁷⁷ Paris, 341.

may find their pride humbled, after experiencing the strength of the West, and be thrust back to their own Tartarus."[78]

As powerful enemies of God, both the Mongols and the Satanic crew in *Paradise Lost* caused great damage and panic in Christendom, which renders it urgent for the Christians to fight back. Satan's two revolts have reduced much of the created world to chaos and subjected the New World to the "misrule" (10.628) of Sin and Death. Likewise, the global ambition of the Mongols threw the whole of Christendom into anarchy. Whereas Satan "drew after him the third part of Heav'n's Host" into Hell, the Mongols succeeded in subduing a host of Christian nations. By 1241, Paris relates, the Tartars had "visited the northern provinces of the Christians" and "reduced to a desert the countries of Friesland, Gothland, Poland, Bohemia, and both divisions of Hungary, slaying or putting to flight princes, prelates, citizens, and rustics." In inflicting "dreadful devastation and destruction," these "barbarous" people had "struck great fear and terror into all Christendom."[79] In a letter to all Western princes, Emperor Frederick warns that by 1243 "six Christian kingdoms have already been destroyed, and the same fate hangs over the others," and now the Tartars are physically stationed at "the door of Christendom," "purposing to enter the boundaries of Germany."[80] Since Satan seeks to "try / In battle, what our Power is, or our right" (5.728), God says to the Son:

> Let us advise, and to this hazard draw
> With speed what force is left, and all imploy
> In our defense, lest unawares we lose
> This our high place, our Sanctuary, our Hill (5.729–32)

God's call for confederation against the "atheist crew" evokes Frederick's urge to form a "potent European empire" against the Mongol invasions. In the same letter to the king of England, Frederick remarks that it is "Satan himself" who "has dragged them [the Mongols] hither to die, before the victorious eagles of the potent European empire."[81] Similarly, Carpini observed that "if Christians wish to save themselves, their country and Christendom, then ought kings, princes, barons, and rulers of countries to assemble together and by common consent send men to fight against the Tartars."[82] By appealing to an imaginary confederation, both the emperor and the pontifical legate meant to mobilize Western nations to battle against the Satanic forces bursting forth from the Far East.

Unlike Satan who ventures out to another world to compete with God for global hegemony, the "Throne / Of *Chaos*" (2.959–60), the personification of the

---

[78] Paris, 346.
[79] Paris, 339, 313. For the nations and regions brought under the Mongol rule also see Dawson ed., 29–32.
[80] Paris, 473, 346.
[81] Paris, 347.
[82] Dawson ed., 45–46.

anarchical forces that threaten the created world, appears a sedentary monarchy wanting in imperial initiatives. In truth, Milton's Chaos is a powerful monarch with a tangible territory bordering Heaven and Hell and a resolute polity to contend with God for dominion. That Chaos resides on the very "Frontiers" of his realm (2.998) shows his constant alert to territorial sovereignty. So rather than a mere "abortive gulf" (2.441), the Chaotic realm features a political entity with a determined purpose to compete with God for "havoc and spoil and ruin."[83]

The subversive strategy Chaos adopts also registers in its Tartarian association. In book VII, Raphael gives a vivid account of how the Son created the world through "the spirit of God" (7.235). As is signified by such instrumental images as "voice" (7.221), "the fervid Wheels," "the golden Compasses" (7.224–25), and the "brooding wings" (7.235), creation is simultaneously a commanding and circumscribing process. All these instruments are adopted by the Son with a definite purpose, that is, to bring under yoke and force to birth the intractable chaos. Most of Chaos gets tamed, but there remain some "black tartareous cold Infernal dregs" that refuse to be warmed to life, whatever device is employed. The lowercase "tartar" denotes "dregs," and it first appeared in *Arderne's Surgery* (c. 1425): "First I made hym ane emplastre of tartare of ale, i.[e]. dreggez."[84] These resistant "tartareous" "dregs" amidst God's creation constitute a fertile site of contention in Milton studies. John Rogers refers to these sediments as physical "tartar," "the inassimilable elements purged from the system in the process of digestion," which "introduce(s) into the otherwise monistic world of the poem a residual race of dualism."[85] For Eric Song, "Despite God's attempt to purge the 'tartareous' dregs from Creation, chaotic elements persist to disrupt an ostensibly monist world by revealing its primordial fissures."[86] I argue that Milton's "tartareous" deposits encode Chaos's remarkable subversive strategy, a tactic adopted by the periphery to contend with the divine center for hegemony and territorial control.

Politically speaking, God's "monistic" economy is erected at the exclusion of the anarchical (Chaos), the nonconformist (rebellious angels), and the incestuous (Sin) "other." Like the Satanic revolt, Chaos's disruption of such an excluding polity symbolizes the rebellion of the periphery. Paris called the Tartars an "inhuman and brutal, outlawed, barbarous, and untamable people" who are fit "to be called monsters than men" or wild "beasts" "thirsting after and drinking blood."[87] Emperor Frederick thought "this race of people" "wild, outlawed, and ignorant of the laws of humanity."[88] For Fletcher, the Tatars had "the most vile and barbarous

---

[83] For a "hostile" chaos see Regina Schwartz, "Milton's Hostile Chaos: ' ... And the Sea Was No More,'" *English Literary History* 52.2 (1985): 337–74.
[84] "tartar, n.1" 2nd ed. 1989. *OED Online*. June 17, 2012.
[85] John Rogers, *The Matter of Revolution: Science, Poetry, and Politics in the Age of Milton* (Ithaca, NY: Cornell UP, 1996), 133, 134.
[86] Song, "Nation, Empire, and the Strange Fire of the Tartars," 119.
[87] Paris, 312.
[88] Paris, 344.

Nation of all the world."[89] In refusing to take on the forms imposed by the creator and sticking to their chaotic state, the tartareous sediments in Milton's epic poem show the very inhuman or "untamable" stubbornness characteristic of the Tartars. Moreover, just as the Tartars were pushing into the heartland of Christendom, Chaos, by condensing itself into some seemingly insignificant deposit amidst creation, manages to lodge his resistance at the very heart of the divine economy. By rejecting being tamed to life by "the spirit of God," Chaos asserts its powerful existence and irreducible part in the creation of the world.

Milton's resistant tartareous dregs elicit in particular the degenerated state of the 10 tribes of Israel, the exiled Jews who disappeared after the Babylonian captivity. The uppercase "Tartar" means "residue or remainder," especially the "residue" of the 10 tribes of Israel. Fletcher remarks that "*Tartar* in the *Syrian* Tongue signifies *Remnants* or *Remainders*," and "the Tartars are the Ten Tribes, who were Carried Captives, and Transplanted by the Assyrians."[90] Similarly, the English antiquary Edward Brerewood (c. 1565–1613) noted that "It is alleaged that the word Tatari, or Totari … signifieth in the Syriaque and Hebrew tongues, a Residue or Remainder such as these Tartars are supposed to bee of the Ten Tribes."[91] The Renaissance association between the Tartars and the 10 tribes was no mere conjecture—the Jews themselves practically made that connection when they learned about the great havoc wrought by the Tartars upon Christendom. According to Paris, the Tartars' invasion uncovered "the enormous wickedness" or "hidden treachery and extraordinary deceit of the Jews." While panic gripped Christendom, Paris says, the Jews looked at the victorious Mongols as "a portion of their race" or "brethren of the tribes of Israel" who came to "bring the whole world to subjection to them and to us." Some Jews even went to the lengths of gathering "all the swords, daggers, and armour" and "assembl[ing] on a general summons in a secret place" to discuss how to welcome the Mongols "with valuable gifts, and receive them with the highest honour."[92] Paris's chronicle of the Jews' enthusiasm for the Tartars had most likely been on Milton's mind when he represented the 10 lost tribes in *Paradise Regained*. One of the reasons Jesus gives for refusing to deliver his fellowmen echoes Paris's disparaging remarks about the 10 tribes. For Paris, what makes the lost Jews most detestable is their apostate ways of "follow[ing] strange gods and unknown customs," which "perverted" them to "an evil way of thinking," "confused" "their heart and language," and "changed" their life "to that of the cruel and irrational wild beast.[93] Similarly, Jesus's critique of the lost tribes also harps on their deviation from the Christian God. That he declines to "delive[r]" his "brethren, those ten Tribes" (PR 3.374), Jesus says, is

---

[89] Berry ed., *Works of Giles Fletcher*, 321.
[90] Berry ed., *Works of Giles Fletcher*, 322.
[91] Edward Brerewood, *Enquiries Touching the Diversity of Languages, and Religions through the Chief Parts of the Worlde* (London, 1614), xiii, 94.
[92] Paris, 357–58.
[93] Paris, 314.

because they have become enemies of God with their "heathenish crimes" (PR 3.419). The worshipping of "all the Idolatries of Heathen round" (PR 3.418) have rendered them "distinguishable scarce / From Gentiles" (PR 3.424–25). Since these "captive Tribes ... wrought their own captivity" (PR 3.414–15), the Savior argues, they are not worthy to be redeemed.

In addition to engineering his own rebellion, Chaos also agrees to ally himself with Satan and is therefore complicit in Satan's imperial project. On the one hand, he obeys the divine behest to provide the "dark materials" of chaos for the creation of "more Worlds" (2.916). But on the other hand, he offers the same "materials" for Satan to fabricate weapons to fight against God. To get a passport to Eden, Satan promises to assist Chaos to win back "all usurpation" by "reduc[ing]" them to their "original darkness" and reasserting the chaotic "sway" and "Standard" (2.983–85). Chaos's endorsement of Satan's plan signifies the joining of hands of the rebellious pair in their revolt against God. Apart from this diplomatic pact, their confederation is also registered in the "Tartarean sulphur" amidst Chaos. During the heavenly war, the Satanic crew turn the tide by resorting to "engines" and "Balls / Of missive ruin" (6.518–19). These destructive weapons were made from the gunpowder or "Sulphurous and Nitrous Foam" dug from the earth (6.512, 516). Moreover, in the "great consult," Moloch proposes "open War" (2.51), suggesting "O'er Heav'n's high Tow'rs to force restless way" (2.62) by, once again, fabricating weapons out of "*Tartarean* sulphur" (2.69). This powerful agent, Moloch remarks, will "mi[x]" and explode "his [God's] throne itself" into "strange fire" (2.68–69). Thus the "Tartarean sulphur" nourished by Chaos provides powerful resources for the rebellion angels to meditate another war against Heaven and thereby negotiate terms of peace with God.

The Threat of Chaos and the "Global Commonwealth" Embodied in the Son's Rule

Fear of Chaos is a chief motivation behind the establishment of empire. Toivo Koivukoski holds that "imperial compulsions" are "moved by a terror of civilizational collapse—a state of being that paradoxically produces a profound level of anxiety regarding potential future threats, while providing a commonsense basis for social cohesion within such large organizations as are empires."[94] Likewise, Munkler maintains that empires "see themselves as creators and guarantors of an order that ultimately depends on them and that they must defend against the outbreak of chaos, which they regard as a constant threat."[95] The Tartarian association of Satanic and Chaotic empires in *Paradise Lost* suggests precisely a "terror of civilizational collapse." Paris records that the

---

[94] Toivo Koivukoski, "Imperial Compulsions," in *Enduring Empire: Ancient Lessons for Global Politics*, ed. David E. Tabachnick and Toivo Koivukoski (Toronto: U of Toronto P, 2009), 98.

[95] Munkler, *World Domination*, viii.

Tartars succeeded in "laying waste the country, committing great slaughter, and striking inexpressible terror and alarm into every one."[96] For Emperor Frederick, the Mongols who caused "a universal desolation of kingdoms" meant "the general ruin of the whole world, especially of Christendom."[97] The "constant threat" of chaos is a chief motif of Milton's epic poems. An anarchical world graphically figures in the "wilderness" in *Paradise Regained*, the background against which the drama of competition for global "lord[ship]" (PR 4.167) between Satan and the Son plays out. The "vast immeasurable Abyss" that lies "Outrageous as a Sea, dark, wasteful, wild" (7.211–12) forms a predominant backdrop of the world represented in *Paradise Lost*. To make things worse, Satan and Chaos's imperial ambitions threaten to thrust the created world back to its uncreated chaotic state. After disrupting the "the great Hierarchical Standard" in Heaven, Satan reduces Eden to the "misrule" of Sin and Death. Not satisfied with ruling over the "Eternal Anarchy" (2.896), Chaos, together with "Night," the "Consort of his Reign" (2.963), aspires to "gain" "Havoc and spoil and ruin" from Satan's imperial adventure. Chaos's chief complaint to Satan is his competition with God for territorial control. Bordering on the edge of Heaven, undermined by "Hell" from beneath, and infiltrated by the newly created world, Chaos complains to Satan, his realm is constantly "encroached on still through our intestine broils" (2.1001), impinged upon by the already created worlds, and above all, tyrannically usurped by God. Chaos and Night obviously do not take things lying down. "The womb / of unoriginal *Night* and *Chaos* wild" (10.476–77) is ever ready to "swallo[w] up" created beings (2.149), "threaten[ing]" the "utter loss of being" with its "abortive gulf" (2.440–41).

Milton highlights the threat of chaos to bring out the necessity of instituting a new sovereignty that can forestall the "civilizational collapse" or "universal ruin" (6.797) threatened by the Satanic revolt. In globalization theory, empire is often regarded as an antidote to chaos. Hardt and Negri assert that "in Empire there is peace, in Empire there is the guarantee of justice for all peoples."[98] For Munkler, "fear of Chaos, and the self-appointed role of defender of order against disorder, good against evil, through which the empire sees and legitimizes itself, are corollaries of the imperial mission, which also represents a fundamental justification for world empire."[99] Milton's God proclaims the Son's rule at once to preempt "the outbreak of chaos" and erect a new "order." What the Son assumes is precisely the "role of defender of order against disorder, good against evil," a role that "legitimizes" the "world empire" he promotes. The Son's power manifests itself most when the world tends to subject to the "misrule" of Chaos. It is at the critical moment when "all Heav'n / Had gone to wrack, with ruin overspread" (6.669–70) that God delegates the Son to "aveng[e] / Upon his enemies" (6.676–

---

[96] Paris, 313.
[97] Paris, 341, 344.
[98] Hardt and Negri, *Empire*, 10.
[99] Munkler, *World Domination*, viii.

77) during the heavenly war. It is to "repair / That detriment" (7.152–53) caused by the fallen angels that God commissions the Son to "create / Another World" (7.154–55). To remedy the havoc wrought by Sin and Death, the Son takes on the role of the "restorer of Mankind" (10.646).

The figure of the Son provides an ideal platform for Milton to imagine a new form of sovereignty that can not only arrest the threat of chaos but also address the limitations of territorial polities, whose rivalry for hegemony proves a major source of widespread chaos. The Son aims at governance beyond national borders. In *Paradise Regained*, Jesus rebukes Satan that "God hath justly giv'n the Nations up / To thy Delusions; justly, since they fell / Idolatrous" (PR 1.442–44). For the two disciples Andrew and Simon, it is because "the kings of th'Earth ... oppress / Thy chosen" that God thinks it "time" to "Send thy Messiah forth" (PR 2.42–45). So the new sovereignty the Son intends to erect is, rather than a kingly rule, a global governance that can "guide Nations in the way of truth" (PR 2.473). Even Satan admits that the Son is "the head of Nations," "Their King, their leader, and Supreme on Earth" (PR 1.98–99). In *Paradise Lost*, God expressly proclaims that the Son is "Anointed universal King" and "Head Supreme," and he will subsume all "Thrones, Princedoms, Powers, Dominions ... In Heaven, or Earth, or under Earth in Hell" (3.317–22) to his own rule.[100] In effect, God institutes the Son's governance with a view to replacing the kingly rule; as God himself puts it, "Then thou thy regal Sceptre shalt lay by, / For regal Sceptre then no more shall need, / God shall be All in All" (3.339–41). The "regal Sceptre" is the archetypical symbol of monarchial rule. Thus the rule of the Son "in whom shall trust / All nations" (12.328–29) intends at once to overcome the limitations of national rule and to govern nations "in the way of truth." By "all nations" Milton means not only "the sons of *Abraham's* loins" but also "the Sons / Of *Abraham's* Faith wherever through the world" (12.447–49). Thus Milton defines nations, rather than as territorial entities, in terms of "faith"—nations will participate in a global commonwealth as "the Sons / Of *Abraham's* Faith."

In seeking to govern nations by spiritual faith or truth and to achieve a "New Heav'n and Earth, wherein the just shall dwell" (3.335), the Son's universal sovereignty recalls both Hardt and Negri's "empire" and Dallmayr's "global commonwealth." For Hardt and Negri, empire is directed by "a unitary power that maintains the social peace and produces its ethical truths," and Dallmayr's global cosmopolis "embrac[es] different cultures and societies and [is] held together ... by lateral connections and bonds of cultural and political interdependence." On the one hand, Satan unwittingly articulates the cosmopolitan nature of the Son's rule when he remarks that the Son resembles his Father who regards it a "glory" to receiv[e] / Promiscuous from all Nations, Jew, or Greek / Or Barbarous, nor exception hath declar'd; / From us his foes pronounc't glory he exacts" (PR 3.117–20). In embracing "promiscuous[ly]" all nations and peoples and even the

---

[100] For the Son's "universal godhead and universal sovereignty" see Stephen M. Buhler, "Kingly States: The Politics in *Paradise Lost*," *Milton Studies* 28 (1992): 49–68.

hostile forces, the universal authority represented by the Son means to refocus the various loyalties and identities once governed by the nation-state toward a new institutional form. On the other hand, the fundamental constitution of the Son's "everlasting Kingdom" (PR 3.199), that is, the "better Cov'nant" (12.302), bears out the top priority the Savior accords to ethical and spiritual truths. God turns evil to good in creating man to fill the "vacant room" left by the rebellious angels; likewise, when Michael tries to distill ethical and political lessons from the sinful history initiated by the fall, divine "wisdom" once again "ordain'd / Good out of evil" (7.187–90). These lessons are epitomized in the new Covenant:

> So Law appears imperfect, and but giv'n
> With purpose to resign them in full time
> Up to a better Cov'nant, disciplin'd
> From shadowy Types to Truth, from Flesh to Spirit,
> From imposition of strict Laws, to free
> Acceptance of large Grace, from servile fear
> To filial, words of Law to works of Faith. (12.300–306)

Typology is used in this passage to signify, among others, two different modes of governance. The new covenant Adam and his offspring are to contract with the Son not only replaces the Mosaic "law" but also derives from and fulfills the old covenant God made with Abraham. The "shadowy Types" in the Old Testament become "truth," the "Flesh" turns into "Spirit," the "imposition of strict laws" is replaced by "acceptance of large Grace," "servile fear" by "filial" love, and "words of law" by "works of Faith." Two different governance structures are evidently juxtaposed and contrasted here. Whereas shadowy types, flesh, strict laws, and servile fear characterize the kingly rule, truth, spirit, filial love, and faith speak of the ethos informing the new governance, an alternative form of sovereignty that symbolizes, as Gills puts it, "our spiritual side and our quest for harmony, moral order, and community." For Milton, the new one is a "better cov'nant."

The global cosmopolis promoted by the Son is far from a mere spiritual empire united by the bonds of "Abraham's Faith" and the new covenant; it is a political commonwealth with its own "Tribunal" (3.326) to "judge," "arraig[n]," and "Sentence" (3.330–33) as well. Robert Fallon holds that "New Heav'n and Earth shall to the Ages rise" (10.647), heralding the end of politics itself, once God's Creation will have achieved a state of existence that need no longer be defined in terms of the governing and the governed."[101] In fact, the rule of the Son does not indicate "the end of politics itself," nor does the Son merely "prefe[r] a metaphorical, inward rule over liberal political might" as Eric Song claims.[102] Rather, as Linda Gregerson argues, "the 'inner man' in question is not merely

---

[101] Fallon, *Divided Empire*, 107.
[102] Song, "Nation, Empire, and the Strange Fire of the Tartars," 136.

the self, a kingdom of one, but the soul of Nations."[103] By "the soul of Nations," Gregerson most likely means the welfare, whether political or spiritual, of nation-states. Thus though propounded as a spiritual principle, the Son's "saving doctrine" has a political mission to regulate not only a private man, a nation or a "selected nation," but also a community of "nations." In *Paradise Regained*, Satan, consistent in his uncanny perception, penetrates the very political nature of the Son's governance. "Should Kings and Nations from thy mouth consult, / Thy Counsel would be as the Oracle" (PR 3.12–13), and "wert thou sought to deeds / That might require th' array of war," Satan says to the Son, "thy skill / Of conduct would be such, that all the world / Could not sustain thy Prowess, or subsist / In battle" (PR 3.16–19). The Son concedes to Satan's view. A peaceful doctrine will be propagated with "winning words" to "conquer willing hearts" (PR 1.222), the Son soliloquizes, but "the stubborn" can "only" be "sudue[d]" (PR 1.226) with "the array of war." Moreover, the Son intends to institute an "everlasting kingdom" that "shall to pieces dash / All Monarchies" (PR 4.149–51), an institution that apparently presupposes armed violence. But the Son does not endorse imperial empires that "once just" and "conquer'd well" but later "govern ill the Nations under yoke" (PR 4.133–35). What he prefers is an institutional form that not only conquers but also governs well, that is, a "global commonwealth" guided by a "saving doctrine."

Milton's imagination of a global sovereignty with distinctive ethical, spiritual, and political rules suggests his contemplation of a world order beyond the governance of republic and monarchy. Milton's institutional model for organizing a world threatened by universal anarchy is empire, not an imperial but a cosmopolitan empire that prioritizes ethical and spiritual values. But it is after an evaluation of the various forms of empire, especially those with imperial and global ambitions, that Milton struck upon the idea of a cosmopolitan empire. The world empire forged by Genghis Khan represented in Milton's figure of the Tartar proved to be one of those global leviathans that tends to thrust the world into chaos, a prospect that made it imperative to institute a "global commonwealth" that can impose a new order upon a chaotic world. A cosmopolitan empire that values ethical and spiritual coherence answers this very purpose. Milton's Tartarian image in *Paradise Lost* brings to light, therefore, the global and cosmopolitan scope of the poet's political thinking and poetic imagination.

---

[103] Linda Gregerson, "Colonials Write the Nation: Spenser, Milton, and England on the Margins," in Rajan and Sauer eds., 169–90, 186.

Conclusion

The global trade networks and the transnational cultural activities accompanying maritime explorations render it pertinent to study East-West contact in the early modern period from a global perspective. Neither Eurocentrism nor sinocentrism can adequately address the cultural traffic between East and West in the Renaissance, since each framework claims a superiority and centrality at the expense of the other. World history is a narrative that comprises the stories of all civilizations, and each story contributes to human progress in its unique way. By the fifteenth century, the Ptolemaic cosmogony and Christian theology had confined the western horizon to Jerusalem and the Mediterranean ring, and racial or ethnical others referred chiefly to the Jews and Muslims. The world beyond the four terminuses delimited by Ptolemy was largely excluded from Western imagination, though the expeditions of the Mongol Tartars did impinge upon the old boundaries. But at that time, the Tartars were commonly regarded as a "brethren of the tribes of Israel." After Columbus and Vasco da Gama's epoch-making discoveries, however, the western horizon started to expand to include the whole world. Consequently, new lands and peoples began to assume a place in the world picture of the West. Thus only a global lens can do justice to the early modern interactions with the new world others, including China.

Liberal cosmopolitanism is at once a central concept governing my discussions of the early modern reception of China and a salient feature characterizing Western minds in the age of discovery. In an increasingly globalized world, imaginary cosmopolitans like Marlowe, Donne, and Milton displayed a remarkable openness towards the various cultural forms transmitted back to Europe by those global travelers. For them, those alien cultures shone a light no less appealing than the recently resurrected classical texts. In effect, the critical discernment shaped by the reading of those ancient texts rendered them the more receptive to the alternative forms of knowledge and historical data provided by the new global others. Bacon's suggestion of building some "ships" of "letters" to propagate learning, Donne's conception of a new global neighborhood, and Milton's proposal to "unite" all "brotherly dissimilitudes" into "one generall and brotherly search after Truth"—all these visions are marked by a notable cosmopolitan spirit.

Despite their liberal intentions, however, Donne and Milton's responses to the new world others entail limitations typical of the era in which they lived. As deeply committed Christians, both authors could not transcend their religious upbringing and the cultural forms they were born with. The central repertoire and concepts they used to interpret the Chinese culture derived from a fundamentally Eurocentric symbolic system. But as is shown in their images of China, they did exhibit admirable endeavors to transcend these limitations, trying to embrace a powerful pagan culture with intellectual grace and maturity. Donne and Milton's receptions of China are exemplary because the issues they raised reflect some typical concerns in the Western encounter with a non-Western other boasting of a high level of civility.

The globalization and liberal cosmopolitanism framework should provide an informative model for East-West contact in modern times. On the one hand, when faced with an advanced civilization once contemporaneous with ancient Greece and Rome, early modern Europeans chose to embrace and engage it with genuine admiration and cosmopolitan generosity. In effect, the liberal cosmopolitanism towards both classical past and the new world cultures proved pivotal to the unparalleled flourishing of Western culture in the Renaissance. If Western countries could, like their early modern predecessors, open up to China and appreciate the strength of alternative political and cultural developments, one could expect a global cultural renaissance in the modern times as well. On the other hand, the model should also offer some inspiration for modern China that is seeking in various ways to engage Western and other countries. In effect, the civilizational thesis proposed by the Chinese president Xi Jinping in his UNESCO speech that emphasizes the necessity of mutual learning and progress among different civilizations gestures towards precisely a liberal cosmopolitanism towards global diversities.

The richness of cultural interactions between China and western Europe that I have identified in Renaissance literary discourse both corroborates recent revisionist claims concerning the centrality of China in early modern history and provides discursive precedents for modern East-West contact from the sixteenth and seventeenth centuries. Since my study captures those early moments when Chinese culture began to influence Western thinking, it will generate discussions on Chinese cultural legacy and its place in the development of world history. Reactionary critics from the latter part of the eighteenth century onwards attempted to deflate China's pretenses to cultural antiquity, a devaluation that tended to be internalized by the Chinese themselves until the nation's re-emergence in the international stage in the past three decades. Whereas recent revisionist historians oblige us to reevaluate China's status in the Renaissance global economy, my study will impel us to reconsider East-West contact in cultural terms, the Chinese contribution to early modern cultural globalization, and the alternative early modernity represented by premodern China.

My discussion of the impact of China upon Renaissance English literature is far from exhaustive. The literary works I have examined are merely exemplary of the early modern imaginative response to the discovery of the Far East, and the themes and motifs I have touched on are representative of a multifaceted communication that involved various aspects of Eastern and Western cultures. Rather than providing a comprehensive picture, this study intends to open up new lines of inquiry for more sophisticated and nuanced engagement with the earlier phase of East-West intercourse.

Bibliography

Primary Sources

Allen, Thomas. *A Chain of Scripture Chronology*. London, 1659.
Ariosto, Ludovico. *Orlando Furioso*. Ferrara, 1516. Trans. Guido Waldman. Oxford: Oxford UP, 1998.
Augustine. *Concerning the City of God against the Pagans*. Trans. Henry Bettenson. London: Penguin, 2003.
Bacon, Francis. *The Advancement of Learning*. 1605. *Francis Bacon: A Critical Edition of the Major Works*. Ed. Brian Vickers. Oxford Authors Series. Oxford, Oxford UP, 2002. 120–299.
———. *New Atlantis*. 1627. *Three Early Modern Utopias*. Ed. Susan Bruce. Oxford: Oxford UP, 1999. 149–85.
———. *Novum Organum*. 1620. *The New Organon, and Related Writings*. Ed. Fulton H. Anderson. Indianapolis: Bobbs-Merrill, 1960. 33–268.
Bañuelos y Carrillo, Hieronimo de. *Relation of the Filipinas Islands*. Mexico, 1638.
Baudouin, Francois. *De institutione historiae universae et ejus cum jurisprudentia conjunctione*. Paris, 1561.
Becher, Johann J. *Character pro Notitia Linguarum Universali*. Frankfurt, 1661.
Beck, Cave. *The Universal Character*. London, 1657.
Beroaldus, M. *Chronicum Scripturae Sacrae*. Geneva, 1575.
Blaeu, Joan. *Atlas Maior*. Amsterdam, 1662.
Blount, Thomas. *Glossographia, or A Dictionary Interpreting all such Hard Words*. London, 1656.
Bodin, Jean. *The Dearness of Things*. Paris, 1568.
———. *Methodus ad facilem historiarum cognitionem*. Paris, 1566. *Method for the Easy Comprehension of History*. Trans. Beatrice Reynolds. New York: Columbia UP, 1945.
Boehme, Jacob. *Mysterium Magnum; or An Exposition of the First Book of Moses Called Genesis*. Trans. John Sparrow. London, 1654.
Botero, Giovanni. *Le relationi universali*. 1591. Trans. Robert Johnson. The Travellers *Breviat*. London, 1630.
Brerewood, Edward. *Enquiries Touching the Diversity of Languages, and Religions through the Chief Parts of the Worlde*. London, 1614.
Burton, Robert. *The Anatomy of Melancholy*. 1621. Ed. A. F. Bullen. London: Bohn's Popular Library, 1923. 3 vols.
Campanella, Tommaso. *De libris propriis et recta ratione studendi syntagma*. Paris, 1642.
Cano, Melchior. *De locis theologicis*. Salamanca, 1563.

Cassian, John. *De Collationes Patrum.* c. 435.
Chaucer, Geoffrey. *The Canterbury Tales.* c. 1400. Oxford: Oxford UP, 1998.
Comenius, John A. *Panorthosia or Universal Reform: Chapters 19 to 26.* Trans. A. M. O. Dobbie. Sheffield: Sheffield Academic, 1993.
———. *The Way of Light.* London, 1668.
Couplet, Philip. *Tabula chronologica monarchiae sinicae.* Paris, 1686.
Cresques, Abraham. *Catalan World Atlas.* 1375.
Cruz, Gaspar da. *Tractado em que se cõtam muito por estêso as cousas da China.* Evora, 1569.
Curio, Iacobus. *Chronologicarum rerum.* Basle, 1557.
Cyprian. *Liber de idolorum vanitate.* AD 247.
Dalgarno, George. *Ars signorum.* London, 1661.
———. *Universal Character and A New Rational Language.* London, 1657.
d'Anghiera, Pietro Martire. *Decades of the New World.* 1555.
Davity [d'Avity], Pierre. *Les Estats, Empires, et Principautez du Monde.* Paris, 1619.
Dee, John. "Preface." Euclid, *The Elements of Geometry.* Trans. Henry Billingsley. London, 1570.
———. *General and Rare Memorials pertayning to the Perfect Arte of Navigation.* London, 1577.
———. *The Great Volume of Famous and Riche Discoveries.* London, 1577.
Descartes, René. *Principles of Philosophy.* 1644–47. René Descartes: *Philosophical Essays and Correspondence.* Ed. Roger Ariew. Indianapolis: Hackett, 2000.
Diodorus, Siculus. *Bibliotheca historica.* c. 36 BC.
Donne, John. *Devotions upon Emergent Occasions and Death's Duel, with the life of Dr. John Donne by Izaak Walton.* Ed. Andrew Motion. New York: Vintage, 1999.
———. *The Elegies and the Songs and Sonnets.* Ed. Helen Gardner. Oxford: Clarendon, 1965.
———. *The Epithalamions, Anniversaries and Epicedes.* Ed. Wesley Milgate. Oxford: Clarendon, 1978.
———. *Essayes in Divinity: Being Several Disquisitions Interwoven with Meditations and Prayers.* Ed. Anthony Raspa. Montreal: McGill-Queen's UP, 2001.
———. *Ignatius his Conclave.* John Donne, Dean of St Paul's: *Complete Poetry and Selected Prose.* Ed. John Hayward. London: Nonesuch, 1967. 357–409.
———. *John Donne: The Divine Poems.* Ed. Gardner. 2nd ed. Oxford: Clarendon, 1978.
———. *Pseudo-Martyr.* Ed. Anthony Raspa. Montreal: McGill-Queen's UP, 1993.
———. *The Satires, Epigrams and Verse Letters.* Ed. Wesley Milgate. Oxford: Clarendon, 1967.
———. *The Sermons of John Donne.* Ed. George R. Potter and Evelyn M. Simpson. Berkeley: U of California P, 1953–62. 10 vols.

Durán, Diego. *Book of the Gods and Rites and the Ancient Calendar*. 1574–76; 1579. Trans. F. Horcasitas and D. Heyden. Norman: U of Oklahoma P, 1971.
Eburne, Richard. *A Plaine Pathway to Plantations*. London, 1624.
Eden, Richard. Trans. *Decades of the New Worlde or West India by Peter Martyr*. 1555.
———. *The History of Travayle in the West and East Indies*. Ed. Richard Willes. London, 1577.
Edmondes, Clement. *Observations upon Caesars Commentaries*. London, 1604.
Edmundson, Henry. *Lingua Linguarum*. London, 1655.
Eusebius, of Caesarea. *Chronicle*. AD 303.
Fletcher, Giles the Elder. *Of the Russe Common Wealth*. 1591. Berry, Works of Giles Fletcher 169–306.
———. *That the Tartars are the Ten Tribes, who were Carried Captives, and Transplanted by the Assyrians*. c. 1610. Berry, Works of Giles Fletcher 318–31.
Franck, Sebastian. *Chronica*. Strasbourg, 1531.
Frisius, Gemma. *De principiis astronomiae*. Antwerp, 1530.
Gastaldi, Giacomo. *Asiae Nova Descriptio*. 1570.
Geoffrey, of Monmouth. *History of the Kings of Britain*. c. 1136.
Gessner, Conrad. *Mithridates*. Tiguri: Excudebat Froschoverus, 1555.
Goropius, Becanus J. *Origines Antwerpianae*. Antwerp, 1569.
Grotius, Hugo. *Adamus Exul*. Leyden, 1601.
———. *H. Grotii et aliorum dissertationes de studiis instituendis*. Amsterdam, 1645.
Hakluyt, Richard. *Principal Navigations, Voiages, Traffiques and Discoveries of the English Nation*. 1589–1600. Glasgow: James Maclehose & Sons, 1903–5. 12 vols.
Helvetius, Christian. *Historical and Chronological Theatre*. London, 1609.
Herodotus. *The Histories*. c. 440 BC. Trans. Aubrey de Sélincourt. New York: Penguin, 2003.
Hetoum or Hayton. *La Fleur des histoires de la terre d'Orient* [*The Flower of the Histories of the East*]. c. 1307. http://rbedrosian.com/hetum3.htm. Accessed May 21, 2013.
Heylyn, Peter. *Cosmographie*. 2nd ed. London: Henry Seile, 1657.
Hooke, Robert. "Some Observations and Conjectures Concerning Chinese Characters." *Philosophical Transactions of the Royal Society* 16 (March–April, 1686): 63–78.
Horn, Georg. *Arca Noae, sive historia imperiorum et regnorum*. Leiden, 1666.
———. *Auctarium defensionis pro vera aetate mundi*. Leiden, 1659.
———. *Defensio dissertationis de vera aetate mundi, contra castigationes Isaaci Vossii*. Leiden, 1659.
Howell, James. *Epistolæ Ho-Elianæ*. London, 1688.
Hugo, Herman. *De prima scribendi origine et universa rei literariae antiquitate*. Antwerp, 1617.

Isaacson, Henry. *Saturni Ephemerides, sive Tabula Historico-chronologica*. London, 1633.
Isidore, of Seville. *Etymologiae*. c. 600.
Jansen [Jansson], Jan. *China Veteribus Sinarum Regio nunc Incolis Tame dicta*. Amsterdam, 1636.
Josephus, Flavius. *Antiquities of the Jews*. Rome, AD 93.
Kircher, Athanasius. *China Illustrata*. 1667. Trans. Charles D. van Tuyl. Baton Rouge: Louisiana UP, 1987.
———. *Polygraphia or A New and Universal writing in Many Languages Revealed by the Combinatory Art*. London, 1663.
Lanquet, Thomas. *An Epitome of Chronicles*. London, 1549.
La Peyrère, Isaac. *Prae-Adamitae*. Amsterdam, 1655. Men before Adam. London, 1656.
———. *A Theological Systeme upon that Presupposition that Men were before Adam*. London, 1656.
Lloyd, Lodowik. *The Consent of Time*. London, 1590.
Lodwick, Francis. *A Common Writing*. London, 1647.
———. *The Ground-Work or Foundation Laid for the Framing of a New Perfect Language*. London, 1652.
Mandeville, Sir John. *Travels*. c. 1356. *The Book of John Mandeville with Related Texts*. Trans. and ed. Iain M. Higgins. Indianapolis: Hackett, 2011.
Maresius [Desmarets], Samuel. *Refutatio fabulae praeadamiticae*. Groningen, 1656.
Martini, Martino. *De Bello Tartarico Historia*. Antwerp, 1654.
———. *Novus Atlas Sinensis*. Amsterdam, 1655.
———. *Sinicae historiae decas prima*. Munich, 1658.
Melanchthon, Philipp. *Sententiae veterum aliquot patrum de caena domini*. Wittenberg, 1530.
Mendoza, Juan González de. *Historia de las cosas más notables del gran Reyno de la China*. Rome, 1585. Venice, 1588. 8 vols. *The History of the Great and Mighty Kingdom of China and the Situation Thereof*. Trans. Robert Parke. 1588. Ed. Sir George T. Staunton. London: Hakluyt Society, 1853. 2 vols.
Mercado, Tomás de. *Suma de Tratos y Contratos* [*Compilation of Deals and Contracts*]. Seville, 1571.
Mercator, Gerald. *Chronologia*. Cologne, 1569.
———. *Historia Mundi, Containing his Cosmographicall Description ... of the World*. Seville, 1535.
Milner, John. *A Defence of Archbishop Usher against Dr. Cary and Dr. Isaac Vossius, together with an Introduction concerning the Uncertainty of Chronology*. Cambridge, 1694.
Milton, John. *The Complete Prose Works of John Milton*. Ed. Don M. Wolfe et al. New Haven: Yale UP, 1953–82. 8 vols.
———. *John Milton, Complete Poems and Major Works*. Ed. Merritt Y. Hughes. New York: Macmillan, 1957. Rpt. 2003.

Montaigne, Michel de. "On Experience." *The Complete Essays*. Trans. and ed. M. A. Screech. London: Penguin, 2003.
More, John. *A Table from the Beginning of the World to this Day*. London, 1593.
Mun, Thomas. *Discovrse of Trade: from England vnto East-Indies: Answering to Diuerse Obiections Which are Usually Made Against the Same*. London, 1621.
Munday, Anthony. *Briefe Chronicle of the Successe of Times from Creation*. London, 1611.
Nicholas, of Lyra. *Postillae perpetuae in universam S. Scripturam*. Rome, 1471.
Nieuhoff, Jean. *An Embassy from the East-India Company of the United Provinces, to the Grand Tartar Cham Emperour of China*. Trans. John Ogilby. London, 1669.
Ortelius, Abraham. *Theatrum orbis terrarium*. 1570.
Paris, Matthew. *Matthew Paris's English History from the Year 1235 to 1273*. Trans. J. A. Giles. Vol. 1. London: Henry G. Bohn. 1852. 3 vols.
Patrizi, Francesco. *Mystica Aegyptiorum et Caldeorum*. Ferrara, 1591.
Pererius, Benedictus. *Commentariorum et Disputationum in Genesim*. Lyons, 1606.
Petavius, Dionysius. *Opus de doctrina temporum*. Paris, 1627.
———. *Rationarium temporum*. Paris, 1633.
Plato. *The Dialogue of Plato*. Trans. Benjamin Jowett. Vol. 3. 1871. 4 vols.
———. *Timaeus*. Trans. R. G. Bury. The Loeb Classical Library. London: William Heinemann, 1929.
Pliny the Elder. *The Natural History*. c. 78. A Selection. Trans. John F. Healy. Harmondsworth: Penguin, 1991.
Polo, Marco. *The Travels of Marco Polo*. c. 1298. Trans. Ronald Latham. London: Penguin, 1958.
Postel, Guillaume. *Cosmographicae disciplinae compendium*. Basle, 1561.
———. *Linguarum duodecim characteribus differentium alphabetum*. Paris, 1538.
Preyel, Adam. *Artificia Hominum, Admiranda Naturae in Sina et Europa. Francofurti ad Moenum*, 1655.
Prideaux, Humphrey. *The Old and New Testament Connected*. London, 1714–18.
Ptolemy. *Geographia*. c. 150.
Purchas, Samuel. *Purchas His Pilgrimage*. London, 1617.
———. *Hakluytus Posthumus or Purchas His Pilgrimes*. 1625. Glasgow: James MacLehose and Sons, 1905–7. 20 vols.
Puttenham, George. *The Arte of English Poesie*. 1589. Ed. Gladys Willcock and Alice Walker. Cambridge: Cambridge UP, 1936.
Ralegh, Sir Walter. *The Discoverie of the Large, Rich, and Beautiful Empire of Guiana*. London, 1595.
———. *History of the World*. London, 1614.
———. *Select Observations relating to Trade, Commerce, and Coin*. London, 1696.
Ramusio, Giovanni Battista. *Delle navigationi et viaggi*. Venice, 1550–54.

Ricci, Matteo. *Complete Map of Mountains, Seas, and Lands*. Beijing, 1602.
———. *De christiana expeditione apud Sinas*. Trans. Nicolas Trigault. Augsburg, 1615. *China in the Sixteenth Century: The Journals of Matthew Ricci: 1583–1610*. Trans. Louis J. Gallagher. S. J. New York: Random, 1953.
Rodrigues, Francisco. *The Atlas*. 1513.
Rushworth, John. *Historical Collections*. London, 1659.
Salmasius, Claude. *De Armis Climaciericis*. London, 1648.
Sande, Duarte de. *An Excellent Treatise of the Kingdom of China*. Macau, 1590.
Scaliger, Joseph. *De emendatione temporum*. Paris, 1583. Rev. ed. Leiden, 1598. Geneva, 1629.
———. *Thesaurus Temporum*. Leiden, 1606.
Schedel, Hartmann. *Nürnberger Chronik*. Nürnberg, 1493.
Semedo, Alvarez. *Imperio de la China*. 1642. *The History of that Great and Renowned Monarchy of China*. Trans. Thomas Henshaw. London, 1655.
Senensis, Sixtus. *Bibliotheca Sancta*. Venice, 1566. Lyons, 1591.
Shakespeare, William. *Measure for Measure*. London, 1604.
———. *Merry Wives of Windsor*. London, 1597–98.
———. *Much Ado about Nothing*. London, 1598–99.
———. *Twelfth Night*. London, c.1600.
Sima, Qian [司马迁]. *Shiji* (史记) *or The Records of the Grand Historian*. c. 109–91 BC.
Smith, John. *The Generall Historie of Virginia, New England, and the Summer Isles*. London, 1624.
Spitzel, Gottlieb [Theophilus Spizelius]. *De re literaria sinensium commentarius* [*Commentary on the Chinese Literature*]. Leiden, 1660.
Sterry, Peter. *A Discourse of the Freedom of the Will*. London, 1675.
Stillingfleet, Edward. *Origines sacrae*. 1666. Oxford: Clarendon, Repr. 1797.
Stubbes, Philip. *The Anatomie of Abuses*. London, 1583.
Synkellos, Geroge. *Ekloge chronographias* [*Extract of Chronography*]. c. 800.
Tatian. *Oratio ad Graecos* [*Address to the Greeks*]. c. 180.
The Secret History of the Mongols. c. 1240. *The Secret History of the Mongols: The Life and Times of Chinggis Khan*. Trans. and ed. Urgunge Onon. London: Routledge, 2001.
Twenty-four Histories of China (二十四史). Vol. 1. Beijing, Zhong Xua Shu Ju, 2000. 63 vols.
Ussher, James. *Annales Veteris et Novi Testamenti*. London, 1650–54.
Van Helmont, Mercurius. *Alphabeti verè Naturalis Hebraici brevissima delineation*. Sulzbach: Abraham Lichtenthaler, 1667.
Vives, Juan Luis. *St. Augustine's "City of God."* Basle, 1522.
Vossius, Gerhard. *De Arte Grammatica Libri Septem*. Amsterdam, 1635.
Vossius, Isaac. *Castigationes ad scriptum Georgii Hornii de Aetate Mundi*. Den Haag, 1659.
———. *De septuaginta interpretibus*. The Hague, 1661.
———. *Dissertatio de vera aetate mundi*. The Hague, 1659.

Walton, Brian. *Biblia Sacra Polyglotta*. London, 1657.
Ward, Seth. *Vindiciae Academiarum*. London, 1654.
Webb, John. *An Historical Essay Endeavoring a Probability That the Language of the Empire of China is the Primitive Language*. London, 1669.
Webster, John. *Academiarum Examen*. London, 1654.
Whitaker, William. *A Disputation on Holy Scripture against the Papists, Especially Bellarmine and Stapleton*. 1595. Trans. and ed. William Fitzgerald. Cambridge: Cambridge UP, 1849.
White, John. *The Planters Plea*. London, 1630.
Wilkins, John. *An Essay towards a Real Character and a Philosophical Language*. London, 1668.
———. *Mercury, or The Secret and Swift Messenger*. London, 1641.
Willes, Richard. "Certaine Other Reasons, or Arguments to Prove a Passage by the Northwest." London, 1576. Hakluyt, *Principal Navigations*. vol. 7. 191–203.
———. Trans. *The History of Travayle in the West and East Indies*. London, 1577.
Winstanley, William. *England's Worthies*. London, 1660.
Yuan Shi [*History of the Yuan Dynasty*]. 1370.

Secondary Sources

Abu-Lughod, Janet L. *Before European Hegemony: The World System A. D. 1250–1350*. Oxford: Oxford UP, 1989.
Achinstein, Sharon. "Imperial Dialectic: Milton and Conquered Peoples." Rajan and Sauer 67–89.
Achinstein, Sharon, and Elizabeth Sauer, eds. *Milton and Toleration*. Oxford: Oxford UP, 2007.
Adler, William, and Paul Tuffin, trans. *The Chronography of George Synkellos: A Byzantine Chronicle of Universal History from the Creation*. Oxford: Oxford UP, 2002.
Akbari, Suzanne C., and Amilcare Iannucci, eds. *Marco Polo and the Encounter of East and West*. Toronto: U of Toronto P, 2008.
Allen, Don C. *The Legend of Noah: Renaissance Rationalism in Art, Science, and Letters*. Urbana: U of Illinois P, 1963.
———. *Mysteriously Meant: The Rediscovery of Pagan Symbolism and Allegorical Interpretation in the Renaissance*. Baltimore: Johns Hopkins UP, 1970.
———. "Some Theories of the Growth and Origin of Language in Milton's Age." *Philological Quarterly* 28 (1949): 5–16.
Almond, Philip. *Adam and Eve in Seventeenth-Century Thought*. New York: Cambridge UP, 1999.
———. "Adam, Pre-Adamites, and Extra-Terrestrial Beings in Early Modern Europe." *Journal of Religious History* 30.2 (2006): 163–74.
Amorose, Thomas. "Milton the Apocalyptic Historian: Competing Genres in Paradise Lost, Books XI–XII." *Milton Studies* 17 (1983): 141–62.

Anderson, Donald K. Jr. "Donne's 'Hymne to God my God, in my Sicknesse' and the T-in-O Maps." *South Atlantic Quarterly* 71 (1972): 465–72.

Appadurai, Arjun. *Modernity at Large: Cultural Dimensions of Globalization*. Minneapolis: U of Minnesota P, 1996.

———, ed. *The Social Life of Things: Commodities in Cultural Perspective*. Cambridge: Cambridge UP, 1986.

Appiah, Kwame A. *Cosmopolitanism: Ethics in a World of Strangers*. New York: Norton, 2006.

Appleton, William W. *A Cycle of Cathay: The Chinese Vogue in England during the Seventeenth and Eighteenth Centuries*. New York: Columbia UP, 1951.

Armitage, David. "The Cromwellian Protectorate and the Language of Empire." *Historical Journal* 35.3 (1992): 531–55.

———. "John Milton: Poet against Empire." *Milton and Republicanism*. Ed. Armitage, Armand Himy, and Quentin Skinner. Cambridge: Cambridge UP, 1995. 206–26.

———. "Literature and Empire." *The Oxford History of the British Empire*. Ed. Roger Louis. vol. 1. *The Origins of Empire: British Overseas Enterprise to the Close of the Seventeenth Century*. Ed. Nicholas Canny and Alaine Low. Oxford: Oxford UP, 1998. 99–123.

Attman, Artur. *American Bullion in the European World Trade, 1600–1800*. Gb'teborg: Kungl. Vetenskaps-och Vitterhets-Samhallet, 1986.

Atwell, William S. "Another Look at Silver Imports into China, ca. 1635–1644." *Journal of World History* 16.4 (2005): 467–89.

———. "International Bullion Flows and the Chinese Economy, circa 1530–1650." Flynn and Giráldez, *Metals and Monies* 141–63.

Baddeley, J. F. "Father Matteo Ricci's Chinese World Maps, 1584–1608." *Geographical Journal* 53 (1919): 254–70.

Baker, David J. *On Demand: Writing for the Market in Early Modern England*. Stanford: Stanford UP, 2010.

Banerjee, Pompa. "Milton's India and Paradise Lost." *Milton Studies* 37 (1999): 142–65.

Barbour, Richard. *Before Orientalism: London's Theatre of the East 1576–1626*. New York: Cambridge UP, 2003.

Barnett, Pamela R. *Theodore Haak, F.R.S. (1605–1690): The First German Translator of Paradise Lost*. The Hague: Mouton, 1962.

Barr, James. "Why the World Was Created in 4004 B.C.: Archbishop Ussher and Biblical Chronology." *Bulletin of the John Rylands University Library of Manchester* 67 (1984–85): 575–608.

Barrett, Ward. "World Bullion Flows: 1450–1800." *The Rise of Merchant Empire: Long-Distance Trade in the Early Modern World, 1350–1750*. Ed. James D. Tracy. New York: Cambridge UP, 1990. 224–54.

Barry, Suzan. "Culture and International Society." *International Affairs* 86.1 (2010): 1–25.

Bartolovich, Crystal. "'Baseless Fabric': London as a World City." *The Tempest and Its Travels*. Ed. Peter Hulme and William Sherman. Philadelphia: U of Pennsylvania P, 2000. 13–26.

———. "Utopian Cosmopolitanism." *Shakespeare Studies* 35 (2007): 47–57.

Batchelor, Robert K. *London: The Selden Map and the Making of a Global City, 1547–1689*. Chicago: U of Chicago P, 2014.

Beazley, Charles Raymond. *The Dawn of Modern Geography*. New York: Peter Smith, 1949. 3 vols.

Beck, Ulrich. *The Cosmopolitan Vision*. Cambridge: Polity, 2006.

Bedford, R. D. "Milton's Journeys North: A Brief History of Moscovia and Paradise Lost." *Renaissance Studies* 7.1 (1993): 71–85.

Belsey, Catherine. *John Milton: Language, Gender, Power*. Oxford: Basil Blackwell, 1988.

Bentley, Jerry H. *Humanists and Holy Writ: New Testament Scholarship in the Renaissance*. Princeton: Princeton UP, 1983.

———. *Old World Encounters: Cross-Cultural Contacts and Exchanges in Pre-Modern Times*. New York: Oxford UP, 1993.

Bernstein, Peter L. *The Power of Gold: The History of an Obsession*. New York: Wiley, 2000.

Berry, Lloyd E., ed. *The English Works of Giles Fletcher, the Elder*. Madison: U of Wisconsin P, 1964.

———. "Giles Fletcher, the Elder, and Milton's A Brief History of Moscovia." *Review of English Studies* 11.42 (1960): 150–56.

Bewley, Marius. ed. *The Selected Poetry of Donne*. New York: Signet Classic, 1966.

Bickerman, Elias J. *Chronology of the Ancient World*. 2nd ed. London: Thames and Hudson, 1980.

Birchwood, Matthew, and Matthew Dimmock, eds. *Cultural Encounters between East and West: 1453–1699*. London: Cambridge Scholars, 2005.

Blair, Emma H., and James A. Robertson, eds. *The Philippine Islands 1493–1898, Explorations by Early Navigators, Descriptions of the Islands and their Peoples*. Vol. 29. Mandaluyong, Rizal: Cachos Hermanos, 1973. 59 vols.

Blaut, James. *The Colonizer's Model of the World: Geographical Diffusionism and Eurocentric History*. New York: Guilford, 1993.

Bold, John. "John Webb: Composite Capitals and the Chinese Language." *Oxford Art Journal* 4.1 Tradition (1981): 9–17.

Boxer, Charles R. *The Great Ships from Amacon: Annals of Macao and the Old Japan Trade, 1555–1640*. Lisbon: Centro de Estudos Historicos Ultramarinos, 1959.

———. "*Plata es Sangre*: Sidelights on the Drain of Spanish-American Silver to the Far East, 1550–1700." *Philippine Studies* 38 (1970): 457–78.

Breitfuss, L. "Early Maps of North-Eastern Asia and of the Lands around the North Pacific Controversy between G. F. Müller and N Delisle." *Imago Mundi* 3 (1939): 87–99.

Brockley, Liam M. *Journey to the East: the Jesuit Mission to China, 1579–1724.* Cambridge, MA: Harvard UP, 2007.
Brook, Timothy. *Mr. Selden's Map of China: Decoding the Secrets of a Vanished Cartographer.* New York: Bloomsbury, 2013.
———. *Vermeer's Hat: The Seventeenth Century and the Dawn of the Global World.* Toronto: Penguin, 2008.
Brown, Pamela A. "'I care not, let naturals love nations': Cosmopolitan Clowning." *Shakespeare Studies* 35 (2007): 66–77.
Bryson, Michael. "'His Tyranny Who Begins': The Biblical Roots of Divine Kingship and Milton's Rejection of Heaven's King." *Milton Studies* 43 (2004): 111–44.
Buhler, Stephen M. "Kingly States: The Politics in Paradise Lost." *Milton Studies* 28 (1992): 49–68.
Burt, Stephen. "Donne the Sea Man." *John Donne Journal* 16 (1997): 137–84.
Burton, Jonathan. *Traffic and Turning: Islam and English Drama, 1579–1624.* Newark: U of Delaware P, 2005.
Butler, Martin. "Jonson's London and Its Theatres." *The Cambridge Companion to Ben Jonson.* Ed. Richard Harp and Stanley Stewart. Cambridge: Cambridge UP, 2000. 15–29.
———, ed. *Re-presenting Ben Jonson: Text, History, Performance.* London: Macmillan, 1999.
Buzan, Barry. "Culture and International Society." *International Affairs* 86.1 (2010): 1–25.
Cain, Tom. "John Donne and the Ideology of Colonization." *English Literary Renaissance* 31 (2001): 440–76.
Campbell, Harry M. "Donne's 'Hymn to God, My God, in My Sickness.'" *College English* 5.4 (1944): 192–96.
Campbell, Mary B. *The Witness and the Other World: Exotic European Travel Writing, 400–1600.* Ithaca, NY: Cornell UP, 1988.
Carey, Daniel, ed. *Asian Travel in the Renaissance.* Oxford: Blackwell, 2004.
Carey, John. "Donne and Coins." *English Renaissance Studies Presented to Dame Helen Gardner in Honour of her Seventieth Birthday.* Ed. Carey and Helen Peters. Oxford: Clarendon, 1980. 151–63.
Carey, John, and Alastair Fowler, eds. *The Poems of John Milton.* London: Longmans, 1968.
Carter, Charles H. *The Secret Diplomacy of the Hapsburgs, 1598–1625.* New York: Columbia UP, 1964.
Cawley, Robert R. *Milton and the Literature of Travel.* Princeton: Princeton UP, 1951.
———. *Unpathed Waters: Studies in the Influence of the Voyagers on Elizabethan Literature.* Princeton: Princeton UP, 1940.
Challis, Christopher. "Currency and the Economy in Mid-Tudor England." 2nd ser. *Economic History Review* 25 (1972): 313–22.
———. *The Tudor Coinage.* Manchester: Manchester UP, 1978.

Chambers, James. *The Devil's Horsemen: The Mongol Invasion of Europe*. 1979. Edison, NJ: Castle Books, 2003.
Chaney, Edward. *The Evolution of the Grand Tour: Anglo-Italian Cultural Relations since the Renaissance*. London: Frank Cass, 1998.
Chang, K. C. [张光直]. *Art, Myth, and Ritual: The Path to Political Authority in Ancient China*. Cambridge, MA: Harvard UP, 1983.
Chang, Y. Z. "Why Did Milton Err on Two Chinas." *Modern Language Review* 65.3 (1970): 493–98.
Chaudhuri, Kirti N. *The Trading World of Asia and the East India Company, 1660–1760*. New York: Cambridge UP, 1978.
Ch'en, Shou-yi, "John Webb, a Forgotten Page in the Early History of Sinology in Europe." Hsia *The Vision of China* 87–114.
———. "Sino-European Cultural Contacts since the Discovery of the Sea Route." *Nankai Social and Economic Quarterly* 8.1 (1935): 44–74.
Chown, John. *A History of Money from AD 800*. London: Routledge, 1994.
Chua, Amy. *How Hyperpowers Rise to Global Dominance—and Why They Fall*. New York: Doubleday, 2007.
Chuan, Hang-Sheng. "The Inflow of American Silver into China from the Late Ming to the Mid-Ch'ing Period." *Journal of the Institute of Chinese Studies of the Chinese University of Hong Kong* 2 (1969): 61–75.
———. "Trade between China, the Philippines and the Americas during the Sixteenth and Seventeenth Centuries." *Proceedings of the International Conference of Sinology: Selection on History and Archaeology*. Taipei: Acedemia Sinica, 1981. 849–54.
Cirillo, Albert R. "Noon-Midnight and the Temporal Structure of Paradise Lost." *English Literary History* 29.4 (1962): 372–95.
Clarke, J. J. *Oriental Enlightenment: The Encounter between Asian and Western Thought*. London: Routledge, 1997.
Clauss, Sidonie. "John Wilkins' Essay toward a Real Character: Its Place in the Seventeenth-Century Episteme." Subbiondo 45–67.
Clossey, Luke. *Salvation and Globalization in the Early Jesuit Missions*. Cambridge: Cambridge UP, 2008.
Cogley, Richard W. "'The Most Vile and Barbarous Nation of all the World': Giles Fletcher the Elder's The Tartars Or, Ten Tribes (ca.1610)." *Renaissance Quarterly* 58.3 (2005): 781–814.
Cohen, Adam M. "Englishing the Globe: Molyneux's Globes and Shakespeare's Theatre Career." *Sixteenth Century Journal* 37 (2006): 963–84.
Cohen, Jonathan. "On the Project of a Universal Character." Subbiondo 237–51.
Cohen, Murray. *Sensible Words: Linguistic Practice in England 1640–1785*. Baltimore: Johns Hopkins UP, 1977.
Cohen, Walter. "The Undiscovered Country: Shakespeare and Mercantile Geography." *Marxist Shakespeares*. Ed. Jean E. Howard and Scott C. Shershow. London: Routledge, 2001. 128–58.

Conkin, George N. *Biblical Criticism and Heresy in Milton.* New York: King's Crown, 1949.
Conlan, J. P. "'Paradise Lost': Milton's Anti-Imperial Epic." *Pacific Coast Philology* 33.1 (1998): 31–43.
Connell, C. W. "Western Views of the Origin of the Tartars: An Example of the Influence of Myth in the Second Half of the Thirteenth Century." *Journal of Medieval and Renaissance Studies* 3 (1973): 115–37.
Connell, Liam, and Nicky Marsh, eds. *Literature and Globalization: A Reader.* London: Routledge, 2011.
Cornelius, Paul E. *Languages in Seventeenth and Early Eighteenth-Century Imaginary Voyages.* Genève: Librairie Droz, 1965.
Crane, Nicholas. *Mercator: The Man Who Mapped the Planet.* London: Phoenix, 2003.
Cram, David, and Jaap Maat, eds. and trans. *George Dalgarno on Universal Language: The Art of Signs (1661), The Deaf and Dumb Man's Tutor (1680), and the Unpublished Papers.* Oxford: Oxford UP, 2001.
Croke, Brian. "The Origins of the Christian World Chronicle." *History and Historians in Late Antiquity.* Ed. Croke and A. Emmett. Sydney: Pergamon, 1983. 116–31.
Cross, Harry E. "South American Bullion Production and Export, 1550–1750." Richards 397–424.
Crump, Galbraith M. *The Mystical Design of "Paradise Lost."* Lewisburg, PA: Bucknell UP, 1975.
Cummins, Juliet, ed. *Milton and the Ends of Time.* Cambridge: Cambridge UP, 2003.
Dallmayr, Fred. "'Empire or Cosmopolis: Civilization at the Crossroads." *Globalizations* 2.1 (2005): 14–30.
Davies, Stevie. *Images of Kingship in Paradise Lost: Milton's Politics and Christian Liberty.* Columbia: U of Missouri P, 1983.
Dawson, Christopher, ed. *The Mongol Mission: Narratives and Letters of the Franciscan Missionaries in Mongolia and China in the Thirteenth and Fourteenth Centuries.* London: Sheed & Ward, 1955.
Dawson, Raymond S. *The Chinese Chameleon: An Analysis of European Conceptions of Chinese Civilization.* London: Oxford UP, 1967.
Dean, L. F. "Bodin's Methodius in England before 1625." *Studies in Philology* 39 (1942): 160–66.
Debus, Allen, ed. *Science and Education in the Seventeenth Century: The Webster-Ward Debate.* London: Macdonald, 1970.
de Grazia, Margreta. "The Secularization of Language in the Seventeenth Century." *Journal of the History of Ideas* 41.2 (1980): 319–29.
DeMott, Benjamin. "The Sources and Development of John Wilkins' Philosophical Language." *Journal of English and Germanic Philology* 57 (1958): 1–13.
Deng, Stephen. *Coinage and State Formation in Early Modern English Literature.* New York: Palgrave, 2011.

Duncan, Joseph E. "Resurrections in Donne's 'A Hymn to God the Father' and 'Hymne to God my God, in my Sicknesse.'" *John Donne Journal* 7.2 (1988): 183–96.

Dunne, George H. S. J. *Generation of Giants: The Story of the Jesuits in China in the Last Decades of the Ming Dynasty*. Notre Dame, IN: U of Notre Dame P, 1962.

Eagle, Christopher. "'Thou Serpent That Name Best': On Adamic Language and Obscurity in Paradise Lost." *Milton Quarterly* 41 (2007): 183–94.

Eckstein, Arthur M. "Rome and the Hellenistic World: Masculinity and Militarism, Monarchy and Republic." *Enduring Empire: Ancient Lessons for Global Politics*. Ed. David E. Tabachnick and Toivo Koivukoski. Toronto: U of Toronto P, 2009.

Eco, Umberto. *The Search for the Perfect Language*. Trans. James Fentress. Oxford: Blackwell, 1995, Repr. 2006.

Edson, Evelyn. *The World Map: 1300–1492: The Persistence of Tradition and Transformation*. Baltimore: Johns Hopkins UP, 2007.

Edwardes, Michael. *East-West Passage*. New York: Taplinger, 1971.

Eldred, Jason. "'The Just will Pay for the Sinners': English Merchants, the Trade with Spain, and Elizabethan Foreign Policy, 1563–1585." *Journal for Early Modern Cultural Studies* 10.1 (2010): 5–28.

Elman, Benjamin A. *On Their Own Terms: Science in China, 1550–1900*. Cambridge, MA: Harvard UP, 2005.

Entzminger, Robert L. *Divine Word: Milton and the Redemption of Language*. Pittsburgh: Duquesne UP, 1985.

Erlichman, Howard J. *Conquest, Tribute, and Trade: The Quest for Precious Metals and the Birth of Globalization*. Amherst, NY: Prometheus Books, 2010.

Evans, Gillian R. *The Language and Logic of the Bible: The Road to Reformation*. New York: Cambridge UP, 1985.

Evans, J. Martin. *Milton's Imperial Epic: "Paradise Lost" and the Discourse of Colonialism*. Ithaca, NY: Cornell UP, 1996.

———. *Paradise Lost and the Genesis Tradition*. Oxford: Clarendon, 1968.

Fallon, Robert T. "Cromwell, Milton, and the Western Design." Rajan and Sauer 33–54.

———. Divided Empire: *Milton's Political Imagery*. University Park: Pennsylvania State UP, 1995.

Farmer, Alan B. "Cosmopolitanism and Foreign Books in Early Modern England." *Shakespeare Studies* 35 (2007): 58–65.

Feavearyear, Albert. *The Pound Sterling: A History of English Money*. 2nd ed. Oxford: Clarendon, 1963.

Ferguson, Arthur B. *Utter Antiquity: Perceptions of Prehistory in Renaissance England*. Durham, NC: Duke UP, 1993.

Ferry, Anne D. *Milton's Epic Voice: The Narrator in "Paradise Lost."* Cambridge, MA: Harvard UP, 1963.

Finegan, Jack. *Handbook of Biblical Chronology*. Princeton: Princeton UP, 1964.

Fischer, Sandra K. *Econolingua: A Glossary of Coins and Economic Language in Renaissance Drama.* Newark: U of Delaware P, 1985.

Fish, Stanley. *Surprised by Sin: The Reader in Paradise Lost.* 2nd ed. Cambridge, MA: Harvard UP, 1997.

Flinker, Noam. "John Donne and the 'Anthropomorphic Map' Tradition." *Applied Semiotics/Sémiotique appliqué* 3.8 (1999): 207–15.

Floyd-Wilson, Mary. *English Ethnicity and Race in Early Modern Drama.* Cambridge: Cambridge UP, 2003.

Flynn, Dennis O., with Arturo Giráldez. "Spanish Profitability in the Pacific: The Philippines in the Sixteenth and Seventeenth Centuries." *Pacific Centuries: Pacific and Pacific Rim History since the Sixteenth Century.* Ed. Flynn, L. Frost, and A. J. H. Latham. London: Routledge, 1999. 23–27.

Flynn, Dennis O., and Arturo Giráldez. "Born with a 'Silver Spoon': The Origin of World Trade in 1571." *Journal of World History* 6.2 (1995): 201–21.

———. *China and the Birth of Globalization in the 16th Century.* Aldershot: Variorum, 2010.

———. "Cycles of Silver: Global Economic Unity through the Mid-Eighteenth Century." *Journal of World History* 13.2 (2002): 391–427.

———, eds. *Metals and Monies in an Emerging Global Economy.* Aldershot: Variorum, 1997.

Flynn, Dennis O, Arturo Giráldez, and Richard von Glahn, eds. *Global Connections and Monetary History 1470–1800.* Aldershot, Ashgate, 2003.

Forman, Valerie. *Tragicomic Redemptions: Global Economics and the Early Modern English Stage.* Philadelphia: U of Pennsylvania P, 2008.

Fowler, Alastair, ed. *Paradise Lost.* London: Longman, 1998.

Frank, Andre Gunder. *ReOrient: Global Economy in the Asian Age.* Berkeley: U of California P, 1988.

Franke, Herbert, and Denis Twitchett, eds. *The Cambridge History of China.* vol. 6, *Alien Regimes and Border States*, 907–1368. Cambridge: Cambridge UP, 1994.

Franklin, Julian H. *Jean Bodin and the Sixteenth-Century Revolution in the Methodology of Law and History.* New York: Columbia UP, 1963.

Fraser, Russell A. *The Language of Adam.* New York: Columbia UP, 1977.

Freer, Coburn. "John Donne and Elizabethan Economic Theory." *Criticism* 38.4 (1996): 497–520.

French, J. Milton, ed. *The Life Records of John Milton.* New Brunswick, NJ: Rutgers UP, 1949–58. 5 vols.

Gaastra, F. S. "The Exports of Precious Metal from Europe to Asia by the Dutch East India Company." Richards 447–75.

Games, Alison. "England's Global Transition and the Cosmopolitans Who Made it Possible." *Shakespeare Studies* 35 (2007): 24–31.

———. *The Web of Empire: English Cosmopolitans in an Age of Expansion, 1560–1660.* New York: Oxford UP, 2008.

Gandelman, Claude. "The Poem as Map: John Donne and the 'Anthropomorphic Landscape' Tradition." *Arcadia: Zeitschrift für Vergleichende Literaturwissenschaft* 19 (1984): 244–51.

Gardner, Helen. *The Limits of Literary Criticism*. Riddell Memorial Lectures. 28th ser. London: Oxford UP, 1956. 40–55.

———. *A Reading of "Paradise Lost."* Oxford: Clarendon, 1965.

Geiss, J. P. "Peking under the Ming, 1368–1644." Diss. Princeton U, 1979.

Gilbert, Allan H. *A Geographical Dictionary of Milton*. New Haven: Yale UP, 1919.

———. "Milton's China." *Modern Language Notes* 26.6 (1911): 199–200.

———. "Pierre Davity: His Geography and Its Use by Milton." *Geographical Review* 7 (1919): 322–38.

Gillies, John. *Shakespeare and the Geography of Difference*. Cambridge: Cambridge UP, 1994.

Gills, Barry K. "'Empire' versus 'Cosmopolis': The Clash of Globalizations." *Globalizations* 2.1 (2005): 5–13.

Glenn, Keith. "Captain John Smith and the Indians." *Virginia Magazine of History and Biography* 52 (1944): 228–48.

Goldberg, Jonathan. "Donne's Journey East: Aspects of a Seventeenth-Century Trope." *Studies in Philology* 68.4 (1971): 470–83.

Golden, Leon, and O. B. Hardison Jr. *Aristotle's Poetics: A Translation and Commentary for Students of Literature*. Tallahassee: UP of Florida, 1981.

Goldstone, Jack A. "East and West in the Seventeenth Century: Political Crises in Stuart England, Ottoman Turkey, and Ming China." *Comparative Studies in Society and History* 30.1 (1988): 103–42.

Goodblatt, Chanita. "From 'Tav' to the Cross: John Donne's Protestant Exegesis and Polemics." Papazian 221–46.

Gottlieb, Sidney. "Milton's Land-Ships and John Wilkins." *Modern Philology* 84.1 (1986): 60–62.

Gouhier, Henri. *Blaise Pascal: Commentaire*. Paris: Vrin, 1971.

Gould, J. D. "Currency and Exchange Rate in Sixteenth-Century England." *Journal of European Economic History* 2 (1973): 149–59.

———. *The Great Debasement: Currency and the Economy in Mid-Tudor England*. Oxford: Clarendon, 1970.

———. "The Great Debasement and the Supply of Money." *Austrian Economic History Review* 13 (1973): 177–89.

Grafton, Anthony. "Dating History: The Renaissance and the Reformation of Chronology." *Daedalus* 132.2 *On Time* (2003): 74–85.

———. *Defenders of the Text: The Traditions of Scholarship in an Age of Science, 1450–1800*. Cambridge, MA: Harvard UP, 1991.

———. "From *De eie natali* to *De emendatione temporum*: The Origins and Setting of Scaliger's Chronology." *Journal of the Warburg and Courtauld Institutes* 45 (1985): 100–43.

———. "Joseph Scaliger and Historical Chronology: The Rise and Fall of a Discipline." *History and Theory* 14 (1975): 156–85.

———. *Joseph Scaliger: A Study in the History of Classical Scholarship*. Vol. 2, *Historical Chronology*. Oxford: Clarendon, 1993. 2 vols.

Greenblatt, Stephen. *Marvelous Possessions: The Wonder of the New World*. Chicago: U of Chicago P, 1992.

Gregerson, Linda. "Colonials Write the Nation: Spenser, Milton, and England on the Margins." Rajan and Sauer 169–90.

Grierson, H. J. C., ed. *The Poems of John Donne*. Oxford: Oxford UP, 1912. 2 vols.

Grossman, Marshall. *"Authors to Themselves": Milton and the Revelation of History*. Cambridge: Cambridge UP, 1987.

Gu, Jiegang. "How Yao, Shun, and Yu are Related to Each Other." *Gu Shi Bian* (古史辨) *or Debates on Ancient History*. Vol. 1. Shanghai: Shanghai Guji, 1982 [first published 1926–41]. 7 vols.

Guibbory, Achsah. *The Map of Time: Seventeenth-Century English Literature and Ideas of Pattern in History*. Urbana: U of Illinois P, 1986. 169–211.

Gunn, Geoffery. *First Globalization: The Eurasian Exchange, 1500–1800*. Lanham, MD: Rowman & Littlefield, 2003.

Gupta, Suman. *Globalization and Literature*. London: Polity, 2009.

Guzman, Gregory G. "Reports of Mongol Cannibalism in the Thirteenth-Century Latin Sources: Oriental Fact or Western Fiction?" *Discovering New Worlds: Essays on Medieval Exploration and Imagination*. Ed. Scott D. Westrem. New York: Garland, 1991. 31–68.

Habib, Imtiaz H. *Black Lives in the English Archives, 1500–1677: Imprints of the Invisible*. Aldershot: Ashgate, 2008.

Hadfield, Andrew. "The English and Other Peoples." *A Companion to Milton*. Ed. Thomas N. Corns. Oxford: Blackwell, 2001.

Hall, Kim. *Things of Darkness: Economies of Race and Gender in Early Modern England*. Ithaca, NY: Cornell UP, 1995.

Halperin, Charles J. "Russia and the Mongols." Kasinec and Polushin 197–207.

Hamilton, Earl J. *American Treasure and the Price Revolution in Spain, 1501–1650*. Cambridge, MA: Harvard UP, 1934.

Hardt, Michael, and Antonio Negri. *Empire*. Cambridge, MA: Harvard UP, 2000.

Harland, Paul W. "Donne and Virginia: The Ideology of Conquest." *John Donne Journal* 18 (1999): 127–52.

Harley, J. B. "Meaning and Ambiguity in Tudor Cartography." Tyacke 22–45.

Harris, Steven J. "Mapping Jesuit Science: The Role of Travel in the Geography of Knowledge." O'Malley et al. 212–40.

Harvey, David. "Time-Space Compression and the Postmodern Condition." Connell and Marsh 6–21.

Hawkes, David. *Idols of the Marketplace: Idolatry and Commodity Fetishism in English Literature, 1580–1680*. 1st ed. New York: Palgrave, 2001.

Hayot, Eric, Haun Saussy, and Steven G. Yao, eds. *Sinographies: Writing China*. Minneapolis: U of Minnesota P, 2008.
Held, David, and Anthony McGrew. *Globalization/Anti-Globalization: Beyond the Great Divide*. 2nd ed. Cambridge: Polity, 2007.
―――. "The Great Globalization Debate: An Introduction." *The Global Transformations Reader: An Introduction to the Globalization Debate*. Ed. Held and McGrew. Cambridge: Polity, 2003. 1–50.
Helgerson, Richard. *Forms of Nationhood*. Chicago: U of Chicago P, 1994.
Hendricks, Margo, and Patricia Parker, eds. *Women, "Race," and Writing in Early Modern England*. London: Routledge, 1994.
Higashibaba, Ikuo. *Christianity in Early Modern Japan: Kirishitan Belief and Practice*. Leiden, Boston & Koln: Brill, 2001.
Hill, Christopher. *The English Bible and the Seventeenth-Century Revolution*. London: Penguin, 1994.
Hirth, Friedrich. *China and the Roman Orient*. Shanghai: Kelly & Walsh, 1885.
Hobson, John M. *The Eastern Origins of Western Civilization*. New York: Cambridge UP, 2004.
Hodgen, Margaret T. *Early Anthropology in the Sixteenth and Seventeenth Centuries*. Philadelphia: U of Pennsylvania P, 1971.
Hollinger, David A. *Postethnic America: Beyond Multiculturalism*. New York: Harper, 1995.
Hon, Tze-Ki. "Ethnic and Cultural Pluralism: Gu Jiegang's Vision of a New China in His Studies of Ancient History." *Modern China* 22.3 (1996): 315–39.
Hsia, Adrian, ed. *Chinesia: The European Construction of China in the Literature of the Seventeenth and Eighteenth Centuries*. Tübingen: Niemeyer, 1998.
―――. *The Vision of China in the English Literature of the Seventeenth and Eighteenth Centuries*. Hong Kong: Hong Kong UP, 1988.
Hsia, R. Po-Chia. *A Jesuit in the Forbidden City: Matteo Ricci, 1552–1610*. Oxford: Oxford UP, 2010.
Huang, Ray. *Taxation and Government Finance in Sixteenth-Century Ming China*. New York: Cambridge UP, 1974.
Hudson, Geoffrey F. *Europe and China: A Survey of their Relations from the Earliest Times to 1800*. London: Arnold, 1931.
Hunt, Clay. *Donne's Poetry: Essays in Literary Analysis*. New Haven: Yale UP, 1954.
Huntley, Frank L. "Milton, Mendoza, and the Chinese Land-Ship." *Modern Language Notes* 69.6 (1954): 404–7.
―――. *Essays in Persuasion: On Seventeenth-Century Literature*. Chicago: U of Chicago P, 1981.
Jackson, Peter. "The Crisis in the Holy Land in 1260." *English Historical Review* 95 (1980): 481–513.
―――. "The Dissolution of the Mongol Empire." *Central Asiatic Journal* 22 (1978): 186–244.

―――. "Jalāl al-Dīn, the Mongols, and the Khwarazmian Conquest of the Panjāb and Sind." *Iran* 28 (1990): 45–54.

Jacob, Margaret. *Strangers Nowhere in the World: The Rise of Cosmopolitanism in Early Modern Europe*. Philadelphia: U of Pennsylvania P, 2006.

Jameson, Fredric, and Masao Miyoshi, eds. *The Cultures of Globalization*. Durham, NC: Duke UP, 1998.

Jenkins, Eugenia Zuroski. *A Taste for China: English Subjectivity and the Prehistory of Orientalism*. New York: Oxford UP, 2013.

Jensen, Lionel M. *Manufacturing Confucianism: Chinese Traditions and Universal Civilization*. Durham, NC: Duke UP. 1997.

Johanyak, Debra, and Walter S. H. Lim, eds. *The English Renaissance, Orientalism, and the Idea of Asia*. New York: Palgrave, 2010.

Johnson, Stanley. "John Donne and the Virginia Company." *English Literary History* 14.2 (1947): 127–38.

Jones, Andrew. *Globalization: Key Thinkers*. Cambridge: Polity, 2010.

Kamen, Henry. *Empire: How Spain Became a World Power 1492–1763*. New York, Perennial: Harper, 2004.

Kasinec, Wendy F., and Michael A. Polushin, eds. *Expanding Empires: Cultural Interaction and Exchange in World Societies from Ancient to Early Modern Times*. Wilmington, DE: SR Books, 2002.

Katz, David S. "The Language of Adam in Seventeenth-Century England." *History and Imagination: Essays in Honour of H. R. Trevor-Roper*. Ed. Hugh Lloyd-Jones, Valerie Pearl, and Blair Worden. London: Duckworth, 1981. 132–45.

Keen, Benjamin, trans. and ed. *The Life of the Admiral Christopher Columbus by His Son Ferdinand*. London: Folio Society, 1960.

Keevak, Michael. *Becoming Yellow: A Short History of Racial Thinking*. Princeton, NJ: Princeton UP, 2011.

Kegley, Charles W. Jr., and Gregory A. Raymond, eds. *Exorcising the Ghost of Westphalia: Building World Order in the New Millennium*. Upper Saddle River, NJ: Prentice Hall, 2002.

Kennedy, D. E. "King James's College of Controversial Divinity at Chelsea." *Grounds of Controversy, Three Studies of Late 16th and Early 17th Century English Polemics*. Ed. D. E. Kennedy. Melbourne: Melbourne UP, 1989. 97–119.

Keuning, Johannes. "Blaeu's 'Atlas.'" *Imago Mundi* 14 (1959): 74–89.

Keynes, Geoffrey. "Doctor Donne and Scaliger." *Times Literary Supplement* (February 21, 1958): 108.

Kidd, Colin. *British Identities before Nationalism: Ethnicity and Nationhood in the Atlantic World, 1600–1800*. New York: Cambridge UP, 1999.

Knoespel, Kenneth J. "Milton and the Hermeneutics of Time: Seventeenth Century Chronologies and the Science of History." *Studies in the Literary Imagination* 22 (1989): 17–35.

―――. "Newton in the School of Time: The Chronology of Ancient Kingdoms Amended and the Crisis of Seventeenth-Century Historiography." *The Eighteenth Century: Theory and Interpretation* 30 (1989): 19–41.

Knowles, James, ed. *Ben Jonson, The Key Keeper: A Masque for the Opening of Britain's Burse April 19, 1609*. Tunbridge Wells: Foundling, 2002.

———. "Cecil's Shopping Centre: The Rediscovery of a Ben Jonson Masque in Praise of Trade." *Times Literary Supplement* (February 7, 1997): 14–15.

———. "Jonson's Entertainment at Britain's Burse." *Re-presenting Ben Jonson: Text, History, Performance*. Ed. Martin Butler. New York: St. Martin's, 1999.

Knowlson, James. *Universal Language Schemes in England and France, 1600–1800*. Toronto: U of Toronto P, 1975.

Kocher, Paul H. *Christopher Marlowe: A Study of His Thought, Learning and Character*. New York: Russel & Russel, 1962.

Koeman, C. "Life and Works of Willem Janszoon Blaeu: New Contributions to the Study of Blaeu, Made during the Last Hundred Years." *Imago Mundi* 26 (1972): 9–16.

Koivukoski, Toivo. "Imperial Compulsions." *Enduring Empire*. Ed. David E. Tabachnick and Toivo Koivukoski. Toronto: U of Toronto P, 2009. 96–113.

Krasner, Stephen. "Compromising Westphalia." *International Security* 20.3 (1995/96): 115–51.

Kurlantzick, Joshua. *Charm Offensive: How China's Soft Power Is Transforming the World*. New Haven: Yale UP, 2007.

Labriola, Albert C. "Altered States in Donne's 'The Canonization': and Alchemy, Mintage, and Transmutation." *John Donne Journal* 27 (2008): 121–30.

Lach, Donald F. *China in the Eyes of Europe: The Sixteenth Century*. Chicago: U of Chicago P, 1965.

Lach, Donald F., and Edwin van Kley. *Asia in the Making of Europe*. Chicago: Chicago UP, 1965–1993. 3 vols.

Lee, Christina H., ed. *Western Visions of the Far East in a Transpacific Age, 1522–1657*. Aldershot: Ashgate, 2012.

Lee, Sue-Im. "'We Are Not the World': Global Village, Universalism, and Karen Tei Yamashita's Tropic of Orange." *Modern Fiction Studies* 52.3 (2007): 501–27.

Lee, Thomas H. C., ed. *China and Europe: Images and Influences in the Sixteenth to Eighteenth Centuries*. Hong Kong: Chinese UP, 1991.

Leibniz, G. W. *Writings on China*. Trans. and ed. Daniel J. Cook and Henry Rosemont Jr. Chicago: Open Court, 1994.

Leonard, John. *Naming in Paradise: Milton and the Language of Adam and Eve*. Oxford: Clarendon, 1990.

LePan, Don. *The Cognitive Revolution in Western Culture*. London: Palgrave, 1989.

Leslie, Michael, Timothy Raylor, and Mark Greengrass, eds. *Samuel Hartlib and Universal Reformation: Studies in Intellectual Communication*. New York: Cambridge UP, 1994.

Lester, Toby. *The Fourth Part of the World: An Astonishing Epic of Global Discovery, Imperial Ambition and the Birth of America*. New York: Free Press, 2009.

Lestringant, Frank. *Mapping the Renaissance World: The Geographical Imagination in the Age of Discovery.* Trans. David Fausett. Berkeley: U of California P, 1994.

Levin, Carole. *Shakespeare's Foreign Worlds: National and Transnational Identities in the Elizabethan Age.* Ithaca, NY: Cornell UP, 2009.

Li, Dan J., trans. *China in Transition, 1517–1911.* New York: Van Nostrand Reinhold, 1969.

Liang, Fang-chung. *The Single-whip Method of Taxation in China.* Trans. Wang Yü-ch'uan. Cambridge, MA: Harvard UP, 1956.

Lim, Walter S. H. "China, India, and the Empire of Commerce in Milton's Paradise Lost." Hayot et al. 115–39.

———. "John Milton, Orientalism, and the Empires of the East in Paradise Lost." Johanyak and Lim 203–35.

Lin, Handa, et al., eds. *Chinese History of Five Thousand Years from Antiquity to Modern Times* (上下五千年). Shanghai: Children's Publisher, 2002.

Lin, Li-Jen. "The Intention to Begin from Huang-Ti in 'Shi-ji Biographic Sketches of Five Emperors.'" *Paper of Humanities and Social Sciences* (人文社會學報) 5 (March 2009): 39–67.

Livingstone, David N. *Adam's Ancestors: Race, Religion, and the Politics of Human Origins.* Baltimore: Johns Hopkins UP, 2008.

Loewenstein, David. *Milton and the Drama of History: Historical Vision, Iconoclasm, and the Literary Imagination.* Cambridge: Cambridge UP, 1990.

Loewenstein, David, and Paul Stevens, eds. *Early Modern Nationalism and Milton's England.* Toronto: U of Toronto P, 2008.

Loomba, Ania. *Colonialism/Postcolonialism.* 2nd ed. London: Routledge, 2005.

———. *Shakespeare, Race, and Colonialism.* Oxford: Oxford UP, 2002.

Lundbaek, Knud. "Imaginary Ancient Chinese Characters." *China Mission Studies (1550–1800)* Bulletin V (1983): 5–23.

Lux, Jonathan E. "'Shot Through with Orient Beams': Restoring the Orient to Milton's Paradise." *Milton Quarterly* 48.4 (2014): 235–47.

Maat, Jaap. *Philosophical Languages in the Seventeenth Century: Dalgarno, Wilkins, Leibniz.* Dordrecht: Academic, 2004.

MacCaffrey, Isabel G. *"Paradise Lost" as "Myth."* Cambridge, MA: Harvard UP, 1959.

MacColley, Grant. *Paradise Lost: An Account of Its Growth and Major Origins, with a Discussion of Milton's Use of Sources and Literary Patterns.* Chicago: U of Chicago P, 1940.

MacDonald, Joyce G. *Women and Race in Early Modern Texts.* Cambridge: Cambridge UP, 2002.

MacPhail, Eric. "The Plot of History from Antiquity to the Renaissance." *Journal of the History of Ideas* 62.1 (2001): 1–16.

Maley, Willy. *Nation, State, and Empire in English Renaissance Literature: Shakespeare to Milton.* New York: Palgrave, 2003.

Manning, Patrick, ed. *Slave Trades, 1500–1800: Globalization of Forced Labour.* Ashgate: Variorum, 1996.

Markley, Robert. "A Brief History of Chronological Time." *Danish Yearbook of Philosophy* 44 (2009): 59–75.

———. "Civility, Ceremony, and Desire at Beijing: Sensibility and the European Quest for 'Free Trade' with China in the Late Seventeenth Century." *Passionate Encounters in a Time of Sensibility.* Ed. Anne Mellor and Maximilian Novak. Newark: U of Delaware P, 2000. 60–88.

———. "'The destin'd Walls / Of Cambalu': Milton, China, and the Ambiguities of the Far East." Rajan and Sauer 191–213.

———. *Fallen Languages: Crises of Representation in Newtonian England, 1660–1740.* Ithaca: Cornell UP, 1993.

———. *The Far East and the English Imagination, 1600–1730.* Cambridge: Cambridge UP, 2006.

———. "Newton, Corruption, and the Tradition of Universal History." *Newton and Religion: Context, Nature, and Influence.* Ed. James E. Force and Richard H. Popkin. Dordrecht: Kluwer, 1999. 123–46.

———. "Riches, Power, Trade, and Religion: The Far East and the English Imagination, 1600–1720." *Renaissance Studies* 17 (2003): 433–55.

Martz, Louis B. *The Poem of the Mind: Essays on Poetry, English and American.* New York: Oxford UP, 1966.

Masson, David. *The Life of John Milton: Narrative in Connexion with the Political, Ecclesiastical, and Literary History of his Time.* Vol. 5. *1654–60.* London: MacMillan, 1877. 7 vols.

Matar, Nabil. *Turks, Moors, and Englishmen in the Age of Discovery.* New York: Columbia UP, 1999.

McCracken, George E. "Athanasius Kircher's Universal Polygraphy." *Isis* 39 (1948): 215–29.

McColley, Diane. *Milton's Eve.* Urbana: U of Illinois P, 1983.

McCulloch, J. R., ed. *Early English Tracts on Commerce.* Cambridge: Cambridge UP, 1970.

McEachern, Claire. *The Poetics of English Nationhood 1590–1612.* Cambridge: Cambridge UP, 1996.

McInnis, David. "The Golden Man and the Golden Age: The Relationship of English Poets and the New World Reconsidered." *Early Modern Literary Studies* 13.1 (2007): 1–19.

McKerrow, Ronald B., ed. *The Works of Thomas Nashe.* 2nd ed. Vol. 2. Oxford: Blackwell, 1958. 5 vols.

McLeod, Bruce. "The 'Lordly eye': Milton and the Strategic Geography of Empire." Rajan and Sauer 48–66.

Milton, Anthony. *Catholic and Reformed: The Roman and Protestant Churches in English Protestant Thought 1600–1640.* Cambridge: U of Cambridge P, 1995.

Mohamed, Feisal G. *Milton and the Post-Secular Present: Ethics, Politics, Terrorism.* Stanford: Stanford UP, 2011.

Moloughney, Brian, and Wenzhong Xia. "Silver and the Fall of the Ming Dynasty: A Reassessment." *Papers on Far Eastern History* 40 (1989): 51–78.

Momigliano, Arnaldo. "Pagan and Christian Historiography in the Fourth Century AD." *The Conflict between Paganism and Christianity in the Fourth Century.* Ed. Momigliano. Oxford: Clarendon, 1963. 79–99.

———. *On Pagans, Jews, and Christians.* Middletown, CT: Wesleyan UP, 1987.

Monroe, Arthur Eli, ed. *Early Economic Thought: Selections from Economic Literature prior to Adam Smith.* Cambridge, MA: Harvard UP, 1924.

Morgan, David. *The Mongols.* 2nd ed. Oxford: Blackwell, 1986.

Morgan, Victor. "The Literary Image of Globes and Maps in Early Modern England." Tyacke 46–56.

Mueller, William R. *John Donne: Preacher.* Princeton: Princeton UP, 1962.

Mungello, David E., ed. *The Chinese Rites Controversy: Its History and Meaning.* Nettetal: Steyler Verlag, 1994.

———. *Curious Land: Jesuit Accommodation and the Origins of Sinology.* Honolulu: U of Hawaii P, 1989.

———. *The Great Encounter of China and the West.* Lanham, MD; Oxford: Rowman & Littlefield, 1999.

Munkler, Herfried. *The Logic of World Domination from Ancient Rome to the United States.* Trans. Patrick Camiller. Cambridge: Polity, 2007.

Murrin, Michael. *Trade and Commerce.* Chicago: Chicago UP, 2014.

Needham, Joseph et al., eds. *Science and Civilisation in China.* Cambridge: Cambridge UP, 1954–2008. 7 vols. Vol. 1. *Introductory Orientations.* Repr. Richmond: Kingprint, 1972.

Neill, S. *A History of Christian Missions.* Harmondsworth: Penguin, 1964.

Northrop, Douglas A. "The Double Structure of Paradise Lost." *Milton Studies* 12 (1978): 75–90.

Nussbaum, Martha. "Kant and Stoic Cosmopolitanism." *Journal of Political Philosophy* 5.1 (1997): 1–25.

Nyquist, Mary. "Contemporary Ancestors of de Bry, Hobbes, and Milton." *University of Toronto Quarterly* 77.3 (2008): 837–75.

———. "The Genesis of Gendered Subjectivity in the Divorce Tracts and in Paradise Lost." *Re-Membering Milton: Essays on the Texts and Traditions.* Ed. Nyquist and Margaret W. Ferguson. New York: Methuen, 1988. 99–127.

Ogborn, Miles. *Indian Ink: Script and Print in the Making of the English East India Company.* Chicago: U of Chicago P, 2008.

O'Malley, John W., Gauvin A. Bailey, and Stephen J. Harris, eds. *The Jesuits: Cultures, Sciences, and the Arts, 1540–1773.* Toronto: U of Toronto P, 1999.

Ostrowski, Donald. *Muscovy and the Mongols: Cross-Cultural Influences on the Steppe Frontier, 1304–1589.* Cambridge: Cambridge UP, 2002.

Otte, Enrique, ed. *Cartas privadas de emigrantes a Indias, 1540–1616* [*Private Letters of the Emigrants to the Indies*]. Seville, Jerez: Escuela de Estudios Hispanoamericanos, 1988.

Outhwaite, R. B. *Inflation in Tudor and Early Stuart England*. 2nd ed. London: Macmillan, 1982.
Owens, Robert R. "The Myth of Anian." *Journal of the History of Ideas* 36.1 (1975): 135–38.
Papazian, Mary A. *John Donne and the Protestant Reformation: New Perspectives*. Detroit: Wayne State UP, 2003.
Parker, Charles H. *Global Interactions in the Early Modern Age, 1400–1800*. New York: Cambridge UP, 2010.
Parks, George B. "The Occasion of Milton's 'Moscovia.'" *Studies in Philology* 40.3 (1943): 399–404.
Parr, Anthony. "John Donne, Travel Writer." *Huntington Library Quarterly* 70.1 (2007): 61–85.
Parry, J. H. *The Spanish Seaborne Empire*. Berkeley: U of California P, 1990.
Patrides, C. A. *Milton and the Christian Tradition*. New York: Oxford UP, 1969.
———. "Renaissance Estimates of the Year of Creation." *Huntington Library Quarterly* 26.4 (1963): 315–22.
———, ed. *Sir Thomas Browne: The Major Works*. London: Penguin, 1977.
Peters, Julie S. "A 'Bridge over Chaos': De Jure Belli, Paradise Lost, Terror, Sovereignty, Globalism, and the Modern Law of Nations." *Comparative Literature* 57.4 (2005): 273–93.
Philips, J. R. S. *The Medieval Expansion of Europe*. 2nd ed. Oxford: Clarendon, 1998.
Pomeranz, Kenneth. *The Great Divergence: China, Europe, and the Making of the Modern World Economy*. Princeton: Princeton UP, 2000.
Pond, Shepard. "The Spanish Dollar: The World's Most Famous Silver Coin." *Bulletin of the Business Historical Society* 15.1 (1941): 12–16.
Poole, Kristen. "Naming, Paradise Lost, and the Gendered Discourse of Perfect Language Schemes." *English Literary Renaissance* 38.3 (2008): 535–60.
Poole, William. "The Divine and the Grammarian: Theological Disputes in the 17th-Century Universal Language Movement." *Historiographica linguistica* 30 (2003): 273–300.
———. "Milton and Science: A Caveat." *Milton Quarterly* 38 (2004): 18–34.
———. "Seventeenth-century Preadamism, and an Anonymous English Preadamist." *Seventeenth Century* 19 (2004): 1–35.
Popkin, Richard H. *Isaac La Peyrère (1596–1676): His Life, Work and Influence*. Leiden: E. J. Brill, 1987.
Porter, David. ed. *Comparative Early Modernities: 1100–1800*. London: Palgrave, 2012.
———. "What Is Universal about Universal Human Rights?" *CICS International Connections* 3.2 (2011): 6–10.
———. *The Chinese Taste in Eighteenth-Century England*. Cambridge: Cambridge UP, 2010.
———. "Sinicizing Early Modernity: The Imperatives of Historical Cosmopolitanism." *Eighteenth-Century Studies* 43.3 (2010): 299–306.

———. *Ideographia: The Chinese Cipher in Early Modern Europe.* Stanford: Stanford UP. 2001.

———. "A Peculiar but Uninteresting Nation: China and the Discourse of Commerce in Eighteenth-Century England." *Eighteenth-Century Studies* 33 (2000): 181–99.

———. "Writing China: Legitimacy and Representation 1606–1773." *Comparative Literature Studies* 33 (1996): 98–101.

Preus, James S. *From Shadow to Promise: Old Testament Interpretation from Augustine to the Young Luther.* Cambridge, MA: Belknap-Harvard UP, 1969.

Puett, Michael. *The Ambivalence of Creation: Debates Concerning Innovation and Artifice in Early China.* Stanford: Stanford UP, 2001.

Qian, Zhongshu, "China in the English Literature of the Seventeenth Century." *Quarterly Bulletin of Chinese Bibliography* 1.4 (1940): 351–84.

Quinn, David B., ed. *New American World: A Documentary History of North America to 1612.* Vol. 4. New York: Arno Press and Hector Bye, 1979. 5 vols.

———, ed. *The Voyages and Colonising Enterprises of Sir Humphrey Gilbert.* London: Hakluyt Society, 1940.

Quinn, Dennis B. "John Donne's Principles of Biblical Exegesis." *Journal of English and German Philology* 61 (1962): 313–29.

Quint, David. *Epic and Empire: Politics and Generic Form from Virgil to Milton.* Princeton: Princeton UP, 1993.

Qvarnstrom, Gunnar. *The Enchanted Palace: Some Structural Aspects of Paradise Lost.* Stockholm: Almqvist & Wiksell, 1967.

Rajan, Balachandra. "Banyan Trees and Fig Leaves: Some Thoughts on Milton's India." *Of Poetry and Politics: New Essays on Milton and His World.* Ed. P. G. Stanwood. Binghamton, NY: Medieval & Renaissance Texts & Studies, 1995. 213–28.

———. "The Imperial Temptation." Rajan and Sauer 294–314.

———. *Under Western Eyes: India from Milton to Macaulay.* Durham, NC: Duke UP, 1999.

Rajan, Balachandra, and Elizabeth Sauer, eds. *Milton and the Imperial Vision.* Pittsburgh: Duquesne UP, 1999.

Raleigh, W. A. *The English Voyages of the Sixteenth Century.* Glasgow, 1905. Hakluyt, Principal Navigations. Vol. 12.

Raman, Shankar. "Can't Buy Me Love: Money, Gender, and Colonialism in Donne's Erotic Verse." *Criticism* 43 (2001): 135–68.

———. *Framing "India": The Colonial Imaginary in Early Modern Culture.* Stanford: Stanford UP, 2002.

Ramsey, Rachel. "China and the Ideal of Order in John Webb's An Historical Essay … ." *Journal of the History of Ideas* 62.3 (2001): 483–503.

Ravenstein, Ernest G. *Martin Behaim, His Life and his Globe.* London: G. Philip & Son, 1908.

Rennie, Neil. *Far-Fetched Facts: The Literature of Travel and the Idea of the South Seas.* Oxford: Clarendon, 1995.

Richards. John F., ed. *Precious Metals in the Later Medieval and Early Modern Worlds*. Durham, NC: Carolina Academic, 1983.

Ricks, Christopher. *Milton's Grand Style*. Oxford: Oxford UP, 1963.

Robertson, Roland. *Globalization: Social Theory and Global Culture*. London: Sage, 1992.

Rogers, John. *The Matter of Revolution: Science, Poetry, and Politics in the Age of Milton*. Ithaca, NY: Cornell UP, 1996.

Ronald, Susan. *The Pirate Queen: Queen Elizabeth I, Her Pirate Adventures, and the Dawn of Empire*. New York: Harper, 2007.

Ross, Andrew C. "Alesssandro Valignano: The Jesuits and Culture in the East." O'Malley et al. 337–51.

Rossi, Paolo. *The Dark Abyss of Time: The History of the Earth and the History of Nations from Hooke to Vico*. Trans. Lydia C. Cochrane. Chicago: U of Chicago P, 1984.

———. *Logic and the Art of Memory: The Quest for a Universal Language*. Trans. Stephen Clucas. Chicago: U of Chicago P, 2000.

Rowbotham, Arnold H. *Missionary and Mandarin: The Jesuits at the Court of China*. Berkeley: U of California P, 1942.

Rubiés, Joan-Pau. "The Spanish Contribution to the Ethnology of Asia in the Sixteenth and Seventeenth Centuries." Carey, *Asian Travel* 93–123.

Rummel, Erika. *Erasmus' Annotations on the New Testament: From Philologist to Theologian*. Erasmus Studies 8. Toronto: U of Toronto P, 1986.

Ryan, Michael T. "Assimilating New World in the Sixteenth and Seventeenth Centuries." *Comparative Studies in Society and History* 23 (1981): 519–38.

Said, Edward W. *Orientalism*. 25th Anniversary Edition. With a New Preface by the Author. New York: Random, 2003.

Salmon, Vivian. *The Study of Language in Seventeenth Century England*. Amsterdam: John Benjamins, 1988.

———. *The Works of Francis Lodwick: A Study of His Writings in the Intellectual Context of the Seventeenth Century*. London: Longman, 1972.

Sanders, Julie. *Ben Jonson in Context*. Cambridge: Cambridge UP, 2010.

Sandler, Florence. "'The Gallery to the New World': Donne, Herbert, and Ferrar on the Virginia Project." *John Donne Journal* 19 (2000): 267–97.

Scheleiner, Winfred. *The Imagery of John Donne's Sermons*. Providence: Brown UP, 1970.

Schurz, William Lytle. *The Manila Galleon*. New York: E. P. Dutton, 1939.

Schwartz, Regina. "Milton's Hostile Chaos: ' … And the Sea Was No More.'" *English Literary History* 52.2 (1985): 337–74.

———. *Remembering and Repeating: Biblical Creation in Paradise Lost*. Cambridge: Cambridge UP, 1988.

Sebek, Barbara, and Stephen Deng, eds. *Global Traffic: Discourses and Practices of Trade in English Literature and Culture from 1550*. New York: Palgrave, 2008.

Sedwick, Daniel, and Frank Sedwick. *The Practical Book of Cobs: Included an Expanded Guide to Shipwrecks*. 4th ed. Winter Park, FL: Daniel Frank Sedwick, 2007.

Shakespeare, William. *The Arden Shakespeare Complete Works*. Ed. Richard Proudfoot, Ann Thompson, and David S. Kastan. 2nd ed. London: Thomson, 2001.

Shambaugh, David. *China Goes Global: The Partial Power*. Oxford: Oxford UP, 2013.

Shami, Jeanne. "John Donne: Geography as Metaphor." *Geography and Literature: A Meeting of the Disciplines*. Ed. William E. Mallory and Paul Simpson-Housley. Syracuse: Syracuse UP, 1987. 161–67.

———. "'Speaking Openly and Speaking First': John Donne, the Synod of Dort, and the Early Stuart Church." Papazian 48–51.

Sharp, Robert L. "Donne's 'Good Morrow' and Cordiform Maps." *Modern Language Notes* 69 (1954): 493–95.

Shaw, W. A. *The History of Currency*. London: Wilsons and Milne, 1895.

Shawcross, John T. ed. *The Complete Poetry of John Donne*. New York: Anchor Books, 1967.

Shuger, Debora K. *The Renaissance Bible: Scholarship, Sacrifice, and Subjectivity*. 1998. Waco: Baylor UP, 2010.

Singer, Thomas C. "Hieroglyphs, Real Characters, and the Idea of Natural Language in English Seventeenth-Century Thought." *Journal of the History of Ideas* 50 (1989): 49–70.

Singh, Jyotsna G. *Colonial Narratives/Cultural Dialogues: "Discoveries" of India in the Language of Colonialism*. London: Routledge, 1996.

Slotkin, James S., ed. *Readings in Early Anthropology*. Chicago: Aldine, 1965.

Smalley, Beryl. *The Study of the Bible in the Middle Ages*. 2nd ed. Notre Dame: U of Notre Dame P, 1964.

Song, Eric B. "Nation, Empire, and the Strange Fire of the Tartars in Milton's Poetry and Prose." *Milton Studies* 47 (2008): 119–44.

Spate, O. H. K. *The Pacific Since Magellan*. Vol. 2. *Monopolists and Freebooters*. Canberra: Australian National UP, 1983.

Spence, Jonathon. *The Chan's Great Continent: China in Western Minds*. London: Penguin, 2000.

Spier, Fred. "Histories Big and Small: A Critique of Wolf Schäfer's New Global History." *Erwägen Wissen Ethik* 14 (2003): 118–20.

Spies, Marijke. *Arctic Routes to Fabled Lands: Olivier Brunel and the Passage to China and Cathay in the Sixteenth Century*. Amsterdam: Amsterdam UP, 2002.

Spooner, Frank. *The International Economy and Monetary Movements in France, 1493–1725*. Cambridge, MA: Harvard UP, 1972.

Standaert, Nicolas. "Jesuit Corporate Culture as Shaped by the Chinese." O'Malley et al. 352–62.

Stanley, Johnson. "John Donne and the Virginia Company." *English Literary History* 14.2 (1947): 127–38.

Steger, Manfred B. *Globalization: A Very Short Introduction*. 2nd ed. Oxford: Oxford UP, 2009.

Steinmetz, David C., ed. *The Bible in the Sixteenth Century*. Durham, NC: Duke UP, 1990.

Stevens, Paul. "'Leviticus Thinking' and the Rhetoric of Early Modern Colonialism." *Criticism* 35 (1993): 441–61.

———. "*Paradise Lost* and the Colonial Imperative." *Milton Studies* 34 (1997): 3–21.

Stevens, Paul, and Rahul Sapra. "Akbar's Dream: Moghul Toleration and English/British Orientalism." *Modern Philology* 104.3 (2007): 379–411.

Stillman, Robert. *The New Philosophy and Universal Languages in Seventeenth-Century England: Bacon, Hobbes, and Wilkins*. Lewisburg: Bucknell UP, 1995.

Stimson, Dorothy L. "Comenius and the Invisible College." *Isis* 23 (1953): 383–88.

Strathmann, Ernest A. *Sir Walter Raleigh: A Study in Elizabethan Skepticism*. New York: Columbia UP, 1951.

Strenski, Ivan. "The Religion in Globalization." *Journal of American Academy of Religion* 72.3 (2004): 631–52.

Stubblefield, Jay. "'I Have Taken a Contrary Way': Identity and Ambiguity in John Donne's Sermon to the Virginia Company." *Renaissance Papers* (2001): 87–106.

———. "'Very Worthily Sett in Printe': Writing the Virginia Company of London." *Renaissance Papers* (2003): 167–87.

Subbiondo, Joseph L., ed. *John Wilkins and 17th Century British Linguistics*. Amsterdam: John Benjamins, 1992.

Sui, Gwee Li. "Westward to the Orient: The Specter of Scientific China in Francis Bacon's New Atlantis." Johanyak and Lim 161–83.

Supple, Berry E. *Commercial Crisis and Change in England 1600–1642: A Study in the Instability of a Mercantile Economy*. Cambridge: Cambridge UP, 1959.

Sure, Donald F., trans., and Ray R. Noll., ed. *100 Roman Documents Relating to the Chinese Rites Controversy (1645–1941)*. San Francisco: Ricci Institute, 1992.

Sutherland, C. H. V. *English Coinage 600–1900*. London: Batsford, 1973.

Synkellos, George. *The Chronography of George Synkellos: A Byzantine Chronicle of Universal History from the Creation*. Trans. William Adler and Paul Tuffin. Oxford: Oxford UP, 2002.

Szcześniak, Boleslaw. "Matteo Ricci's Maps of China." *Imago Mundi* 11 (1954): 127–36.

———. "The Seventeenth Century Maps of China: An Inquiry into the Compilations of European Cartographers." *Imago Mundi* 13 (1956): 116–36.

Taylor, E. G. R. "John Dee and the Map of North-East Asia." *Imago Mundi* 12 (1955): 103–6.

———. "A Letter Dated 1577 from Mercator to John Dee." *Imago Mundi* 13 (1956): 56–68.
TePaske, John J. "New World Silver, Castile, and the Philippines, 1590–1800." Richards 397–424.
Teschke, Benno. *The Myth of 1648: Class, Geopolitics, and the Making of Modern International Relations*. London: Verso, 2003.
Thrash, Cheryl. "'How cam'st thou speakable of mute?': Learning Words in Milton's Paradise." *Milton Quarterly* 31 (1997): 42–61.
Tomlinson, John. *Globalization and Culture*. Chicago: U of Chicago P: 1999.
Trevor-Roper, Hugh. *Catholics, Anglicans, and Puritans*. London: Secker & Warburg, 1987.
Trubowitz, Rachel. "'The people of Asia and with them the Jews': Israel, Asia, and England in Milton's Writings." *Milton and the Jews*. Ed. Douglas A. Brooks. Cambridge: Cambridge UP, 2008. 151–77.
Turnbull, G. H. *Hartlib, Dury and Comenius: Gleanings from Hartlib's Papers*. Liverpool: Liverpool UP, 1947.
Turner, Bryan S. *Globalization East and West*. London: Sage, 2010.
Tyacke, Sarah, ed. *English Map-Making 1500–1650: Historical Essays*. London: British Library, 1983.
van Creveld, Martin. *The Rise and Decline of the State*. New York: Cambridge UP, 1999.
van der Krogt, Peter. *Globi Neerlandici: The Production of Globes in the Low Countries*. Utrecht: HES, 1993.
van Kley, Edwin J. "Europe's 'Discovery' of China and the Writing of World History." *American Historical Review* 76.2 (1971): 358–85.
———. "News from China: Seventeenth-Century European Notices of the Manchu Conquest." *Journal of Modern History* 45.4 (1973): 561–82.
Vaughan, Alden T. "'Expulsion of the Savages': English Policy and the Virginia Massacre of 1622." *William and Mary Quarterly* 35.1 (1978): 57–84.
Vitkus, Daniel. "Introduction: Toward a New Globalism in Early Modern Studies." *Journal for Early Modern Cultural Studies* 2.1 (2002): v–viii.
Von Glahn, Richard. *Fountain of Fortune: Money and Monetary Policy in China, 1000–1700*. Berkeley: U of California P, 1996.
Wadkins, T. H. "Theological Polemic and Religious Culture in Early Stuart England." Diss. Graduate Theological Union, U of California, Berkeley, 1988.
Wallis, Helen. "England's Search for the Northern Passages in the Sixteenth and Early Seventeenth Centuries." *Arctic* 37.4 (1984): 453–72.
Walton, Timothy R. *The Spanish Treasure Fleets*. Florida: Pineapple, 1994.
Watson, Adam. *The Evolution of International Society: A Comparative Historical Analysis*. 1992. Intro. Barry Buzan and Richard Little. London: Routledge, 2009.
Weatherford, Jack. *Genghis Khan and the Making of the Modern World*. New York: Three Rivers, 2004.

Weigand, Hermann J. "The Two and Seventy Languages of the World." *Germanic Review* 17 (1942): 241–60.
Welch, Anthony K. "Reconsidering Chronology in Paradise Lost." *Milton Studies* 41 (2002): 1–17.
Wetsel, David. "'Histoire de la China': Pascal and the Challenge to Biblical Time." *Journal of Religion* 69.2 (1989): 199–219.
Whiting, George W. *Milton and This Pedant World*. Austin: U of Texas P, 1958.
Wilcox, Donald J. *The Measure of Times Past: Pre-Newtonian Chronologies and the Rhetoric of Relative Time*. Chicago: U of Chicago P, 1987.
Williams, Arnold. *The Common Expositor: An Account of the Commentaries on Genesis 1527–1633*. Chapel Hill: U of North Carolina P, 1948.
Wills, John E. Jr., ed. *China and Maritime Europe, 1500–1800: Trade, Settlement, Diplomacy, and Missions*. New York: Cambridge UP, 2011.
Winter, Heinrich. "Catalan Portolan Maps and Their Place in the Total View of Cartographic Development." *Imago Mundi* 11 (1954): 1–12.
———. "Francisco Rodrigues' Atlas of ca. 1513." *Imago Mundi* 6 (1949): 20–26.
Wolf, Eric R. *Europe and the People without History*. Foreword. Thomas H. Eriksen. 2nd ed. Berkeley: U of California P, 2010.
Wong, Roy Bin. *China Transformed: Historical Change and the Limits of European Experience*. Ithaca, NY: Cornell UP, 1997.
Wood, James D. *The Interpretation of the Bible*. London: Gerald Duckworth, 1958.
Woolley, Benjamin. *Savage Kingdom: The True Story of Jamestown, 1607, and the Settlement of America*. New York: Harper, 2008.
Yang, Chi-ming. *Performing China: Virtue, Commerce and Orientalism in Eighteenth-Century England, 1660–1760*. Baltimore: Johns Hopkins UP, 2011.
Young, R. V. "'My America, My New-found-land': Pornography and Imperial Politics in Donne's Elegies." *South Central Review* 4.2 (1987): 35–48.
Yule, Sir Henry, trans. and ed. *Cathay and the Way Thither: Being a Collection of Medieval Notices of China*. Taipei: Ch'eng-Wen, 1966. 4 vols.
Zheng, Jiexiang (郑杰祥). *Huangdi and Leizu* (黄帝与嫘祖). Zhengzhou: Zhongzhou Antiquity Publisher [中州古籍出版社], 2005.
———. *Xinzhou, Huangdi's Hometown and Capital* (黄帝故里故都在新郑). Zhengzhou: Zhongzhou Antiquity Publisher [中州古籍出版社], 2005.
Zivley, Sherry L. "The Thirty-Three Days of Paradise Lost." *Milton Quarterly* 34:4 (2000): 117–27.

Index

Abu-Lughod, Janet L. 31
Achinstein, Sharon 134, 173
Akbari, Suzanne C. 8
Allen, Don C. 83, 87, 102, 144, 145
Anyan 32, 57–75
apologetic agenda 81, 82, 114, 144, 146
Appadurai, Arjun 6, 25
Appiah, Kwame A. 26
Appleton, William W. 15
Ariosto, Ludovico 12, 133, 188
Aristotle, 100, 130
Armitage, David 174
Attman, Artur, 42, 43
Atwell, William S. 38, 41, 42
Augustine 82, 86, 87, 99, 102, 142, 168

Bacon, Francis 8, 12, 15, 20, 28, 77, 87, 91, 111, 136, 141, 142, 148, 149, 151, 152, 155, 158, 160, 166, 201
Baker, David J. 4, 16, 24
Banerjee, Pompa 113
Bartolovich, Crystal 63
Batchelor, Robert K. 31
Beazley, Charles Raymond 65
Beck, Ulrich 182
Berry, Lloyd E. 186, 187, 192
Bodin, Jean 50, 85, 89–93, 100, 106, 133, 134, 141, 150, 172, 203
Boehme, Jacob 142, 143
Brook, Timothy 32
bullion 38, 39, 40–48, 51–54

Cambalu 112, 132, 133, 136, 138, 173, 180, 184, 187
Carpini, John of Plano 8, 17, 187, 191, 193
Cataia (n) 55, 60, 66, 67, 68
Cathaia(n) 17, 66, 68, 111, 132, 133, 173, 178, 184
Cathayan 12, 27
Cawley, Robert R. 12, 124

Chaldean 85, 87, 98, 99, 100, 115, 154
Challis, Christopher 56, 60
Chaucer, Geoffrey 187, 188
Chaudhuri, Kirti N. 43
Ch'en, Shou-yi 10, 118, 145, 146
Chinese antiquity 32, 83, 86, 88, 92, 98, 107, 109, 111–39
Chinese chronology 81, 83–107, 116–22, 141, 153, 155
Clossey, Luke 25
Cogley, Richard W.177
Cohen, Jonathan 151, 153, 156
Cohen, Walter 12
colonialism: 18, 20, 21, 26, 30, 38, 113, 134, 174, 188
Columbus 20, 41, 71, 72
Comenius, John A. 152, 156, 170, 171, 186
Confucius 23, 95, 96
Cornelius, Paul 116, 143, 151, 169
cosmopolis 33, 175, 182, 198, 199
cosmopolitanism 14, 26, 27–32, 56–58, 63, 74, 75, 77, 79, 107, 110, 111, 114, 127, 134, 139, 173, 175, 201, 202
cultural pluralism 26, 28, 31, 59, 63, 97, 120

da Cruz, Gaspar 146, 197
Da Gama, Vasco 6, 201
d'Avity, Pierre 136, 137
Dalgarno, George 142, 151, 152, 154, 156
Dallmayr, Fred 175
Dawson, Christopher 8, 179, 193
Dawson, Raymond S. 10
Dee, John 61, 65, 68
de Grazia, Margreta 150
DeMott, Benjamin 143, 171
Deng, Stephen 5, 36, 47
Desmarets [Maresius] Samuel, 115, 116
Dunne, George 10, 19, 29, 182
Dury, John 156, 171, 186
the Dutch 29, 38, 56, 123, 145

East-West contact 1, 3, 5
Eagle, Christopher 159
Eco, Umberto 143
Eden, Richard 52, 55, 65, 83
Edson, Evelyn 65
Edwardes, Michael 1
Egyptians 99, 100, 106, 115, 117, 154
Entzminger, Robert L. 158
Erlichman, Howard J., 24
Eurocentric 2, 17, 26, 31, 64, 81, 112, 139, 172, 201
Eusebius, of Caesarea 85, 89, 91, 94
Evans, J. Martin 79, 113, 174
exegesis: 32, 82, 102, 104, 114, 129

Feavearyear, Sir Albert 48
Fish, Stanley 158
Fletcher, Giles the Elder 177, 186, 187, 192, 194, 195
Flinker, Noam 58
Floyd-Wilson, Mary 19
Flynn, Dennis O. 24, 25, 37, 38, 41, 42, 53, 56
Fowler, Alastair 128, 177
Frank, Andre Gunder 24
Emperor Frederick II 179, 191–93, 197
Freer, Coburn 38
Frobisher, Sir Martin 41, 68
King Fuxi 118, 119, 120, 126

Gallagher, Louis J. 9
Games, Alison 28, 33, 63
Gandelman, Claude 58
Gardner, Helen 36, 37, 72, 83
Gastaldi, Giacomo 17, 60, 67
Genghis Khan 173, 178, 180, 183, 185, 186, 200
Gilbert, Allan H. 112
Gilbert, Sir Humphrey 3, 17, 18, 55, 60, 61, 65, 66, 67, 68, 70
Gillies, John 58, 73
Gills, Barry K. 175
Giráldez, Arturo 24, 25, 37, 38, 41, 42, 43, 53, 54, 56
globalization 1, 16, 23–26, 30, 31, 35, 38, 56, 59, 62, 113, 151, 175–77, 182, 202
global trade 2, 4, 26, 36, 39, 57, 201

gold 2, 35–56, 133
Goldstone, Jack A. 54
Goodblatt, Chanita 83, 103
Goropius, Becanus J. 85, 100, 150
Gould, J. D. 43, 50
Grafton, Anthony 8, 84, 85, 88, 90, 91, 92, 93, 94, 97, 98, 100, 135
Greenblatt, Stephen 1
Gregerson, Linda 199, 200
Grossman, Marshall 129
Grotius, Hugo 60, 63, 94, 129
Gunn, Geoffery 25
Gupta, Suman 26
Guyuk Khan 179, 180

Haak, Theodore 156, 157, 186
Habib, Imtiaz H. 19
Hakluyt, Richard 10, 14, 30, 32, 35, 40, 54, 55, 57, 59, 60, 65, 66, 90, 134, 186
Hall, Kim, 19
Hardt, Michael 176, 181, 197
Harris, Steven J. 11
Hartlib, Samuel, 156, 157, 171, 172, 186
Hawkes, David 6, 49
Hayot, Eric, 16, 29
Hebrew history 86, 109, 111, 114, 117, 122, 126, 127, 129, 130, 132, 135, 139
Hebrew [language]: 142, 145, 150, 153, 154, 164, 172
Held, David 59, 182
Helgerson, Richard 31
Heylyn, Peter 10, 14, 155, 186
Hobson, John M. 1, 11, 24, 31, 40
Hodgen, Margaret T. 17, 21
Hollinger, David A. 74
Hondius, Henricus 125
Hsia, Adrian 15
Hsia, R. Po-Chia, 10
Huangdi [Yellow Emperor] 84, 95, 96, 97
Huang, Ray 53
Hudson, Geoffrey F. 10
Hughes, Merritt Y. 109, 110
Huntley, Frank L. 113

Jackson, Peter 180, 181
Jacob, Margaret 63
Jameson, Fredric 25

Jenkins, Eugenia Zuroski 16
Jensen, Lionel M. 10
the Jesuits 2, 10, 13, 14, 22, 23, 25, 26, 29, 40, 78, 79, 87
Johanyak, Debra 16, 19
Jones, Andrew 176
Jonson, Ben 3–12, 17, 40
Julian period 93, 94

Kamen, Henry 43, 50
Kasinec, Wendy F. 25
Katz, David S. 150
Keevak, Michael 19, 26
Keuning, Johannes 116
Keynes, Sir Geoffrey 101
Khwarizmi Empire 183, 184
Kidd, Colin 88
Kircher, Athanasius 120, 136, 141, 148, 154, 155, 156
Knoespel, Kenneth J. 121, 128
Knowles, James 4, 16
Knowlson, James 146, 148, 151, 155, 156
Koivukoski, Toivo, 43, 196

la Peyrère, Isaac de 88, 98, 116, 117, 118, 121, 127, 141
Labriola, Albert C. 37
Lach, Donald F. 10, 11, 12
Lee, Christina H. 29
Leibniz, Gottfried W.118
Leonard, John 145, 158, 159, 160, 166
LePan, Don 84
Lester, Toby 17, 62
Lestringant, Frank 25
liberal cosmopolitanism 14, 26, 27, 29, 32, 63, 107, 111, 114, 134, 139, 173, 201, 202
Lim, Walter S. H. 16, 19, 113, 134
Livingstone, David N. 72, 88
Lodwick, Francis 156
Loewenstein, David 113
Loomba, Ania 18, 19, 20
Lundbaek, Knud 151
Lux, Jonathan E. 16

Maat, Jaap 151
McCulloch, J. R. 49
MacDonald, Joyce G. 19

McGrew, Anthony 59, 182
McLeod, Bruce 174
MacPhail, Eric 130
Magellan 56, 57, 59, 62, 64, 66, 68, 69, 70, 72, 73
Mandeville, Sir John 8, 9, 20, 41, 136, 180, 187
Manetho, 85, 94
Mangi(a), 8, 61, 68, 137
Manila 20, 24, 37, 38, 42
Manila galleons 24, 48
Manning, Patrick 25
Markley, Robert 3, 5, 16, 56, 84, 112, 113, 125, 126, 135, 137, 151, 171, 186
Marlowe, Christopher, 33, 87, 185, 201
Marsh, Nicky 7, 26
Martini, Martino, 10, 83, 112, 115–26, 129, 136–38, 141, 148, 153–55, 180, 185, 186, 206
Masson, David 123
Matar, Nabil 19
Mauro, Fra 71, 72, 75
Mendoza, González de 7, 10, 20, 32, 83–85, 94–96, 98, 106, 114, 118, 121, 136, 146, 147, 155, 179, 187
Mercator, Gerard, 65–67, 83, 91
Middle Kingdom 2, 9, 18, 19, 21, 22
Milgate, Wesley 36
Milton, Anthony 13
mines 2, 15, 38–45, 52
Ming Empire 9, 15, 53, 60, 84, 96, 186
Miyoshi, Masao 25
Mohamed, Feisal G. 111
Moloughney, Brian 38
Momigliano, Arnaldo 86, 89
Mongol Empire 173, 178, 181
the Mongols 8, 17, 33, 173, 178, 179, 183–87, 191–95
Monroe, Arthur Eli 44
Montaigne, Michel de 8, 15
Morgan, David, 178, 181, 183, 185
Mungello, David E. 10, 119, 148
Munkler, Herfried 182, 196, 197
Murrin, Michael 16

nationalism 31, 113, 182
natural language 143, 150, 158
Needham, Joseph 10, 97

Negri, Antonio 176, 181, 197
Nicholas of Lyra 102, 103, 104
Nieuhoff, Jean 119, 120, 123, 153
Noachian flood 119, 163
Northeast [North-east] passage 32, 40, 54–56, 59, 62, 64–66, 70, 110
Northwest [North-west] Passage 32, 40, 41, 54, 55–57, 59, 61, 62, 64–70
Nyquist, Mary 21, 158

Oldenburg, Henry, 112, 114–18, 119, 123–25, 186
Orientalism 16, 18, 19, 21, 113
Ortelius, Abraham 17, 66, 67
Outhwaite, R. B. 48, 51
Owens, Robert R. 58, 60

Paquin 133, 136, 138, 173, 180, 184,
Paracelsus 88, 141
Paris, Matthew 91, 178, 183, 184, 186, 191–95
Parry, J. H. 44
Patrides, C. A., 69, 84, 91, 92, 114, 120, 130
Petavius, Dionysius 89, 90
Peters, Julie S. 114, 134
pistolet 37, 40, 44, 45, 50, 52, 54
Polo, Marco 8, 9, 17, 20, 40, 41, 60, 136, 137, 187
Polushin, Michael A. 25, 185
Pomeranz, Kenneth 40
Poole, Kristen 142, 144, 145, 160
Poole, William 88, 117, 151
Popkin, Richard H. 88, 116, 117, 118, 135
Porter, David 2, 3, 5, 7, 15, 16, 23, 56, 143, 144, 148, 151, 155, 163, 170
the Portuguese 4, 20, 22, 38, 42, 148
primitive language 15, 32, 109, 141, 145, 152, 157–59, 162, 164, 170, 172
profane history[histories] 82, 83, 84, 89, 93, 106, 107, 129, 131
proleptic time 92, 98, 121, 124, 131
Ptolemy 62, 125, 201
Purchas, Samuel 9, 10, 14, 137, 155, 156, 157, 184, 186, 187

Quinn, David B. 18, 65
Quinn, Dennis B. 83, 103
Quinzay 60, 68

Rabelais, Francois 12
Rajan, Balachandra 112, 113, 174, 200
Ralegh, Sir Walter 41, 44, 46, 48, 50, 91, 125, 126, 155
Raleigh, W. A. 3, 33, 35, 40, 58
Raman, Shankar 38, 113
Ramsey, Rachel 118, 145
Ramusio, Giovanni Battista 9
Raspa, Anthony 22, 81, 83, 99, 105
real character 30, 142–44, 148, 152, 155, 156, 158, 164, 170
Ricci, Matteo 9, 10, 11, 18, 20, 21, 22, 84, 126, 137, 146, 147, 153, 155, 157, 171, 187
Richards, John F. 37, 47
Rossi, Paolo 121, 143
Rubruck, William of 8, 17, 187, 192
Ryan, Michael T. 87

sacred history 82, 93, 135
Said, Edward W. 18, 21
Salmon, Vivian 151, 156
Sauer, Elizabeth 112, 134, 174, 200
Saussy, Haun 12
Scaliger, Joseph, 8, 15, 32, 83–87, 90, 91–101, 104, 121, 124, 130, 131, 134, 150, 172
scriptural chronology 81, 82, 85, 86, 89, 99, 100, 107, 122, 127–34
Sebek, Barbara 5
Sedwick, Daniel 36, 39, 47
Semedo, Alvaro 119, 141, 148, 153–55
Shakespeare, William 6, 12, 33
Shami, Jeanne 63, 83
Sharp, Robert L. 58
Shuger, Debora K. 102, 104
silver 2, 24, 35–56
Sima, Qian, 95–97
Simpson, Evelyn M. 36
Singh, Jyotsna G. 113
Slotkin, James S. 87
Song, Eric B. 194
the Spanish 4, 20, 22, 29, 36–57, 76, 83, 84, 95, 97, 179
Spanish coins 36, 50, 58
Spanish Empire 54, 179
Spanish pesos 38, 45, 47, 50
Spanish stamps 36, 37, 38, 39, 53

Spate, O. H. K. 3
Spence, Jonathon 10
Spier, Fred 25
Spies, Marijke 59
Steger, Manfred B. 23
Stevens, Paul 31, 113, 134
Stillman, Robert 142
Subbiondo, Joseph L. 150
Sui, Gwee Li 16
Supple, Berry E. 50
Syncellus, George 84, 124

Tabachnick, David E. 190, 196
Tamerlane 185, 186
Tartar: 8, 9, 15, 33, 55, 95, 115, 116, 123, 137, 138, 173, 177–200, 201
Tartary 12, 177, 188, 192
Taylor, E. G. R. 65
TePaske, John J. 37
theological: 13, 15, 17, 32, 49, 57–79, 107, 111, 116, 117, 126, 146, 170
Thrash, Cheryl 159
Tomlinson, John 25
Tracy, James D. 42
Trigault, Nicholas, 9, 11, 18, 20, 21, 22, 84, 126, 147, 148, 153, 155, 157, 171, 185, 187
Turnbull, G. H. 156, 186
Twitchett, Denis 178
Tyacke, Sarah 25

universal chronology 88, 134, 139
universal history 88, 89, 91, 130, 133, 135, 172
universal language 142, 151, 152, 155, 156
Ussher, James 118–21, 128, 129

Valignano, Alessandro 10, 11, 22
van der Krogt, Peter, 67
van Kley, Edwin J. 10, 11, 12, 83, 92, 119
Vitkus, Daniel 23
von Glahn, Richard 25, 41
Vossius, Isaac 72, 115, 118, 120, 122, 150, 153, 154, 155

Walton, Timothy R. 37, 39
Watson, Adam 175–76
Weatherford, Jack 178
Webb, John 32, 109, 118–23, 126, 137, 141–72
Webster, John 142, 143, 164–66
Welch, Anthony K. 128
Westrem, Scott D. 17
Wetsel, David, 121–22
whelps 44–46, 52, 54
Whitaker, William 89, 102, 103, 104, 120, 150
Wilcox, Donald J. 84, 90, 91, 93, 98
Wilkins, John 30, 113, 142, 143, 145, 150, 152, 154, 155, 156, 165, 170, 172
Willes, Richard 55, 61, 65, 66, 67, 70, 83
Wills, John E. Jr. 10
Winter, Heinrich 17
Wolf, Eric R. 2
Wong, Roy Bin 31

Yang, Chi-ming 16
King Yao [Jaus, Yaus], 96, 97, 119, 120, 126
Yao, Steven G. 16
Yuan Empire 41, 180, 184
Yule, Sir Henry 10, 65